Corporations and Disability Rights

Corporations and Disability Rights

Bridging the Digital Divide

Neha Pathakji

OXFORD
UNIVERSITY PRESS

OXFORD
UNIVERSITY PRESS

Oxford University Press is a department of the University of Oxford.
It furthers the University's objective of excellence in research, scholarship,
and education by publishing worldwide. Oxford is a registered trademark of
Oxford University Press in the UK and in certain other countries.

Published in India by
Oxford University Press
2/11 Ground Floor, Ansari Road, Daryaganj, New Delhi 110 002, India

ISBN-13 (print edition): 978-0-19-948523-9
ISBN-10 (print edition): 0-19-948523-2

ISBN-13 (eBook): 978-0-19-909188-1
ISBN-10 (eBook): 0-19-909188-9

Typeset in Goudy Old Style 11/13
by Tranistics Data Technologies, New Delhi 110 044
Printed in India by Rakmo Press, New Delhi 110 020

Contents

Figures

Table of Cases

Table of Statutes

Foreword

Persons with disabilities are integral members of humanity; hence, their concerns need to be woven into the original design of any theory of social justice and cannot be an afterthought. John Rawls in his theory of justice excluded persons with disabilities from the original contract. Rawlsian exclusion stemmed from the deficiencies of reason and understanding associated with disability, especially mental, intellectual, and developmental disabilities.[1] Martha Nussbaum questioned this justification by pointing out that reason may be required to enter into a contract but is not needed to be a beneficiary; hence Rawls has been unfair in excluding persons with disabilities from the original position.[2] I refer to this difference of opinion between Nussbaum and Rawls at the start of this foreword because it sheds light on the critical concern of this book on how exclusion occurs and when should inclusion happen?

Rawls excludes by the way he constructs contractual capacity. Nussbaum does not question the requirement of reason but finds a way to include the concerns of persons with disabilities in the original position, only not on an equal basis with others. Instead she adopts the standard of as equal as possible.

Rawls was not unique in denying the status of being rights bearers to persons with disabilities. Such deprivation was routinely inflicted on them in laws, policies, and social practices

---

[1] John Rawls, A Theory of Justice (Harvard University Press 1971).

[2] Martha Nussbaum, Frontiers of Justice: Disability, Nationality, Species Membership (Harvard University Press 2006).

across nations.[3] This near all-pervasive discrimination prompted the move to set up an ad hoc committee in the United Nations to undertake the task of drafting a Convention on the Rights of Persons with Disabilities (CRPD). Though the State of Mexico took the initiative to have a committee set up to deliberate on a Disability Rights Convention, the functioning of the committee was primarily driven by persons with disabilities, who participated in the deliberations in large numbers as members of state and non-state delegations, as also in their individual capacity. Nothing about us without us became the operative credo of the ad hoc committee, which was largely engaged in providing a level playing field to persons with disabilities. Equality and non-discrimination were the major rights drivers of the Convention. The articles on awareness raising and accessibility were included as cross-cutting rights to address the exclusion practised by prejudicial attitudes and an ableist infrastructure. The Convention is a course corrector, which is attempting to remodel the world in order to make it disability inclusive. This task of modifying the normative and physical world in order to make it disability inclusive has been arduous. It brings home the difficulties of rectifying the inequity of design after it has been executed and is no longer on the drawing table. This learning needs to be continually kept in view to appreciate Neha Pathakji's insistence in this book that if persons with disabilities are not to lose out a second time, then the Internet must from the very beginning be designed as a disability inclusive space. This insistence has to be placed alongside the fact that the commitments of the Convention, with a record number of ratifications, obtained large scale endorsement of the international community.[4] Despite this wide endorsement, the task of realising the goals of the Convention has been an uphill task because inclusion is faced with the barrier of prejudice and a disability excluding lived environment. Inclusion

[3] Amita Dhanda, 'Legal Capacity in the Disability Rights Convention: Stranglehold of the Past or Lodestar for the Future', 34 *Syracuse J of International law and Commerce* 429 (2006–7).

[4] The Convention has been signed by 160 countries and ratified by 168 of them. Available at http://fra.europa.eu/en/theme/people-disabilities/ratified-crpd (last visited 12 January 2018).

should be part of original design as once barriers are created, they are difficult to dismantle.[5]

It may be contended that this pragmatic argument of Pathakji has been rendered redundant by the CRPD which in article 9 requires, 'States Parties (to) take appropriate measures to ensure to persons with disabilities access, on an equal basis with others, to the physical environment, to transportation, to information and communications, including information and communications technologies and systems...' and 'to promote access for persons with disabilities to new information and communications technologies and systems, **including the Internet**'. In article 21 State parties have been asked to urge private parties who provide services through the Internet to do so in accessible and usable formats for persons with disabilities. A similar request has been made in relation to mass media who provide their services through the Internet. The point of redundancy can be made if the Internet is only viewed as a medium of communication and not as an alternative living space. Pathakji takes the view that the Internet is alternative living space hence deliberations on its accessibility should be undertaken accordingly. It is from that perspective that she holds that right to the Internet is not just a right to enable the fulfilment of other rights but a right in itself.[6] In contending that the right to the Internet is not just an enabling right, the author is raising the stakes of non-discriminatory access.

Scholars who view the right to the Internet as only enabling, rely in the first place upon the text of the CRPD. Both articles 9 and 21 refer to the Internet in the enabling mode and this express mention in their view settles the matter on the nature of the right. In article 9, the Internet was mentioned illustratively to underscore the point that the obligations of inclusion are not restricted to old mediums of communication but also extend to new technologies such as the Internet. In article 21 again the Internet was referred to for similar reasons. Disabled people and their organizations who, as I have already mentioned, were key players in the drafting of the Convention wished

---

[5] The concluding observations of the committee even on physical accessibility provide evidence of this fact.

[6] See chapter 1.

to guard against the emergence of new barriers to freedom of speech and expression and this prompted the inclusion of the reference to the Internet in article 21. For the text of the Convention to settle the 'nature of right controversy', it is important that the deliberations in the ad hoc committee occurred distinguishing between Internet as living space and as medium of communication. As both observer and participant in the proceedings, I can vouch that the nature of the Internet space was not deliberated in the Committee.[7] To make the ambiguous text of CRPD determinative of a question which was not deliberated in the Committee is not in accord with the canons of interpretations of treaties.

The second objection to Neha Pathakji's advocacy of the right to the Internet is that if the contention is accepted, then persons with disabilities would be holders of more rights than are available to non-disabled people. The CRPD aims to usher equality and non-discrimination for persons with disabilities, it cannot be used to invent new rights for this excluded population. However, is Pathakji's contention introducing new rights or is it ensuring that persons with disabilities people the Internet on an equal basis with others? Unless persons with disabilities are counted in from the start, the Internet will be only designed for the non-disabled, with the concerns of persons with disabilities as in the construction of the physical world, will only bring up the rear. It may be pertinent to note that the right to equality and non-discrimination in the CRPD has been designed differently from how the right has been extended to persons with disabilities under other human rights instruments. In the other instruments, the right to reasonable accommodation was continually interpreted in ableist terms. In those instruments, persons with disabilities are entitled to reasonable accommodation provided including them does not place a disproportionate burden on the non-disabled. If the burden is disproportionate then exclusion is conceded. In comparison to 'will do our best approach', the CRPD declares that denial of reasonable accommodation would be perceived as discrimination on the basis of disability, which means that in no case can a person with disability denied

---

[7] I participated in the deliberations of the ad hoc committee as a member of the delegation of the World Network of Users and Survivors of Psychiatry.

reasonable accommodation. Reasonable Accommodation in the CRPD aims to accommodate the diversity in disability so that no one is left behind. Reasonable Accommodation is thus the safety net to prevent exclusion; not the primary medium to effect inclusion. Inclusion is to be brought in through universal design and such design would be created if persons with disabilities are seen as peopling the Internet from the beginning. Unlike non-disabled persons, this would not happen on its own for persons with disabilities. For that position to be conceded, it is important to use the language of rights and assert that persons with disabilities have a right to the Internet. Persons with disabilities would be brought at par with the non-disabled only when it is asserted that they have a right to the Internet. In contending that the Internet is a core human right and not just enabling right, Neha Pathakji is only applying the right to equality and non-discrimination to persons with disabilities, in such a manner that there is equality of outcome between disabled and non-disabled people. She is not seeking a new right for persons with disabilities; instead she is attempting to ensure that persons with disabilities also obtain what is provided as a matter of course to the non-disabled.

Whilst making my presentation before the CRPD Committee in its day of general discussion in preparation for the General Comment on article 5,[8] I made a similar submission. Virginia Gomez, the Chair of the Committee in Economic Social and Cultural Rights, was of the view that whilst my argument was conceptually attractive, it would be difficult if not impossible to have any state party accept it. Pragmatism, she opined, was the bulwark of UN human rights jurisprudence; but such pragmatism should not be allowed to function in peace. Instead it should be continually challenged by values-driven contentions so that the gap between norm and reality continues to trouble both the UN Bodies and the State parties. As only such discomfiture would bring change.

It has often been found that both advocates and researchers on human rights make detailed justifications on why particular rights

---

[8] Amita Dhanda, 'In a Class of My Own: Reasonable Accommodation from a Disability Perspective', Presentation made to the CRPD on 25 August 2017 on its day of general discussion.

claims should be admitted; but do not then reflect on how those rights shall be realized. Henry Shue in his seminal work on basic rights has opined that something can be claimed to be a right if the substance of the right is socially guaranteed against standard threats.[9] Neha Pathakji has departed from this trend of normative ambitiousness often encountered in Indian scholarship by not just asserting that right to the Internet is a core human right for persons with disabilities; but also expounded on how this right can be realized. She has designed implementation and not just demanded it.

The Internet is controlled by private players and not by the State. It is for this reason that the CRPD could only ask State parties to persuade the private players to provide access. Pathakji again moves beyond the CRPD to set up an argument of corporate accountability.[10] She holds that as the power wielded by corporations increases; both procedural and normative mechanisms of accountability need to be created. Human rights are a powerful source of seeking such accountability. This accountability cannot be obtained in the same manner in which it is sought from the State. Pathakji suggests a mix of strategies which range from regulation to persuasion to reflexive operation driven by market operations. Pathakji's Interconnected Pentagon Model (IPM) aims to demonstrate that all goals cannot be achieved by similar procedures. It is important to customize strategies to needs and not let one size fit all. With the IPM,[11] the author is asking academicians to not just concern themselves with the normative but also worry on how the normative can be rendered real. Rule implementing like rule making needs to be designed. In the absence of such design, scholastic berating of poor implementation would invite strict scrutiny. Pathakji's work has provided the parameters for conducting such scrutiny.

Disability Human Rights are late entrants in the pantheon of Human Rights. As late entrants either they can either be continually employed play catch up; or they can provide justification for being

---

[9] Henry Shue, *Basic Rights: Subsistence Affluence and US Foreign Policy* (Princeton University Press 1988).

[10] See chapters 2 to 4 of this book.

[11] Interconnected Pentagon Model, chapter 5.

included at inception in all spaces opening up after the CRPD. Neha Pathakji has taken the second option. Her highly persuasive argument for a right to the Internet should be read both literally and metaphorically. All human growth and development post the admission of disability human rights needs to be disability inclusive from its inception, remedial measures adopted subsequently may provide superficial relief but leave the embedded discrimination undisturbed. This book sets up a powerful argument for a policy of original inclusion.

12 January 2018   Amita Dhanda
Hyderabad   Professor of Law, NALSAR

Preface

The idea of this book was implanted somewhere in the year 2010 during my involvement with the legislation drafting of the new Indian Disability Law in compliance with the United Nations Convention on Rights of Persons with Disabilities (UNCRPD) to which India is a signatory. As a researcher with the Legal Consultant to the Drafting Committee appointed by the Central Government of India, I witnessed the dialogues and deliberations of the committee members who included persons with disabilities, NGOs, and experts from the disability sector. Consequent to the consultations carried out by the Committee through the length and breadth of the country, what came to the drawing board were the aspirations and expectations, apprehensions and frustrations voiced by persons with disabilities. The lived experience of persons with disabilities, not only in India but across the world, informed that persons with disabilities could not realize rights guaranteed to them to the fullest extent owing to the prevalent physical, social, and attitudinal barriers. While this dialogue of ushering rights based disability law was harping upon eliminating physical and infrastructural barriers, the implications of inaccessible technology on lives of persons with disabilities and barriers existing in the virtual world was escaping attention.

As a law person in the room with specialization in business laws, I was hit hard by the realization that the design of virtual world would be immensely critical in shaping lives of persons with disabilities. However, it was not the government but corporations, who as architects of virtual world, could respond to the impending digital divide. Yet, corporation was conspicuously missing from the scene. It was this anxiousness that led to the present inquiry probing the creation of an accessible, inclusive, and participative virtual world for persons with disabilities and the extent of corporate participation.

This book sets out to explore the interplay between human rights of persons with disabilities and corporate obligation in a technologically advanced society. With the progressive shift of human functionality from the real physical world to the virtual world, access to the Internet would determine the quality of life and autonomy guaranteed to persons with disabilities. Corporations as gatekeepers of the virtual world need to proactively engage in dismantling barriers to access the Internet. The contemporary discourse about the nature of the right to access the Internet when contextualized in terms of disability rights jurisprudence offers a complex challenge. Even as corporations hold the key to gates of the virtual world and clearly emerge as a new addressee under human rights and technology discourse, the state continues to remain a duty-bearer of human rights, despite being a marginal player on the Internet. This calls for re-conceptualizing normative and theoretical justifications for corporate obligation with respect to human rights and developing innovative regulatory strategy of seeking compliance. Instead of deploying classical deter or co-operate techniques of compliance, a web of influences that engages multiple institutions and instrumentalities in various combinations at institutional, domestic, and international level offers better scheme of compliance.

I thank all those enlightened beings who have helped me in diverse ways during this project. First and foremost, I thank Amita Dhanda, my PhD supervisor, for her continuous guidance and critical insights not particularly limited to my academic struggles alone. She provided me all the support that I could ask for and the ones I could not ask. This book would not have taken shape without her engagement. I also thank her as my senior most colleague, friend, philosopher, and guide whose presence in my life has molded me as a scholar and made an indelible mark on me as a professor and an individual.

I express my sincere gratitude to Faizan Mustafa whose effervescent personality keeps me encouraged to accomplish higher goals. I see this book impossible without his unflinching support and faith in my capabilities.

Thanks to all those illuminated beings who crossed my path during this study. This book has benefited from discussions with them. I would like to particularly extend my gratitude to Gerard Quinn, whose gently expressed counter views to my propositions nudged me to think deeper on the issue. I extend my heartfelt thanks to Francisco Javier Zamora Cabot, who alerted me about the ground realities of business world, yet expressed his confidence in my overall proposition. I am thankful to Karen Topaz Druckman, who provided me with the necessary insight that helped to shape my understanding. I express warm gratitude to Victoria Lee for having shared her experience as a disability rights activist and her constant endeavours to keep me alert on the ongoing formal discourse that further advanced my knowledge.

I express my gratitude to Andrew Clapham, who responded to my desperate emails and bailed me out from some very particular scholastic struggles. I will always regret the fact that I did not have the fortune to meet and interact with Prof. Clapham personally during my stay in Lausanne.

I fondly remember meetings of the working group of the drafting Committee for the Disability Rights Bill. I am particularly thankful to Sudha Kaul, chairperson of the Drafting Committee and distinguished committee members, whose discussions and deliberations contributed towards my own sensitization to disability. The drafting of the Disability Rights Bill was a humbling experience for me in several ways and enabled me to internalize the lived-experience of persons with disabilities and put the things in a new perspective. I have equally gained from my research and writing of India's First Country Report to the UNCRPD Committee. I am thankful to Nilesh Singit who provided me first lessons on accessibility. It was during these projects that I could closely observe and witness a live discourse between the state, disability groups, and society.

I express my gratitude to the Swiss Institute of Comparative Law, Lausanne, Switzerland for their generous 'van Calker' scholarship that enabled me to undertake an intensive and extensive research at the institute. This work has benefited largely from the research at the Institute. I am thankful to Sadri Saieb and the library staff of the Swiss Institute. My three months' research at the Institute would not have been as pleasant without the company of the good-natured staff and attorneys at the institute. I am particularly thankful to Martin Schyhold, my mentor at the Swiss Institute and Karim el Chazli, Stephannie Dycker, Johanna for their kindness and affection. I am grateful to Christiane Serkis, Martin Do-Spitteler, and Magadalena for their warm-heartedness.

I am thankful to the NALSAR University of Law for granting my sabbatical leave for completing this work. I am also thankful to students who signed up for my seminar course on Reflexive Law and Corporations at NALSAR University of Law Hyderabad and participated in stimulating discussions, questioning the theory, and its practicality allowed me to test ideas. I am thankful to the Editorial Board of the *Queensland University of Technology Law Review* and the anonymous referees who very closely questioned some of my initial propositions and provided me critical insights.

I am thankful to Kusum Dhanania and Nikhil Kejriwal for their kindness and support during my stay in Lausanne. It was sheer serendipity that I befriended Kusum Dhanania, yet she was instrumental in many ways in my seeking the scholarship in Lausanne.

This long endeavour would not have been possible without unconditional love and support of my friends and family. I thank Pranshu Bhutra, Prajwal Gyawali, Akshaya Kamalnath, and Manav Kapur for their irreplaceable friendship and reliable presence in my life. I express my gratitude to my mother and sister, the winds beneath my wings. I am thankful to my sister for having rubbed her kindness, humility, and compassion on me. It has made me a better person than I am. I express my gratitude to my mother for having infused in me the ability to battle one's way out from the toughest struggles without losing liveliness of the spirit. I also express my gratitude to my ancestors whose values have been guiding me.

Abbreviations

ACB	American Council of the Blind
ADA	Americans with Disabilities Act, 1990
AODA	Accessibility for Ontarians with Disabilities Act, 2005
ASU	Arizona State University
CEDAW	Convention on the Elimination of All Forms of Discrimination Against Women
COP	Communication of Policy
CSR	Corporate Social Responsibility
CVAA	21st Century Communications and Video Accessibility Act, 2010
DDA	Disability Discrimination Act, 1992
DPA	Disabled Person's Act
EQA	Equality Act, 2010
FCC	Federal Communications Commission
G3ict	Global Initiative for Inclusive Information and Communication Technologies
HRC	Human Rights Council
HREOC	Human Rights and the Equal Opportunities Commission
IBS	Internet Backbone Providers
ICERD	International Convention on the Elimination of All Forms of Racial Discrimination
ICT	Information and Communication Technology
IETF	Internet Engineering Task Force
IGF	Internet Governance Forum
IGWG	Intergovernmental Working Group
ILO	International Labour Organization

IPM	Interconnected Pentagon Model
ISPs	Internet Service Providers
ITU	International Telecommunication Union
ODA	Ontarians with Disabilities Act, 2001
OECD	Organisation of Economic Co-operation and Development
OSPs	Online Service Providers
SRSG	Special Representative to the Secretary General
TNCs	Transnational Corporations
UDHR	Universal Declaration of Human Rights
UNCRPD	United Nations Convention on Rights of Persons of Disabilities
UNESCO	United Nations Educational, Scientific and Cultural Organization
UNDESA	United Nations Department for Economic and Social Affairs
UN GP	United Nations Guiding Principles
UNITAR	United Nations Institute for Training and Research
UN PRR	United Nations Framework of Protect, Respect and Remedy
WBU	World Blind Union
WCAG	Web Content Accessibility Guidelines
WIPO	World Intellectual Property Organisation
WSIS	World Summit on Information Society
W3C	World Wide Web Consortium

Introduction

Persons with disabilities, it has been contended, even prior to the adoption of the Convention on the Rights of Persons with Disabilities (CRPD), in principle were entitled to the full gamut of civil, economic, political, cultural, and social rights. Real-life evidence from across the world, however, demonstrated that persons with disabilities were routinely denied equality and non-discrimination. It was progressively realized that persons with disabilities constituted the largest minority in the world, whose marginalization and exclusion from the world order needed to cease. This isolation ended when the United Nations Convention on the Rights of Persons with Disabilities (UNCPD) unequivocally recognized the rights of persons with disabilities to dignity, to live in the community on an equal basis with others. The CRPD puts in place an authoritative text of global legal standards on disability rights. Disability rights' scholars have long before asserted and now also supported by the authoritative text of CRPD that 'right of persons with disabilities to live in the world also encompasses the right to live in the virtual world'.[1]

It is remarkable how the borderless, compact, cost-effective Internet, and technology can dismantle the barriers created in the

---

[1] Bradley A. Areheart and Michael Ashley Stein, *Integrating the Internet*, 83 George Washington L. REV. 449 (2015). Available at http://ssrn.com/abstract=2420510 (arguing that the right to live in the world, naturally encompasses the right to live in the virtual world. The article develops a claim that the Internet place of public accommodation, which must be integrated. The issue is, however, even more pressing as the Internet is broad enough to encompass all of the traditional categories of public accommodations—as well as social arenas like education and work).

physical world. It is, however, worrisome that the Internet is not living up to the promises it initially made. With the advancement in technology and increased diversity in participation in the virtual world, persons with disabilities have been crowded out. With the digital divide opening up before them, there is a danger that the exclusion faced by persons with disabilities in the physical world may be replayed in virtual space. Since the Internet is largely dominated by corporations, this digital divide cannot be bridged without questioning their role.

Access to the Internet is the new source of power, corporations as providers of access, as architects of the Internet emerged as a private authority. Corporations and the technology they create hold the key to access the virtual world and create better life and living experiences for persons with disabilities. It is therefore critical to bring corporation on board not only in their capacity as architects of the Internet but also as private authority vested with implicit legitimacy of governance in the virtual world. However, corporations in general have proved to be slippery targets of regulation and seeking compliance, especially on social and human rights issues have been a daunting task both under domestic laws and international regimes.

Here, then lies the challenge. Rights of persons with disabilities to an accessible virtual world need to be recognized and realized so that they can lead an autonomous and fuller life. However, realization of this right cannot be possible without summoning corporation. For commitment made to persons with disabilities, compliance has to be sought from corporation, yet there exists normative, theoretical, and regulatory challenges. How should the concern about the rights of persons with disabilities to accessible Internet be approached? What justifications can be accorded to get the corporation involved to ensure that these rights are realized? How should a compliance strategy be designed? Should legislations carry a mandate that corporations must create virtual world or should some persuasive techniques be deployed?

This book engages with the contemporary discourse about the nature of the right to access the Internet and contextualizes the same with emerging 'disability rights jurisprudence'. It articulates existing digital divide as an extension of social injustice to persons with disabilities. It is argued that conceptualizing right to access the Internet as merely an enabling right is an oversimplification of an otherwise complex issue. The right to access the Internet deserves to be examined under the human rights lens. In this context, the book questions and investigates the role of corporations in bridging the digital divide and raises pertinent questions on the extent and scope of corporate human rights obligations.

Thus, the book makes two claims—one, that the right to access the Internet is a human right which cannot be realized unless corporations are recognized as duty bearers and entrusted with positive obligations towards accessibility; two, the evolving nature of the virtual world and disability rights jurisprudence demands new legal and strategic framework to obtain proactive corporate compliance.

In order to address systemic discrimination faced by persons with disabilities, the book proposes a strategic approach to combat the prevalence of structural discrimination. A plausible solution is offered in the form of Interconnected Pentagon Model (IPM) of regulatory approach. The IPM is a detailed and complex mix of actors and their instrumentalities. The five points of the pentagon represents five pressure points—the State, corporation, community, markets, and international organizations. Each commands a certain amount of leverage over some instrumentalities. Instead of looking for formally recognized actors as authorities, the interconnected pentagon looks at many disaggregated sources whose webs of influence provoke and guide the effective implementation of the right to access the Internet.

Human Rights in a Technologically Advanced Society

Life today is unimaginable without the Internet. Almost everything that human life could possibly demand in terms of materialistic comforts, intellectual stimulations, professional and socializing opportunities and even spiritual quests can be availed on the Internet. We are paying bills, reading newspapers, shopping grocery and apparels, filling applications for jobs and education, writing exams, mailing, and socializing through the Internet.

There has been a steady growth in the percentage of individuals using the Internet (defined as those who have used the Internet at least once in the last three months) and of households with Internet access. According to an estimate released by the International Telecommunication Union (ITU), globally, 3.6 billion people had been using the Internet by the end of 2017 of which 2.6 billion were from developing countries.[2] There is an obvious increase in the absolute number of Internet users across the globe from 1 billion in 2005 to 3.6 billion in 2017. However, it is important to note that whereas the number of individuals using the Internet in the developed countries increased by 406 million during 2005–17, the developing countries registered about 2148 million increase during this time period.[3] A region-wise break-up

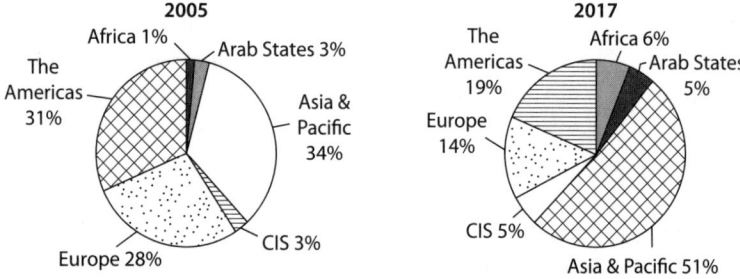

Figure I.1   Individual Internet users in the world (in millions) by regions in 2005 and 2017 (estimate)[4]
Source: International Telecommunication Union World Telecommunication/ICT Indicators database.

    [2] Available at http://www.itu.int/en/ITU-D/Statistics/Pages/stat/default. aspx (last visited 30 August 2017).
    [3] Whereas the number of individuals using Internet (in million) in the developed countries were 617 in 2005, it was 1023 in 2017, the same for developing countries were 407 in 2005 and 2,555 in 2017. Available at http://www.itu.int/en/ITU-D/Statistics/Pages/stat/default.aspx (last visited 30 August 2017). The developed/developing country classifications are based on the UN M49, see http://www.itu.int/en/ITU-D/Statistics/Pages/ definitions/regions.aspx (last visited 30 August 2017).
    [4] Created from the data collected from the ITU World Telecommunication/ ICT Indicators database. Regions in this table are based on the ITU regions, available at http://www.itu.int/en/ITU-D/Statistics/Pages/ definitions/regions.aspx (last visited 30 August 2017).

of the Internet users demonstrates that a larger pie is now shared by the Asia and Pacific and African countries.

In addition to computers, the Internet can also be accessed through mobile-broadband connection. According to ITU's estimate mobile broadband connection penetration will be touching 56 per cent in 2017, a value that increased 14 times since 2007.[5] Hence, it will be relevant to have a region wise break-up of users with active mobile-broadband subscription as depicted in Figure I.2.

It may be noted that in the year 2007, out of the total active broadband mobile subscribers 38 per cent were from Asia and Pacific and African nations. In the year 2017, subscribers from these nations comprised of 58 per cent of the total. Thus, percentage of subscribers in Asia and Pacific and African nations, both in terms of the Internet and mobile-broadband connections have steeply risen by the year 2017. These also happen to be amongst thickly populated continents of the world and comprise of either developing countries or those which are emerging economies of the world. Consequently, they also offer the most lucrative markets for the evolving technologies. What do these facts and figures suggest? Simply one

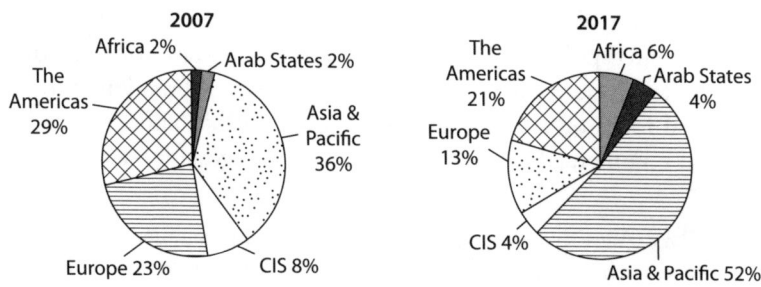

Figure I.2 Active mobile-broadband subscription in the world (in millions) by region in 2007 and 2017 (estimate)[6]
Source: International Telecommunication Union World Telecommunication/ICT Indicators database.

[5] Whereas active mobile broadband connection in the year 2007 per 100 inhabitants was 4.0 that in 2017 increased to 56.4. Available at http://www.itu.int/en/ITU-D/Statistics/Pages/definitions/regions.aspx (last visited 30 August 2017).

[6] Created from the data collected from the ITU World Telecommunication/ICT Indicators database.

thing: the world is speedily advancing towards a digital society and developing countries are moving even faster.

From its beginning in the early 1970s to its massive worldwide expansion in the 1990s and 2000s, the Internet has phenomenally evolved from a research project to an integral part of the human community. The Internet was first conceived in the United States in early 1960s in the form of a first high-speed computer network, ARPANET, possessed by the military, defence contractors, and university laboratories performing defence–related research.[7] In early 1970s, ARPANET grew from four hosts at US campuses (in 1969) to 23 hosts connecting universities and government research centers around the United States. Towards the late 1970s and during the 1980s, ARPANET moved away from its military/research roots, however the traffic on the Internet was still restricted by the National Science Foundation's Backbone.[8] However, with commercial interested piqued in the Internet during the late 1980s and early 1990s, the NSF permitted commercial use of the Internet and lifted restrictions on traffic.

As Chinoy and Salo note, during the 1990s, the evolution of the US portion of the Internet has, to a very large extent, been driven by two related policies: commercialization and privatization. Under commercialization, the mission of the Internet was broadened from its initial focus on supporting research, education, and defence to include commercial (as well as nearly any imaginable) activity. At

---

[7] ARPA (Advanced Research Projects Agency) was founded in 1958 to support research and development in technology, to confront the perceived threat of Soviet technological advantage. It was later commissioned by the United States Defense Department's Advanced Research Project Agency in December 1969. See Richard T. Griffiths, 'History of the Internet, Internet for Historians, Chapter Two: From ARPANET to World Wide Web' (2002), available at http://www.let.leidenuniv.nl/history/ivh/chap2.html (last visited 25 May 2016).

[8] NAFNET was basically program of co-ordinated, evolving projects sponsored by the National Science Foundation that was initiated in 1985 to support and promote advanced networking among US research and education institutions. See http://www.nsfnet-legacy.org/about.php (last visited 24 May 2016).

the same time, privatization shifted responsibility for the design, implementation, operation, and funding of the Internet from the Federal government to the private sector.[9]

It is this decision of privatization and commercialization of the Internet that has shaped the Internet we know today. It may be however, noted that while the Internet has become the nucleus of our daily functionalities, it is nevertheless relatively young and so are the companies that offer a range of online services, products, and facilities on the Internet. Amazon.com begun in 1995, allowing people to order through its digital shop; e-Bay was born in 1996 and grew to become a virtual market place. Google was launched in 1998, LinkedIn in 2003, Facebook in 2004, and YouTube did not exist until 2005 and Twitter until 2006. It may be observed that most of these companies are less than fifteen years old and yet, the way these have impacted human lives is unprecedented.

This increasingly pervasive, unpredictable, and rapidly changing interaction between the Internet and individuals has deeply affected and fundamentally reshaped almost every aspect of human life. For instance, the Internet offered an alternative to the infrastructure of discourse and as it was progressively absorbed and developed, it reshaped the idea of community, leading to the creation of an online community.[10] Perceived as an element of what Habermas calls the 'public sphere',[11] the virtual world offers a sphere where citizens can engage freely in public debate, free from the control of the government, or market physical place where the debate has

---

[9] See Bilal Chinoy and Tim Salo, 'Internet Exchanges: Policy Driven Evolution', https://www.caida.org/publications/papers/1996/nap/nap.html (last visited 24 May 2016). For detailed analysis on the graduated privatization and commercialization of the Internet in the US, see Brett Frischmann, *Privatisation and Commercialisation of the Internet Infrastructure: Rethinking Market Intervention into Government and Government Intervention into the Market*, 2 COLUM. SCI. & TECH. L. REV. 1 (2000-1).

[10] M. Price, 'Free Expression and Digital Dreams: The Open and Closed Terrain of Speech', *Critical Inquiry* 64: 69-70 (1995).

[11] J. Habermas, 'The Structural Transformation of the Public Sphere: An Inquiry into a Category of Bougeois Society' (1996); J. Habermas, 'Between Facts and Norms' (1992).

consequences.[12] However, different regimes have adopted different approaches to the Internet. Some of the regimes have resorted to completely blocking access or filtering technologies to limit access to specific websites on the Internet and thereby infringing their citizens' basic human right to freedom of speech and expression.[13] There are others that have recognized the citizen's right to access to the Internet as a fundamental right.[14]

[12] Price, 'Free Expression and Digital Dreams'.

[13] In Egypt, prior to the overthrow of Mubarak in 2011, politically sensitive websites were blocked. While no law specifically gave the government power to filter such websites, the Penal Code and the Emergency Law provided the government with the authority to restrict and monitor communications. Bruce Etling, Robert Faris, and John Palfrey, 'Political Change in the Digital Age. The Fragility and Promise of Online Organizing', 30 SAIS REV 37 (Summer-Fall 2010), available at http://dash.harvard.edu/handle/1/4609956 (last visited 25 May 2016); During the Arab Spring uprisings in early 2011, for example, the governments of China and Iran attempted to block the flow of images and information of the uprisings on their news networks and Internet. In China, the reaction was strong because the government feared a 'Jasmine Revolution' modeled on the pro-democracy protests that were spreading across the Arab world. Simon Cottle, *Media and the Arab Uprisings of 2011: Research Notes*, 12 Journalism 647: p. 654 (2011), available at http://www.contexting.me/files/CottleMediaandtheArabUprising.pdf (last visited 25 May 2016) cited in Young Joon Lim and Sarah E. Sexton, *Internet as a Human Right: A Practical Legal Framework to Address the Unique Nature of the Medium and to promote development*, 7 WASH. J.L. TECH. & Arts 295 (2011–12).

[14] For instance, in May 2009, the French parliament passed a new online copyright infringement law known as HADOPI, which gave power to a government agency to cut off people's Internet access for repeated copyright infringement. A month later, the country's Conseil Constitutionnel, or national constitutional court, found this power to cut off Internet connectivity an unconstitutional restriction on citizens' right to 'freedom of expression and communication'. *French Online Copyright Infringement Law Faces Challenges but May Create Business Opportunities*, TELECOMM., MEDIA & ENT. UPDATE (Hogan & Hartson LLP, D.C.), 1 (21 May 2009), available at http://www.hoganlovells.de/files/Publication/b3773467-7d3c-4d28-8546-be4e4952fba9/Presentation/PublicationAttachment/51918c8f-410b-4d7c-89c1-c40a85947978/TME_May2109.pdf (last visited 25 May 2016); In October 2009, the Finnish government passed a law making it a 'right' not only for its citizens

It has been progressively realized that the access to the Internet and rights share remarkably deeper relationship than earlier thought.[15] Access to the Internet and its transformative potentials can be critical in the advancement or retardation of human rights.[16] Those who have access to the virtual world find themselves better situated to seek, exercise, claim, and receive their needs and get to define the economic, social, and political landscape. For instance, in the context of the rights encapsulated in the Universal Declaration of Human Rights (UDHR), the Internet was found to be having significant effect in increasing the ability to exercise the right 'to hold opinions without interference and to seek, receive and impart information' and the right 'to freedom of peaceful assembly and association' recognized under Articles 19 and 20 of the UDHR. On the one hand, the Internet ensures the citizens' right to participation in government and equal access to public service (where the service is provided through the Internet) as stipulated in Article 21. On the other hand,

---

to have Internet access, but that the service provided by telecommunications companies must offer connectivity speeds of at least one megabit-per-second (Mbps). Conseil constitutionnel [CC] [Constitutional Court] decision No. 2009-580DC, 10 June 2009, J.O. 9675 (Fr.), *translated in Act Furthering the Diffusion and Protection of Creation on the Internet*, Decision no 2009-580, 4 (June 10, 2009) cited in Jonathon W. Penney, *Internet Access Rights: A Brief History and Intellectual Origins*, 38 WM. MITCHELL L. REV. 10 (2011-12).

[15] The international rights regime is a complex framework of inter-related rights articulated in a series of international agreements that share a number of common principles. These include the International Bill of Human Rights (the UDHR, ICCPR, ICESCR), regional Conventions, and a group of additional global Conventions concerned with the rights of women (CEDAW), children (CRC), people with disabilities (CRPD) and migrant workers (ICRMW), and with issues of racial discrimination (ICERD), torture (CAT) and disappearance (CPED). For an excellent and detailed impact assessment of internet on several human rights conventions and rights guaranteed there under, see Human Rights and the Internet: A Review of Perceptions in Human Rights Organisations, David Souter, Report to the Association for Progressive Communications (APC), available at http://www.apc.org/en/system/files/HumanRightsAndTheInternet_20120637.pdf (last visited 17 August 2014).

[16] APC Report, 'Human Rights and the Internet'.

threats from the Internet including cybercrime and surveillance pose new challenges to the 'security of person' under Article 3 as well as compromises on individuals' protection from 'arbitrary interference with his privacy, family, home, or correspondence, and from attacks upon his honour and reputation' enshrined in Article 12. Disparities in access to the Internet within a nation state can be held as violating an individual's right to employment (Article 23), right to education (Article 26) as well as right to freely participate in cultural life of community (Article 27), and most importantly right to equality (Article 2). Thus, the Internet occupies central position in empowering people to claim their basic human rights.

Consequent to exploring deeper convergences between the Internet and human rights, discussions surrounding access to the Internet have slowly gained momentum in recent years.[17] Taking cognizance of the significance of the Internet in human rights context, in his 2011 report to the United Nations General Assembly, the UN Special Rapporteur on Freedom of Expression,

---

[17] These developments are witnessed in academic exercises, domestic legislatures as well as international fora. See generally, Steven Hick, Edward Halpin, and Eric Hoskins, Human Rights and the Internet (2000); Michael L. Best, *Can the Internet Be a Human Right?*, 4 'Human Rights and Human Welfare' 23, p. 24 (2004); Alberto J Certa Silva, *Internet Freedom is not enough: Towards an Internet based on human rights*, 18 SUR-INT'L J. ON Human Rights 17 (2013). At domestic level, refer to law on access to the Internet access as a right in Estonia and Finland. In April 2014, Brazil passed a groundbreaking legislation touted as Brazil's 'Internet Constitution' that guarantees equal access to the Internet and protects privacy of Brazilian users. The French online copyright infringement law known as HADOPI passed in May 2009 which gave power to a government agency to cut off people's Internet access for repeated copyright infringement ran into difficulties. A month after passing the law, the country's Conseil Constitutionnel, or national constitutional court, found this power to cut off Internet connectivity an unconstitutional restriction on citizens' right to freedom of expression and communication. In New Zealand, back in 2008, Internet access was likened to a basic human right by key government officials. At international level, range of charters and principle initiatives are emerging in international bodies and regional bodies such as IGF, the Council of Europe.

Frank La Rue, suggested that ensuring access to the Internet should be a 'priority' for the States, and reminded the government 'of their positive obligation to promote or to facilitate the enjoyment of the right to freedom of expression and the means necessary to exercise this right, including the Internet'.[18]

Whereas the Internet has positively transformed lives of many, lives and living for several others have remained untouched. According to ITU, 3.9 billion people, more than half the world's total population, are still offline.[19] Access to the Internet has not occurred uniformly across the globe. There are disparities in its geographical and demographical reach. Various factors, including socio-economic status, education level, geography, age, disability, language, and literacy, leave large numbers of people underserved, disadvantaged, or underrepresented in the access to the Internet and their knowledge of how to use this technology.[20]

This disparity has led to a digital divide. Those on the wrong side of the divide are rendered heavily disempowered. For persons with disabilities, the digital divide amounts to an extension of their exclusion and marginalization from the physical world to the virtual world. Whereas the Internet was initially credited as holding the potential to dismantle the barriers and be the greatest mechanism for inclusion of person with disabilities ever invented,[21] a constantly expanding and inaccessible Internet creates new barriers for persons with disabilities.

[18] Human Rights Council, Special Rapporteur on the Promotion and Protection of the Right to Freedom of Opinion and Expression, *Report of the Special Rapporteur on Key Trends and Challenges to the Right of all Individuals to Seek, Receive and Impart Information and Ideas of All Kinds Through the Internet* (By Frank La Rue) UN Doc. A/HRC/17/27.

[19] *Measuring the Information Society Report 2016*, International Telecommunication Union, available at http://www.itu.int/en/ITU-D/Statistics/Pages/publications/mis2016.aspx (last visited 31 August, 2017).

[20] Paul T. Jaeger, John Carlo Bertot, Kim M. Thompson, Sarah M. Katz, and Elizabeth J. DeCoster, 'The Intersection of Public Policy and Public Access: Digital Divides, Digital Literacy, Digital Inclusion, and Public Libraries', Public Library Quarterly 31 (1) (2012) DOI:10.1080/01616846.2012.654728

[21] Paul T. Jaeger, 'Disability and the Internet: Confronting a Digital Divide' 33 (2012).

The Internet Rhetoric and Rights of Persons with Disabilities

'The Internet is not just a window on the world, but more and more the Internet is the world. It is where we talk, it is where we shop, and it is where we make our living.'[22] These are words of Gary Wunder, a visually impaired American, who was advocating for Internet accessibility for the blind at the 2000 House Judiciary Hearing on the Americans with Disabilities Act (ADA) and the Internet.

The emergence of a decentralized, fragmented, and low-cost Internet held promises for persons with disabilities to lead an autonomous and inclusive life which was denied to them in the physical world. The Internet opened up the possibilities for people to attend classes, find jobs, bank, transact business, read newspapers, shop, meet new people, converse with friends and family, and watch movies. However, advancements in information and communication technologies belied initial promises it made and progressively failed the aspirations of persons with disabilities. For instance, some individuals with disabilities, such as those with visual, auditory, or muscular impairments are unable to access many features of today's Internet.[23] Their exclusion from information is exacerbated by the difficulty of obtaining material in alternative formats.[24] Lessing,

---

[22] Applicability of the Americans with Disabilities Act (ADA) to Private Internet Sites: Hearing before the H.R. Subcomm. on Constitution of the H. Comm. on the Judiciary, 106th Cong. 16 (2000).

[23] See Jeffrey Scott Ranen, 'Was Blind but Now I See: The Argument for ADA Applicability to the Internet', Boston College Third World. 389 (2002): 390 (noting that 98 per cent of websites 'are to some extent inaccessible to the visually disabled'); Applicability of the ADA to Private Internet Sites: Hearings before the House Subcomm. on the Constitution of the House Comm. on the Judiciary, 106th Cong. (2000): 31-2, available at http://www.house.gov/judiciary/2.htm (last visited 17 May 2016).

[24] Anna Lawson, *Challenging Disabling Barriers to Information and Communication Technology in the Information Society: A United Kingdom Perspective,* in European Yearbook of Disability Law 2 131 (Lisa Waddington and Gerard Quinn eds) 2010.

a leading internet scholar lamented 'when graphics entered the Net... the blind became "blind" again'.[25]

Progressive crowding of the virtual world led to crowding out of persons with disabilities. The inequalities, stereotypes, and attitudes of the physical world replicated in the virtual world with growing community participation. Just as most people ordinarily do not think about ramps or elevators when approaching a building, most people on the Internet do not consider structural issues relating to accessibility. Failure to provide Internet access is not analogous to a city's reluctance to retrofit a historical building. It has more serious ramifications on rights of persons with disabilities. For instance, while persons without disabilities are progressively applying for and finding jobs, educational positions, health care online, persons with disabilities face significant barriers to availing these opportunities due to inaccessible features of the Internet. Besides accessibility, the availability, affordability, and usability of the products and services in general and those availed on and from the Internet, in particular, are a matter of concern.

In a virtual manifestation of social injustice, the interests and inclusion of persons with disabilities on the Internet were soon invisiblized. This exclusion resulted in a second round of exclusion, this time from the virtual world[26] rendering them disempowered.

Social justice theorists have come under attack for having excluded persons with disabilities from initial social contracting and consequently providing an inferior, segregated structure in subsequent stages.[27] It has been argued that persons with

---

[25] Lawrence Lessig, Code and Other Laws of Cyberspace 66 (1999).

[26] Jaeger, 'Disability and the Internet', p. 177.

[27] Maratha Nussabaum, *Frontiers of Justice: Disability, Nationality, Species Membership* (2006) (this work comprise a deeply thought critique of social justice theorists especially that of Rawls. The author challenges the social justice theories restriction on participation in the initial social contracting. It is argued that such restrictive process for mutual advantage cannot do justice to the persons with disabilities. The social contract theory is charged with creating an 'outlier problem' and resulting in 'unsolved problems on which justice as fairness may fail'. The author offers an alternative 'capabilities approach' which develops a non-contractarian idea of justice centered on human dignity. The capabilities approach proffers the widest possible distribution (at least

disabilities have a right to live in the world in an inclusive and participatory manner on an equal basis with others.[28] Full and effective realization of this right, nevertheless, requires dismantling social and attitudinal barriers including those to the Internet. While demands for dismantling physical barriers have long existed, increasingly attention is gathered to barriers to and in the virtual world.

Accessibility has been at the heart of disability rights as long as persons with disabilities have demanded equal treatment. Disability rights movement has been crusading for years to ensure inclusion, access and participation in society, culminating into an express recognition of their human rights by the CRPD. Primarily based on substantive equality, CRPD aims to ensure 'respect for difference'.[29] The concept of substantive equality reconfigures equality so that the norm itself is refashioned to incorporate social diversity. Accordingly, it entails a proactive approach so to tackle 'systemic forms of discrimination rooted in society'. Persons with disabilities have remained a discrete and insular minority, who has suffered from a history of discrimination and who are relatively powerless politically and are socially excluded. Mindful of this exclusion, CRPD mandates removal of barriers which in interaction with impairments hinder full and effective

---

among humankind) of all the capabilities, each to be attained at least to the threshold level required for a dignified life).

[28] Jacobus ten Broek, 'The Right to Live in the World: The Disabled in the Law of Torts', 54 CAL. L. REV. 841 (1966): 841–52 (arguing for the right of people with disabilities to live in the world. This right required access to 'common modes of transportation, communication and interchange', including 'full and equal access to places of public accommodation', which enable communal interaction for disability. It was therefore, suggested to have integration as 'the policy of the nation' that would further require legal innovations to effectuate the right of people with disabilities 'to live in the world'. The policy of integrationism as 'a policy entitling the disabled to full participation in the life of the community and encouraging and enabling them to do so . . . .').

[29] D. Chalmers, G. Davies, and G. Monti, *European Union Law: Cases and Materials* (2011).

participation of person with disability in society on an equal basis with others.[30]

It needs to be appreciated that human rights guaranteed to persons with disabilities has to be realized in societies that are fast getting digitalized. Even where CRPD recognizes a full range of civil, political, economic, and socio-cultural rights, effective realization of rights may not be possible unless access to the Internet is ensured. The rise of the Internet points towards future issues, for society, for architects of virtual society, and persons with disabilities.[31]

State and Corporation in the Information Age

Forces of globalization riding on the tide of information and technological revolution propelled by the Internet has not only broadened and deepened cross border transactions between different economies but has also increased levels of complexity and interdependencies. Reinicke notes that 'spatial reorganization of corporate activity leads to the emergence of a single, integrated economic geography defined by the reach of corporate industrial networks and their financial relationships. These networks and relationships cut across multiple political geographies, challenging the operational dimension of internal sovereignty, as governments no longer have a monopoly of the legitimate power over the territory within which these private sector actors organize themselves'.[32] While forces of globalization and privatization and their

---

[30] Article 9 stipulates: 'to enable persons with disabilities to live independently and participate fully in all aspects of life, States Parties shall take appropriate measures to ensure to persons with disabilities access, on an equal basis with others, to the physical environment, to transportation, to information and communications, including information and communications technologies and systems, and to other facilities and services open or provided to the public, both in urban and in rural areas.'

[31] Paul T. Jaeger and Cynthia Ann Bowman, *Understanding Disbaility: Inclusion, Access, Diversity and Civil Rights* (2005).

[32] Wolfgang Reinicke, 'Global Public Policy: Governing without Government.' 7(1998) (emphasis in the original).

implications on the state, community, authority, and relationships are still being fully understood, the digital revolution and rise of the Internet completely changed the power dynamics. Economic interdependence, deregulation, and dominance of markets and networked society have together curtailed the powers of states.

Historical literature on the Internet informs us that while the state discharged a fundamental role in the initiation of the Internet, later development was carried out by private and commercial players. The result of the commercialization and privatization process is that '[v]ery little of the current Internet is owned, operated, or even controlled by governmental bodies. Today large part of provisioning of Internet communication services, regardless of use, is being handled by commercial firms on a profit-making basis.'[33] Corporations in the information economy, in which information is a central resource, turn out to be highly mobile and independent of any specific location. The ability to convey information and knowledge easily allowed corporations to organize themselves across national borders, thereby decreasing the dominance of the State in organizing economic relations.[34]

The growth and proliferation of the Internet re-conceptualized and redefined the relationship between the public-private, state-citizen, and domestic-international, at the same time challenging the role of the state as the only legitimate policy and decision maker. Non-state actors, especially corporations, became new repositories of private authority and economic power. Furthermore, the design of the technology—or code—provided private companies with regulatory power to shape the information environment.[35] Overall, the private sector in the digital environment enjoys more power in setting the agenda and shaping the priorities.

[33] Robert E. Kahn, 'The Role of Government in the Evolution of the Internet', in *Revolution in the US Information Infrastructure* 13 (1995): 13.

[34] See Christopher May, *The Information Society: A Sceptical View*, pp. 114–48 (2002) (arguing that 'the suggestion that states are likely to decline in importance in the information age is mistaken').

[35] Lessig, Code and Other Laws of Cyberspace (1999); Joel Reidenberg, *Lex Informatica: The Formulation of Information Policy Rules through Technology*, 76 TEX. L. REV. 553 (1998).

Since the Internet and its designs, architecture, and services are virtually corporate colonies of private authority; corporations remain the gatekeepers to the Internet. This combination of authority and capability of corporations empowers them to make a positive change by advancing access and thereby the realm of all civil, political, social, economical, cultural, constitutional, and human rights on the Internet, of the Internet and related to the Internet.

Therefore, there are renewed claims to corporate obligations. If corporations hold the key to access the Internet instead of the State, is it not obvious that corporations are duty bearers? The profit driven corporations may be inclined to promote access to the Internet to such areas and population which hold promise of surest returns on investment at lowest possible risk. However, human rights dimension holds interest in ensuring access to the most disadvantaged members of society whose rights may be jeopardized in the absence of access. This situation is further complicated by the fact that the nature and scope of corporation's direct obligation under international human rights law is unsettled, even where corporations themselves have progressively accepted their societal obligation.

Corporation's Societal and Human Rights Obligations

Ever since corporations first emerged more than a century and a half ago, the relationship between the state, corporations, and wider society has undergone frequent transformation. During these years the nature and scope of corporations, their scale of functioning, their governance structures, and their interactions with multiple stakeholders have undergone a major overhaul. Corporations have achieved vast wealth and immense influence.[36] They exercise

---

[36] See generally, United Nations Conference on Trade and Development, *The Universe of the Largest Transnational Corporations*, UN Doc. UNCTAD/ ITE/IIA/2007/2 (2007) available at http://www.unctad.org/en/docs/ iteiia20072_en.pdf (last visited 10 April 2015) (compiling a list of the 100 largest non-financial transnational corporations and the top fifty transnational corporations from developing countries).

economic, political, and legal influence in home countries, the country of incorporation, and host countries—the country in which assets or operations are located.

Examining the historical and theoretical development of metaphysical theories of the corporation suggests that questions about 'what corporations are' has engendered a longstanding debate about 'what ought to be their role in society'.[37] This debate played out along legal, political, economic, and social lines. Participants to this debate grouped themselves as contractarians and communitarians. According to contractarian view various participants in corporate activity specify their respective rights and obligations through contract. The state corporate law provides the terms of the contract by which shareholders purchase management's undivided loyalty to their welfare. The key term is management's fiduciary duty to direct the corporation so as to maximize shareholder wealth.[38] Communitarians believe since individuals including corporations are members of shared community, they owe obligations to each other irrespective and independent of any contract.

The Corporate Social Responsibility debate began as early as 1930 with an exchange of views between Professors Merrick Dodd and Adolf Berle on the corporation as an economic entity versus a social entity.[39] Some recent debates have reshaped the issue as competing claims between shareholders versus stakeholder interests.

---

[37] See generally, Morton J. Horwitz, 'Santa Clara Revisited: The Development of Corporate Theory', 88 W. VA. L. REV. 173 (1985).

[38] David K. Millon, 'New Directions in Corporate Law communitarians, Contractarians, and the crisis in Corporate Law', 50 WASH. & LEE L. REV. 1373 (1993): 1378.

[39] See E. Merrick Dodd, Jr., 'For Whom are Corporate Managers Trustees?', 45 HARV. L. REV. 1145, 1162 (1932); Adolph A. Berle, Jr., 'For Whom are Corporate Managers Trustees: A Note', 45 HARV. L. REV. 1365, 1368 (1932). Analyzing the fiduciary duties of the board of directors from the perspective of the nature of corporation Dodd and Berle applied different perspectives of the nature of corporation and developed different implications about the fiduciary duties of the board of directors depending upon such nature. Thus, Berle argued that the powers granted to the board are necessarily exercisable only for the benefit of the all the shareholders. Dodd countered this position

It has been argued *ad nauseam* that corporations are primarily designed to serve economic purposes of profit maximization, rather than assuming broad-based welfare functions.[40] Yet there are counter-voices that dismiss shareholder primacy perception of the corporation on the basis that corporations is an instance of team production, requiring the firm-specific inputs of various constituents, including employees, middle managers, and the

---

with a view that the modern corporation is a quasi-public entity, and that the board of directors had quasi-public responsibilities to multiple constituencies.

[40] Most prominent amongst these is Milton Friedman. In his celebrated book *Capitalism and Freedom*, Friedman briefly dealt with the question of corporate social responsibility. He elaborated his views on the topic in 1970 is the essay 'The Social Responsibility of Business is to Increase its Profits', *The New York Times Magazine*, 13 September, 1970. (It is argued that the view that corporate officials and labour leaders have a 'social responsibility' that goes beyond serving the interests of their stockholders or their members is a fundamental misconception of the character and nature of a free market economy. In such an economy, there is one and only one social responsibility of business-to use its resources and engage in activities designed to increase its profits so long as it stays within the rules of the game, which is to say, engage in open and free competition, without deception or fraud). Ronald Coase developed an alternative paradigm to Friedman's understanding of how businesses should act, arguing that businesses are best understood by observing carefully their actual conduct rather than creating artificial models of how they ought to act. See Ronald Harry Coase, *The Firm, the Market, and the Law* (1988). The past fifteen years have demonstrated that major businesses are, in fact, becoming aware of the interplay between their businesses and their impact on individuals, communities, and the environment; they realize that respect for human rights leads to better business performance and find it beneficial to issue their own codes of conduct that go far beyond a narrow profit motive or legal mandates. Hence, the creation of human rights standards that help attract the best and brightest employees, solicit investments from investors who place at least some socially responsible screen on their stock holdings, and attract consumers who prefer to purchase goods made without child labor or unnecessarily soiling the environment are not contrary to the primary purpose of transnational corporations and other business enterprises. The creation of a uniform set of international human rights standards would aid in this process by helping to make clear what human rights standards a company should follow and which business enterprises are meeting those standards.

communities in which business operations are located.[41] Therefore, interests of stakeholders must be taken on board.

The contractarian versus communitarian debate on corporations takes on harder questions on international human rights law. It examines whether there are theoretical grounds for constructing affirmative corporate human rights obligations. Is there any basis for imposing duties on corporations to mitigate any potential harm they might be causing by violating human rights? Is it feasible to entrust positive human rights obligations to corporations to ensure advancement of human rights?

International human rights law has been oscillating between the need to respond to the growing disparities between private power and public authority and classical understanding of violators and protectors of human rights. Modern human rights law does not generally directly regulate corporations. International human rights agreements are—by definition—agreements between nation states. Thus, international human rights documents having recorded an understanding of human rights and human dignity; place obligations on the doorstep of the State to realize the goals by enacting and enforcing laws that protect human rights. This understanding about the protector and promoter of human rights is heavily influenced by the twentieth century's exposure to human destruction in the World Wars at the hands of the State. According to this classical understanding, corporations cannot create customary international law which is only a prerogative of the states and merely based on their importance, a corporation cannot be automatically imposed with duties.[42] Another objection that fortifies this argument is the claim that corporations were not traditionally recognized as

---

[41] Margaret M. Blair and Lynn A. Stout, *A Team Production Theory of the Corporation*, 85 VA. L. REV. 247 (1999): 280, 288 (fiduciary duties of directors extend to corporation, not to shareholders per se).

[42] A.C. Arend, *Legal Rules and International Society* (1999) argues that even though non-state actors exist, and in some cases these non-state actors have entered into international agreements, these actors do not enter the process of creating general international law in an unmediated fashion. The interactions of non-state actors with each other and with states do not produce customary international law.

subjects of international law and therefore they cannot be imposed with obligations.[43] Others support this view on grounds that in the absence of enforcement mechanism, no obligations can be imposed on corporations.[44]

Times have changed and so have the realization and the reality that corporations are equally capable of interfering with human rights. First, corporations can be direct violators of human rights. This 'negative' focus has been prompted by apparently increasing instance, and certainly visibility, of such examples of human rights abuse as sweatshop labour in the footwear and apparel industries; environmental, health and cultural degradation in the extractive industries; and personal integrity and freedoms abuses by security forces guarding infrastructure, factories, and other installations of corporations in various fields of enterprise.[45] Second, they can indirectly violate human rights by supporting a regime that violates human rights. Third, besides the fact that they may threaten an effective enjoyment of human rights, they can also have a positive role in advancing human rights.[46] To say that corporations abstain from abusing/violating and thereby retarding human rights is one

---

[43] For introduction to the debate as to whether non-state actors should fit in a theory of international relations, see A.Weenink, 'The Relevance of Being Important or the Importance of Being Relevant? State and Non-State Actors in International Relations Theory', in Non-state Actors in International Relations (B. Arts, M. Noortmann and B. Reinalda eds, 2001); D. Thureer, 'The Emergence of Non-Governmental Organisations and Transnational Enterprises in International Law and the Changing Role of the State', in Non-State Actors as New Subjects of International Law: International Law from Traditional State Order towards the Law of the Global Community (R. Hoffmann ed., 1999).

[44] Carlos M. Vazquez, 'Direct vs. Indirect Obligations of Corporations under International Law', *Georgetown University Law Centre*, 43 colum. J. Transnatl' L. 927 (2005): 940-1.

[45] David Kinely and Rachel Chambers, 'The UN Human Rights Norms for Corporations: The Private Implications of Public International Law', 6 HUM. RTS. L. REV. 447 (2006).

[46] O. de. Schutter, 'Transnational Corporations as Instruments of Human Development', in *Human Rights and Development: Towards Mutual Reinforcement*, pp. 403-44 (P. Alston and M. Robinson eds, 2005).

thing; to command its proactive engagement in protection and advancement of human rights is another.

Consequently, a contrary view has emerged which contends that international human rights laws can be extended to corporations.[47] It is argued that international law is becoming a less state-centric legal regime, allowing the possibility to identify new duty holders in the area of human rights. This view has provoked thinking about human rights law in new ways to meet challenges posed by private actors[48] and espoused theorizing on

[47] J.A. Zerk, *Multinationals and Corporate Social Responsibility: Limitations and Opportunities in International Law* (2006) (arguing that soft law tradition of international law has the potential to develop into hard law. She argues that the states are capable of developing regulatory framework based on the soft law experience. Zerk acknowledges that while it may be problematic to negotiate an overarching treaty on CSR, devising international regimes to tackle specific CSR issues may be more feasible.) Rosalyn Higgins, *Problems and Process: International Law and How We Use It* (1994) (arguing that it is better to speak of international participants rather than subjects).

[48] Ralph G. Steinhardt, 'Corporate Responsibility and the International Law of Human Rights: The New Lex Mercatoria', in Non-State Actors and Human Rights 177, pp. 180–7 (Philip Alston ed., 2005) (arguing that that subjectivity under international law does not serve as a barrier through both historical and current models. Steinhardt argues that an artificial distinction between the realms of the public (human rights) and private (corporate activities) molded about the state-centric international legal model results in a misinterpretation of corporate and human rights interactions unreflective of contemporary reality and inhibitive of future productive legal discourse. Corporations have become obligation-bearers under the international human rights regime for negative and positive rights); A. Clapham, *Human Rights in the Private Sphere* (1993) (arguing that international human rights laws demands states protect individuals from private acts which threaten their rights. Where the state so fails to protect, it amounts violation of international obligations. Acknowledging the progressive difficulty in differentiating between private and public sphere, it is suggested that in certain circumstances, human rights obligations may give rise to directly enforceable duties on the private actors themselves. It is therefore, emphasized that we need to reconceptualize our understanding about human rights); A. Clapham, *Human Rights Obligations of Non-State Actors* (2006) (examining the recent human rights cases, the book elaborate ideas to develop an understanding of the importance of

corporate responsibility.[49] Paradoxically, while understanding of nexus between human rights and corporate have deepened with the privatized, globalized, and technological advanced world order; expectations from the States to meet human rights obligations have not yet been modified. Although a process has already been initiated to create an international legally binding instrument to regulate, in international human rights law, the activities of transnational corporations (TNCs) and other business enterprises;[50] the work

---

human rights accountability for corporations and other non-state actors. Such paradigm shift from state-centric approach to human rights protection, requires developing a framework for non-state actors and the distinctions between the state and non-state activity). David Kinley and Junko Tadaki, 'From Talk to Walk: The Emergence of Human Rights Responsibilities for Corporations at International Law', 44 VA. J. INT'L L. (2004): 931 (Professor Kinley and Barrister Tadaki extrapolate more specific duties and argue for more positive rights obligations to be required of the TNC).

[49] Steven R. Ratner, 'Corporations and Human Rights: A Theory of Legal Responsibility', 111 YALE L.J. 443 (2001): 459. (Ratner has developed 'concentric circles' theory which takes into account the 'diverse structures' of corporations as well as unique 'modes of operating' employed by businesses in a particular country. These are elaborated as (a) the nexus between the corporation and the government, (b) the nexus between the corporation and the affected population, and (c) the substantive human rights at issue and (d) where the corporation acts as an agent of the State. This theory has been found to be of particular relevance in areas such as labour law and environmental law. Susan Strange, *The Retreat of the State: The Diffusion of Power in the World Economy*, pp. 16–43 (1996) (concluding that globalization is marked by a fragmentation of authority and that economic power likely matters more than political power, thus markets are more important sources of power than states).

[50] Human Rights Council, Resolution 26/9, 'Elaboration of an internationally legally binding instrument on transnational corporations and other business enterprises with respect to human rights', 26th Sess., June 10–27, 2014, A/HRC/26/L.22/Rev.1 para 1(26 June 2014). The resolution was tabled by Ecuador and South Africa, co-sponsored by Bolivia, Cuba, and Venezuela and supported coalition of civil society organizations who formed a 'Treaty Alliance'. The proposal was highly divisive within the 47-members-large Human Rights Council with 20 member states supporting, 14 states (including the United States and the Member States of the European Union) opposing and 13 member states abstaining.

is in its early stage and substantive contents, procedures are far from settled. In the meantime, existing international human rights law do not in effect have any mechanism in place which regulates corporations' negative duties towards human rights—duty not to violate human rights. It is left to states to effectively regulate corporations within their domestic laws. Thus, a primary regulatory gap emerge from the fact that corporations are multinational while legal systems are still largely national, creating disconnect between international corporate structures and the law.

While corporations have long been under the gaze of society and international human rights for good or bad reasons, the attention they garner in the virtual world is more recent. Thus, corporations in the virtual world were found to be equally potent to retard or advance human rights. Corporations as direct violators of human rights could heavily curtail and compromise the freedom of speech, privacy, and of the Internet participants. Indeed, if the information technology can function as a tool of the oppressed, it can just as much serve the oppressor—'technologies of freedom' can just as easily become technologies of abuse. The amounts of publicly available information on every aspect of a person's life, from commercial activities, to medical treatment or associations and memberships can become an incredibly powerful tool which governments, businesses, and individuals can exploit at the expense of individual rights and privacy.[51] There have been instances when corporations have indirectly violated human rights by supporting a regime that violated human rights. Besides the fact that they may threaten an effective enjoyment of human rights, they can also have a positive role in advancing human rights.[52]

However, corporations have proven to be too complicated target of social regulation both at the domestic and international

---

[51] See, for example, Fred Weingarten, *Communications Technology: New Challenges to Privacy*, 21 JOHN MARSHALL L. REV. 735 (1988); Mark Fall, *Privacy Projections of Computerized Information*, 2 S. CAL. Interdisciplinary J. 170 (1993); David Flaherty, *Protecting Privacy in Surveillance Societies: The Federal Republic of Germany, Sweden, France, Canada, and the United States* 1 (1989).

[52] Schutter, 'Transnational Corporations as Instruments of Human Development'.

level. Whereas initial regulatory practices applied various instrumentalities (hard law/soft law) and approaches (deterrence/co-operation) as alternatives to one another, more recent regulatory scholarship has taken a more innovative approach to regulation. In consideration of the increasing complexity of the societal problems and corporate structures and way of functioning, the new regulatory techniques have engaged with the mapping and understanding the expansion of state, market, and civil society based regulation at local, national, and transnational levels.[53] Prominent among these works is the Ayres and Braithwaites enforcement pyramid which applies combination of persuasion and punishment in a gradation style,[54] others suggest matching regulatory tools to the

[53] John Braithwaite and Peter Drahos, 'Global Business Regulation' (2008) (demonstrating how patterns of regulation emerge and arguing how business regulation has shifted from national to global regulation); John Braithwaite, *Regulatory Capitalism: How it Works, Ideas for Making it Work Better* (2008); Benjamin, 'Legitimacy and the Privatisation of Environmental Governance: How Non-state Market-driven Governance (NSMD) Systems Gain Rule-making Authority', in *Responsible Business: Self-Governance and Law in Transnational Economic Transaction* (Olaf Dilling, Martin Herberg and Gerd Winter eds, 2008); Jacint Jordana and David Levi-Faur, *The Politics of Regulation Institutions and Regulatory Reforms for the New Age Governance* (2004) (investigating the evolution in the manner and extent of governance through regulation); Christaine Parkers, *The Open Corporation: Effective Self-Regulation and Democracy* (2002) (arguing that law and regulators need to focus on meta regulation of corporation in order to advance democratic control of corporation).

[54] Amongst the most influential regulatory theories has been the seminal work of Ian Ayres and John Braithwaite, *Responsive Regulation: Transcending The Deregulation Debate* (1992) (Moving the debate beyond 'deterrence' v. 'co-operation', Ian Ayres and John Braithwaite introduced the model of 'responsive regulation'. According to this model the trick of successful regulation is to establish a synergy between punishment and persuasion.[54] Ayres and Braithwaite argue that regulatory sanctions and strategies should be aligned to the mixed motives or objectives of corporate actors in order to ensure an effective and efficient regulatory framework); N. Gunningham, P. Grobosky, and D. Sinclair, *Smart Regulation: Designing Environment Policy* (1998) (Unlike the Ayres and Briathwaite pyramid which is concerned with the interaction only between the State and business; Smart regulation considers

task.[55] Most of these regulatory models have primarily been designed to address health care, environment, labour related issues. There exists a governance gap between realities of the present technology driven societies and human rights expectations from the States. This gap widens in the context of human rights associated with the virtual world where corporations occupy a dominating position than the state.

Corporations, Disability Rights, and the Internet access

Even as disability rights scholars assert that right of persons with disabilities to live in the world also encompasses the right to live

---

third set of players. Accordingly, regulation can be carried out not merely by the State but by businesses themselves and by quasi-regulators such as public interest groups, professional bodies and industry associations); R. Baldwin and J. Black, 'Really Responsive Regulation', 71 MODERN L. REV 59 (2008) (the really responsive framework set out to offer a framework for considering how in any given context, the main challenges of design can be addressed and how issues of regulatory mix can be analysed. It takes on board not only the issues of institutional and instrumental variety but also the significance of variations in regulatees and regulators as well as the difficulties of effecting performance assessments. It has two main considerations on focus—One, that in designing and developing regulatory systems and especially complex, multi-actor regimes, attention has to be paid to five essential factors. These are the behaviour, attitudes, and cultures of regulatory actors; the institutional settings of the different regulators; the different logics of regulatory tools and strategies and how these interact; the regime's own performance over time and finally changes in each of these elements. Two, the main tasks of the regulators comprise in detecting non-compliant behaviour, development, enforcement, assessment, and modification of tools and strategies. The regulatory designs and developments, therefore, should take on board the regulatory challenges that are likely to be encountered by the regulators in carrying out these tasks).

[55] M. Sparrow, *The Regulatory Craft* (2003) (Central to Sparrow's approach is the need to pick the most important task and then decide on the important tools, rather than 'decide on the important tools and pick the tasks to fit. Such problem centered approach assumes that regulation can be parceled into problems and projects to be addressed by project teams. Sparrow tells us to

in the virtual world,[56] and worried about the divide, the rights and the divide is narrowly scoped in terms of accessible websites,[57] or contents or inaccessible products or services. The digital divide continues to be seen as a technical infrastructural problem to be sorted out at the domestic level. At the most, it is viewed as a socio-economic problem, rarely as a human rights issue. Moreover, while corporate human rights obligations have been discussed *ad nauseam* in popular contexts such as environmental issues, indigenous labour, its theoretical and regulatory implications requires a closer scrutiny in a society which is soon advancing towards digitalization.

---

target key problems and solve these by developing solutions or interventions and implementing the plan. It separates out the stages of problem solving and stresses the need to define problems precisely to monitor and measure performance and to adjust strategy on the basis of performance assessments).

[56] Bradley A. Areheart and Michael Ashley Stein, *Integrating the Internet*, 83 George Washington L. REV. 449 (2015). Available at http://ssrn.com/ abstract=2420510 (arguing that the right to live in the world, naturally encompasses the right to live in the virtual world. The article develops a claim that the Internet is a place of public accommodation, which must be integrated. The issue is, however, even more pressing as the Internet is broad enough to encompass all of the traditional categories of public accommodations—as well as social arenas like education and work).

[57] Peter Blanck, *eQuality: The Struggle for Web Accessibility by Persons With Cognitive Disabilities* (2014) (providing a highly comprehensive and recent position pertaining to the web accessibility with particular focus on persons with cognitive disabilities); Paul T. Jaeger, *Disability and the Internet: Bridging The Digital Divide* (arguing that access to the Internet is integral for persons with disabilities and traces the historical, legal evolution of the digital disability divide in education, work, social life and culture); Mark N. Cooper, 'Symposium: Bridging the Digital Divide: Equality in the Information Age: Why the Digital Divide Deserves All the Attention it Gets', 20 Cardozo Arts & ENT. LJ 73 (2002). (Deepening the discussion of the digital divide debate by digging beneath the surface indicators of the divide, computer ownership and Internet connectivity, and boring down into behavioral implications, such as civic participation, as well as examining the underlying causative trends of the divide. The article presents empirical discussions of the nature of the transformation of society, the causes of the digital divide, and the technology experience of societies and households (not only ownership, but also use of and attitudes towards computers and the Internet); Gary Annable, Gerard

It is therefore important to worry about the ways and means of attaining accessibility rights of persons with disabilities who are the most recent entrants to human rights. Can corporation be recognized as new addressee of human rights? How do we seek their compliance and involvement with emerging human rights goals? Do we need new normative and theoretical framework of corporation's obligations? Is it possible to identify areas and issues where direct human rights obligations can be imposed on corporations? Do we need new laws, a new legal system, or a different approach to seek corporate compliance? This book examines emerging disability rights and technologically advanced Internet society and undertakes an interrogation of corporate obligation.

Major Claims

In this backdrop, this book advances two claims. CRPD embraces substantive equality model and aims at dismantling general social

---

Goggin and Deborah Stienstra, 'Accessibility, Disability, and Inclusion in Information Technologies: Introduction', 23, *The Information Society: An International Journal* 145 (2007) DOI:10.1080/01972240701323523 (observing how with the rise of concepts of the information society and developments with convergent information and communications technologies, questions have been raised on accessibility and inclusion by disability. Although the topic has gradually become visible and legible to scholars, policymakers, scientists and technologists, businesspeople, and civil society organizations; it still has not received, however, the sustained study, analysis, and debate it merits.) Joshua L. Friedman and Gary C. Norman, 'The Norman/Friedman Principle: Equal Rights to Information and Technology Access', 18 TEX. J. ON C.L. & C.R. 47(2012) (arguing that in Information Age, a society that does not commit itself to a proactive effort respecting information and digital access propagates injustice, denigrates affirmative civil rights already on the books. The article contributes to a dialogue about the problem of accessibility. It puts forth a broader understanding of constitutional jurisprudence, in the context of the US Constitution that arguable supports an affirmative right to information and technology access. The authors also posit that, regardless of whether the US Supreme Court declares the existence of the right to technology access, positive legislation on the state and local levels will provide much-needed progress towards protecting the civil rights of the disabled).

and attitudinal barriers to participation and inclusion of persons with disabilities. Insofar as the accessibility barriers to the virtual world are concerned, the dismantling has to happen at the corporate end. The **prefatory claim** is that under disability rights jurisprudence, the right to access the Internet is a human right which cannot be realized unless corporations are also recognized as duty bearers and entrusted with positive obligations towards accessibility.

Considering the progressive shift in power and resources to corporations, their roles must inevitably be scrutinized under the rubric of human rights more conscientiously—not because corporations did not have obligations prior to this point, (all actors capable of effecting the dignity of the individual have such obligations)—but because their potential to either promote the realization of human rights or harm that realization and escape liability for doing so has exponentially increased. It is problematic when international human rights focus and impose duties singularly upon the State leading to breakdown of effective realization of human rights in those areas where corporations have an obvious control.

However, there exists normative and enforcement inadequacies in international human rights frameworks in so recognizing corporations as duty bearers. At the same time most domestic anti-discrimination laws pre-date the Internet age and rely on reactive approach based on individual litigation; they are ill-equipped to address systemic discrimination meted out to persons with disabilities.

The **central claim** is that the evolving nature of the virtual world and disability rights jurisprudence demands new legal and strategic framework to obtain proactive corporate compliance. An 'Interconnected Pentagon Model' offers a regulatory web of influences to obtain the corporate compliance and its proactive engagement to the attainment of goals of substantive equality and inclusion of persons with disabilities in the virtual world.

The arguments regarding the aforesaid claims have been neatly sequenced. After scoping the right to access the Internet as human right and what precisely could be the contents of this right, the next logical step identifies corporations as duty bearers of the right to access along with states and why should corporations be held obligable. This is followed by a detailed analysis of the available regulatory approaches, strategies, instrumentalities at international and national level and finally provides an interconnected pentagon model to seek corporate compliance. The book is divided into seven chapters including this introductory chapter. A brief narration of each chapter will follow next.

Even where the significance of the right to access the Internet is widely acknowledged, contesting claims prevail regarding the exact scope and nature of this right. The next chapter aims to offer an understanding about deeper convergences between the Internet and human rights with the specific context of accessibility concerns of persons with disabilities. The chapter begins by introducing the crusade of the disability rights towards inclusion and participation which now extends to the virtual world. However, there exists an ongoing controversy whether the right to access the Internet for persons with disabilities in itself is a human right or merely an enabling right. The underlying purpose is to draw a conclusion about the status of the right to access the Internet vis-a-vis disability. The inquiry is one of primary concern since responses and the urgency of action will be directly proportionate to the stature so accorded to the right to access. It is argued that reading the right to access merely as an enabling right is oversimplification of an otherwise complex issue, especially in the context of disability rights. The naturalist theories of human right are invoked in favour of right to access the Internet and the same examined under equality-anti-discrimination approach, autonomy approach and active citizenship approach.

In the backdrop of the foundation of the right to access the Internet as a human right, Chapter 2 moves on to answer the next logical question—against whom is this right available? Who is the duty bearer for ensuring these rights? This chapter examines whether a traditional state-centric approach could be successfully transplanted to technology and human rights discourse, in particular, the right to access the Internet. An answer to this question requires an insight to the virtual world to facilitate identification of the dominant nodes of power and determination of the duty bearer. Accordingly, this chapter undertakes two tasks—first, it maps the virtual world terrain to decipher the dominant player; two, having thus identified the corporation as a dominant player, it proceeds to establish normative and theoretical framework for the duty bearer.

While it is acknowledged that corporations hold the Midas touch to the effective realization of the right to access the Internet, it is critical to question how the Midas touch should be obtained. As such, it has been quite challenging, for international human rights law as well as the state, to regulate corporate conduct vis-a-vis human rights. Past experience of deterrence-based and cooperation-based regulatory approaches have resulted in a Goldilocks dilemma. Chapter 3 analyses prevalent regulatory experiments with respect to corporations' human rights conduct at international level. The international human rights law appears to have resolved the Goldilocks dilemma and offered certain soft law instrumentalities to obtain compliance from corporations. The chapter assesses the adequacy and effectiveness of these soft law instrumentalities.

Having explored the regulatory support from international level, Chapter 4 surveys variety of instrumentalities deployed by States to implement the rights of persons with disabilities, in general and the right to access the Internet, in particular. This exercise is helpful in assessing the sufficiency and efficiency of domestic instrumentalities towards attainment of the right to access the Internet. At the same time it also informs the present study about crucial legal and practical difficulties that may be encountered whilst mandating accessibility to private players.

While international human rights law mostly placed relevance on soft law instrumentalities, it presumed that if corporations wish to retain their 'social license' to operate, they would be self-motivated to adopt a human rights–compliant behaviour. Domestic laws, on the other hand, offered limited persuasions in the form of public procurement and taxation which appealed only to limited participants in the Internet. For the rest, anti-discrimination laws were considered to be sufficient enough to obtain the requisite compliance. Chapter 5 identifies a problem that persuasion and punishment when applied in a disjunctive fashion failed to create the requisite proactive response from corporations. This chapter engages with more recent regulatory approaches to corporate regulation, especially the popular and influential enforcement pyramid model developed by Ayres and Braithwaite. This chapter assesses the application of Ayres and Braithwaite enforcement pyramid to ensure the right to access the Internet. It is argued that responsive regulation offers a combination of enforcement options to regulators, yet it is not suitable for application in a multi-regulatee regulatory regime. The enforcement pyramid operates in a linear fashion which is not useful to address the complexity of a polycentric virtual world with multi regulatees. The chapter introduces an interconnected pentagon model (IPM) which entails multi-regulators and multi-regulatees. Drawing connects between instrumentalities and joining the dots backwards, the IPM aims to provide a mix of instrumentalities and institutions to attain desirable outcomes by creating webs of influences.

The concluding chapter serves as a vantage point to take a view of larger findings, learning, and conclusions from this study.

Conceptual Guideposts

Digital Divide

It is difficult to trace the exact origin of the term digital divide, nevertheless, the term is mostly understood to describe an 'uneven diffusion of information and communication technology'.[58] When the digital divide first caught people's attention, it was focused on the inequalities of technological resources, such as phone lines, computer hardware, network connections, and information technology skills. As time passed, however, policymakers and scholars have expanded the definition of the digital divide to cover the disparity of accessible Internet content.[59] Broadly speaking, the perceived gap which surfaced between those who have access to information technology and those who do not is referred to as the digital divide.[60] However, as observed by the ITU and the United Nations Conference on Trade and Development (UNCTAD)[61]

---

[58] United Nations Development Program, 'Making New Technologies Work For Human Development', Human Development Report 38 (2001).

[59] Peter K. Yu, 'Bridging the Digital Divide: Equality in the Information Age: Forward', 20 CARDOZO ARTS & ENT.LJ 1 (2002).

[60] Weber Rolf, Meoud Valeri, 'The Information Society and the Digital Divide: Legal Strategies to Finance Global Access', 4 (2008).

[61] ITU/UNCTAD, 'World Information Society Report 2007: Beyond WSIS' (2007).

digital divide is a dynamic concept, which evolves over time and there is no single divide, but rather multiple divides are to be differentiated.

On similar lines, Andrew Celli and Kenneth Dreifach point out that the digital divide is a multifaceted problem representing a 'convergence of several fault lines'.[62] It encompasses a wide spectrum of disparities and differences existing along wealth, gender, geographical, and social lines within states.[63] For the purposes of this book, the term digital divide is to be understood as referring to the rift existing between persons with disabilities and those without disabilities in full and effective access to, participation in and experience of the Internet.

The Internet

Different terminologies are used to address and scope the Internet. While some of these terms address the Internet from a technical perspective, others have taken a broader approach, often connecting it with the creation of intangible space. Thus, under a technical understanding, the Internet represents a giant network which connects innumerable smaller groups of linked computer networks. What results is a seamless web of communications networks, computers, databases, and consumer electronics that will put vast amounts of information at the user's fingertips.[64] Simply

[62] Andrew Celli and Kenneth Dreifach, 'Postcards from the Edge: Surveying the Digital Divide', 20 CARDOZO ARTS and ENT. L.J. 53 (2002): 54. In addition to the access divide, which has captured both national and international attention, Celli and Dreifach discuss two additional divides. The capital divide reflects the inequalities in raising start-up money for business ventures on the Internet, while the treatment divide discriminates consumers based on their Internet browsing habits and purchasing preferences.

[63] Rue, 'Report of the Special Rapporteur on Key Trends and Challenges to the Right of all Individuals to Seek, Receive and Impart Information and Ideas of All Kinds Through the Internet.'

[64] See Llewellyn Joseph Gibbons, 'No Regulation, Government Regulation, or Self-Regulation: Social Enforcement or Social Contracting for Governance in Cyberspace', 6 Cornell J. L. and Pub. Pol'y 475 (1996).

put, the Internet 'is merely a simple computer protocol, a piece of code that permits computer users to transmit data between their computers using existing communications networks'.[65] Such technical understanding accords a narrow conception to the term 'Internet' encompassing a global network of networks which includes hardware and software technical infrastructure, applications, and content that is communicated or generated using those applications.[66]

In a broad sense the Internet is often equated to cyberspace, information society, information highway; often the explanation of one term leading to the evolution of the other. The term 'cyberspace' was first used by Gibson in a specific way and was later introduced by Barlow as the name for the new technology-driven electronic 'place'. Gibson, as the originator of the term 'cyberspace' did not view this as an autonomous place, but as a 'consensual hallucination' in this world.[67] This book adopts a broader understanding of the term

---

[65] Mark A. Lemley, 'Place and Cyberspace', 91 CAL. L. REV. 521 (2003): 523.

[66] The application that is most commonly associated with the Internet is the World Wide Web, which utilizes HTTP. But the Internet is not identical to the World Wide Web. See Lawrence Solumn, 'Models of Internet Governance', Research Paper, University of Illinois, 7–25, available at http://ssrn.com/abstract=1136825. The Internet is viewed as different from other electronic information and communication networks (telecommunications and broadcasting). Rather than being a single, centrally controlled network designed to deliver one service to 'dumb' terminals, it is a 'network of networks' that is controlled from the 'edge' by users on an 'end-to-end' basis, using intelligent terminals across a dumb network to access and provide a wide range of services which, although functionally similar in some cases to the services provided by other networks and media, are inherently different for multiple reasons including technology, design, capability, control, and economics. Don MacLean, *Herding Schrodinger's Cats: Some Conceptual Tools for Thinking about Internet Governance* (ITU, Background Paper for the ITU Workshop on Internet Governance Geneva, pp. 26–7, February 2004).

[67] Gibson William, 'Neuromancer' (1984). Another term used to describe the global network is 'information superhighway', an expression introduced into political discourse by former US Vice-President Albert Gore. In several speeches, Gore outlined the notion that the speedy transmission of information is replacing the physical carriage of people or goods. The

Internet instead of confining it to a technical meaning. Accordingly, for the purposes of this book, the Internet is understood as a virtual community which offers a new and democratic public sphere that thrives on a participative and inclusive online culture.[68]

Accessibility

One of the difficulties worth highlighting at the beginning is the problematic nature of accessibility as a concept. Accessibility, whether in the physical or online world, commonly refers to the use of modifications and accommodations to make service and goods comparably enjoyable by individuals with and without disabilities.[69] In the online sphere, this may include the provisions of captioning for hearing impaired individuals or text-to-speech capacity for individuals with visual impairments. It may necessitate that a website be operable with screen reader software so an individual with a visual disability may access web content.[70]

---

new infrastructure is particularly designed for the conduct of business, in other words, commerce is using not only asphalt highways but information highways as well.

[68] The culture metaphor is reflected in a large body of research that explores the Internet from the perspective of its cultural practices, focusing on various examples of internet communities, including their norms and values, identity formation, sharing and collaboration, means of social control, and so forth. See generally, S.Turkle, *Life on the Screen: Identity in the Age of the Internet* (1995); D. Silver, 'Looking Backwards, Looking Forward: Cyberculture Studies', in *Web Studies: Rewiring Media Studies for the Digital Age*, pp. 19–30 (Gauntlett ed., 2000); C. Shirky, *Here Comes Everybody: The Power of Organizing Without Organisations* (2008).

[69] W3C. *Semantic Web*. W3C, 2013, available at http://www.w3.org/2001/sw/ (last visited 5 November 2014).

[70] Often the terms accessibility and usability are used interchangeably. Usability is a collection of dynamic and contextual considerations for functioning, such as user satisfaction, ease of use, comprehensibility, efficiency, and achievement of user purpose. There are multiple ways to approach the user experience, depending upon individual, technological, and environmental factors. For further discussion, see Blanck, 'eQuality'.

CRPD does not define accessibility, however, one can take some leads from other parallel developments. The ITU defines accessibility as a measure of the extent to which a product or service can be used by a person with a disability as effectively as it can be used by a person without that disability.[71] Accordingly, accessibility is diversified to deal with the needs and abilities of persons with disabilities and expressed in degrees. Accessibility is therefore, graded as being 'fully accessible', to 'partially accessible', to 'completely inaccessible', for a specified user group. The same is progressively gaining acceptance amongst several jurisdictions while formulating an e-inclusion policy or accessibility policy. For instance, the Indian policy on e-accessibility has adopted this understanding of the ITU.[72] European Union adopts a comprehensive perspective. In keeping with the ideology that disability is a life condition, EU policy targets its policy initiatives at groups other than persons with disabilities as well. Thus, for EU 'eAccessibility' concerns the design of Information and Communication Technology (ICT) products and services, so that they can be used by persons with disabilities, whether of a permanent or temporary nature, and by older people with age-related changes in functional capacities.

Whereas these definitions of accessibility are more or less confined to accessibility of products/services through the Internet; the one developed by the World Wide Web Consortium (W3C) adopts a more comprehensive approach. According to the Web Accessibility Initiative (WAI) of the W3C, web accessibility means that persons with disabilities can perceive, understand, navigate, and interact with the web, and that they can contribute to the web.[73] The narrowly defined conception of the term accessibility,

---

[71] Available at http://www.e-accessibilitytoolkit.org/toolkit/eaccessibility_basics/introduction_to_e-accessibility%20basics (last visited 5 November 2014).

[72] For instance, the e-Accessibility Toolkit for Policy Makers defines accessibility as a measure of the extent to which a product or service can be used by a person with a disability as effectively as it can be used by a person without that disability.

[73] Available at http://www.w3.org/WAI/intro/accessibility.php (last visited 22 March 2015).

as developed by the ITU, perceives access as limited to availability of goods or services from the Internet. As a consequence, this definition overlooks the growing significance of the Internet as a virtual community and at the same time unintentionally tends to diminish persons with disabilities as mere customers. The definition of accessibility by W3C appears broader in its scope and perception than the one forwarded by the ITU by emphasizing accessibility as the instructiveness of the Internet for persons with disabilities.

In certain ways, the concept is also closely related to the Universal design as defined by CRPD. This means designing such products, environments, programmes, and services to be usable by all people, to the greatest extent possible, without the need for adaptation or specialized design.[74] Blanck rightly observes that accessibility and usability are often used interchangeably.[75]

While the ITU definition of accessibility is more concerned with quantifying usability of goods and services; the W3C and Universal Design of accessibility focuses on the usability of the web. The difficulty with each of these definitions is that they fail to articulate participatory justice and inclusiveness in the virtual world. Consequently, the situation has led to a lack of principled application of these terms in practice.[76]

A broad understanding of the Internet already adopted earlier in this book that symbolizes the Internet as a culture, a public sphere, and a community does not allow accessibility to be perceived as particularly restricted to the usability of goods or services through the Internet. Rather, accessibility in the present context entails ensuring participatory justice and inclusion of persons with disabilities in the virtual world on an equal basis with others. The aim is to accord recognition to persons with disabilities as parties in the original

---

[74] Article 2 Definitions—'Universal design' means the design of products, environments, programmes, and services to be usable by all people, to the greatest extent possible, without the need for adaptation or specialized design. 'Universal design' shall not exclude assistive devices for particular groups of persons with disabilities where this is needed.

[75] Blanck, 'eQuality', p. 45.

[76] Blanck, 'eQuality', p. 45.

position in Rawlsian understanding[77] who have an equal voice in designing principles of the virtual world.

For the purposes of this book, accessibility refers to the extent a person with disability can participate, interact and experience the Internet as effectively as it can be participated, interacted and experienced by a person without disability. This includes availing and consuming products and/or services through or from the Internet. Such participation, interaction, and experience occur in combination with such user interface which has operable, perceivable, and understandable contents and components available at affordable cost and compatible with assistive technologies.[78]

From a commercial standpoint, the technical definition of accessibility ought to be repackaged as 'offering such components to, contents of, goods and services through or from the Internet which can be availed or consumed or experienced by anyone, anytime, anywhere irrespective of the Internet participant's abilities'.[79] This kind of 'Anytime, Anywhere, Anyone (AAA)' branding[80] meets a fundamental business goal—that of enabling customers and users to receive the benefits of products and services without barriers due to location, time, or device capability.

---

[77] Refer Chapter 1 for elaboration.

[78] The present definition has been drafted in combination of the ITU definition with the Web Content Accessibility Guidelines by the World Wide Web Consortium. The definition of accessibility drafted for this study may also be rooted in the concept of active citizenship that seeks to advance broader engagement of persons with disabilities in valued forms of participation. Rather than limiting the scope of accessibility to products and services that unknowingly tends to diminish persons with disabilities as mere customers, the present definition pushes the boundaries of the virtual world.

[79] I develop this definition from the one given by E.T. Loiacono, Scott McCoy, and Nicholas C. Romano, *Information Technology Systems Accessibility*, Universal Access in the info. Soc'y 5(1) (2006). Accessibility in commercial terms is thus defined as 'the possibility, regardless of specific user's abilities, to easily access information in any form, structure or presentation'.

[80] Helen Maskery, 'Crossing the Digital Divide—Possibilities for Influencing the Private-Sector Business Case', 23 *The Information Society: An International Journal*, 187 (2007) DOI: 10.1080/01972240701323614.

Corporation

A 'corporation' implies an organization of persons and material resources included with, with a distinct legal personality, of limited liability and licensed by the state for the purpose of conducting profit-seeking business activities, by whatever name, whether TNCs, multinational corporations (MNCs), business, and enterprise.[81] Whereas an MNC (also called a TNC or MNE) is a business with the characteristics of a 'certain minimum size, if it controls production or service plants outside its home state and if it incorporates these plants into a unified corporate strategy';[82] for the purposes of the present study I focus on all corporations including those operating within one country. It particularly refers to terms chosen in current international discourse involving business and human rights issues. It is clear that many important legal considerations applicable to multinational corporations apply equally to those with domestic operations. For instance, the duty to promote and protect human rights under the language of the Preamble to the UDHR applies to all corporations, as important 'organs of society' regardless of the range of their operations. Furthermore, contextualizing the same in the virtual world, physical territories appear to be of little consequence. Thus, the model I develop is, applicable to business enterprises in whatever form or degree of trans nationality. I use a variety of terms interchangeably without attempting to draw distinctions among such entities.

Persons with Disabilities

The concept of 'persons with disabilities' in this book is in line with CRPD. Accordingly, persons with disabilities include those who have long-term physical, mental, intellectual, or sensory impairments which in interaction with various barriers may hinder

[81] Markos Karavias, 'Corporate Obligations under International Law', 4 (2013).

[82] L. Wildhaber, 'Some Aspects of the Transnational Corporation in Interntional Law', 27 NETH. INT'L L. REV. 79 (1980).

their full and effective participation in society on an equal basis with others. This conception of 'disability' is premised on the social model which views disability to arise from attitudinal bias and the impact between impairment and default in constructions of the built and social environment. Whilst this does not imply that persons with disabilities do not have any physical or mental impairments. Rather, it recognizes that given aspects of our social environment can be reconfigured and attitudinal barriers deriving from stigma and prejudice can be challenged, in order to make mainstream participation at previously thought impossible levels possible.[83]

Some Caveats

Before beginning, it is worthwhile to clearly set out certain caveats.

First, the issues pertaining to accessibility rights of persons with disabilities study should not be seen as being confined to Western liberal democracies and their perceptions of disability, especially in the context of the right to access the Internet and disabilities. The positive connection between disability and poverty may give an impression that the right to access the Internet may be a problem only for liberal Western democracies. However, I underscore, here, the fact that technological advancement and reduction of costs means that the Internet is proliferating in Asian, African, and Latin American countries at a much faster pace. For instance, Blanck in his recent book notes that web usage is expected to accelerate for those who have previously faced barriers to it, including those with disabilities, those living in poverty, those who face economic and political restrictions.[84] Accessibility to the Internet, therefore is a question not only for Western democracies but also for others who are tapping this opportunity. Hence, everyone needs to worry about it, and worry about it now.

Second, the present study proposes a normative and theoretical conception of accessibility rooted in participatory justice and substantive equality. It is conceded that accessibility requirements

[83] Oliver Smith, *Disability Discrimination Law* (2010).
[84] See Blanck, 'eQuality'.

of persons with disabilities may differ depending upon the nature of impairment. While this variation in impairments will necessitate lending definition of accessibility based on applied science, such technical finesse of accessibility is beyond the scope of this book.

Third, the key goal of a digital divide problem addressed here is to lend human rights perspectives to the issue of prevailing inequities in access to the Internet so as to ensure full and meaningful participation in the digital revolution. However, it needs to be acknowledged that different communities have different conditions and thus require different solutions to address digital divide. A definition that is useful in one community may be irrelevant in another. As a result, we should be sensitive to particular conditions of a community and constantly evaluate whether the definition makes sense in light of those conditions.

Fourth, while the book focuses on corporate forms that dominate the virtual world and investigates their role in ensuring accessibility, certain other unincorporated forms of private entities wielding considerable influence on the Internet cannot be ruled out. Whereas these latter entities have not been a part of analysis in the present study, there is nothing which prevents extending domestic regulations to such private entities, especially if they are discharging services for or on behalf of or in partnership with the governments. Even where these private entities have not been explicitly referred under the present form of analysis, the underlying purpose and objective of the model proposed here is to eradicate systemic discrimination by addressing structural and attitudinal changes. The goal is to create positive web of influence by evoking reflexive and responsive solutions from the actors operational on the Internet, which although may not be expected overnight but definitely in a progressive fashion.

Fifth, the interconnected pentagon approach developed here to the creation of an accessible virtual world is largely specific to disability rights. Whilst this strategy has been crafted focusing on disability jurisprudence, application of this regulatory approach can be extended to any other mutli-regulator, polycentric sector.

Sixth, attempts have been made to draw from several theoretical and normative sources under international law, the Internet and human rights. However, the same should in no way suggest any sort of unilateral imposition of rules on corporations. Whilst emphasis is placed on the key role assigned to a corporation, the same does not preclude in any which way, the role of the state in developing norms and enforcement mechanisms to suit its own situation.

Finally, it needs to be emphasized that the suggested model does not purport to explain all legal rules that regulates the virtual world, nor does it purport to explain all practices that have developed. The argument in this book has been limited to a narrow—though highly important and emerging—segment of disability rights and corporate obligations towards access to the virtual world as a human rights issue. The digital environment is a highly complex space, where many ultra-dynamic factors and forces are at constant work. Therefore, the best possible mix of available options is suggested here. Finally, this is not a comparative study or a comprehensive survey of all disability related laws passed in recent years, and it does not provide a full description of the Internet regulatory regime either. The book has simply drawn attention to several examples identified as significant and believe should be studied.

Evidently, private forces and markets have made an immense contribution to the evolution, growth, and proliferation of the Internet and virtual world. The State's light-handed approach to regulation has given participants of the virtual world substantial freedom to innovate, operate and self-regulate numerous issues. This book does not challenge any of the settled positions. Nor does it advocate increased state regulation. Rather, the objective is to underscore significant role to be played by the private sector especially corporation towards attainment of accessibility rights of persons with disabilities in consonance with CRPD mandate that ensures living an independent and meaningful life.

1

Embedding the Right to Access the Internet in Human Rights Framework

Even where significance and emancipator potentials of the right to access the Internet vis-à-vis rights of persons with disabilities are widely acknowledged, contesting claims prevail regarding the exact scope and nature of this right. Applying naturalist theories of human rights, a more orthodox approach is often resorted to argue that the right to access the Internet cannot be a human right in itself. Such contestation pegs the right to access as an enabling right, the one that enables realization of other human rights, important but relatively humble and non-urgent. A relatively practical view that stems from political approach to human rights accords functional purposes of human rights to protect urgent individual rights in any decent society. I argue that the conception we have chosen to describe the Internet guides us in how we scope the nature of this right. In order to fully appreciate the nature of this right, one has to conceptualize the Internet in a broad and imaginative manner. This chapter first provides a detailed narrative of the exclusionary experiences of persons with disabilities and their crusade towards establishing a rights-based regime. Further, the chapter assesses dichotomous claims in relation to the right to access the Internet in relation to disability rights jurisprudence. The inquiry is important because responses and the urgency of action will be directly proportionate to the stature accorded to the right to access. It is argued that CRPD cannot augment substantive equality, participatory justice, and a rights based regime for persons with disabilities if it trivializes the right to access the Internet as a mere enabling right.

Exclusionary Experience of the Physical World

When rational people in an asocial state of nature first entered into social cooperation, their underlying motivation was to seek mutual advantage.[1] The very logic of a contract for mutual advantage was predicted on social cooperation being optional, though highly desirable, and could be avoided with people from whom no benefits were gained. Thus, one would not include in the first place agents whose contribution to overall social well-being was likely to be dramatically lower than that of others.[2] Social cooperation was believed to take place only amongst those who were 'normal and fully cooperating member[s] of society over a complete life'.[3] In other words, it was assumed that such contract to cooperate was only among people who are 'roughly similar' in mental and physical powers, and that there are no relations of justice with people who are substantially weaker than others.[4] Thus, in order to settle the

---

[1] See generally, John Rawls, A Theory of Justice (1971). Society, according to Rawls, is a 'co-operative venture for mutual advantage', which is characterized by an identity of interests, since a co-operative scheme is better for each member of society than no scheme at all. The idea is that since everyone's well-being depends upon a scheme of cooperation without which no one could have a satisfactory life, the division of advantages should be such as to draw forth the willing co-operation of everyone taking part in it, including those less well situated.

[2] See generally, John Rawls, A Theory of Justice, 53 (REV. ed. 1999); Samuel Freeman, 'Reason and Agreements in Social Contract Views', in Justice and the Social Contract: Essays on Rawlsian Political Philosophy, 17 (2006): 18–20.

[3] Rawls, A Theory of Justice, p. 10.

[4] See Maratha Nussabaum, Frontiers of Justice: Disability, Nationality, Species Membership (2006).

basic structure and principles of society in a 'clear and uncluttered' manner only 'normal functioning members' participated in initial social contracting restricting 'others' who could not so co-operate.[5] This selective participation in initial bargaining then crystallizes into the problem of outliers whereby certain groups including persons with disabilities are not considered as subjects of justice.

Thus, provisioning of justice, specific questions and public policy for 'other' persons and interests, their unusual needs of care, among other issues becomes 'a pressing practical question' which was postponed to a later stage. All unusual needs of persons with disabilities were to be considered only after society's basic structure had been designed. It was premised that parties in the original position would want to appropriately address concerns of these groups subsequently. Thus, parties in the original position now posed as 'trustee' or 'representatives' of the 'other' persons. It was presumed that beneficiaries may be so incapacitated that they would be unable to make rational decisions about their own medical treatment, living arrangements, education, and so on. The parties to the original position, therefore, assume a self-imposed responsibility to choose for others as they would choose for themselves, if they were of the age of reason and capable of deciding rationally. As a consequence of such an approach, persons with disabilities were subjugated, by what social justice theorists term as 'cultural imperialism'. This is a process whereby abilities of the excluded group are dictated by how the dominant group perceived them. On account of such cultural imperialism persons with disabilities and their aspirations were rendered invisible, and were stereotyped them in accordance with the beliefs and perceptions of the dominant group.[6]

---

[5] Rawls calls this the position of origin where none knows all her personal strengths and deficits, or her actual social and economic positioning, so none can say whether, as an individual, she will be helped or hindered by a proposed principle. Absent information about one's own differences and therefore, about which social arrangements will be most facilitative to one's own self, the most advantageous strategy for any one seems to be whatever will be most advantageous for each one alike, regardless of who one is and what one's social and economic position turns out to be.

[6] Claire H. Liachowitz, *Disability as a Social Construct: Legislative Roots*, 11 (1988) (avers how medical model of disability stigmatizes persons with

Clearly, initial societal foundations and principles were neither designed 'by' persons with disabilities nor designed 'for' persons with disabilities. Even where parties in the original position promised to make practical arrangements for the needs of those who were not included in the original contracting group including persons with disabilities; they were not at liberty to redesign the principles of justice themselves. So that persons with disabilities were to adapt themselves so as to enable to function in the world around them. At the most certain nominal adjustments were sought to be forwarded to persons with disabilities as a charitable response by 'doing special things'. Accordingly, law-makers were presumed to have enough information about the prevalence of types of severe disabilities so to be well-situated to work out appropriate policies and procedures for caring for them in keeping with the costs of accommodations. This omission of persons with disabilities from making choice of basic principles both at initial stage and a subsequent stage had consequences in terms of their exclusion and marginalization from the mainstream society. Yet, exclusion and marginalization were deemed a natural result of their impairments.

In furtherance of the perception of disability as a problematic category, the medical model of disability identified persons with disabilities as 'abnormal objects' with functional limitations.[7] It focused on the impairment of an individual and while the cause of impairment varied, the individual was viewed as innately, biologically different, and inferior. The medical model offered an artificially-constructed notion of normality, deviation from which was highly undesirable and consequently, proponents of the medical model encouraged regulators to devote resources to preventive, curative

---

disabilities by conditioning their inclusion only on the terms of the able-bodied majority); Maria C. Lugones and Elizabeth V. Spelman, 'Have We Got a Theory for You!', Feminist Theory, Cultural Imperialism and the Demand for 'The Woman Voice', cited in Amita Dhanda, *Legal Capacity in the Disability Rights Convention: Stranglehold of the Past or Lodestar for the Future?* 34 Syracruse J. Int'l. and com. 429 (2007).

[7] See Michael Oliver, *Understanding Disability: From Theory to Practice*, 17 (1996).

and ultimately rehabilitative endeavours.[8] The medical model took paternalistic overtones calling for interventions that required the State to 'protect' persons with disabilities from society. As a result, persons with disabilities were systemically excluded from social opportunities and offered social welfare benefits in lieu of employment or accorded limited participation in those opportunities, for instance having their education circumscribed in separate schools. The society and legislation perceived an individual with disability as an unfortunate victim of some twist of fate not ascribable to any social cause.[9] This approach on the one hand, induced a state-sponsored welfarist approach heavily discounting their autonomy, self-determination, and dignity and on the other segregated them from the mainstream thereby deepening the exclusion and marginalization.

The growing dissatisfaction with the medical model of disability led to the search for alternative conceptualization of disability which saw the creation and development of the social model of disability. As per this model, it is the physically engineered environment, and the attitudes that are reflected in its construction, that play a central role in creating the condition termed 'disability'.[10] It asserts that impairment alone is not disabling. Rather, disabilities are created

[8] Lisa Waddington and Matthew Diller, 'Tensions and Coherence in Disability Policy: The Uneasy Relationship Between Social Welfare and Civil Rights Models of Disability in American, European and International Employment Law', in *Disability Rights Law and Policy: International and National Perspectives* 241, 244 (Mary Lou Breslin and Silvia Yee eds, 2002), available at http://www.dredf.org/international/waddington.html. (last visited 27 August 2017) Waddington and Diller analyse the relationship between the social welfare/ medical model and civil rights model of disability policy and consider whether the dissonance between the two can be resolved or reduced, to what extent the tension is a problem, and whether a new disability policy model is needed.

[9] Oliver, *Understanding Disability*, p. 32.

[10] A defining statement of this model was articulated in 1976 by a British group called the Union of the Physically Impaired against Segregation (UPIAS): In our view it is society which disables physically impaired people. Disability is something imposed on top of our impairments by the way we are unnecessarily isolated and excluded from full participation in society. Disabled people are therefore an oppressed group in society. Colin Barne and Geof Mercer, *Exploring Disability: A Sociological Introduction*, 31 (2nd ed., 2010).

and perpetuated through societal process which isolates, excludes, and stigmatizes people who have physical or mental impairments.[11] Since disabilities are caused by the constructed environment, they are induced, and that it is society's ethical or moral duty to change that environment to provide equal access and equal functioning to all its members.[12] While the main thrust of disability policy under the medical model was to get rid of disability by attempting to cure or rehabilitate the individual, the main thrust of policy under the social model is to get rid of disability by 'rehabilitating' the social and physical structures and systems that serve to impose disadvantages on persons with disabilities.[13] The 'core of the social

[11] In order to focus attention on the disabling impact of society, many adherents of social model favour the term 'disabled people' (in the sense of the disablement caused by the society) over that of 'people with disabilities.' Gerard Quinn, 'The Human Rights of People with Disabilities under EU Law', in *The EU and Human Rights* 281, p. 285 (Philip Alston et al. eds, 1999).

[12] See generally, Saad Z. Nagi, *Disability and Rehabilitation: Legal, Clinical and Self-Concepts and Measurement* (1969); Micahel Oliver, *The Politics of Disablement: A Sociological Approach* (1990); Jacobus tenBroek, 'The Right to Live in the World: The Disabled in the Law of Torts', 54 CAL. L. REV. 841 (1966); Mary Crossley, 'The Disability Kaleidoscope', 74 Notre Dame L. REV. 621 (1999). The social model has often been criticized for failing to recognize the importance of impairments in the experiences of those living with a disability. More broadly, Shakespeare, who had been an advocate of the social model, later criticized it for being overly simplistic. He questioned the distinction the social model makes between impairment and disability, and pointed out that it is not just the environment that causes disability. Many disabilities are inherently associated with pain, fatigue, or other physical or mental difficulties, irrespective of social arrangements and attitudes. Similarly, Scotch and Schriner observe that real aspects of disability require social responses, and these characteristics shift over time, but they are nonetheless real. Many people with disabilities have problems in functioning that will not disappear even if prejudice and discrimination are eliminated. See generally, Tom Shakespeare, *Disability Rights and Wrongs* (2006); R.K. Scotch and K. Schriner, 'Disability as Human Variation: Implications for Policy', 549 *The Annals of the American Academy of Political and Social Science* 148(1997).

[13] Harlan Hahn, 'Feminist Perspectives, Disability, Sexuality and Law: New Issues and Agendas', 4 S. CAL. REV. L and Women's Studies 97, p. 104.

model' aims for the ideal that '[i]t is society that has to change not individuals'.[14]

An offshoot of the social model also resulted in the minority model of disability that attributed marginalization experienced by persons with disabilities to their minority social status.[15] According to the minority model of disability, persons with disabilities were perceived to be a minority group and social institutions were designed for and around needs of those without disability while a separate and inferior system was established to cater to the specific needs of persons with disabilities.[16] Consequently, persons with disabilities faced barriers to participation in society on account of patterns of hierarchy and subordination based on physical differences.[17] This model challenged the existing features of architectural design, job requirements, and daily life as discriminatory practices towards persons with disabilities and demanded formal equality and inclusion through a reactive approach.[18]

Crusade towards Human Rights Regime

Adopting the social model and minority model did not always result in equal treatment.[19] Anti-discrimination laws focused on

[14] Oliver, *Understanding Disability*, p. 37.

[15] Often dubbed as 'cultural imperialism', the aspirations of the excluded group are rendered invisible, along with stereotyping them in accordance with the beliefs and perceptions of the dominant group.

[16] Anita Silvers, 'Disability Rights', in *Encyclopedia of Applied Ethics* 48, p. 781 (1998). Silver hypothesizes how our social landscape would look different if a dominant group in society used wheelchairs and what social arrangements would be in place were persons with disabilities dominant rather than suppressed.

[17] Jonathan C. Drimmer, 'Cripples, Overcomers, and Civil Rights: Tracing the Evolution of Federal Legislation and Social Policy for People with Disability', 40 UCLA L. REV. 1341 (1993).

[18] Drimmer, 'Cripples, Overcomers, and Civil Rights', p. 164.

[19] Paul Harpur, 'Time to be Heard: How Advocates can use the Convention on the Rights of Persons with Disabilities to Drive Change', 45 VAL.U.L.REV. 1271 (2011).

negative rights without elaborating the positive rights. Equality of treatment, therefore, privileged over a more substantive equality of opportunity. Consequently, despite being guaranteed rights, persons with disabilities were routinely denied the effective realization of those rights and continued to face marginalization and exclusion. It was progressively recognized that the oppression and exclusion of persons with disabilities must be viewed through the prism of human rights to provide a holistic approach to their rights.[20] People are to be valued not just because they have functional utility but because they have inherent self-worth. Recognition of the value of human dignity serves as a powerful reminder that persons with disabilities have a stake in and a claim on society that must be honoured quite apart from any considerations of social or economic utility.[21] Thus, the impetus provided by human rights approach to disability culminated into adoption of the (CRPD or Convention) by the UN General Assembly in 2006.[22] CRPD, the first human rights

[20] Michael Ashley Stein and Penelope J.S. Stein, 'Beyond Disability Civil Rights', 58 Hastings L.J. 1203 (2007) (advocating for a disability human rights paradigm which combines the best aspects of the social model of disability, the human right to development, and ultimately the capabilities approach, to create a holistic and comprehensive rights theory).

[21] Gerard Quinn and Theresia Degener, *Human Rights and Disability: The Current Use and Future Potential of United Nations Human Rights Instruments in the Context of Disability* (2002).

[22] CRPD owes itself to many years of work within the UN system to place disability rights on the international agenda and to fully integrate disability issues into the broader human rights and international development frameworks. The early efforts began in the 1970s, when the UN adopted the Declaration on the Rights of Mentally Retarded Persons followed by the Declaration on the Rights of Disabled Persons. (Declaration on the Rights of Mentally Retarded Persons, G.A. res. 2856 (XXVI), 26 U.N. GAOR Supp. (No. 29), p. 93, U.N. Doc. A/8429 (1971). Article 1, Preamble 5; Declaration on the Rights of Disabled Persons, G.A. res. 3447 (XXX), 30 U.N. GAOR Supp. (No. 34) at p. 88, UN Doc. A/10034 (1975). The next level of impetus was provided when the year 1981 was designated as the International Year of Disabled Persons. International Year of Disabled Persons, G.A. Res. 36/77, at p.176, UN GAOR, 36th Sess., Supp.No.77, U.N. Doc.A/RES/36/77 (1981). The year 1982 saw the adoption of the non-binding World Programme of Action in 1982 by the

treaty of the twenty-first century, re-conceptualized the discourse surrounding the meaning and construction of 'disability' as well as notions of equality, discrimination and exclusion.[23] Based on the concepts of justice, human dignity and autonomy, CRPD visualizes persons with disabilities as 'subjects of rights' rather than 'objects of charity'.[24] Predominantly hailed for the paradigm shift it brings for persons with disabilities, CRPD saw discourse on disability move away from the medical model which was located in the impairments of an individual, towards a social model that views disability as a social construct created through social barriers.[25] It combines human rights paradigm with anti-discrimination protections

---

General Assembly to encourage national-level progammes to achieve equality of persons with disabilities. See World Programme of Action 1982, at paras. 87–90. The Decade of Disabled Persons (1983–92) culminated in the adoption of the Standard Rules on the Equalization of Opportunities for Persons with Disabilities by the General Assembly on 4 March 1994. See Decade of Disabled Persons, GA Res. 48/96, U.N. Doc. A/RES/48/96 (4 March 1993), which annexed thereto (resolution 48/96 annex, 20 December 1993), available at http://www1.umn.edu/humanrts/instree/disabilitystandards.html (last visited 24 September 2014).

[23] UN Convention on the Rights of Persons with Disabilities, G.A. Res. 61/106, U.N. Doc. A/61/611 (13 December 2006), *opened for signature* 30 March 2007, 46 I.L.M. 433 [hereinafter Convention or CRPD]. An Optional Protocol providing for additional monitoring mechanisms was adopted at the same time. Optional Protocol to the Convention on the Rights of Persons with Disabilities, *opened for signature* 30 March 2007, 46 I.L.M. 433 [hereinafter Optional Protocol]. The CRPD text, along with its drafting history, resolutions and updated list of signatories and States Parties, is posted on the United Nations Enable website at http://www.un.org/esa/socdev/enable/rights/convtexte.htm (last visited 24 September 2014).

[24] The UN High Commissioner for Human Rights emphasized this shift to a rights-oriented perspective on the adoption of the CRPD in December 2006. See UN High Commissioner for Human Rights, Statement by UN High Commissioner for Human Rights on Convention on Rights of Persons with Disabilities, delivered at the adoption of the convention in December 2006 (6 December 2006), available at: http://www.ohchr.org/English/issues/disability/docs/statementhcdec06.doc (last visited 24 September 2014).

[25] See Victor Finkelstein, 'Attitudes and Disabled People: Issues for Discussion' (1980); Michael Oliver, 'The Politics of Disablement' (1990);

that the social model created with rights found under human rights regimes.

CRPD essentially entails that the society ought to perceive disability as a part of human diversity and towards that end make a major departure from formal equality to substantive equality.[26] The formal approach to equality believes that social structures are constant and cannot be changed. It, thereby, places emphasis on prohibiting distinctions on the basis of personal characteristics. The substantive approach to equality, on the other hand, stresses on removing obstacles in society so as to allow full participation of persons with certain characteristics. Thus, the general principles of CRPD inter alia enunciates respect for individual dignity, autonomy, and independence, respect for difference and acceptance of disability as part of human diversity as its general principles. The Preamble of the CRPD emphasizes the importance of mainstreaming disability issues as an integral part of relevant strategies of sustainable development. In a move to eliminate discriminatory treatment meted out to persons with disabilities, Article 5 requires States Parties to ensure equality of persons with disabilities in their societies while also prohibiting all types of discrimination 'on the basis of disability'. Thus, CRPD proffers a human rights and social model of disability seeking substantive equality for persons with disabilities.

Emergence of the Virtual World

Just about the time when disability rights movement was gaining momentum and human rights of persons with disabilities were being asserted to offset exclusionary practices from the past, the

---

Michale Oliver, *Understanding Disability: From Theory to Practice* (1996); Jenny Morris, 'Pride Against Prejudice' (1991). Michael Ashley Stein, 'Disability Human Rights', 95 CAL. L. REV. 75 (2007).

[26] A formal equality model is based on an idea of 'sameness' or a 'symmetrical approach', assuming that all persons should be treated in the same way or are 'symmetrical' irrespective of the unequal consequences of this

world was gearing up for yet another phenomenal change—the era of the Internet. In what had begun as a research project in the 1970s, the Internet and its exponential growth during the 1990s changed the way the real world operated.[27] The proliferation of computers and the Internet at an unprecedented level and as an online mode of operation had a profound impact on economies, politics, culture, communication, and societal opportunities around the world.

Whereas in the initial stages, the Internet was perceived as just another medium to facilitate communication, soon it was realized that unlike other traditional mediums of communication, the Internet had a global reach, dialogic interaction, and plurality of contents which led to creation of an open-ended space. This was a space which enabled participants not only to passively receive information but also actively engage in dialogues and discourses beyond local and regional contexts. The emerging publicness was further harnessed to mobilize political opinions, expression, and diversity of voices. At the same time, the Internet captured the imagination of the private sector which saw it as a market without borders, free from regulations. The world quickly realigned itself around Internet based products, services, and activities. For others it offered an alternative space where real life individuals could routinely interact, share, participate, socialize, and perform a range activities from personal interaction to business, work, culture, communication, social movements, and politics.[28] As virtual communities became central to everyday activities of the connected individuals; they created a richer choice of

---

treatment. This approach is formal in character, in the sense that it does not require a substantive or a normative test of the contents of the treatment as long as there is consistency in treatment. It therefore, does not address structural disadvantages facing persons belonging to certain groups and consequently equality sought to be achieved by disregarding a certain characteristic.

[27] In the late 1960s, the US government sponsored the development of the Defense Advanced Research Project Network (DARPA Net), a resilient communication resource. By the mid-1970s, with the invention of TCP/IP protocol, this network evolved in what is known today as the Internet.

[28] Social Network Sites are web-based services that allow individuals to (1) construct a public or semi-public profile within a bounded system, (2)

communities to which they may belong, and that online spaces potentially revitalize the notion of community. Thus, based on the transformation of space, work and economic activity, culture and communication, what emerged is a new social structure, the Internet, as a global network society, characterized by the rise of a new culture and community. Manuel Castells identifies six types of autonomies that were promised by the Internet—autonomy of professional development, communication, entrepreneurship, autonomy of the body, socio-political participation, and personal individual autonomy. The more a person was autonomous, the more she/he used the web; the more she/he used the web, the more autonomous she/he became.[29]

Creating a Disability-Inclusive Virtual World

The advent of the Internet and the virtual world offered the chance to sidestep barriers created in the physical world. It promised to redress the exclusion experienced by persons with disabilities on account of social contracting of the physical world. Access to the Internet was the key to inclusion. To have 'access' to the Internet, was to have access to the de facto political, economic, social, informational authority in any given context.[30] Having access to the Internet and consequently to the virtual world, persons with disabilities found themselves better situated to seek, exercise, claim, and receive their needs. They got, theoretically a chance, to define the economic, social, and political landscape and participate in the

---

articulate a list of other users with whom they share a connection, and (3) view and traverse their list of connections and those made by others within the system. See Danah M. Boyd and Nicole B. Ellison, 'Social Network Sites: Definition, History, and Scholarship', *Journal of Computer-Mediated Comm.* 13(1) (2007).

[29] Manuel Castells, 'The Impact of the Internet on Society: A Global Perspective', available at https://www.bbvaopenmind.com/en/book/19-key-essays-on-how-internet-is-changing-our-lives/ (last visited 2 May 2015).

[30] Rikke Frank Jørgensen, *Framing the Net: The Internet and Human Rights* (2013).

political, economic, social, educational, employment opportunities created and available in the virtual world. When the Internet and its related technology initially developed; the mainstream access was feasible for all.

However, with technological advancements and complicated applications, there has been a widespread adoption of inaccessible technology. Concerns of usability and accessibility have now often been side tracked. The Internet now seamlessly control, manipulate, and wield power over the way human life is lived and experienced, altering, and reshaping the idea of a community.[31] Being locked out of electronic gates of the virtual world would mean being excluded from the virtual community. Evidently, while access to the virtual world initially empowered persons with disabilities, the subsequent differential to access has resulted in deprivation of their right to education, employment, leisure, and participation. In a sequel to the social contract which had debarred persons with disabilities from participating in designing the basic social structure as well as participation in the physical world, the virtual world has been oblivious to the accessibility concerns, resulting in a digital divide and a second round of exclusion, this time from the virtual world. For persons with disabilities living on the wrong side of the digital divide means denial of a whole range of opportunities and possibilities to live an inclusive and autonomous life. Unlike structures of the real world; the virtual world is currently under construction. The classic postponement approach is not available this time since the Internet is taking shape every day. It is, therefore, indefensible if the virtual world is constructed in a total disregard to accessibility concerns of persons with disabilities.

It needs to be underscored that persons with disabilities have a right to live in the world and to have equally meaningful contact with the population and community at large. Thus, the right to live in the world entails not only physical access to areas of public accommodation,[32] but even more appreciably 'a basic right

---

[31] M. Price, 'Free Expression and Digital Dreams: The Open and Closed Terrain of Speech', *Critical Inquiry* 64 (1995).

[32] Jacobus tenBroek, 'The Right to Live in the World: The Disabled in the Law of Torts', 54 CAL. L. REV. (1966), 841, 848.

indispensable to participation in the community, a substantive right to which all are fully and equally entitled'.[33] It, therefore, becomes a human rights issue as well as a social justice issue to ensure participation and inclusion of persons with disabilities to the virtual world. This participative justice calls for not only removing unneeded obstacles, but also making 'participation a moral imperative'.[34] 'If persons with disabilities have the right to live in the world, they must have the right to make their way into it and therefore, must be entitled to use all indispensable means of access, and to use them on terms that will make the original right effective.'[35]

If the Internet is a requirement of modern living so much so that non-access tantamount to non-existence, one must ask how virtual exclusion exemplified in the Internet is sought to be ensured. Does CRPD that holds high promises for eliminating the marginalized living have sufficient responses to the accessibility concerns to the Internet?

Decoding the CRPD Mandate on Access to the Internet

CRPD acknowledges that accessibility is a precondition to the full and effective realization of participation and other substantive rights. Thus, the Preamble recognizes the importance of accessibility to the physical, social, economic, and cultural environment, to health and education and to information and communication, *in enabling* persons with disabilities to fully enjoy all human rights and fundamental freedoms (emphasis supplied). Conscious of the attitudinal and social barriers in society towards persons with disabilities, CRPD seeks to dismantle the same and advance a disability inclusive citizenship. The same is reiterated in the general principle as well as several other Articles in CRPD. Article 8 targets the underlying attitudinal causes of disability-based discrimination by requiring States Parties

[33] tenBroek, 'The Right to Live in the World', p. 858.
[34] Michael Ashley Stein, 'Disability Human Rights', 95 CAL. L. REV. 75 (2007): 102.
[35] tenBroek, 'The Right to Live in the World', p. 814.

to raise public awareness, and provides a list of illustrative measures. Article 9 seeks to dismantle barriers created by discriminatory attitudes by promoting access including access to the Internet. In furtherance of this mandate, Article 21(c) urges private entities that provide services to general public through the Internet to provide the same in accessible and usable formats for persons with disabilities. The General Comment on Article 9 of CRPD provides an elaboration of the mandate and the expectations on the accessibility front. Whereas CRPD as well as the General Comment make sporadic references to the Internet, it may be worthwhile to understand the mandate in terms of accessibility which extends to the Internet.

Accordingly, it is reiterated that accessibility is one of its key underlying principles—a *vital precondition* for the effective and equal enjoyment of different civil, political, economic, social, and cultural rights by persons with disabilities (emphasis supplied).[36] It has been conceded that accessibility is all-encompassing; however, often it is understood too narrowly in terms of physical environment alone. CRPD does not favour reading accessibility either in a restricted view or in isolation from other rights. Thus, a conjunctive reading of general principles (including accessibility and awareness-raising) together with articles of general and cross-cutting application (Articles 3 to 9) serves as a guide to interpretation of the accessibility mandate.[37]

Accordingly, state parties should strive systematically and continuously to raise awareness about accessibility among all stakeholders. Whereas Article 9 does not attempt to enumerate any exhaustive list of relevant stakeholders, the General Comment clarifies that the duty to observe accessibility standards applies equally to the public sector as well as private sector. CRPD makes a clear shift in focus from the nature of the service provider to the nature of the service. In other words, it has been categorically explained that

---

[36] General comment on Article 9: Accessibility, Committee on the Rights of Persons with Disabilities, CRPD/C/11/3.

[37] It has been the basic scheme of the CRPD that all other articles specifying substantive rights covering civil, political, economic, social, and cultural rights are to be read in conjunction with the cross-cutting articles so as to advance the core principles of autonomy and participation.

where goods, products, or services are available to general public, the same must be accessible irrespective of the legal personality of the provider. Denial to access should be an act of disability discrimination prohibited by law.

Having thus indicated a broad conception of accessibility and imposing duties both on public authority as well as private individuals, CRPD draws distinctions between obligations to ensure access to newly designed or built infrastructure and products/services and obligations to remove barriers and ensure access to the existing ones. Insofar as the newly designed or constructed infrastructure, objects, products, goods or services are concerned, CRPD mandates that all these should be fully accessible for persons with disabilities. Accordingly, ensuring accessibility *pro futuro* should be viewed in the context of implementing the general obligation to develop universally designed goods, services, equipment, and facilities.[38] For existing infrastructures and products/services, state parties are mandated to adopt action plans and strategies to identify existing barriers to accessibility, set time frames with specific deadlines and provide both the human and material resources necessary to remove the barriers.

CRPD thus, neatly chalks out the mandate on accessibility. It addresses not only existing structures and their barriers but also the ones that are yet under construction and may be designed in future. Yet, there are two difficulties. One, whereas CRPD has recognized the right to access in general, it has not engaged with the nature of the right to access and made passing references to the Internet and the virtual world. Two, despite being ambitious in the mandate, as far as the scope and application to the right to access is concerned, CRPD takes a position that the Convention does not create any new rights. The General Comment clarifies that accessibility should be seen as 'a disability-specific reaffirmation of the right of access'. In order to draw support for this 'reaffirmation', the General Comment

---

[38] Article 4(f) To undertake or promote research and development of universally designed goods, services, equipment, and facilities, as defined in article 2 of the present Convention, which should require the minimum possible adaptation and the least cost to meet the specific needs of a person with disabilities, to promote their availability and use, and to promote universal design in the development of standards and guidelines.

provides references to other human rights instruments. Thus, it is claimed that historically, access to the physical environment and public transport for persons with disabilities was a precondition for freedom of movement, as guaranteed under Article 13 of the UDHR and Article 12 of the International Covenant on Civil and Political Rights (ICCPR). Similarly, access to information and communication is seen as a precondition for freedom of opinion and expression, as guaranteed under Article 19 of the UDHR and Article 19, paragraph 2, of the International Covenant on Civil and Political Rights. In a similar fashion CRPD also emphasizes that accessibility is a precondition for persons with disabilities to live independently and participate fully and equally in society.

A plain reading of relevant human rights instruments and CRPD demonstrates that the right to access is persistently described as a precondition to the effective realization of other substantive rights. Such selective reading gives an impression that the right to access is nothing more than an enabling right. A primary problem with this perception is that it fails to fully imagine implications of the right to access the Internet and its translation to the set of rights guaranteed to persons with disabilities by CRPD.

Adopting Human Rights Approach to the Internet

Evidently, inquiries pertaining to the exact nature and scope of the right to access the Internet are not unique to disability rights jurisprudence and are also found to have occurred elsewhere. Since most international human rights instruments are open textured, the same have been read so to include references to access to the Internet. For instance, Article 19 of the UDHR stipulates that everyone has the right to 'hold opinions without interference and to seek, receive, and impart information and ideas through any media regardless of frontiers'. This was interpreted to include the Internet. When Article 19 further stipulated that people should have the right to 'the widest possible access to sources and information, to travel unhampered in pursuit thereof, and to transmit copy without unreasonable or discriminatory limitation.....' it was again seen as making references to the Internet as a new source of information.

The problem is that such interpretations, necessarily rooted in the Internet as medium metaphor, take a constricted view of the problem. Consequently, the right to access the Internet is understood merely as an enabling right, important but less urgent. Thus, even where the enabling approach concedes that international instruments may be read in broad conceptual terms so as to include references to the Internet, it is not willing to contextualize the right to access the Internet as a human right. Enabler theorists argue that human rights more or less remain constant and technology for exercising and enforcing these generic rights is susceptible to change over time. Therefore, what qualifies as a human right is the right per se and not the means through which such rights are enabled. The Internet in that sense is viewed only as an indispensable tool for attaining range of human rights.[39]

Supporting this view, Vinton Cerf,[40] who is regarded as one of the inventors of the worldwide website, made a public claim that it would be erroneous to regard the Internet as a human right, as the 'technology is an enabler of rights, not a right itself'. He recommends that the Internet should be regarded as a constitutional right and an enabler of rights (a term also used by the UN Special Rapporteur) rather than as a human right per se.[41] Cerf advocates that in order to qualify something as a human right the bar needs to be set high. It, therefore, must be among the things that we need to lead

[39] The Special Rapporteur reiterates that the framework of international human rights law, in particular the provisions relating to the right to freedom of expression, continues to remain relevant and applicable to the Internet. Indeed, by explicitly providing that everyone has the right to freedom of expression through any media of choice, regardless of frontiers, articles 19 of the Universal Declaration of Human Rights and the International Covenant on Civil and Political Rights were drafted with the foresight to include and accommodate future technological developments through which individuals may exercise this right. Frank La Rue, 'Report of the Special Rapporteur on Key Trends and Challenges to the Right of all Individuals to Seek, Receive and Impart Information and Ideas of All Kinds through the Internet'.

[40] See http://www.nytimes.com/2012/01/05/opinion/internet-access-is-not-a-human-right.html (last visited 27 August 2017).

[41] A commentary from Joy Liddicoat of APC can be found at http://www.apc.org/en/news/access-internet-and-human-rights-thanks-vint (last visited 17 August 2014).

healthy, meaningful lives. Thus, the best way to characterize human rights is to identify the outcomes that we are trying to ensure. These include critical freedoms like the freedom of speech and freedom of access to information—and those are not necessarily bound to any particular technology at any particular time. He further illustrates his position. At one time if you didn't have a horse it was hard to make a living. But the most important right in that case was the right to make a living, not the right to a horse.

Accordingly, access to the Internet is regarded as merely a tool for facilitating other more important human rights, including civil, political rights, and freedoms. Therefore, Cerf concedes that the argument that it is a civil right is a stronger one than that it is a human right. In a more recent attempt, Brian Skepys argued there is no such a thing called human right to the Internet access. Whilst he saw human rights as instrumentally necessary for the membership in an organized and decent political society, he argued that the Internet access even though instrumentally valuable for this membership, is not necessary for membership. Therefore, the Internet should not be seen as a human right in and of itself because it is not necessary for membership. Instead its denial should be seen as a potentially urgent threat to a more basic list of human rights.[42] It is often suggested that civil rights, after all, are different from human rights because they are conferred upon us by law, not intrinsic to us as human beings. Besides, one may ask whether access to the Internet is more important than access to water, food, medicine, or freedom from torture. If not, can it be a human right?

This perception is largely influenced by the naturalist theories of human rights that views human rights derived from 'a theological, philosophical, or moral conception of the nature of the human person'. Accordingly, human rights are those rights that all human beings possess simply in 'virtue of their humanity'.[43] It is a right that is believed to exist in a state of nature where there are no established

[42] Brian Skepys, 'Is There a Human Right to the Internet?' 5 J. POL. & L. 15 (2012).

[43] A. John Simmons, 'Human Rights and World Citizenship: The Universality of Human Rights in Kant and Locke', in *Justification and Legitimacy: Essays on Rights and Obligations*, 185 (2001) (emphasis in original; the order of the passages has been reversed).

social conventions or institutionalized patterns of reciprocity. Thus, these rights exist regardless of the prevailing legal or social structures, and attach to all persons notwithstanding their spatial or temporal locations.[44] If we transplant this argument in the present context, the enabling approach attempts to forbid the diversity of rights, suggesting hierarchies of rights. It clearly suggests that while certain rights are 'basic' others are negotiable, even dispensable.

Purely assessed under this section, right to access the Internet can be conveniently disqualified from the catalogue of human rights. These arguments amassed by the enabler approach sounds convincing at first blush. In fact, a selective reading of Article 21 of CRPD which pertains to ensuring access may also yield a conclusion compatible to the enabler approach. The problem of this reductionist reasoning is that it overwhelmingly emphasizes on a few most basic human rights and seriously neglects the urgent need of the specification of basic human rights in current human right practice.[45]

However, it is also imperative to acknowledge that the very term 'human rights' is problematic deeply as it straddles several universes of discourse. While moral philosophers attribute it to a set of ethical imperatives that contribute to making the basic structure of society and state; international lawyers regard human rights as a set of norms and standards having some sort of binding effect on the behaviour of States and regional and international organizations. Baxi cautions that it would be fallacious to reduce the abundance of meaning to some 'false totality' such as 'basic human rights'. He argues and rightly so, that all human rights are basic to those who are deprived, disadvantaged and dispossessed. The diverse range of human rights resists encapsulation in any formula.[46]

According to the political approach to human rights, human rights come from a 'proper subset' of the rights required by justice

---

[44] See generally, A. Gewirth, *Human Rights: Essays on Justification and Applications* (1982), J. Griffin, *On Human Rights* (2008), J. Donnelly, *Universal Human Rights in Theory and Practice* (2003).

[45] Xiaowei Wang, 'Time to Think about Human Right to the Internet Access: A Beitz's Approach', 6 J. POL. & L. 67 (2013) (justifies that the right to access the Internet is a human right using Beitz theory and contrasting the naturalist theory of human rights).

[46] Upendra Baxi, 'The Future of Human Rights', 5 (2002).

in liberal and 'decent' societies, so they are a 'special class of urgent rights'.[47] Accordingly, for a right to be a human right by the political approach standard, it must have some practical weight on the international level.[48] Beitz argues that the practice and discourse of international human rights are aimed at protecting individuals' most urgent interests from the acts and omissions of states. Thus, Beitz puts forward what he considers a 'practical' approach to international human rights.[49] Human rights are requirements whose object is to protect urgent individual interests against certain predictable dangers ('standard threats') to which they are vulnerable under typical circumstances of life in a modern world order composed of states. An 'urgent' interest is one that would be recognizable as important in a wide range of typical lives that occur in contemporary societies. However, I find this approach problematic in that determination of the norms that should be regarded as politically 'urgent' enough to be considered human rights is left upon global public reason. To be considered urgent by a standard of global public reason, the interest in question needs to be shown as urgent for any decent society. And yet again the determination of what is or is not intrinsically urgent for a decent society would largely depend upon the membership that composes this society. This very much leads to a similar problem of exclusion as in social contracting theory.

It needs to be recounted that social justice to persons with disabilities has been long delayed. The concern to extend education, health care, political rights and liberties to persons with disabilities are even more urgent now than ever before since the world is all set on a transition phase—transition from the physical to the virtual, from offline to online. The Internet holds potential to realize a world that is just as whole, in which accidents of birth and national

---

[47] John Rawls, 'The Law of Peoples with "The Idea of Public Reason Revisited"', 79 (1999).

[48] Wang, 'Time to Think about Human Right to the Internet Access'.

[49] A practical conception takes the doctrine and practice of human rights as they are found in international political life as the source materials for constructing a conception of human rights. Charles Beitz, *The Idea of Human Rights*, 102 (2009).

origin do not warp people's life chances.[50] This emancipator potential cannot be allowed to fizzle out. I apprehend that if the right to access the Internet is not fully appreciated by the society and its urgency for persons with disabilities overlooked, it will have an adverse impact on realization of the rights ensured to persons with disabilities.

Full and effective realization of the rights of persons with disabilities in the Information Age requires reshaping theoretical structures of human rights and re-conceptualizing perceptions about the right to access the Internet. My premise here, then, is that the conception we have chosen to describe human rights as well as the Internet reveals not only how we conceptualize the Internet, but also, and more importantly, how we scope the nature of the right to access the Internet and the normative and legal framework we create for the right to access to the Internet.[51] If the Internet is understood as infrastructure, it necessarily falls within the description of an underlying foundation, a basic framework to reach a certain end. It thus, only remains a means rather than an end in itself. The conclusion then reached by the enabling approach might be a sufficient response to the right to access. However, it needs to be underscored that the Internet is not merely infrastructure. In a progressively popular conception, the Internet constitutes a culture, a public sphere and a community.[52] In these terms, if the Internet is a symbol of a new and more democratic frontier of civilization, then it can be conveniently argued that the Internet provides individuals with a richer choice of communities and online spaces

[50] Nussabaum, 'Frontiers of Justice', p. 2.

[51] Colin Crawford, 'Cyberplace: Defining a Right to Internet Access through Public Accommodation Law', 76 Temp. L. Rev. 225 (2003).

[52] The culture metaphor is reflected in a large body of research that explores the internet from the perspective of its cultural practices, focusing on various examples of internet communities, including their norms and values, identity formation, sharing and collaboration, means of social control, and so forth. See generally, S. Turkle, *Life on the Screen: Identity in the Age of the Internet*, (Simon and Schuster, 1995); D. Silver, 'Looking Backwards, Looking Forward: Cyberculture Studies', in *WebStudies: Rewiring Media Studies for the Digital Age*, 19–30 (Gauntlett ed., 2000); C. Shirky, *Here Comes Everybody: The Power of Organizing without Organisations* (2008).

that revitalize the notion of community. This articulation of the Internet necessarily involves a space of empowerment and creativity.

While CRPD makes an attempt in this regard, it is very crucial to be fully alert to what is being asked and offered. I am, therefore, compelled to call in question the perception of CRPD that the right to access the Internet is merely an enabling right. I argue that the right to access the Internet under disability lens is a human right. CRPD needs to shed its inhibitions in claiming that the right to access in general and right to access the Internet in particular is a new right. I would therefore, establish how naturalist theories of human rights can be favourably applied to hold that the right to access the Internet is a human right.

Access to the Internet—A Human Right

According to the naturalist theories human rights apply to all people equally, regardless of their nationality, religion, and so on, and holds these rights to be pre-institutional, where no legal institution needs to exist to declare or protect these rights in order for them to exist.[53] Human rights, therefore ought to be conceptualized as a means of ensuring general human flourishing.[54] In order to attain 'truly human functioning',[55] there are certain 'central human capabilities'. People ought to have the freedom to function as they choose. Amartya Sen

[53] Skepys, 'Is There a Human Right to the Internet?', p. 16.

[54] Stein and Stein, 'Beyond Disability Civil Rights', p. 1218.

[55] The central capabilities (with rights necessary for them in parentheses) are: (a) living a normal life span; (b) bodily health, including (rights to) adequate nourishment; (c) bodily integrity (including freedom of movement and security against assault, as well as freedom of choice in reproduction and in sexual relations); (d) being able to use the senses, the imagination, and thought (including freedom of expression and religious exercise, and adequate education), and being able to have pleasurable experiences; (e) experiencing normal human emotions, including longing, grief, anger, etc., and having emotional attachments to others (that is, love, friendships, and the normal range of affective emotions); (f) development of one's capacities for practical reason, including the capacity of critical reflection upon one's good or plan of life (protected by liberty of conscience and religious freedom, among other

calls 'effective freedoms', and not simply well-being or functioning; all persons are equally entitled to the necessities of living a good life. All individuals require both resources and the opportunity to utilize those resources to achieve their potential. According to the capabilities approach, there are certain basic human needs and the capacities that must be realized to a minimum degree if human beings are to live a decent life consonant with human dignity and flourish. It is this provisioning of capabilities and sufficiency of resources which enable a person to exercise developed capacities and live a truly human life.[56] Equality of capability is an essential social goal where its absence would be connected with a deficit in dignity and self-respect and it is the equal dignity of human beings that demands recognition.[57]

That the right to access the Internet is a human right thus springs from three strands of arguments derived from naturalist theorists.[58] One strand emerges from the equality-non-discrimination approach, and the second and the third strands emerge from autonomy approach and active citizenship approach, respectively. While my arguments here are strictly made under the disability lens, there is nothing which prevents their extension to more generic audience so as to build case that right to access the Internet is necessarily a human right.

Equality and Non-Discrimination Argument

Equality and non-discrimination are amongst the core principles of human rights and it may not be an exaggeration to say that they form

---

rights); (g) capabilities for affiliation (including both having the capacities to care for and commiserate with others, and having social bases of self-respect and non-humiliation (with rights to non-discrimination on the basis of race, sex, sexual orientation, ethnicity, caste, religion, and national origin)); (h) living with other species; (i) play, including the ability to enjoy recreational activities; (j) control over one's environment (including rights to political participation, freedom of association, and having property rights on an equal basis with others and equal opportunities). See Nussbaum, 'Frontiers of Justice', pp. 76-8.

[56] See Nussbaum, 'Frontiers of Justice', p. 77.

[57] Nussbaum, 'Frontiers of Justice'.

[58] Jonathan W. Penney, 'Internet Access Rights: A Brief History and Intellectual Origins', 38 WM. Mitchell L. REV. 10 (2011-12).

the central tenets of international human rights law and Constitutions of several countries in the world. I argue that when the denial to right to access the Internet leads to inequality and discrimination, how can it be disqualified as a human right. Let me elaborate.

Article 2 of the UDHR[59] stipulates that 'everyone is entitled to all the rights and freedoms....without distinction of any kind....', becomes relevant when persons with disabilities are distinguished and excluded by denying them access to the Internet and their rights and freedoms thereto. It also impinges on the limitation of access to informational resources when denial to the Internet can increase underprivileged status of persons with disabilities. Similarly, when Article 26(1) of the UDHR guarantees that everyone has the right to education and further stipulates that higher education shall be equally accessible to all on the basis of merit; such right to education cannot be ensured unless read in conjunction with access to the Internet. While most opportunities of education, scholarship, research, admissions and examinations are progressively taking place online; the right to access to study components and other processes has to be available to all in an accessible manner otherwise the same would amount to inequality in opportunities and result into discrimination.

Similarly, Article 25(c) of the ICCPR enshrines the right of every citizen to have access, on general terms of equality, to public service in his or her country can be read in conjunction with Article 21(c) of CRPD. The International Convention on the Elimination of All Forms of Racial Discrimination by virtue of Article 5(f) guarantees everyone the right of access to any place or service intended for use by the general public, such as transport hotels, restaurants, cafes, theatres, and parks. This right to access can be extended to the right of persons with disabilities to have access to the virtual world and their right to be included in the community under Article 19 of CRPD. Such construction of treaties and convention make oblique references to the right to access as an important basis of wholesome enjoyment of rights. When these treaties are read under the disability lens, they yield result compatible to the mandate of CRPD.

---

[59] Universal Declaration of Human Rights, G.A. Res. 217A (III), Article 26, U.N. Doc.A/810 (10 December 1948).

As society is progressively depending upon the Internet, political, economic, social consequences of access to the Internet or otherwise are becoming more obvious. Increasingly there has been a demand to create a level playing field for everyone in the Information Society. The proponents of the 'equality and non-discrimination' approach to the Internet emphasize that edifice of a modern egalitarian society in Information age is bound to have right to access the Internet as a fundamental right.

It needs to be recounted that CRPD does not allow a disjunctive reading of Articles. Accordingly, a combined reading of Article 3, Article 4,[60] Article 5,[61] and Article 9[62] of CRPD creates obligations on State Parties to ensure full realization of all human rights for persons with disabilities without discrimination so that they may live independently and participate fully in all aspects of life in a dignified and autonomous manner. The general obligation is further entwined with other specific rights guaranteed in other parts of CRPD. Thus, when Article 19 guarantees the right of persons with disabilities to live independently and to be included in the community, it extends to the virtual world and its implementation in an inclusive manner which respects diversity. In a similar breath, the right to be educated in an inclusive and non-discriminatory manner under Article 24 entails ensuring that education opportunities, information, admission process, online examinations are made available to persons with disabilities on an equal basis with others.

Accordingly, where denial of the access to the Internet leads to any exclusion or restriction on grounds of disability and has the effect of impairing or nullifying the enjoyment or exercise of human

---

[60] Article 4(1) stipulates that, 'States Parties undertake to ensure and promote the full realisation of all human rights and fundamental freedoms for all persons with disabilities without discrimination of any kind on the basis of disability.'

[61] Article 5(1) provides that, 'States Parties recognize that all persons are equal before and under the law and are entitled without any discrimination to the equal protection and equal benefit of the law.'

[62] Article 9(1) stipulates: 'To enable persons with disabilities to live independently and participate fully in all aspects of life, States Parties shall take appropriate measures to ensure to persons with disabilities access, on an equal

rights; it amounts to discrimination and a breach of obligation under CRPD.[63] Take for instance a situation where a user with visual impairment interacts with websites with the aid of a screen reader inbuilt in computer and derives range of information including education, employment, or social networking. The screen reader reads aloud text or magnify image on the screen or provide Braille, but this tool alone cannot do the job unless the digital information provided on the website or e-book is accessible. Thus, if the user could not have access to website say for example pertaining to education on an equal basis with others, it amounts to discrimination and inequality, denial of rights guaranteed, and a breach of international obligation by the State.

In a progressively technological advanced world where real world individuals are expected to make transitions to the virtual world for their basic civic transactions, including education, banking, and finance and, accessing public information, does not interference with or denial of access to the Internet become a human rights issue? Is it not troublesome when technology results in jeopardizing the universal and the indivisible core to the most basic and primary human rights?

---

basis with others, to the physical environment, transportation, information, and communications, including information and communications technologies and systems, and to other facilities and services open or provided to the public, both in urban and in rural areas. These measures, which shall include the identification and elimination of obstacles and barriers to accessibility, shall apply to, inter alia: (a) Buildings, roads, transportation, and other indoor and outdoor facilities, including schools, housing, medical facilities, and workplaces; (b) Information, communications, and other services, including electronic services and emergency services.'

[63] Article 2 stipulates: 'Discrimination on the basis of disability' means any distinction, exclusion or restriction on the basis of disability which has the purpose or effect of impairing or nullifying the recognition, enjoyment or exercise, on an equal basis with others, of all human rights and fundamental freedoms in the political, economic, social, cultural, civil, or any other field. It includes all forms of discrimination, including denial of reasonable accommodation. Note that the preambular paragraphs of the CRPD reference equality and non-discrimination and Article 1 declares the purpose of the CRPD, and Article 3 articulates non-discrimination as a general principle.

Autonomy Approach

Autonomy is often equated with individuality, freedom of the will, integrity, independence, self-knowledge, responsibility, freedom from obligation, self-assertion, critical reflection, and absence of external causation.[64] Thus, it is fairly accepted that autonomy is a norm that is valuable and worthy of protection under the naturalist theory of human rights. It has been elaborately discussed how advent of the Internet helped persons with disabilities to sidestep the barriers existing in physical world, leading to promises of an autonomous life and living. An individual without access to the Internet in today's society can be easily likened to the proverbial 'The Man in the Pit' sketched by Joseph Raz.[65] Accordingly, a man who falls down a pit is stuck there for his entire life with enough food to keep him alive without suffering (after he gets used it). His only choices are when to eat and when to sleep. Raz argues that this man is void of autonomy because his options are those that concern his most basic of needs.[66] A fundamental feature of autonomy, as suggested by Raz, is the presence of choices and options to an individual.[67] This definition of autonomy also finds tacit endorsement by the prescribed intrinsic values of Griffin.[68] Raz argues that failure to promote autonomy would constitute harm, when someone makes him worse off than he is 'entitled' to be[69] or when one fails in one's duty 'to' him to improve his situation.[70]

Evidently, today a person with disability cannot be expected to live autonomously and exercise full range of other rights unless the right to access the Internet is accorded equal priority and urgency.

---

[64] Onora O'neill, 'Bounds of Justice', 30 (2000).

[65] Joseph Raz, *The Morality of Freedom* (1986).

[66] Raz, *The Morality of Freedom*, p. 373.

[67] Raz, *The Morality of Freedom*, p. 373.

[68] Accordingly, autonomy rights are those that are necessary for forming a conception of a worthwhile life. However such autonomy requires anti-determinist free-will, at least, if it is to have intrinsic value. Griffin, 'On Human Rights', pp. 155, 157.

[69] Raz, *The Morality of Freedom*, p. 414.

[70] Raz, *The Morality of Freedom*, p. 416.

One has to bear in mind the overarching general principles and cross cutting articles which guides interpretation of substantive rights. Such conjunctive reading of Article 3, Article 4, Article 5, and Article 9 of the CRPD with other articles demonstrates that access to the Internet and the capabilities are so intertwined that denial of rights status to the Internet access diminishes or denies the associated capabilities.[71]

Active Citizenship Approach

Governments have also proclaimed their 'commitment to build a people-centered, inclusive and development-oriented Information Society, where everyone can create, access, utilize and share information and knowledge'.[72] The UN Special Rapporteur on the Promotion and Protection of the Right to Freedom of Opinion and Expression has stressed that he believes the Internet to be one of the most powerful instruments of the twenty-first century for 'increasing transparency in the conduct of the powerful, access to information, and for facilitating active citizen participation in building democratic societies'. Elaborating on participation in the online sphere, the Council of Europe in its contribution to the first Internet Governance Forum in Athens, emphasizes that the right to participate in the information society includes 'not only the right to be connected to infrastructure, not only the right to gain access to the informational richness on the Net, but also the possibility for everybody to take part in the large discussion forum which the Internet does constitute'.[73]

[71] Stephen B. Wicker and Stephanie M. Santoso, 'Access to the Internet is a Human Right', 56(6) COMMUN. ACM. 43 (2013) DOI: 10.1145/2461256.2461271.

[72] World Summit on the Information Society, Plan of Action, Geneva, 12 December 2003, WSIS-03/GENEVA/DOC/5-E, available at www.itu.int/wsis/docs/geneva/official/poa.html (last visited 2 April 2015).

[73] Council of Europe Blogged Submission to the Internet Governance Forum (30 October to 2 November 2006) available at http://igf.wgig.org/cmsold/2011-igf-nairobi/w2011/107-athens-preparatory-contributions (last visited 1 May 2015).

Thus, we see that many governments, scholars and activists speak of the Internet as an extended public sphere where citizens actively participate and articulate their opinions, priorities and criticism with respect to the democratic rule of a country.[74] The active citizenship approach[75] challenges socially constructed barriers, behaviours and attitudes which continue to deny full citizenship. It, therefore, calls for promoting a life in the community and engaging all the users of the Internet as citizens of the Internet as citizens of cyberspace by providing the supports needed to enable people to realize their citizenship. Whereas in the narrow sense such engagement refers to political participation, its broader connotation includes range of ways by which citizens engage in public services. The active citizenship approach to right to access the Internet refers to a broader engagement. According to this approach, the right to take part in the conduct of public affairs is a right on its own merits, as well as a right that is closely related to several other rights.

Evidently, 'access to technology is one determinant of who can participate in the social, cultural, political and economic facets of a society'.[76] Accordingly, effective access to information is 'a prerequisite for any meaningful concept of citizenship', as the media provide the public with necessary information to be involved in civil society.[77] Such approach to the Internet is crucial in that it prioritizes citizenship interests over commercial interests and ensures that persons with disabilities are perceived not as disempowered victims

---

[74] According to Smith (1983), participation refers to various procedures designed to consult, involve, and inform the public to allow those affected by a decision to have an input into that decision.

[75] The term citizenship entails wide definition of citizenship, based on the values associated with this concept, including all residents within a community. It thereby reflects 'the actual practice and experience of what might be called citizenship', including participation in society. See Eliz Varney, *Disability and Information Technology: A Comparative Study in Media Regulation* (2014).

[76] J.L. Gregg, 'Policy-making in the Public Interests: A Contextual Analysis in the Passage of Closed-captioning Policy', *Disability and Society*, 21(5) 537 (2006).

[77] M. Feintuc and M. Varney, 'Media Regulation, Public Interest and the Law', 250 (2nd ed., 2006).

but as citizens with full entitlements in society.[78] Any narrower approach tends to diminish persons with disabilities from being citizens to merely being 'consumers', 'customers', or 'end users'. Consequentially, commercial players driven by financial advantage may not place sufficient weight on accessibility considerations that facilitate equal access to information for persons with disabilities and thereby detriment their 'ability to participate in democratic deliberations and debate'.[79]

The right to access the Internet when translated into disability rights language necessitates grounding in human rights. This grounding lends a human dignity approach to the whole issue. It can thus be seen that applying a human rights framework tends to rectify the deficits in access and ensure equality, at the same time promoting a citizenship base to deprived groups. It has been predicted that progressively the Internet will become so pervasive in every facet of our lives that will effectively 'disappear' in the background.[80] It will be a part of our presence all the time. It is, therefore absolutely essential that the right to access the Internet is pitched on a human rights note. Advancement in cyberspace lead to a movement towards redefinitions of impoverishment: poverty is no longer to be identified in terms of material deprivations but in terms of access to information to cyberspace. Thus, one hears of 'dead' or 'wild' zones of the urban impoverishment in terms of cyber-poverty, rather than in those of the right to food, housing, and health.[81]

While drafting CRPD it was conceded that disability jurisprudence was only reiterating and elaborating on the human

---

[78] D. Chalmers, G. Davies, and G. Monti, *European Union Law: Cases and Materials* (2011).

[79] Anthony E. Varona, 'Changing Channels and Bridging Divides: The Failure and Redemption of American Broadcast Television Regulation', 6 MINN. J. L., SCI. & TEC.1, 99 (2004).

[80] Google boss Eric Schmidt opines predicted that the Internet will soon be so pervasive in every facet of our lives that it will effectively 'disappear' into the background, Google boss Eric Schmidt at the World Economic Forum at Davos, at the summit, a panel brought together the heads of Google, Microsoft, and Vodafone, *The Hindu*, 24 January 2015.

[81] U. Baxi, 'The Future of Human Rights', 160 (2002).

rights of persons with disabilities and not creating any new rights. In the main, persons with disabilities were assuring the international community that what they were asking for was nothing new, it was merely what others already had. However, as Eric Schmidt puts it, 'The Internet is the first thing that humanity has built that humanity doesn't understand, the largest experiment in anarchy that we have ever had.'[82] Unless current Internet regulators, infrastructure architects, and disability constituency perceive the Internet in a broad fashion; they may never realize what is lost.

It needs to be understood that so far as the right to access to the Internet is concerned, disability rights jurisprudence cannot take the line of construction similar to other human rights instruments primarily for the reason that concerns and apprehensions of persons with disabilities are different from other groups. Other excluded groups, say women or racial minority, will automatically seek entry into the virtual world once geographic, income, gender, and broadband divides are bridged. However, persons with disabilities will still be left out of the electronic gates of the virtual world if the very design and basic principles of the virtual world are not inclusive. The disability jurisprudence cannot afford to adopt a weaker plank of enabling right and must necessarily pitch the right to access as a human right even if it amounts to claiming a 'new right'. If the General Comments on CRPD insist on construing right to access against disability perspective, this necessarily has to be a demand of a new right. The right to access the Internet has to clearly powerfully sharply be articulated as a human right of persons with disabilities. Any other compromise or pragmatic attempt will rather result into disability constituency excluding itself from the virtual community.

While CRPD and General Comments have been sharing concerns of other human rights treaties with regards to access, pioneering a human rights claim to the right to access the Internet by the ones at the outermost periphery of the virtual world, will enable include other marginalized groups as well. Only then can CRPD claim to be a truly 'remarkable and forward-looking document' which heralds

---

[82] Eric Schmidt quoted in Andrew Murray, *The Regulation of Cyberspace: Control in the Online Environment*, 233 (2007).

'the dawn of a new era—an era in which disabled people will no longer have to endure the discriminatory practices and attitudes that have been permitted to prevail for all too long'.[83]

Progressive Acceptance of the Right to Access the Internet as Fundamental Right

Constitution of some countries explicitly guarantees equality to persons with disabilities and consequently the right to access resources on equal basis with others. Disability is, therefore, a ground of non-discrimination in such countries. While some constitutions address discrimination against persons with disabilities in an explicit manner some others adopt a generic manner by including disability on a list of protected groups, together with race, religion, and political beliefs.[84] Say for instance, Italy, in accordance to the principle of equality enshrined in Article 3 of the Constitution, the right of persons with disabilities to access to all sources of information and for their pertinent services is recognized.

The Canadian Charter of Rights and Freedoms Canada is possibly the first country to have adopted in its Constitution an explicit equality guarantee for persons with disabilities.[85] Section 15(1) of the Canadian Charter of Rights and Freedoms[86] stipulates

[83] Message, The Secretary-General, 'Secretary-General's Message on the Adoption of the Convention of the Rights of Persons with Disabilities, delivered by Mr. Mark MallochBrown, Deputy Secretary General', U.N. Doc. SG/SM!10797, HR/491 1, L/T/4400 (13 December.2006), available at http://www.un.org/News/Press/docs/2006/sgsm10797.doc.htm (last visited 2 April 2015).

[84] See for example, Aus. Const. (Constitution Act, 1983); Braz. Const. (Constitution Act, 1988); Can. Const. (Constitution Act of 1982); Switz. Const. (Constitution Act, 2000); Uganda Const. (Constitution Act, 1995), Article 21. For comprehensive details see Arlene Kanter, 'The Globalisation of Disability Rights Law', 30 SYRACUSE J. INT'L L. & COM. 241 (2003).

[85] F.L. Pickering and A. Silvers, 'Americans with Disabilities: Exploring Implications of the Law for Individuals and Institutions', 339 (2000).

[86] The Canadian Constitution includes the Constitution Act, the Canadian Charter of Rights and Freedoms and the British North America

that 'every individual is equal before and under the law and has the right to the equal protection and equal benefit of the law without discrimination and, in particular, without discrimination based [inter alia] on mental or physical disability.'[87]

While the Charter does not make any specific reference to access to the Internet or virtual world, section 15(1) of this instrument indirectly protects these rights due to its 'considerable moral impact in establishing the expectations of non-discrimination in the country'.[88] Such provisions in the Constitution reflect a substantive vision of equality,[89] requiring a proactive approach to safeguarding the rights of persons with disabilities, and have been invoked to tackle the accessibility barriers faced by persons with disabilities.

For instance, in *Donnna Jodhan v. Attorney General of Canada*,[90] the applicant who was a professional with visual impairment brought the matter that despite the Communications Policy of the Government of Canada making federal institutions subject to the *Common Look and Feel for the Internet: Standards and Guidelines* (CLF 1.0 Standard) which guarantees universal accessibility and equitable access to all content on Government of Canada websites; the government website was not accessible. The applicant successfully argued that such denial to access to government information and service constitutes a breach of the applicant's rights to equal treatment under section 15(1) of the Canadian Charter of Rights and Freedoms. As stressed by Justice Kelen,

> for the blind and visually impaired, accessing information and services online gives them independence, self-reliance, control, ease of access, dignity and self-esteem. A person is not handicapped if she does not need help. Making the government online information and services accessible provides the visually impaired with 'substantive equality'.

Act. See Mooney Cotter, 'This Ability: An International Legal Perspective of Disability Discrimination', 155 (2007).

[87] Charter, section 15(1).

[88] See Meac, 'Measuring Progress of e-accessibility in Europe, Assessment of the Status of E-accessibility in Europe', 250 (2007).

[89] R.V. Kapp (2008) 2 S.C.R. 483.

[90] (2011) 2 F.C.R. 355.

This is like the ramp to permit wheelchair access to a building. It is a ramp for the blind to access online services.[91]

A handful of countries have been experimenting with different notions of the Internet rights. In 2000 Estonia declared Internet access to be a human right 'essential for life in the 21st century'.[92] The practical entitlement, however, only extends to free Internet access at public libraries.[93]

***

When disability rights icon Jacobusten Broek argued nearly 50 years ago for the right of people with disabilities 'to live in the world',[94] perhaps no one contemplated about a future virtual world. Nonetheless his call to attain participatory justice for persons with disabilities by 'integrationalism' can be validly extended to the virtual world.[95] As Stein puts it—Jacobus tenBroek's focus on the right of people with disabilities 'to live in the world' naturally encompasses their 'right to live in the internet'.[96] In terms of biological metaphor, cyberspace [is] a social petri dish, the [Intern]et [is] the agar medium, and virtual communities, in all their diversity, [are] the colonies of microorganisms that grow in petri dishes. Each of the colonies of a microorganism the communities

---

[91] (2011) 2 F.C.R. 355 paragraph 179 (10).

[92] Colin Woodard, *Estonia, Where Being Wired Is a Human Right* (2003) Christian Science Monitor 7, available at http://www.csmonitor.com/2003/0701/p07s01-woeu.html (last visited 31 March 2015).

[93] Public Information Act (Estonia); and section 44 Constitution of Estonia.

[94] tenBroek, 'The Right to Live in the World' ('If the disabled have the right to live in the world, they must have the right to make their way into it and therefore, must be entitled to use the indispensable means of access, and to use them on terms that will make the original right effective').

[95] tenBroek, 'The Right to Live in the World', 'integrationism'—system wide policies 'entitling the disabled to full participation in the life of the community and encouraging and enabling them to do so'.

[96] Brad Areheart and Michael Ashley Stein, 'Integrating the Internet', 83 George Washington L. REV. 449 (2015).

on the [Intern]et—is a social experiment that nobody planned but that is happening nevertheless.[97] If it is a social experiment, it is essential that disability community participate in this experiment and insert an element thereto.

Shutting out persons with disabilities from the virtual world implies denial of opportunity of living an independent life with dignity and self-respect. CRPD cannot serve its purpose of mainstreaming persons with disabilities from marginalization unless it fully realizes the potentials and implications of the access to the Internet. An examination of the right to access to the Internet under disability rights jurisprudence opens up a discourse more complex than the one led by enabler theorists. While a constricted view of the enabling approach perceives the Internet as merely a catalyst, a facilitator to the attainment of other rights; a broader conception leads to different conclusion. Insofar as the Internet is crucial for 'normal social functioning', deprived access could entail social exclusion and arguably amount to a human rights violation.

If the Internet is an inevitable part of the Information Society, a culture, a community, it is vital to raise questions on the position taken by CRPD. It can be concluded from aforesaid discussion that CRPD cannot advance the rights and fulfil the promises if it continues with a complacent, convenient position on the right to access the Internet—uncontroversial but incomplete. The goals of substantive equality and a rights based regime that CRPD augments cannot be advanced if access to the Internet is trivialized as an enabling right. Based on this understanding, the right to access has to necessarily be rooted in human rights jurisprudence besides being supported by active citizenship and equality-non-discrimination approach. It, thereby assumes criticality as a human right that requires immediate attention and action rather than being pegged as merely an enabling right. As pointed out by Nussbaum, upholding the dignity of the rights of persons with disabilities and according recognition necessitates central human capabilities to be perceived not simply as desirable social goals but urgent entitlements grounded in justice.

[97] Howard Rheingold, 'The Virtual Community: A Homesteading on the Electronic Frontier', 6 (1993).

Having embedded the right to access the Internet in human rights framework, it is trite to emphasize that this right entails negative duties as well as positive duties. This raises questions as to what is the nature of the duty, whom should it be attributed. The next chapters will elaborate on this aspect.

2

Re-conceptualizing the Corporate Human Rights Obligation

Having established that the right to access to the Internet is essentially a core human right, the next logical question that follows is against whom is this right available? Who is the duty bearer for ensuring that this right is realized? As such the State is considered to be the addressee of human rights obligations and as a corollary; the State is the duty bearer of the rights of persons with disabilities to access the Internet. This understanding stands challenged in a technology driven world of the Internet where the emergence of powerful non-State actors, especially corporation, has marginalized the State from its central position. In this backdrop, I shall interrogate the transplantation of traditional state-centric approach to the technology and human rights discourse, in particular the right to access to the Internet. However, this interrogation cannot be complete without an insight into the virtual world. Accordingly, this chapter undertakes two tasks; first, it maps the virtual world terrain to decipher the dominant player; second, having thus, identified the player the latter part of the chapter proceeds to establish normative and theoretical framework for the duty bearer.

Limits of the State as the Sole Duty-Bearer of Human Rights Obligation

If the right to access the Internet is a human right, is it not logical that the existing framework of human rights law becomes applicable? Under the state-centric international human rights law, the State is considered to be the primary duty bearer of human rights obligations. This is the classical approach, largely guided by the Westphalian hypothesis, which fundamentally assumes international system to be anarchic, lacking any centric authority and recognizing States as the only actors. Consequently actors other than the State are diminished as mere instruments of governments, and therefore unimportant in their own right. Thus, traditionally, human rights are addressed to states and have been intended principally to regulate relations between individuals and the state.

The classical state-centric approach is largely guided by a basic assumption that the amount of power a sovereign State wields renders it more capable not only of inflicting systematic abuse but at the same time also of promoting human rights. Thus, it is presumed that threat to human rights violation emanate only from the State and the State being classic effective regulator, vested with legitimacy and authority, is well situated to redress human rights concerns. Consequently, regardless of the fact whether the human right is 'negative', commanding abstinence from arbitrary interference with rights or 'positive', requiring to ensure the well-being of its nationals, the State is the addressee of human rights obligations. Insofar as obligations of non-state actors are concerned, these are essentially a matter of domestic civil or criminal law, backed by international legal obligation of the state to ensure effective protection of human rights of individuals under its jurisdiction.

Thus, the State is the best medium to tackle the threats emanating from non-state actors under their territorial jurisdiction.[1]

---

[1] It is often apprehended that attempting to extend legal duties under human rights law to non-state actors bestows legitimacy on such actors which will undermine the authority of the State and dilute their responsibilities towards human rights obligation. See generally Andrew Clapham, *Human Rights Obligations of Non-State Actors* (2006).

Consequently, most human rights treaties adopt an indirect approach so far as non-state actors are concerned. Under Indirect Approach, international law imposes duties directly on state and most obligations are placed indirectly on private actors through the state. For instance, Article 2(1)(d) of International Convention on the Elimination of all Forms of Racial Discrimination[2] (CERD) and Article 2(e) of Convention on the Elimination of all forms of Discrimination Against Women[3] (CEDAW). Both articles mandate the state to take 'all appropriate measures' to eliminate discrimination. Thus, Article 2(e) of CEDAW requires the state 'to take all appropriate measures to eliminate discrimination against women by any person, organisation or enterprise'. Similarly, CERD Article2(1)(d) obliges states to 'prohibit and bring to an end... racial discrimination by any persons, group organisation'. The Convention itself also obliges states to criminalize the spreading of ideas of racial superiority and inciting others to racial discrimination and violence and make racist organizations illegal (Article 4); states must also protect against racially motivated violence 'whether inflicted by government officials or by any individual group or institution' (Article 5(b)). States must ensure that victims of racial discrimination have effective remedies, including compensation (Article 6). An advantage of this indirect approach of accountability is that it is non-controversial being firmly within human rights legal tradition.

Applying this approach, if rights of persons with disabilities to access the Internet are to be ensured, duties ought to be imposed directly on the State. The most convenient mode is thus, to entrust States with the obligation to restrict private actions that interfere with enjoyment of accessibility rights of persons with disabilities, and place most obligations indirectly on private actors through the State. This is the route preferred by CRPD when it mandates State Parties under Article 3 to take all appropriate measures

[2] UDHR, G.A. Res. 217A (III), Article 26, UN Doc.A/810 (10 December 1948).

[3] Convention on Elimination of all forms of Discrimination against Women, GA res. 34/180, 34 UN GAOR Supp. (No. 46), p. 193, UN Doc. A/34/46.

to eliminate discrimination on the basis of disability by any person, organization, or private enterprise.[4] Whereas this route is convenient, prior to accepting this position at its face value, it would be pertinent to be informed of ground realities.

Both these perceptions about the State power stands challenged in the present world order of globalization and privatization. First, it is observed that globalization has not only broadened and deepened cross border transactions between different economies but also has a multidimensional impact on various systems, institutions, law, and policies of the international community. Economic interdependence, deregulation and dominance of markets have resulted in the curtailment of States powers.[5] The emergence of corporations and their economic power dwarfed the power of certain States. Rather, States are often caught between the need to choose between development and individual rights with most states opting for the former thereby abdicating their responsibilities to protect their own citizens in the short term.[6] This is also indicative of the lack of willingness and capacity of states to regulate corporate human rights conduct. Soft borders and attractive investment destinations mean corporations shift their activities to states with fewer regulatory burdens, including human rights regulations. Apart from the quantitative aspect of economic capacity, corporations began to exercise functions comparable to those of the State.[7] Thus, with the rise of corporations as private authority, States were dislocated from its exclusive regulatory power.

[4] CRPD, Article 3.

[5] See generally Paul Redmond, 'Transnational Enterprise and Human Rights: Options for Standard Settings and Compliance', 37 INT'L L. 69 (2003).

[6] Christen Broecker, '"Better the Devil You Know": Home State approaches to Transnational Corporate Accountability', 41 N.Y.U. J. INT'L L. and POL. 159, p. 161 (2008).

[7] The most commented example of a situation in which traditional state functions have been delegated to private companies is peacekeeping, security, and the running of detention facilities in post-conflict situations. See generally, S. Chesterman and C. Lehnardt, From Mercenaries to Market: Rise and Regulation of Private Military Companies (2007).

Second, progressively it has been realized that threats to human rights violation may not emanate only from States.[8] Corporations now wield such power that their conduct poses a threat to enjoyment of most human rights as well as have a positive influence on advancement of human rights. As a result, ideological, social, and international pressure has been mounting to entrust human rights obligations to corporations. Thus, there is a growing demand to hold corporations directly accountable under international human rights laws.[9] A rich and expansive debate surrounding theoretical and practical implications of ascribing liability for human rights violations to corporate entities has emerged during the past twenty years.[10] However, consensus is still lacking whether existing normative and enforcement framework of international human rights laws allows direct imposition of obligations on corporations.

Thus, any inquiry on the issue of the right to access the Internet and its duty bearer cannot be made in oblivion to the aforementioned turmoil within international human rights law. Prior to applying classical understanding based on exclusive State obligation, it is crucial to pose certain questions. It is pertinent to ask whether the State wields the power in the virtual world to

---

[8] The same holds true for the Internet related issues. Several occasions in the past have raised public concerns about the role of private players in the virtual world. Yahoo! settled a lawsuit brought in the US by several Chinese dissidents who alleged they were persecuted for political speech after Yahoo! revealed their identities to the Chinese government. Available at http://business-humanrights.org/en/yahoo-lawsuit-re-china-0#c9340 (last visited 2 December 2014).

[9] Under Direct Approach human rights law directly places duties on private actors, with enforcement of those duties left to domestic laws or international tribunals. The most prominent example of this is found in Genocide Convention where Article 4 provides that '[p]ersons committing genocide . . . shall be punished, whether they are . . . public officials or private individuals'. The UN Norms on the Responsibilities of Transnational Corporations and Other Business Entities, drafted by the UN Sub-Commission on the Promotion and Protection of Human Rights is amongst earliest attempts to directly hold corporations accountable under international law.

[10] This debate can be tracked both in academia as well as real world discourses. At international level this debate can be neatly identified in phases

the same extent as contemplated in the physical world. Is the State well situated to address the goals of CRPD? If the issue of right to access was merely confined to a negative duty on the State to not to violate accessibility rights, perhaps the classical approach would comprise a sufficient response. However, the problem is that CRPD and its accessibility mandate details not only negative duties but also positive duties. It not only envisions refraining from discrimination but also proactively seek to address discrimination so as to bring about systemic change in attitude towards disability. Given this mandate of CRPD, I probe into the following questions. Does the State have the technical prowess and regulatory reach to ensure creation of an accessible virtual world for persons with

---

culminating into UN Compact, UN Norms, and UN Framework. Discussed at greater details in later chapter. For academic discussions, see Steven R. Ratner, 'Corporations and Human Rights: A Theory of Legal Responsibility', 111 YALE L.J. 443 (2001). Other scholars have also joined the discussion over the years. See, for example, Nien-Hsieh, 'The Obligations of Transnational Corporations: Rawlsian Justice and the Duty of Assistance', 14 Bus. Ethics Q. 643 (2004); Kenneth Paul Kinyua, 'The Accountability of Multinational Corporations for Human Rights Violations: A Critical Analysis of Select Mechanisms and Their Potential to Protect Economic, Social and Cultural Rights in Developing Countries', Working Paper Series, No. K33 (2009), available at http://papers.ssrn.com/sol3/papers.cfm?abstract_id=1599842 (critically analyzing the effectiveness of the U.N. Human Rights Norms as a development in customary international law); David Kinley and Junko Tadaki, 'From Talk to Walk: The Emergence of Human Rights Responsibilities for Corporations at International Law', 44 VA. J. INT'L L. 931 (2004) (arguing that the current state-based framework for human rights accountability is inadequate and duties for TNCs under international law should be implemented); Paul Redmond, 'Transnational Enterprise and Human Rights: Options for Standard Setting and Compliance', 37 INT'L LAW. 69 (2003) (arguing for an international legal framework for TNCs); Larissa van den Herikv and V. Jernejv Netmarv Cernic, 'Régulating Corporations Under International Law: From Human Rights to International Criminal Law and Back Again', 8 J. INT'L CRIM. JUST. 725 (2010) (exploring the idea of bringing corporate human rights responsibility into an international criminal law paradigm to remedy the existing enforcement gap); Rachel J. Anderson, 'Reimagining Human Rights Law: Toward Global Regulation of Transnational Corporations', 88 DENV. U. L. REV. 183 (2010) (arguing for

disabilities? Whether classical state-centric approach could be successfully applied to the technology and human rights discourse? Will it not amount to transplanting problems of existing framework to a relatively new human right? Does it require re-conceptualizing existing framework? A satisfactory and wholesome answer to these questions requires obtaining an insight into the Internet.

Mapping the Virtual World Terrain

The virtual world with the Internet[11] as its technical backbone is a giant network of interconnected computers where real life persons and entities engage a range of social, economic, political activities.[12] The evolution of the Internet owed itself to the State initiatives.[13]

---

the creation of global human rights law, as distinct from international human rights law, to be the law paradigm for TNCs); Cynthia Williams, 'Corporate Social Responsibility in an Era of Economic Globalisation', 35 U.C. DAVIS L. REV. 705 (2002) (arguing that a new paradigm needs to be created that incorporates the reality of how corporations do business today).

[11] Rather than being a single, centrally controlled network designed to deliver one service to terminals, it is a 'network of networks' that is controlled from the 'edge' by users on an 'end-to-end' basis, using terminals across a network to access and provide a wide range of services. Don MacLean, 'Herding Schrodinger's Cats: Some Thinking Tools about the Internet Governance', in *The Internet Governance: A Grand Collaboration* 77 (Don MacLean ed., 2004)

[12] Technically, the Internet can be viewed as a system of communication in the virtual world which comprise of six layers. The Content Layer—the symbols and images that are communicated; The Application Layer—the programs that use the Internet, for example the Web; The Transport Layer—TCP, which breaks the data into packets; The Internet Protocol Layer—IP, handles the flow of data over the network; The Link Layer—the interface between users' computers and the physical layer; The Physical Layer—the copper wire, optical cable, satellite links, and so on. For detailed understanding about the Internet architecture. See Lawrence B. Solum and Minn Chung, 'The Layers Principle: Internet Architecture and the Law', Public Law and Legal Theory Research Paper, University of San Diego School of Law 55 (2003), available at http://ssrn.com/abstract=416263.

[13] Robert Hobbes' Zakon, 'Hobbes' Internet Timeline' v6.1 (2003), available at http://www.zakon.org/robert/internet/timeline/(last visited

The early phases of the Internet spans the period between 1960–85 where government research was based primarily on three objectives: (a) to establish a secure, reliable communications and control system for national defence purposes, (b) to facilitate co-operative research among government agencies and among academic institutions, and (c) to advance the computing and networking technologies themselves. Thus, in the early days, the government efforts focused on creating interconnections between government and academic networks for certain predetermined objectives.[14]

With realization of the apparent potential of the technology commercial interests in the Internet began to blossom in the late 1980s and early 1990s. The emergence of unanticipated, yet extremely attractive, applications forced a shift from public funding and public management of its research results towards commercialization and privatization. The US policy of commercialization and privatization of the Internet led to two broad consequences: first, broadening the focus from academic and military research purposes to commercial exploitation of the emerging virtual space; second, shifting the responsibility to for the design, implementation, operation, and funding of the Internet from the Federal government to the private sector.[15]

The Internet as we know it today has a host of communications, entertainment, electronic commerce, information, multimedia, and other applications. These have emerged from the interconnection of multitudinous, different networks, serving different sets of end-users with different end-uses.[16] Market actors have contributed immensely to the evolution of the Internet in terms of investment, products, services, and infrastructure. There has been a rise of new

---

10 March 2015); Richard T. Griffiths, *History of the Internet, Internet for Historians, Chapter Two: From ARPANET to World Wide Web* (2002), available at http://www.let.leidenuniv.nl/history/ivh/chap2.htm (last visited 10 March 2015).

[14] For detailed history of the Internet, see Chapter 1.

[15] Chinoy and Salo, *Internet Exchanges*, 9.

[16] Although the Internet depends on physical media for implementation, it does not consist of a physical infrastructure of wires, radio waves, cables, or terminals. What we call 'the Internet' is really a standardized set of software instructions (known as protocols) for sending data over a network, and a global

players, such as Internet Service Providers (ISPs), search engines, content producers, application designers, and other Online Service Providers (OSPs). Thus, actual networks on which communication on the Internet occurs are privately owned and administered networks. They are heterogeneous, belonging to households, small businesses, large enterprises, non-profit organizations, and the (usually privately owned) commercial networks of Internet service providers.[17] The Internet is thus a web of actors. It is often thought of as a hierarchy consisting of three levels of participants: end users, ISPs, and Internet Backbone Providers (IBPs).[18]

The flow chart below attempts to provide general upstream-downstream relationship of the Internet participants. While it may not be possible to detail out every kind of participant and its function, the figure offers a fair idea of a range of entities involved and their mutual dependence upon each other.

Top tier comprise of providers of the Internet infrastructure and other support services; the middle tier has actors including companies that are the intermediaries who use the infrastructure and provide various internet dependent public and private goods and services. At the bottom are actors that are consumers of internet dependent goods and services or end-users of the Internet based products and services. Increasingly, provision of Internet service is

---

set of unique addresses so the data can be told where to go. Using the Internet protocols, pre-existing networks can communicate with each other, giving users the functionality of a global network, even though there is only a standard-enabled cross-network communication capacity. See Michael Kende, *The Digital Handshake: Connecting Internet Backbones*, OPP Working Paper, Federal Communications Commission, No. 32 (2000), available at http://www.fcc. gov/working-papers/digital-handshake-connecting-internet-backbones.

[17] Milton Mueller, John Mathiason, and Hans Klein, *The Internet and Global Governance: Principles and Norms for a New Regime*, 13 Global Governance 237 (2007).

[18] 'IBPs own or lease high speed fiber optic networks connected together by routers, which they use to deliver traffic to and from their customers. IBPs primarily sell wholesale Internet connectivity to ISPs that essentially resell this connectivity to their customers....' Michael Kende and Jason Oxman, *The Information Interchange: Interconnection on the Internet*, Proceedings of the 27th Annual Telecommunications Policy Research Conference, 1999.

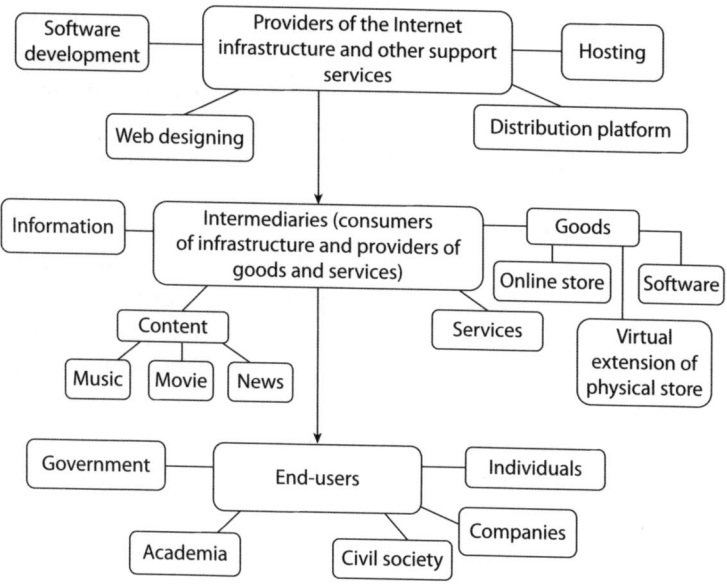

Figure 2.1   Flow chart of the Internet participants
Source: Author.

being handled by commercial firms on a profit-making basis,[19] who have gained power and control in the information environment. The profit motivated corporations occupy much larger space in the Internet, both as providers of infrastructures, end-users.[20] It is important to note that the transactions between the providers of

[19] Robert E. Kahn, 'The Role of Government in the Evolution of the Internet', in Revolution in the US Information Infrastructure 13 (1995).

[20] Google's search market share in the USA in early 2012 was more than 66 per cent, followed by Bing (15.3 per cent) and Yahoo (13.9 per cent), Danny Goodwin, 'Yahoo Search Share Sinks, Google, Bing Rise in February 2012' (New York, 12 March 2012) available at http://searchenginewatch.com/article/2158888/Yahoo-Search-Share-Sinks-Google-Bing-Rise-in-February-2012 (last visited 10 March 2015); while in the UK in April 2012 Google accounted for more than 90 per cent of all searches with the remainder being shared between Yahoo, Bing, and Ask. Experian Hitwise, 'Data Center—Top Sites & Engines', available at http://www.hitwise.com/uk/datacentre/main/dashboard-7323.html (last visited 10 March 2015).

the Internet infrastructure and intermediaries could be B2B (that is, business to business) or B2C (that is, business to consumer) or B2G (that is, business to government). The transaction between intermediaries and end-users are usually B2C.

For the sake of convenience I broadly categorized these into the following:

1) Supply companies—Those companies which are on supply side of the Internet, that is, companies engaged in providing infrastructure providing services of transmission, routing and receipt of messages. These are known as search engines, ISPs, Operating Systems Providers (OSPs), web developers, application developers, hardware manufacturers, and so on. Corporations such as Google, Yahoo, Microsoft, fall under this category.[21]

[21] **Infrastructure and Network Providers**—The core infrastructure of the Internet consist largely of routers (computers designed to receive and forward packets of data), hosts (which store programs and data) and pipes (telecommunications connections which link the hosts and routers together). Hosts and routers are owned by various government and private organizations whose computers are fully connected into the Internet. Many of the pipes tend to be owned by telecommunications companies who typically provide internet compliant routing and switching facilities themselves or lease capacity to network providers who add those facilities to create sections of the Internet. The telecommunication companies, especially American ones such as sprint and MCI are intimately involved with the Internet. **Content Providers**—They range from multinational companies to individuals. Content comes in many forms. It generally divides into real-time and downloadable content. Real-time content is that which can be viewed or heard as the user accesses it. A page of text on the World Wide Web is an example of real-time content. Downloadable content takes the form of a file which can be copied form the Internet site to the user's own computer. The user uses his own applications to read, view or play the file. **Host**—A host is a storage place accessible via the Internet. Hosts are often referred to as servers. The owner host has a spectrum of possible relationships to the data stored on the host. It may own and actively control all the data or may have only a tenuous connection with the stored content. The legal responsibility of the host will vary according to the exact nature of the role that it has assumed. It is impossible to generalize about these responsibilities and they have to be analysed separately for each type of right and liability. One specialized variety of host plays an important role in

2) Consumer companies—These are companies that remain on demand side of the Internet. These may be end-users themselves or who have virtual world presence to influence their real world business or are engaged in business that primarily uses the Internet and related services to conduct their operations. Companies such as Amazon, e-Bay, and so on form this latter category. Most companies these days have the Internet presence given a range of online facilities. A sub category is also such companies that function in partnership with the State or at times function as state agencies.

Supply companies establish network protocols and play a key role between interworks. These often help consumer companies create and develop visual representation of information on the Internet which is made available through web pages within websites. The World Wide Web is accessible by the identities of domain names and site addresses and through the use of search engines.[22]

The result of commercialization and privatization process is that very little of the current Internet is owned and operated by governmental bodies. The government's light-handed approach to regulation has given producers and consumers substantial freedom to innovate. The Internet is susceptible to various types of private ordering. In fact, private ordering is progressively performing Internet governance functions.[23] Given the Internet's openness, its global interconnectedness, its decentralized nature, and the

---

the functioning of the Internet is the domain name server. Domain names are allocated by various organizations connected with the Internet society.

[22] See generally, Teresa Fuentes-Camacho, *The International Dimensions of Cyberspace Law* (2000).

[23] David R. Johnson and David G. Post, 'Law and Borders—The Rise of Law in Cyberspace', 48 *Stanford Law Review* 1367, pp. 1378-9 (1996). This is considered to be a groundbreaking work wherein authors for the first time set out a legal interpretation of the cyber libertarian contention that regulation founded upon traditional state sovereignty cannot function effectively in cyberspace. It is argued that as individuals in cyberspace may move seamlessly between zones governed by differing regulatory regimes in accordance with their personal preferences, it was impossible to effectively regulate the activities of these individuals.

interrelationships among the players, it is remarkably resistant to traditional tools of state governance.[24] Unlike other forms of traditional communications—print, common carriers, and broadcast media that the State could easily regulate and control as owner or regulator, intangible cyberspace pose new challenges before the State. Challenges somewhat similar to the authority of the State in international order were experienced in the virtual world order as well. The legitimacy of the State regulation which would otherwise be justifiable within territorial borders was seen to be questioned by the global intangible nature of the Internet.[25] Since the Internet activities were not restricted to any geographical area, enforceability of laws imposed by the State was weakened. The accelerating pace of technological change further impaired the effectiveness of State regulation, making it almost impossible for regulators to keep up with a technology that reinvents itself every few months. While on the one hand, States were having their own struggles with the Internet, on the other hand, corporations seemed to riding the tide. Corporations in the information economy, where information is a central resource, turn out to be highly mobile and independent of any specific location. The ability to convey information and knowledge easily allowed multinational corporations to organize themselves across national borders, thereby decreasing the dominance of the State in regulating economic relations.[26]

[24] Joe Waz and Phil Weiser, 'Internet Governance: The Role of Multistakeholder Organisations', 10 J. On telecomm. and high tech L. 331 (2012).

[25] Cyberspace was perceived as a new, different, separate space outside physical space—one devoid of scarcity, whose boundless possibilities would provide better rules than any state-made law. This utopian vision delegitimized the role of state law in regulating cyberspace and asserted that self-rule of autonomous virtual communities was both freer and more legitimate than any law imposed by the territorial state. See David R. Johnson and David G. Post, 'Law and Borders—The Rise of Law in Cyberspace', 48 STAN. L. REV. 1367 (1995); David G. Post, 'The Unsettled Paradox: The Internet, the State, and the Consent of the Governed', 5 Ind. J. Global Legal Stud. 521 (1997) Nicolas P. Suzor, 'The Role of the Rule of Law in Virtual Communities', 25 Berkeley Tech. L. J. 1818 (2010).

[26] The services and companies we think of now as being an integral part of the digital realm are relatively recent. Amazon.com began in 1995,

Furthermore, the design of the technology—or code—accorded private companies with regulatory power in shaping the information environment.[27] As Lessig describes the constraints of architecture of the Internet became new law. These constraints impose conditions on the way in which users can operate online. Lessig gives numerous examples of this: such as requirement of an access password; the ability to participate anonymously or to have multiple e-mail identities. Rather, it was asserted that of all the forces such as law, social norms, market that could influence an individuals' behaviour in the virtual world, the code was most effective. [28] While the direct effect of the law was to suffer a sanction or penalize a particular behaviour if it violated a directive under that law for example, copyright infringement, defamation laws; social norms regulate behaviour by threatening an adverse consequence to be imposed by society or community. Markets also regulate in that they constraint individual and collective behaviour. For instance, pricing structures such as access charges to certain information on the Web and to Internet services as well as factors such as congestion, influencing choices that cyberspace consumers make are all examples of cyberspace market regulation.

However, Lessig asserted that Code determines what actions are feasible and what options become available, and therefore, may prove more effective than legal rules in directing human behaviour.[29] It was predicted that code can achieve a nearly perfect control in cyberspace; architecture becomes the most powerful regulator. It was construed that there is a 'relationship between the values imbedded in a particular cyberspace place and the code that

---

letting people order through its digital shopfront from what was effectively a warehouse system. In the same year, eBay was born, hosting 250,000 auctions in 1996 and 2m in 1997. Google was incorporated in 1998. The first iPod was sold in 2001, and the iTunes store opened its online doors in 2003. Facebook went live in 2004. YouTube did not exist until 2005. Nick Harkaway, *The Blind Giant: Being Human in a Digital World* p. 22 (2012).

[27] See generally, Lawrence Lessig, *Code and Other Laws of Cyberspace*.

[28] Lessig, *Code and Other Laws of Cyberspace*.

[29] Lessig, *Code and Other Laws of Cyberspace*.

makes those values possible'.[30] Moreover it was envisaged that the code can and increasingly will displace law leading to a world where effective regulatory power shifts from law to code, from sovereigns to software.[31] Overall, the private sector in the digital environment enjoyed more power in setting the agenda and shaping priorities.[32]

A dynamic interaction between code and the law is quite visible with the State seeking alliance with private nodes of power to formulate effective regulation.[33] While the law attempts to adopt itself to the fast-changing technology and offer new rules that would

[30] Lessig, 'The Law of the Horse: What Cyberlaw Might Teach', 113 HARV. L. REV. 501 (1999). He illustrates this by reference to the rules of various online services. For example, a service may stipulate that participants in a discussion group must have only one cyber-identity and that this must be the user's true identity. While in one sense this may constrain users in what they feel free to discuss, it also manifests a value where 'individuals are tied to their real space reputation; where that reputation is used, in a sense, to moderate or control the conversation of that space.

[31] Lessig, 'The Law of the Horse', p. 206.

[32] Lessig, *Code and Other Laws of Cyberspace*, p. 88. Lessig's work could be read in conjunction with Castells theory. Perhaps the question of power as traditionally formulated does not make sense in the network society, but new forms of domination and determination are critical in shaping peoples' lives regardless of their will. So, there are power relationships at work, albeit in new forms and with new kinds of actors. The most crucial forms of power follow the logic of network-making power. In a world of networks, the ability to exercise control over others depends on two basic mechanisms: (a) the ability to constitute network(s) and to program/reprogram the network(s) in terms of the goals assigned to the network; and (b) the ability to connect and ensure the cooperation of different networks by sharing common goals and combining resources while fending off competition from other networks by setting up strategic cooperation.

[33] For instance, the USA Patriot Act in the United States (as amended in 2002 by the Homeland Security Act), the Antiterrorism Act in the United Kingdom, and the Convention on Cybercrime, initiated by the Council of Europe mandate the Internet intermediaries to track down the alleged criminal activities of the users. For a comprehensive understanding on the internet intermediaries and their use by the State as gatekeepers, see Uta Kohl, 'Google: the rise and rise of online intermediaries in the governance of the Internet and beyond (Part 2)', Int J Law Info Tech 21(2) 187 (2013); Kohl, 'The

govern the new information landscape; the law was identifying existing nodes of control such as infrastructure designers, access providers, and facilitators of online services and utilizing their prerogative.[34] These dynamics gave rise to an 'invisible handshake' between the State and corporations. [35]

This cooperation between the State and corporations, whether voluntary or forced, is seen as enabling the State in seizing control and exercising power in the decentralized borderless information environment. At the same time it is apprehended that use of private parties for executing government roles may create an *unholy alliance* between governments that wish to exercise their power and large online players that seek to maintain and strengthen their dominant role in the market.[36] Unlike other participants to the Internet, corporations are essentially found to be in a dominating position. Concerns were raised about the role of companies in violation of human rights in complicity with certain governments. There have been problems of governments using censorship, blocking, and surveillance as powerful weapons of repression and the private sector being an accomplice intentionally or unintentionally.[37]

Rise and Rise of Online Intermediaries in the Governance of the Internet and Beyond—Connectivity Intermediaries', 26 Int'l Rev. of Law, Computers, and Tech 185 (2012).

[34] Lessig, Code and Other Laws of Cyberspace, p. 2, Joel Reidenberg, 'Lex Informatica: The Formulation of Information Policy Rules through Technology', 76 TEX. L. REV. 553 (1998).

[35] Michael D. Birnhack and Niva Elkin-Koren, 'The Invisible Handshake: The Reemergence of the State in the Digital Environment', 8 VA. J.L. & TECH. 6 (2003).

[36] Yahoo! settled a lawsuit brought in the US by several Chinese dissidents who alleged they were persecuted for political speech after Yahoo! revealed their identities to the Chinese government. The United States government asked Twitter to delay scheduled service maintenance during the protests following the 2009 Iranian presidential election so that online dissent and citizen journalism could continue unabated. Google initially took criticism from international human rights organizations for complying with requests to delete politically sensitive YouTube videos or to filter content. Birnhack and Elkin-Koren, 'The Invisible Handshake', p. 205.

[37] For instance, China initiated regulations on the Internet architectural arrangements, which leads to curtailment of freedom and expression and

The role and responsibility of the private sector were put under a scanner and uncomfortable questions began to be raised. Thus, possibility of human rights violations or abuses by private sector either when it acts in conjunction with the State or on its own accord could not be ruled out.

Corporation as New Addressee of Human Rights Obligation

Thus, the premise and perceptions of classical state-centric international human rights law once again stands seriously challenged on similar grounds, this time with reference to the Internet. One, the threat to the human rights in the Internet emanates not only from the State but also corporations. Two, most States lack technical capabilities to condition the operation of the Internet. The State is merely a marginal player with private industry playing crucial role in designing the Internet.

Further, the virtual world order reflects 'a growing recognition of degrees of order and institutionalized, patterned interaction within the international system'.[38] Such a development indicates the proliferation of non-state actors, including private standard-setting institutions, non-governmental organizations (NGOs), and global

---

human rights violations. Technically, the ISPs in China are required to block all traffic from or to specific IP addresses handed down by the government. The Chinese authorities monitor and filter all Internet traffic going through China's eight primary gateways to the global Internet. Presumably, the packets from the banned IP addresses are dropped at these backbone gateways. At the other end of the ISPs, installation of site-blocking software is required on all end-user computers with public access, such as those in Internet cafés. See Philip Sohmen, 'Taming the Dragon: China's Efforts to Regulate the Internet', 1 Stan. J. of East Asian Affairs', 17 (2001); Ronald J. Deibert, John G. Palfrey, Rafal Rohozinski, and Jonathan Zittrain (eds), *Access Denied: The Practice and Policy of Global Internet Filtering*, pp. 263–71 (2008).

[38] Rodney Bruce Hall and Thomas J. Biersteker, 'The Emergence of Private Authority in the International System', in *The Emergence of Private Authority in Global Governance* 4 (Hall and Bierstker eds, 2002).

market forces, that appear to have taken on authoritative roles and functions.[39] Such actors wield 'authority', like that of any State, built on the legitimacy of their claims to power, emanating from some form of normative, uncoerced consent or recognition of authority on the part of the regulated or governed.[40] Even states have largely conceded that the 'Internet governance is the development and application by Governments, the private sector and civil society, in their respective roles, of shared principles, norms, rules, decision-making procedures, and programmes that shape the evolution and utilisation of the Internet.'[41]

Thus, I answer most questions posed before this inquiry in negation. The State does not wield power and authority to the same extent in the virtual world as in the physical world. Even where the State may enforce its negative duty mandated under CRPD, positive duties with regards to ensuring access to the Internet cannot be shouldered by the State alone. As the State may not prove to be too effective a regulator of the Internet, classical approach cannot be transplanted to the current discourse. Rather the problems in that approach are replicating in the virtual world as well.

Disability right jurisprudence and international human rights law converge in their turmoil over corporations and human rights obligations; their expectations from the corporation substantially diverge. First, international human rights law mostly seek to impose corporations with negative obligations—an obligation not to abuse/violate human right. Its energies, therefore, are focused on how to bring corporations to book, what should be an ideal framework of accountability. Disability human rights seek to engage corporations with a positive obligation to advance right to access the Internet. Its interest, therefore, is how to get the corporations

[39] Hall and Biersteker, 'The Emergence of Private Authority in the International System', pp. 4–5.

[40] Robert O. Keohane and Joseph S. Nye, Jr., *Introduction*, in Governance in a Globalizing World 1, 20 (Joseph S. Nye, Jr. and John D. Donahue eds, 2000).

[41] ITU, Working Group on Internet Governance, Report from the Working Group on Internet Governance 10 Document WSIS-II/PC-3/DOC/5-E (June 2005) available at www.wgig.org/docs/BackgroundReport. doc (last visited 3 April 2015).

to proactively engage with their rights. Second, disability rights decipher relatively stronger connect between right to access the Internet and corporations. As discussed, States seek corporate alliance to effectively regulate the Internet and so far as accessibility is concerned corporations have emerged as private authority. Viewed from disability rights angle, this position can be exploited by corporations to either advance or retard accessibility rights.

Two approaches are available—either disability jurisprudence remain within the existing framework—consider the State as duty bearer of the right to access the Internet. This will be a pragmatic line but not an effective one. And certainly not the one yielding results. Or disability jurisprudence approach corporations directly and ask for creation of an accessible virtual world.[42] This will be a radical line, the one that has so far met with little success when tried by others. There is a third line, recommended by Clapham which is a system where human rights obligations attach both to states and to non-state actors. Clapham suggests that at the beginning of the twenty first century we need a paradigm shift in our understanding of the power and utility of human rights. He asks why not imagine a system where human rights obligations attach both to states and to non-state actors?[43]

In this study, I follow the third approach. I argue that by blinkering our outlook so as to focus on governments and excluding actual players, we blind ourselves to opportunities presented by including corporations. In the current scenario, by striking out corporations from human rights obligations on right to

---

[42] Besides the general question of whether an international corporation can be the bearer of human rights obligations, transnational corporations present an additional challenge in respect of applying human rights law. Unlike international organizations, we have noted that it is generally admitted that corporations do not, in principle, have international legal personality. Corporations therefore cannot, under the current conception of international law, be seen as having rights and duties under international law, nor can such obligations be imposed on corporations without granting them a (limited) status under international law. The absence of international legal personality poses a problem in ensuring that corporations can be held directly accountable for violations of international law.

[43] See Clapham, *Human Rights Obligations of Non-State Actors*, p. 28.

access the Internet, disability rights movement would be unable to accommodate their main concerns. It is my view that a handshake is needed between the State and corporation to advance right to access the Internet for persons with disabilities. The right of persons with disabilities to access the Internet cannot be made an obligation only of the State. Especially, if the goal is to inculcate systemic changes to create an inclusive and participative world, the Internet cannot be made inclusive for persons with disabilities without bringing corporations on board.

Even where it is broadly accepted that corporations hold answers to accessibility issues and range of connected rights guaranteed to persons with disabilities; it is crucial to be informed about several theoretical and practical challenges that lies ahead in fixing obligations on corporation. An application of human rights obligations on corporations is dismissed by an orthodox understanding of human rights law as well as corporations. On the one hand, scholars of human rights law are not in agreement with one another to extend obligations on corporations in the absence of their recognition as subjects of international law and formal enforcement mechanism. On the other hand, corporate law theorists and scholars are deeply divided on the lines of communitarian understanding of corporation and the contractarian perception of the same. The combined forces of these perceptions have led to a never ending debate surrounding human rights obligations of corporations and the scope and extent of their duties towards society. I will respond to both sets of objections in order to make a case for human rights obligations of the corporation with specific reference to the right to access the Internet.

Overcoming Theoretical Barriers in International Human Rights Law

The issue of corporation as a bearer of human rights obligations is correlated with the issue of international legal personality of the corporation. Thus, claims of imposing human rights obligations on corporations has often been resisted on the basis that corporations are not subjects of the international law. In the absence of subjectivity of corporations, unlike states, no duties could be placed on corporations by international law. It has been argued by some scholars that in principle corporations do not have international personality. Even where they enjoy certain rights under international laws these are temporary and limited.[44] Others argue that corporations have been certainly enjoying rights under international human rights law and also been entrusted with duties.[45] Clapham counters that if non-state entities do not enjoy all competences, privileges, and rights that states enjoy under international law; even states do not have all rights that individuals have under international law. We need to admit that international rights and duties depend on the capacity of the entity to enjoy those rights and bear those obligations; such rights and obligations do not depend on the mysteries of subjectivity.[46]

For some scholars existence of an international enforcement framework is quintessential for placing duties on corporations. Carlos Vazquez, for example, suggests that an international norm applies directly to non-state actors only if 'an international

[44] According to Cassese, despite the fact that MNEs can conclude transactions with States and their disputes with States can be submitted to international tribunals they have not been upgraded by States as proper international subjects. He concludes that multinational corporations possess no international rights and duties; they are only subjects to municipal and transnational law. A. Cassese, *International Law in a Divided World* 103 (1989). Similarly, according to Malanczuk the fact that individuals or companies are the beneficiaries of many rules of international law does not mean that these rules create rights for the individual companies, in much the same way as laws prohibiting cruelty to animals do not create rights for animals. See P. Malanczuk, 'Globalisation and the Future Role of Sovereign States', in *International Economic Law with a Human Face* 100 (F. Weiss et. al. eds, 1998). In contrast Henkin maintains that in a privatized world the company may prove to be the essential unit of the world economy. It may be time for the system solely to re-conceive the company and rethink the notion of nationality of companies. See L. Henkin, 'International Law: Politics And Values', 24, 159 (1995): 17.

[45] For example, corporations have been imposed duties not to commit war crimes, crimes against humanity or genocide.

[46] Clapham, *Human Rights Obligations of Non-State Actors*, pp. 68–9.

mechanism is established for enforcing' it, or if there is 'language in dictating an intent to subject [the actors] to international enforcement mechanisms in the future'.[47] So that for Vazquez, even if the language of a treaty appears to establish a direct obligation of private parties, he would not treat it as such if its enforcement appears to be left to domestic law.[48] But, as Ratner has written, this approach 'confuses the existence of responsibility with the mode of implementing it'.[49] Treaties that purport to place duties directly on private actors should be read as meaning what they say, just as any other treaties would be. What needs to be appreciated is that international law has legal capacity to place direct horizontal duties on all private actors not to violate one another's human rights. What it lacks is the practical and political capacity to enforce those duties. However, the absence of enforcement framework should not negate existence of a just obligation. Instead, if obligations are created, enforcement mechanism can be developed at a later stage.

In yet another set of objections, application of human rights on corporation is seen as trivializing human rights and ignoring the historical pedigree of human rights. It is argued that the grand concept of human rights relates to only serious abuses of state power and this is what distinguished human rights from ordinary breaches of the law. The trivialization argument is based on an assumption that human rights as a rule are only actionable against the state and that exceptions to this rule have been explicitly spelt out. Clapham suggests that instead of perceiving human rights obligation on corporations as trivializing, it should be seen as a shift in human rights discourse from the realms of rhetoric and ideology into the sphere of daily reality and social progress. Thus, one can turn the current perception head on heels if human rights are to be respected by all persons, groups, and states and that exceptional additional duty have been articulated for the state.[50]

[47] Carlos M. Vazquez, 'Direct vs. Indirect Obligations of Corporations under International Law', 43 colum. J. Transnatl'l. 927, pp. 940–1 (2005).

[48] Vazquez, 'Direct vs. Indirect Obligations of Corporations under International Law', p. 934.

[49] Steven R. Ratner, 'Corporations and Human Rights: A Theory of Legal Responsibility', 111 YALE L.J. 443 (2001): p. 481.

[50] Ratner, 'Corporations and Human Rights'.

The idea that protection of human rights is too important to be left exclusively to nation states and rather necessitates joint and several liabilities of all is gaining ground. Further international law has full potential to expand its scope so as to include a corporation. In what is considered to be the most popular legal source of corporate human rights duties is the Preamble of the UDHR–'every individual and every organ of society....shall strive' to promote respect for human rights and to secure their recognition and observance.[51] Louis Henkin interprets it as excluding 'no one, no company, no market, no cyberspace'.[52] Article 29 of UDHR specifies that 'everyone (including non-state actors) has duties to the community'[53] and Article 30 prohibits 'any State, group or person' from engaging in 'any activity or performing any act aimed at the destruction of any of the rights and freedoms in the Declaration.'[54] When this is read in combination to the Article 2 which refers to everyone's entitlement to 'all the rights and freedoms.... without distinction of any kind.....' we can construct a statement of obligation for the non-state actors.[55]

It needs to be underscored that human rights concept has its origin in social contract tradition. If that be the case then duties are imposed on all members of the society and the State. Wilson argues that applying the terms of social contracts, even corporations are understood to operate under an unwritten but critically important social charter. It is the unwritten charter of social expectations that determines values to which the corporation must adhere and sets the terms under which the public grants legitimacy to the corporation.[56] The terms of this social contract have become

[51] UDHR, G.A. Res. 217A (III), Article 26, U.N. Doc.A/810 (10 December 1948).

[52] Louis Henkin, 'Keynote Address: The Universal Declaration at 50 and the Challenge of Global Markets', 25 BROOK. J. INT'L. L.17, p. 25 (1999).

[53] UDHR, G.A. Res. 217A (III), Article 26, U.N. Doc.A/810, Article 29, p. 1.

[54] UDHR, G.A. Res. 217A (III), Article 26, U.N. Doc.A/810, Article 30.

[55] However, in terms of the international law, the UDHR provides a very fragile base, since it is merely a 'declaration'. Even where it speaks volumes about the aspirations of the drafters of the UDHR; there needs to be a more direct and legal instrumentality for corporate human right obligation.

[56] I. Wilson, *The New Rules of Corporate Conduct: Rewriting the Social Charter* 3 (2000).

more complex with the increase in stakeholders in corporations. According to Wilson,

> This expansion of constituencies and interests has progressively enlarged the social role and importance of the corporation, broadened its responsibilities, and underscored the fact that it must reflect the society's shared values—social, moral, political and legal as well as economic. Building the corporation on a foundation of economic values alone has never been a satisfying solution, either for its members or society. Now it is not even a viable option.[57]

It has been acknowledged that 'it may be desirable in some circumstances for corporations to become direct bearers of international human rights obligations, especially where host Governments cannot or will not enforce their obligations and where classical international human rights regime, therefore, cannot possibly be expected to function as intended'.[58] Having examined and answered the objections of international human rights law, I now proceed to examine the resistance coming from corporations.

Corporations and Their Bystander Rhetoric

When called upon to fulfil human rights responsibilities, corporations largely play the bystander rhetoric.[59] Since the economic objective of maximization of corporate profit and wealth

---

[57] Wilson, *The New Rules of Corporate Conduct*, p. 4.

[58] Commission on Human Rights, *Promotion and Protection of Human Rights*, U.N. Doc. E/CN.4/2006/97 (22 February 2006), available at https://documents-dds-ny.un.org/doc/UNDOC/GEN/G06/110/27/PDF/G0611027.pdf?OpenElement (last visited 26 August 2017) (Interim Report 2006 Report summarized factors that led to the shifting landscape of international law, specifically with regard to business and human rights with globalization as one of the most factors).

[59] Jena Martin Amerson, *The End of the Beginning?: A Comprehensive Look at the U.N.'s Business and Human Rights Agenda from a Bystander Perspective*, 17 FORDHAM J. CORP. and FIN. L. 871 (2012). The author labels bystander rhetoric indicative one of the several means of escaping human rights violation liability by Corporation.

creation for its shareholders more than often takes precedence over likely goals of social amelioration; corporate law looks inwards to govern *inter alia* the relationship between those who contributed the capital and those managing it. The resulting ethic of corporate law is one of vicarious acquisitiveness, respecting its core function of protecting the deployment of other people's money. Human rights concerns are, for the most part, extraneous to corporate regulation, culture, and doctrines.[60]

Consequently, corporations conveniently embrace bystander rhetoric in the wake of human rights abuses. Even where the corporation acknowledges that there are human rights abuses occurring around them, it disclaims any and all involvement with the acts. In essence, corporation assumes no responsibility for human rights abuse and casts itself as no more than a witness or a bystander to the acts of abuse.

In the virtual world corporations not only occupy a larger space in terms of participation when compared to the State but also wield greater control. Hence, they cannot assume bystander position whilst explaining the happenings in the virtual world. Technical agencies that manage network resources, transatlantic communications providers, and telecommunications service providers, corporate network access, content providers, and online services are mainly private entities. In the context of this study simply put, these are supply companies and consumer companies. Furthermore, the design of the technology or code accord private companies with regulatory power in shaping the virtual world.[61] Overall, the private sector in the digital environment enjoys more power in setting the agenda and shaping priorities. Consequently, concerns have been growing about the role that corporation have in violating or denying human rights exercised through or from the virtual world.

Since corporation is a dominant player, it can no longer claim to be an innocent bystander—who was merely witnessing struggle between persons with disabilities and the State. Especially in the

---

[60] Paul Redmond, 'Transnational Enterprise and Human Rights: Options for Standard Setting and Compliance', 37 INT'L LAW 69 (2003).

[61] For detailed discussion, see Lessig, *Code and Other Laws of Cyberspace*.

present context when supply companies are providers and creators of the virtual world architecture while consumer companies set out to offer a range of experiences, products, services including those offered to the State and the public at large the bystander rhetoric hardly comes to the rescue of corporations. Having validly dismissed the corporate bystander rhetoric, it is next essential to engage with the claims that resist corporate involvement with the social and human rights concerns.

The Unresolved Dispute between Contractarians and Communitarians

It has been discussed already how it has been quite a while now that possibilities to get corporations on board on human rights have been explored. This inquiry was primarily guided by the fact that corporations are ubiquitous and outperform states in terms of economic wealth and jurisdictional outreach (and in this case even the technological and regulatory expertise). It is, therefore, expected that corporation and corporate law should be responsive to public interest concerns. Such inquires, however, are watered down on the grounds that corporations and corporate law ought to govern private relations between shareholders and management. There is a long standing debate whether corporations should be responsive to social performance or concentrate on economic performance alone.

The participants in this debate are primarily classified as contractarians and communitarians. Contractarians start from a presumption that people ought to be free to make their own choices about how to live their lives (subject to an overriding duty not to harm others). Legal rules that redistribute wealth, mandate particular forms of behaviour, or prevent people from making bargains they would otherwise choose to make are presumptively objectionable because they interfere with people's ability to live their own lives according to their own preferences, structuring their relationships with others and defining their duties toward them by means of consent.[62] Contractarians are willing to accept State

---

[62] See Milton Freedman, *Capitalism and Freedom* (1962).

interference only to the extent it facilitates markets and provides requisite law and order situation. Deriving from nexus-of-contracts theory,[63] contractarians propose that because corporation is a legal fiction, it is incapable of having social or moral obligations much in the same way that inanimate objects are incapable of having these obligations.[64]

In this proposition contractarians have been mainly guided by the notion that shareholders own corporations. The influential work of Berle and Means[65] that emphasized the separation of ownership and control ensured that a corporation is seen as the private property of its stockholder-owners. Accordingly, the purpose of the corporation is to advance purposes of these owners (predominantly to increase their wealth). The function of the company's management, as agents of the owners, is to faithfully advance the financial interests of the owners.[66] Thus, corporate law employs its language from agency and trust law, and rooted in property law and contract law in particular. Under this view, corporations meet their proper social responsibilities by excelling in their economic activities, which then contributes to a well-functioning economy by employing people, by providing needed (and some unneeded) goods and services and by contributing to social welfare through paying taxes. The most widely quoted exemplar of this view is Professor Milton Freedman,

[63] The nexus of contracts theory conceives the company as a vehicle for contracting in which each constituency is placed within a contractual paradigm that only recognizes bargained rights. Thus, the sole purpose of the corporation is to maximize shareholder's profit. All other constituencies within the corporation are protected to the extent of the provisions of the term of their contracts. I. Lynch Fannon, *Working within Two Kinds of Capitalism: Corporate Governance and Employer Stakeholding: Us and EU Perspectives*, pp. 77-8 (2003).

[64] D.R. Fischel, 'The Corporate Governance Movement', 35 VANDERBILT L. REV. 1259 (1982). They often take the irresponsibility position suggesting that corporate managers do not even have a social or moral obligation to follow the law when violations are profitable.

[65] A. Berle and G. Means, *The Modern Corporation and Private Property*, 275 (1932).

[66] William T. Allen, 'Our Schizophrenic Conception of the Business Corporation', 14 CARDOZO L. REV. 261, pp. 264-5 (1992).

who has stated that in a free economy 'there is one and only one social responsibility of business—to use its resources and engage in activities designed to increase its profits so long as it stays within the rules of the game, which is to say, engages in open and free competition, without deception or fraud'.[67]

The communitarians approach to the corporation proposes that since individuals are members of shared community, they owe obligations to each other irrespective and independent of any contract. It is this membership that predominantly guides their behaviour towards fellow being. The State can, therefore, enforce such duties on them that ensure proper and adequate discharge of this obligation. The 'shareholders wealth' structure of corporations has recently been challenged by Professors Margaret Blair and Lynn Stout, who suggest that as an economic matter, the fundamental nature of the public business corporation is as an instance of team production, requiring the firm-specific inputs of various constituents, including employees, middle managers, and perhaps the communities in which business operations are located.[68] Under the 'team production' model of the public corporation, all constituents other than shareholders cannot fairly be treated as outsiders to the corporate enterprise, both because their inputs into the corporate enterprise are necessary to its success, and because many of these other constituents are also residual claimants to the wealth created in the corporate enterprise. With the advent of tiered ownership through nominees and multi layered mutual funds finance portfolio of corporation, the property law perception of corporation has come under an attack. It is argued that with the diversification of corporate finances; present time shareholders are not exclusive contributors of capital.[69]

---

[67] Milton Friedman, *Capitalism and Freedom* 133 (1962); see also Friedman, 'The Social Responsibility of Business Is to Increase Its Profits', *N. Y. Times Magazine*, 13 September 1970, p. 32.

[68] Margaret M. Blair and Lynn A. Stout, *A Team Production Theory of the Corporation*, 85 VA. L. REV. 247, pp. 280, 288 (1999) (fiduciary duties of directors extend to corporation, not to shareholders per se).

[69] Corporate laws these days have begun to confer broader scope to management to take on board concerns and interests of constituencies other than shareholders. While the management still remains within their functional framework, they are accorded with more space to take decisions.

A similar case can be made out for companies participating in the virtual world. While one concedes that in the virtual world and social networking sites, the technology to create the platform is often the result of significant expenditure on behalf of the developer; it can be strongly argued that a very significant part of the value of the platform comes from the social network provided by the participants. The network effects which distinguish successful communities from virtual ghost towns are the result of social interactions, but these are often disregarded in overall negotiations. Consequently, when accessibility is discussed under the property paradigm, the value that the participant brings to the system is not easily recognized within this framework.[70] Rather, it has been claimed that in the virtual world, the relationship between platform owners and players is not simply the one between producers and consumers. Rather, it is often a relationship of governors to citizens. Communities that grow and thrive in the virtual world may not have been foreseeable or controlled even by the platform developer. Virtual world, therefore, quickly becomes joint project between platform owners and players.[71] Applying this logic, it is in the self-interest of the corporations, whether supply companies or consumer companies, to address accessibility concerns of its users.

Theorizing the Corporate Obligation

Having demystified the objections to imposition of obligations on corporation, in this part, I further substantiate the rational for imposition of such obligations. I draw from Ratner's work[72] that comprehensively devises a method for translating duties under current human rights law to private context. Ratner's theory of responsibility undertakes this conversion with the help of four factors: the corporation's 'relationship with the government,

---

[70] Sal Humphreys, 'Productive Users, Intellectual Property and Governance: The Challenges of Computer Games', 10 MEDIA AND ARTS L. REV. 299 (2005).

[71] See Jack M. Balkin, 'Virtual Liberty: Freedom to Design and Freedom to Play in Virtual Worlds', 90 VA. L. REV. (2004): 2043, 2046, 2082.

[72] Ratner, 'Corporations and Human Rights', p. 181.

its nexus to affected populations, the particular human right at issue, and the place of individuals violating human rights within the corporate structure'.[73] Ratner does not attempt to spell out how these factors would work in every case. Instead, he offers his proposal as a kind of conversion machine, with which interested parties could begin 'to develop a corpus of law that would recognize obligations on businesses to protect human rights'.[74] I seek to apply his factors in the context of rights of virtual accessibility under the CRPD and the resultant delineation of corporate obligation.

Corporations' Relationship with the State

Taking the minimum common denominator, it can be safely assumed that even where the State remains significant actor, the international system is no longer state-centric. Multiple non-state actors, particularly corporation assume legitimate authority and wield power to participate in 'the formulation and implementation of rules in policy areas that were once the sole responsibility of the state or international governmental organisations.'[75] One of the most influential works of political economist Susane Strange proposed that retreat of the State has resulted into diffusion of power and authority to other institutions.[76] In a globalized world order private authority, such as corporations may be seen as an agent of public authority which exercise authority over some significant

---

[73] Ratner, 'Corporations and Human Rights', p. 649.

[74] Almost closely associated with the attempt of present research, Miltello applies the concentric circles framework of Ratner to the problem of Internet and Telecommunication Companies who divulge private information to authoritative governments, in order to determine the nature of obligations on ITCs to protect human rights. Emily C. Miletello, 'The Page You Are Attempting to Access Has Been Blocked in Accordance with National Laws: Applying a Corporate Responsibility Framework to Human Rights Issues Facing Internet Companies', 11 PGH. J. TECH. L. and POL'Y 1 (2011).

[75] Guido Palazzo and Andreas G. Scherer, 'Corporative Legitimacy as Deliberation: A Communicative Framework', 66 J. BUS. ETHICS Q. 71 (2006).

[76] See generally, Susane Strange, *The Retreat of the State: The Diffusion of Power in the World Economy* (1996).

issue or domain. Dilution of the public-private sphere of operation between the State and corporation, corporations are either delegated functions by the State itself, or appointed as agents. Thus, as per Ratner's theory where the corporation has close ties with the government, it has prima facie a greater set of obligations in the area of human rights. Hence, it becomes essential to consider the relationships that States and corporations are most likely to have and legal ramifications of these relationships for the company.

First, state responsibility has a mirror effect on corporation duties. Since international law and treaty obligations make the State liable for the acts of some private actors; private actors functional within that State can also be held liable for the same conduct. Such replication of duties exist even where there exists no defined relationship between the State and corporation. Second, where corporations act as agents of the State; responsibility of the principal entails the responsibility of the agent. Thus, where the State outsources its functions to a corporation or appoints a corporation as its formal agents, accessibility obligations on state as principal has its implications for corporations to follow the same as agents. Where a corporation is the accomplice of the State[77] for instance, this is a regular feature when public-private partnerships are entered into for the discharge of certain sovereign functions. One may rely on joint and several liabilities to consider duties of the State under international obligations to be a part of contract and hence becomes duties of its accomplice. It is crucial to note that recognizing importance of non-state actors and their influence do not necessarily suggest that they have achieved the role of lawmaker. Their activity and their interaction with states and others are examined to determine duties and rights that states have fixed on them. Such an examination elevates them to subjects of interest without any automatic legitimizing effect.[78]

---

[77] For the purposes of the inquiry under consideration, I tweak the version of state-corporate complicity as given by Ratner. Whilst Ratner's notion of complicity means one entity engaging in otherwise lawful conduct that serves to aid other entities in violating norms, I seek to use it in term of complicity in partnership.

[78] Clapham, *Human Rights Obligations of Non-State Actors*, p. 142.

Corporations' Nexus to Affected Population

Simply extending human rights obligations of the State to corporations tend to undermine the differences essential in the nature and functionality of the State and corporations. Whereas the norm that all organs of society ought to cultivate respect towards all human rights have gained widespread acceptance, it is a felt need that under certain circumstances, individuals and corporations owe greater duties in their 'spheres of influence'.[79] The sphere of influence operates on the nexus factor and suggests that duties of the corporation are directly related to the proximity of circles.

Accordingly, sphere of influence is described and envisaged in concentric circles, where influence diminishes as the circles get bigger. The smallest circle includes a company's core business activities in the workplace and marketplace. This is where a company has the greatest control in affecting ESG (environmental, social, and governance) performance. The next circle covers the supply chain. Control is weakened here, but in some cases the influence can be significant. The third circle includes a company's community interaction, social investment, and philanthropy activities. And the final circle of influence is a company's engagement in public policy dialogue and advocacy activities.[80]

In the context of corporations, the ties are viewed as concentric circles emanating from the enterprise with spheres enlarging from shareholders, employees, creditors, investors, customers, citizens, locality, and community and so on. But in general, as the circles widen, duties of the corporation will diminish. These circles represent social groupings, with inner circles, having stronger bonds and weaker with the ones that lie towards the outside. The concept of

---

[79] United Nations Global Compact, 'The Ten Principles', http://www.unglobalcompact.org/aboutthegc/thetenprinciples/index.html (last visited 3 April 2015) (although the Global Compact is non-binding, it is considered *soft law*, thus it does warrant consideration on an international level even though it does not impose binding obligations on corporations).

[80] UN Norms co-opted this term from the voluntary Global Compact, applying and expanding it to a *mandatory* accountability mechanism for TNCs. Specifically, the norms state that within their 'respective spheres of activity and influence', TNCs must respect and promote human rights.

a 'sphere' reflects two core propositions: first, that organizations have the ability, within certain limits, to influence actions and outcomes outside their own organizational boundaries through their relationships with other actors, and secondly, that business firms and States perform distinct social functions in distinct social domains, giving rise to distinct roles and responsibilities.[81]

Ratner further classifies this nexus in terms of purely territorial elements, such that a corporation's duties depends upon the extent to which corporation physically controls a certain area. Thus, where an enterprise effectively manages a particular piece of territory, as in the case of mineral or timber concessions, it would have a certain, presumably larger, set of duties to those living within that territory, distinct from those to persons living outside it. However, the tendency to operationalize the sphere of influence in terms of geographic proximity is often misleading since the companies' activities can have effects very far away.[82] Hence, it is not proximity that determines whether or not a human rights impact falls within the responsibility to respect, but rather the company's web of activities and relationships.[83]

If one draws an analogy from this proposition, it can easily be inferred that corporations dominate a large part of the virtual world territory. This brings corporations in close proximity to every such user of the Internet so as to create an obligation. Although the responsibility to ensure affordability of such use remains with the State, designing a virtual world which is accessible to a person with disability lies with the corporation.

Substantive Rights at Issue

Ratner distinguishes between the rights that a corporation can directly infringe and those that only government can directly

---

[81] O. de. Schutter, 'Transnational Corporations as Instruments of Human Development', in *Human Rights and Development: Towards Mutual Reinforcement* (P. Alston and M. Robinson eds, 2005), p. 12.

[82] Anthony Tusler, 'How to Make Technology Work: A Study of Best Practices in United States Electronic and Information Technology Companies', *Disability Studies Quarterly* 25(2) (2005), available at http://dsq-sds.org/article/view/551/728 (last visited 16 May 2016).

[83] Tusler, 'How to Make Technology Work'.

infringe. Two distinct sets of duties that are identified for corporations are: to respect human rights 'within their sphere of influence' and to avoid being 'complicit in human rights abuses'— the latter term refers to the corporate involvement in governmental action.[84] This perception ties up closely to the one proposed by Kinley and Tadaki in the form of core rights and direct impact rights.[85] Translating corporate duties in the context of accessibility rights requires corporations to engage in proactive commission rather than omission, that is, in addition to respect of right within its sphere of influence, it is essential that corporations act to provide accessibility to persons with disabilities and not just limit itself by non-involvement in government action. Hence, where corporations enjoy control over the virtual world equivalent to the extent of that of the territory of a State, it has duties akin to those of the States. It would also have duties to protect the welfare of those closest to it.

Attributing Responsibility to the Controlling Corporation

Corporations comprise of complex relationships between employees, shareholders, investors, and customers. Besides, relationships between two or more corporations per se is equally complex. For instance, corporations in joint ventures, subsidiary-holding companies, group companies, licensees or franchises, suppliers or sub-contractors pose difficulties while attributing corporate duties. Thus, even where corporate ties with government have been identified and its sphere of influence defined, fixating duties is a challenging task given various forms of corporate structure. The problem further aggravates with globalization, where jurisdictional boundaries are fluid, more specifically in terms of the virtual world where the boundaries are per se non-existent. Ratner's theory suggests that the touchstone for determining duties must be the element of control. Thus, one may identify 'authority relations' which arise due to economic dependence of one party

---

[84] Humphreys, *Productive Users, Intellectual Property and Governance.*

[85] David Kinley and Junko Tadaki, 'From Talk to Walk: The Emergence of Human Rights Responsibilities for Corporations at International Law', 44 VA. J. INT'L L. 931 (2004).

upon the other effectively requires compliance with the dominant party's wishes.[86] In such situations, actions of controlled entity can be appropriately attributed to the controller. In the virtual world context, where corporations are calling shots in terms of design, technology, access, and so on, it is apt to attribute duties to such controller, that is, corporation.

Thus, a logical extension of Ratner's framework to disability rights jurisprudence in the context of virtual accessibility helps us to derive a set of duties for corporations. It can be safely confirmed that duties of the corporation are a direct function of its capacity to dominate and design virtual world. This obligation of corporations is further consolidated by its nexus of the affected populations and disability rights at issue.

Leverage-based Responsibility

The current proposition also gains strengths from leverage-based responsibility whereby a specific agent may not only have a responsibility to exercise power responsibility (that is, not to do harm) but that under certain conditions, there may be an actual responsibility actively to make use of its power for the benefit of others.[87]

When denial of access to the virtual world is examined under the non-discrimination rubric, it imposes obligations on corporations requiring them to take appropriate measures to prevent discrimination based on disability. This ties up with substantive equality goals set out by CRPD which then enables us to draw reasonable justification for positive engagement of corporations to accessibility concerns. First, corporations have obligation to create an accessible virtual world for persons with disabilities because they are in a position that effectively allows them to do so. There is a reasonable and realistic chance that their influence

---

[86] Hugh Collins, 'Ascription of Legal Responsibility to Groups in Complex Patterns of Economic Integration', 53 MOD. L. REV. 731 (1990) as cited in Ratner, 'Corporations and Human Rights', p. 519.

[87] Stephan Wood, 'Leverage-Based Corporate Human Rights Responsibility', 22 *Business Ethics Quarterly*, 63 (2012).

and efforts will lead to an actual improvement in access. Thus, a positive relationship exists between the exercise of influence and the potential improvement in access. This holds true for supply companies as well as consumer companies. Second, the normative burden for an agent to meet an obligation, corporation in this case, could be considered as a justifiably reasonable one in proportion to the obligation at stake. Thus, creating accessible virtual world and designing products and components at the outset, not only benefit persons with disabilities but also those without disabilities. Third, there exists a significant connection between corporation and accessibility concerns.

Delineating Accessibility Rights Agenda

Apart from theoretical and normative issues on corporate obligation, there prevails ambiguity about precisely defined human rights agenda for corporations within human rights treaties and conventions. With international human rights law providing little guidance to corporations regarding the norms that should frame their human rights observance and define their responsibilities; standard setting becomes even more difficult. As Professor John Ruggie explains, simply placing the same duties on corporations as those already imposed on states might undermine both corporate entrepreneurship and government responsibility, and generate 'endless strategic gaming' between the two as to who is more responsible for fulfilling human rights in a particular situation.[88] Therefore, the challenge before scholars and advocates is not only whether it is judicious to expand the scope of international law to include corporations, how to posit corporations in overall legal framework of international human rights laws but also how to delineate duties between state and corporations.

---

[88] Human Rights Council, 'Interim Report 2007 Business and Human Rights: Mapping International Standards of Responsibility and Accountability for Corporate Acts', UN Doc. A/HRC/4/035 (9 February 2007) (by John Ruggie), available at http://www.business-manrights.org/SpecialRepPortal/Home/ReportstoUNHumanRightsCouncil/2007 (last visited 25 August 2014).

Insofar as the right to access to the Internet is concerned, the creation, proliferation, and operation of accessible technology rest with the corporations. As suppliers of the Internet services and controls of the architecture, larger set of duties lies at the door step of corporations.

As propounded by Henry Shue, complete fulfilment of each kind of right involves the performance of multiple kinds of duties. Thus, each right can be seen to have at least three types of derivative duties emanating from it. Such duties include duties to avoid depriving an individual of a right (these are largely 'negative' in character); duties to protect individuals from the deprivation of their rights (these arise largely in order to ensure that duties to avoid depriving and to aid are enforced); and duties to aid the deprived (these are largely 'positive' in character and require active steps to be taken to fulfil the rights).[89]

Thus, we identify two sets of duties: a positive duty and a negative duty. A negative duty is a duty to do no harm. This involves passive duty, that is, to abstain from harmful action. This often extends to mitigating or preventing harm taking place. It needs to be underscored that the requirement of taking positive steps to prevent such harm from occurring does not turn the duty itself into a positive one. A positive duty, on the other hand, is a duty to improve a given state of affairs or to come to the assistance. It is thus, a duty to do good rather than not to harm. As such, it requires an idea of desirable or obligatory ends. Positive responsibilities also presuppose certain capacities which are concentrated in a specific agent and not shared equally by all agents. Therefore, such duties are specific and not universal. Unlike negative duties that apply equally to everyone at all the times, positive duties apply to specific agents in specific contexts and to varying degrees and extents. Positive responsibilities are grounded in teleological thinking, since these aim at the improvement of a given state of affairs and hinge on a vision of the good in society. Brian Skepys neatly chalks out the negative and positive duties associated with the right to access the Internet—a negative obligation not to interfere with the proliferation of ICTs and infrastructure required to access the Internet and thereby not to

---

[89] See generally Henry Shue, *Basic Rights* (2nd ed., 1996).

adversely impact the access to the Internet and a positive obligation to foster, encourage, and ensure conducive conditions where Internet access and ICT proliferation can occur.[90]

In terms of the access to the Internet, therefore what is required is a positive responsibility from a corporation rather than mere abstention from violation. In fact, in this particular context, not taking positive action in itself would culminate into violation of the rights of persons with disabilities to access the Internet. It needs to be underscored that corporations ought to be allotted human rights duties which are appropriate and proportionate to their own nature and activities; more so if corporations are expected to have positive duties instead of mere negative ones. Kinley and Tadaki undertake delineation of such 'appropriate' human rights duties to corporations.[91] For this purpose they create two categories of rights—a) core rights and b) direct impact rights. Core rights encompass fundamental rights, including the right to life, liberty, and physical integrity. These rights require to be protected from the infringement by the State as well as corporations. Thus, core rights impose duties on the corporations. As the nomenclature itself suggests, the direct impact rights are those rights which are most directly affected by the corporate action to the associated group such as employees, their families, and members of local communities. The labour rights, environmental rights, rights of indigenous peoples fall under this category. Thus, corporations can be imposed with human rights obligations pertaining to these rights as well. In the light of the discussion already undertaken in the earlier chapter, one may conveniently categorize access to the Internet as core rights as well as direct impact rights. Hence, corporations' human rights obligation is the clearest and most direct when it comes to the Internet. CRPD contemplates correlative duties on States and private entities. The General comments on Article 9 also clearly support this. Therefore, insofar as the virtual accessibility rights are concerned, the State and corporation share a joint and several responsibilities.

**

[90] Skepys, 'Is There a Human Right to the Internet?', p. 19.
[91] Kinley and Tadaki , 'From Talk to Walk', p. 695.

Prof. Alston rightly cautions that 'the international human rights regime's aspiration to ensure the accountability of all major actors will be severely compromised in the years ahead if it does not succeed in devising a considerably more effective framework than currently exists in order to take adequate account of the roles played by some non-state actors'.[92] The rights of persons with disabilities will stand heavily compromised unless one creates a paradigm of joint and several responsibilities on the state and corporation for right to access the Internet.

Such an attempt may encounter tremendous resistance from the State as well as corporations. While States may see this as undermining of their authority and sovereignty; corporations may desire to slip away from a formal commitment. One can always argue that an extension of international law has already been witnessed to inter-governmental organizations, and there is a reason why the same cannot be extended to the corporation. There is no evidence that the international legal order cannot accommodate duties for other kinds of actor. Lack of international jurisdiction to try a corporation does not mean that corporation is under no international legal obligation. [93]

Most people's historical understanding of rights is that rights are embodied in a contract between government and the individual, and that rights protect individuals and private groups from state interference in a number of specified domains. This understanding requires to be reconceptualized in the context of the right to access the Internet, which is emerging as a new human right of the twenty-first century. It necessarily creates a tripartite relationship between the individuals, the State and the corporation. The new dynamics require new responses and new frameworks. In keeping with these developments, CRPD will have to be fully conscious about the emergence of new fragmented centres of power and the possible repression and alienation of individuals through this variety of new

[92] Philip Alston, 'The "Not-a-cat" Syndrome: Can the Human Rights Regime Accommodate Non-State Actors', in *Non-State Actors and Human Rights* (P. Alston 2005).

[93] Clapham, *Human Rights Obligations of Non-State Actors*, p. 142.

bodies.[94] It thus, can be concluded that insofar as the right to access the Internet is concerned, the corporation and the state are joint and several duty bearers.

So far the 'what' and the 'why' part of the issue has been answered. The next two chapters will set out to explore how this right could be materialized. What options and instrumentalities are available at international and domestic level.

---

[94] Andrew Clapham, *Human Rights in the Private Sphere*, pp. 89–133, 137 (1993).

3

Corporations and the Goldilocks Dilemma of International Human Rights Laws

The earlier chapters have clearly outlined the nature and scope of the right to access the Internet as a human right, furnished the rational for the same, and identified corporations as the duty bearers of this right. Having dealt with the 'what', 'why', and 'who' aspect of the human right to access the Internet, I next proceed to explore 'how' the right of persons with disabilities to access the Internet could be realized. If the goal is to bring about a systemic change in the overall perception towards disability and removing barriers by inculcating accessibility concerns in the DNA of corporations,[1] it calls for intensive and extensive strategies to obtain compliance from corporations. Two regulatory approaches are quite popular to seek corporate compliance—either deter or co-operate.

The next two chapters will explore available techniques of corporate regulation both under international human rights laws and domestic laws. This chapter will mainly focus on the

[1] Anthony Tusler, 'How to Make Technology Work: A Study of Best Practices in United States Electronic and Information Technology Companies', *Disability Studies Quarterly* 25(2) (2005), available at http://dsq-sds.org/article/view/551/728 (last visited 16 May 2016).

dialogic co-operation approach and soft-laws evolved under existing international human rights framework and critically analyse its applicability to the issue on hand. The next chapter will elaborate on the state instrumentalities primarily in the form of anti-discrimination laws and other persuasive measures adopted towards ensuring accessibility. Together, these chapters will undertake an assessment of the adequacy and effectiveness of various legal and non-legal instrumentalities and regulatory options available at international and domestic levels to ensuring corporation's proactive engagement in realizing access to the Internet as a human right.

Deter or Co-operate: Two Ends of the Regulatory Spectrum

As such, it has been quite challenging, both for the international human rights regime as well as the State, to regulate corporate conduct from the perspective of human rights. Two major regulatory approaches have been developed throughout the years as to the optimal design of regulatory regime—the deterrence-based approach and the cooperation-based approach. While both schools share the same objective, that is, ensuring regulatory compliance in a socially desirable manner; each school endorses different enforcement styles in achieving this objective. The deterrence-based approach coerces compliance through a confrontational enforcement style centered upon sanctioning violators. In contrast, co-operative enforcement fosters regulatory compliance through co-operative governance, bargaining, and persuasive methods. This dichotomy of approaches has resulted in what I refer to as the Goldilocks dilemma—either corporation are too strongly coerced or too mildly nudged to cooperate.

The deterrence-based enforcement approach originates in economics literature that analyses behavioural decision-making processes,[2] the most dominant being rational choice

---

[2] See Charles De Second Motesqieu, *The Spirit of Laws* (1748); Cesare Beccaria, *On Crime and Punishment and Other Writings* (1995); Jeremy Bentahm, *An Introduction to the Principles of Morals and Legislations* (1973).

theory.[3] The basic idea is that when would-be offenders know that law breaking triggers sanctions, then they may be deterred from breaking the law.[4] Based on certain assumptions,[5] rational choice theory postulates that actors make decisions according to a cost–benefit analysis. According to Becker,[6] actors are rational, 'amoral calculators who compare their expected compliance utility, that is, the payoffs expected to be obtained when they obey the law, with their expected violation utility, that is, the expected payoffs when they violate the law. Accordingly, actors commit crimes only

[3] At the heart of the rational choice theory rests the fundamental idea that actors' behaviour in society reflects their conscious choices made to achieve their own greatest satisfaction.

[4] Under this approach when crafting regulations, policymakers may control several important variables such as kind of the sanction imposed, severity of the sanction, and the probability of violation detection and sanctioning. It is through these variables that the level of deterrence is determined. At the same time, it is equally vital that optimal deterrence level is attained since under-deterrence or over-deterrence may adversely affect the social welfare goals. In that, *under-deterrence* implies that regulatory subjects are insufficiently motivated to comply with regulatory orders while *over-deterrence* may imply that some regulatees are induced to takeover-precautions, or are deterred from engaging in productive activities that could otherwise increase social welfare.

[5] The rational choice theory is based on certain core assumptions. First, actors in marketplace strive to maximize its own objectives and there may be difference between objectives of one actor from other. This assumption is known as Utility Maximization Assumption. Second, when provided with finite set of choices, actors can indicate ranked order of preference of choices but may also remain indifferent to choices. This is known as Completeness Assumption. Third, actors' choices are transitive, that is, if actors prefer A to B, and B to C, they necessarily prefer A to C. This is referred to as Transitivity Assumption. For a general overview of the rational choice theory see, for instance, Michael Allingham, *Rational Choice* 143 (1999); Margaret S. Archer and Jonathan Q. Tritter, *Rational Choice Theory: Resisting Colonization* 257(2001).

[6] Becker is considered to be the first to formalize the deterrence hypothesis. He analysed offenders' behavioral choices as decisions made by rational agents weighing the costs and benefits of their actions when deciding whether to commit a crime. See Gary S. Becker, 'Crime and Punishment: An Economic Approach', 76 *Journal of Political Economy* 169 (1968).

when their expected violation utility is greater than their expected compliance utility.[7] Hence, according to Becker's contribution, punishment may efficiently deter actors from committing crimes by changing the cost of the crime. Therefore, regulatory policies must deter market players from law-breaking by creating an environment that makes market players better off by obeying the law rather than violating it.[8]

Since the deterrence-based approach seeks compliance through coercion by sanctioning regulatory violations, it is confrontational by nature. As such, the deterrence approach endorses a regulatory 'cat-and-mouse' game between law enforcers and regulatory targets.[9] This involves certain administrative costs to the public enforcement system, along with litigation costs. The deterrence approach more often applies a top-down 'command-control' technique of regulation. This approach is compliance-oriented wherein rule-making, monitoring, and enforcement are all designed to elicit a particular regulatory objective.[10]

The cooperative enforcement approach, on the other hand, departs from the presumption of rationality that deterrence-based model relies on. Instead, this approach hinges upon the regulatees' nature as law-abiding creatures and powerfully motivates them to obey the law, even in the absence of significant threats of punishment. According to the co-operative approach, compliance can best be achieved through persuasion rather than through threat of sanctions. Therefore, under cooperative approach enforcement

[7] Becker, 'Crime and Punishment'.

[8] See Anthony Ogus, 'Enforcing Regulation: Do We Need the Criminal Law?' in *New Perspectives on Economic Crime*, pp. 42–55 (H. Sjögren and G. Skogh, eds, 2004).

[9] Analysing pitfalls of deterrence-based enforcement, Sharon Oded observes how the deterrence approach endorses a regulatory 'cat-and-mouse' game between law enforcers and regulatory targets. Enforcers invest their resources in pursuing potential wrongdoers, while the wrongdoers invest in minimizing their expected liability. Sharon Oded, *Corporate Compliance: New Approaches to Regulatory Enforcement* 36 (2013).

[10] C. Parker, 'Reinventing Regulation within the Corporation: Compliance-Oriented Regulatory Innovation', 32 *Administration and Society* 529 (2000).

policies accentuate cooperation, rather than confrontation, and conciliation, rather than coercion.

The proponents of the cooperative school of thought are mindful of the fact that business corporations may sometimes succumb to the temptation of misbehaviour when encountered with an opportunity to gain,[11] nevertheless, their approach presumes that most regulatees are 'good apples', whose inclination to comply with the law increases when they perceive themselves fairly treated by a reasonable enforcement policy.[12]

Cooperative approach merits virtue of cost effectiveness that relinquishes some of the costs associated with the regulatory 'cat-and-mouse' game, typically endorsed by the deterrence-based enforcement approach. Further, it generates a higher level of regulatory compliance. The co-operative approach usually applies in a bottoms-up manner, encouraging firms to rectify themselves through self-regulation and incentivizing them to define and develop their own norms and rules. Consequently, the legislature avoids specifying detailed regulations and simply provides broad objectives to be achieved and leaves decisions about attaining objectives to each firm. Since private firms, as insiders know the sector better than the government that seeks to regulate them as an outsider; they can design better means to attain objectives than those prescribed by the State. They can design rules in accordance with market possibilities and thus enhance investment and technological development without hurting these processes.

International human rights law has been attempting to evolve some sort of voluntary-based regulation of corporations.[13] Under

[11] See Robert A. Kagan and John Scholz, 'The "Criminology of the Corporation" and Regulatory Enforcement Strategies', in Enforcing Regulation 71 (Keith Hawkins and John M. Thomas, eds, 1984).

[12] See Eugene Bardach and Kagan, Going by the Book: The Problem of Regulatory Unreasonableness, pp. 59–61, 66 (1982).

[13] The attempts to draft comprehensive set of rules governing transnational corporations began as early as the 1970s and 1980s. However, more successful attempts were made through non-legal, non-binding instruments. Towards this end, two significant attempts have been made in the form of the Organisation for Economic Cooperation and Development (OECD) Guidelines for MNEs and the ILO Tripartite Declaration.

this regime, the UN Global Compact can be fairly considered an experiment with the cooperative approach.[14] In 2000, the UN launched the Global Compact to engage with non-state actors and push for a public-private partnership making globalization more inclusive and equitable.[15] It asked 'companies to embrace, support and enact, within their sphere of influence, a set of core values of human rights, labour standards, the environment and

[14] The UN Global Compact is preceded by the voluntary, non-binding guidelines by the OECD and the ILO. The OECD Guidelines for Multinational Enterprises emanated as recommendations addressed by industrialized States to multinational enterprises. The Guidelines are statement of the standards expected by home governments of their corporations operating abroad. The Guidelines are voluntary and are not legally enforceable. For the initial draft see, 'OECD Declaration on International Investment and Multinational Enterprises', 21 June 1976, reprinted in 1976 ILM, vol. 15, 967. The Guidelines have been revised in order to keep them in alignment with international developments. For the revised guideline see OECD Guidelines for Multinational Enterprises, Recommendations for Responsible Business conduct in a Global Context, OECD Ministerial Meeting, 25 May 2011 available at www.oecd.org/dataoecd/43/29/48004323.pdf (last visited 3 April 2015). In another initiative, the ILO adopted a Tripartite Declaration of Principles concerning Multinational Enterprises and Social Policy in 1977. The ILO Declaration offers a set of core principles and guidelines for corporations with respect to employment, training, working conditions, and industrial relations. The instrument is voluntary in nature. See Tripartite Declaration of Principles Concerning Multinational Enterprises and Social Policy, ILO, 204th Sess., 16 November 1977, reprinted in 1978, ILM, vol. 17, p. 422. The same has been revised in 2000. See International Labour Organisation, Tripartite Declaration of Principles concerning Multinational Enterprises and Social Policy adopted by the Governing Body of the International Labour Office at its 204th Session (Geneva, November 1977) as amended in its 279th (November 2000) and 295th Session (March 2006).

[15] Unlike many of the initiatives that came after this, the Global Compact originally began as an initiative from then Secretary-General Kofi-Annan. During an economic meeting in Switzerland, Kofi Annan gave a speech in which he discussed a global compact between the UN and businesses that would encourage businesses to infuse their companies with the values of human rights norms. At its heart, the Compact encouraged businesses to pledge to honour ten principles that surround human rights issues.

anti-corruption'.[16] This was purely a voluntary initiative aiming to engage businesses in a wide-ranging societal agenda. While this initiative may not be directly relevant to seek compliance from corporations in the context of the right to access the Internet, its study is no doubt important to examine the impact of its approach.

As part of the Global Compact, business leaders voluntarily agreed to first, make efforts to internalize the Global Compact principles as a part of business strategy and operations and second, to facilitate a co-operative and collective problem-solving between different stakeholders. The UN Global Compact looked towards a partnership oriented model of problem solving and set a Ten Principle goal setting for corporations.[17]

As the Global Compact was envisioned as a learning dialogue and a platform of action, it relied on a range of unconventional means and strategies to promote respect for its principles. These include principle-based change, risk management, public accountability, enlightened self-interest of companies, sharing best practices, and partnerships.[18] The UN Global Compact came under heavy criticism owing to its voluntarism and alleged non-seriousness on the part of the company which despite announcing their allegiance to the Compact Principle, failed to provide assessable information on compliance. The participants to UN Global Compact were required to provide Communication of Progress (COP). COP is mainly a public disclosure to stakeholders (for example, investors, consumers, civil society, governments, and so on) on progress made

[16] United Nations Global Compact, 'The Ten Principles', available at http://www.unglobalcompact.org/aboutthegc/thetenprinciples/index.html (last visited 3 April 2015).

[17] These ten principles try to fill the void between regulatory regimes, at one end of the spectrum, and voluntary codes of industry conduct, at the other. Only two of the ten principles explicitly fall under the rubric of human rights: '(1) Businesses should support and respect the protection of internationally proclaimed human rights; and (2) make sure that they are not complicit in human rights abuses.'

[18] Price Waterhousecoopers, 'The UN Global Compact: Moving to the Business Mainstream', An Interview with George Kell, Corporate Responsibility Report (2005) available at www.unglobalcompact.org/docs/new_events/9.5/pwc_int_2005.pdf (last visited 25 August 2014).

in implementing the ten principles of the UN Global Compact, and in supporting broader UN development goals. Thus, the only sanction that the UN Global Compact provided was delisting of a corporation for failure to file a COP. However, this was found to be too mild in its impact, unless being delisted evoked strong market reactions or reputational harm. Even where a COP was filed, the claims of corporations could not be verified without any independent monitoring mechanisms. Consequently, it was believed that COP could turn out to be a mere public relations exercise.[19] This experience demonstrates that a purely voluntary initiative, without any legal binding or monitoring mechanism, may create an initial buzz but cannot be relied on to bring any effectively visible outcome.

Contemporaneously, with the development of the Global Compact, another UN initiative was taking shape elsewhere. In 1998, the UN Sub-Commission on the Promotion and Protection of Human Rights established a working group on the activities of TNCs which was asked to 'contribute to the drafting of relevant norms concerning human rights and TNCs and other economic units whose activities have an impact on human rights'.[20] The working group formulated the Norms on the Responsibilities of TNCs and Other Business Enterprises with Regard to Human Rights. Dissatisfaction with the UN Global Compact led to experimentation with the deterrence based approach. Thus, the UN Norms took another extreme position, aiming strongly to devise an accountability mechanism for corporations on human rights violations.[21] This was basically confrontational in nature, operating

[19] G. Kell, 'The Global Compact: Origins, Operations, Progress, Challenges', 1 *Journal of Corporate Citizenship* 35 (2003). Since the Global Compact was a learning dialogue and a platform of action, it relied on a range of unconventional means and strategies to promote respect for its principles. These include principle-based change, risk management, public accountability, the enlightened self-interest of companies, sharing good practices, and partnerships.

[20] UN Doc. E/CN.4/Sub.2/RES/2001/3.

[21] Commission on Human Rights, Sub-commission, 55th Sess., 'Norms on the Responsibilities of Transnational Corporations and other Business Enterprises with Regard to Human Rights', UN Doc. E/CN.4/

in a top-down manner. Two particularly controversial aspects included: one, the mandate for the corporations to implement the principles embodied in the Norms and two, the review of application of the Norms by UN monitoring body.[22] Thus, the Norms included almost anything and everything under the human rights to be corporate concern.[23]

The Sub-Commission outlined a six-step process in a Commentary to ensure that TNCs implemented these rules. These included distribution of internal operational rules of the company to all relevant stakeholders, the provision of training

---

Sub.2/2003/12/Rev.2 (13 August 2003). The UN Norms coupled with the commentary appended to them, provided a comprehensive statement of corporate human rights obligations and also outlined the procedure for their implementation.

[22] Putting aside the spirit of the monitoring process, the language in the Norms regarding monitoring is problematic. What exactly should the UN monitor? How should TNCs apply the Norms to their internal mechanisms? How should particular Norms apply, at any given period in time, to a TNC? The Norms are silent as to these questions. Likewise, the Norms Commentary sheds no light on this subject. Rather, the Commentary simply states that the Council should 'receive information and take effective action when enterprises fail to comply with the Norms.' Commission on Human Rights, Sub-commission, 'Commentary on the Norms on the Responsibilities of Transnational Corporations and Other Business Enterprises with Regard to Human Rights', P 16(b), U.N. Doc. E/CN.4/Sub.2/2003/38/Rev.2 (26 August 2003), available at http://www.unhchr.ch/Huridocda/Huridoca. nsf/e06a5300f90fa0238025668700518ca4/293378ff2003ceb0cl256d790031 0d90/ILE/G0316018.pdf (last visited 25 August 2014).

[23] The Norms was drawn upon numerous human rights treaties. The Norms refer to approximately thirty transnational instruments as the sources from which they derive their authority for TNCs and human rights issues. The Norms were not 'an international treaty open to ratification by States', they would not be 'legally binding' on either States or TNCs. Nevertheless, as a purported restatement of the law regarding TNCs and human rights abuses, if adopted, the Norms could have been a powerful accountability tool for human rights advocates and victims of human rights abuses. Int'l Network On Forecon., Society and Cultural Rights, UN Human Rights Norms for Business: Briefing Kit 4 (January 2005), available at http://www.escr-net.org/ usr_doc/Briefing_Kit.pdf (last visited 25 August 2015).

on implementation of these rules, increasing transparency by disclosing information regarding company's performance, and financial situation, informing the affected communities about its activities and continually working on improving the Norms.[24] Further, a TNC would need to integrate human rights issues into all aspects of its operations for the implementation program to be successful, rather than simply relegating the subject to its corporate social responsibility department.

Besides placing a heavy burden on the corporations to demonstrate how their activities either benefited or harmed the human rights of groups and communities, this implementation strategy virtually sought to replace company management. When the Human Rights Council took up the Norms in 2004, it 'expressed [its] appreciation to the Sub-Commission for the work it had undertaken in preparing [the Norms]. . . . It affirmed, however, that the document had not been requested and . . . had no legal standing'.[25]

The UN Global Compact and the UN Norms are prototypes of two ends of the regulatory spectrum. Whilst the former was a pure voluntary, bottom up approach with hardly any effective implementation mechanism, the latter was an absolute top-down mandatory approach, with such strict implementation that, it invaded the corporate functionality. It is often alleged that the UN Norms were too ambitious to leave no stone unturned for corporate accountability,[26] however, in the process ended up becoming engulfed by their own doctrinal excesses.

---

[24] 'Commentary on the Norms on the Responsibilities of Transnational Corporations and Other Business Enterprises with Regard to Human Rights'.

[25] Commission on Human Rights, 'Summaries of Post-Sessional Meetings and Other Activities of the Expanded Bureau During the Period from May to September 2004, transmitted by Note of the Secretariat', UN Doc. E/CN.4/ IM/2004/2 (28 September 2004): 27, available at http://www2.ohchr.org/ english/bodies/chr/informal/documents.htm (last visited 27 February 2015).

[26] For instance, paragraph 12 of the UN Norms stated that companies shall respect economic, social, and cultural rights as well as civil and political rights and contribute to their realization, in particular the rights to development, adequate food and drinking water, the highest attainable standard of physical and mental health, adequate housing, privacy, education, freedom of thought, conscience, and religion and freedom of opinion and expression.

The experience of international human rights law informs us that seeking human rights compliance for the corporations is a complex exercise. Corporations are either too slippery or too stubborn to be formally entrusted with human rights obligations. Any voluntary bottom-up approach is not taken very seriously; conversely a top-down mandatory approach is met with rejection.[27] Neither of the two approaches, therefore, can garner adequate and real support from corporations on human rights. Thus, learning from the past suggests that if the right to access the Internet is attempted to be attained at an international level from a full range of corporations involved therein, the co-operative approach will be too mild while the top-down approach will be perceived as uncalled interference and can result in alienating corporations from disability rights rather than actively involving them. It is somewhat a similar situation which Goldilocks found the options before her to be too hard or too soft, too hot, or too cold until she found herself the one that was just right.

In an endeavour to resolve such Goldilocks dilemma prevailing in international human rights law, in 2005, the Human Rights Council asked the Secretary General Kofi Annan to appoint a Special Representative to report to the Council on human rights issues and TNCs.[28] Prof. John Ruggie was appointed as the Special

---

[27] An unsuccessful effort was made during the 1970s and 1980s to draft a comprehensive set of rules governing transnational corporation. In 1972, the UN Economic and Social Council (ECOSOC) appointed a 'Group of Eminent Persons' to advise on matters related to transnational corporations and their impact on the development process. In 1974 the UN established the Centre on Transnational Corporations which by 1977 was co-coordinating the negotiation of a Draft Code of Conduct on Transnational Corporations (Draft Code). Negotiations lingered until the early 1990s but no final agreement was concluded. Due to political disagreements between States, the Draft Code was never officially adopted and its legal nature was never established. See UN Draft Code of Conduct on Transnational Corporations, UN Doc E/1990/94 (1990).

[28] Commission on Human Rights, Human Rights Res. 2005/69: 'Human Rights and Transnational Corporations and Other Business Enterprises', 59th mtg., U.N. Doc. E/CN.4/RES/2005/69 (20 April 2005), available at www.unhcr.org/refworld/doci d/45377c80c.html (last visited 27 August 2014).

Rapporteur to the Secretary-General.[29] The mandate culminated in the UN Protect, Respect and Remedy Framework in 2008.[30] The PRR Framework is operationalized through a set of Guiding Principles, submitted to the Human Rights Council in 2011. [31]

UN PRR Framework: Averting the Goldilocks Dilemma

The PRR Framework rests on three essential pillars: (a) the State's legal duty to protect individuals and communities from human rights abuses committed by others, including corporations; (b) the

[29] Ruggie's original mandate was to identify standards regarding human rights affecting TNCs; discuss the role of State in regulating human rights abuses within their borders; research and clarify application of the terms 'complicity' and 'sphere of influence' to TNCs; develop materials to assist TNCs in implementing human rights impact assessments; and compile a 'compendium of best practices' for both States and TNCs to follow. What followed were six years of annual reports that had two key milestones: the development of the Respect Framework in 2008 and the U.N. Human Rights Council's approval of the Guiding Principles in 2011. There had been two Interim Reports in 2006 and 2007. Interim Report 2006 Report summarized factors that led to the shifting landscape of international law, specifically with regard to business and human rights with globalization as one of the most factors. Commission on Human Rights, 'Promotion and Protection of Human Rights', UN Doc. E/CN.4/2006/97 (22 February 2006), available at http://daccess-dds-y. un.org/doc/UNDOC/GEN/GO6/110/27/PDF/G0611027.pdf (last visited 25 August 2014); 'Mapping International Standards of Responsibility and Accountability for Corporate Acts', U.N. Doc. A/HRC/4/035, Interim Report 2007 Business and Human Rights, Human Rights Council (9 February 2007) (by John Ruggie), available at http://www.business-humanrights.org/ SpecialRepPortal/Home/ReportstoUNHumanRightsCouncil/2007 (last visited 25 August 2014).

[30] Human Rights Council, 'Protect, Respect and Remedy: A Framework for Business and Human Rights', UN Doc. A/HRC/8/5 (7 April 2008) (by John Ruggie), available at http://www.unglobalcompact.org/docs/issues_doc/ human_rights/Human_Rights_Working_Group/29Apr08_7_Report_of_ SRSG_to_HRC.pdf (last visited 27 August 2014) (the PRR FRAMEWORK).

[31] Human Rights Council, 'Guiding Principles on Business and Human Rights: Implementing the United Nations "Protect, Respect and

responsibility of corporations to respect human rights; and (c) an amelioration of current remedial mechanisms when dealing with human rights abuses. The PRR Framework reaffirms a non-legal accountability framework for corporations by explaining 'the responsibility of business enterprises to respect human rights'.[32] This responsibility of business enterprises to respect human rights is distinct from issues of legal liability and enforcement, which remain defined largely by national law provisions in relevant jurisdictions.[33]

The PRR Framework effects a strict separation between the State and corporate obligations towards human rights. Whilst the PRR Framework concedes that corporations may be 'organs of society', it emphatically states that they are specialized economic organs, not democratic public interest institutions.[34] The PRR Framework stipulates that corporations lack any binding legal obligations in relation to human rights and any responsibility to respect flow from the 'social expectations' rationale.[35]

The framework thus encourages companies to reflect upon their human rights impact and address the same; although without creating a legal obligation. Guided by 'principled pragmatism'.[36]

Remedy" Framework', UN Doc.A/HRC/17/31 (21 March 2011) (by John Ruggie), available at http://www.ohchr.org/Documents/Issues/Business/A-HRC-17-31_AEV.pdf (last visited 27 August 2014) (the Guiding Principles).

[32] Human Rights Council, 'Guiding Principles on Business and Human Rights', § II.A, para 12, at p. 13. It needs to be pointed that the PRR Framework uses the term 'responsibility' instead of the term 'duty', 'obligation' or 'accountability' that is indicative that corporations does not have any legally binding duty.

[33] Human Rights Council, 'Guiding Principles on Business and Human Rights', pp. 13–14.

[34] Human Rights Council, 'Protect, Respect and Remedy', para 54.

[35] Human Rights Council, 'Protect, Respect and Remedy', § III.A, para 54. This notion of social expectation is then linked to the self-interest of the corporation—how failure to meet responsibility can subject companies to the 'courts of public opinion' and deprive them of a 'social license to operate'.[308] Such a proposition is thus rooted in making a 'business case for human rights' arguing why it is in the corporation's own self-interest to avoid harming rights and to contribute towards their realization.

[36] Principled pragmatism views international law as a tool for collective problem solving, not an end in itself. It recognizes that the development of

the PRR Framework and the Guiding Principles (GPs) refer both to co-operative approach as well as deterrence approach, albeit in a disjointed fashion, to address human rights obligations. While corporations are expected to cooperate, States are required to deter or themselves arrive at a 'smart mix' to attain compliance from corporations.[37] The GPs do not elaborate on the latter, however, they do neatly outline steps that corporations may take to avoid infringing on human rights of others and addressing adverse human rights impact with which they are involved.[38]

The GPs stipulate that corporations should demonstrate a firm commitment to the human rights issues by having a human rights policy. In addition, corporations must conduct due diligence, assess human rights impacts of company activities,[39] integrate those values and findings into corporate cultures and management systems,[40] and track as well as report performance,[41] in consultation with experts and other stakeholders. Thus, the GPs provide for a fully self-driven initiative from corporations to 'respect' human rights and tend to excessively rely on dialogic co-operation from them.[42]

---

any international legal instrument requires a certain degree of consensus among states.

[37] Human Rights Council, 'Guiding Principles on Business and Human Rights', p. 8.

[38] Human Rights Council, 'Guiding Principles on Business and Human Rights', para 6.

[39] Human Rights Council, 'Guiding Principles on Business and Human Rights', § II.B, para 17, p. 16.

[40] Human Rights Council, 'Guiding Principles on Business and Human Rights', § II.B, para 16.

[41] Human Rights Council, 'Business and Human Rights: Towards Operationalising the "Protect, Respect and Remedy" Framework', A/HRC/11/13, 2009 (22 April 2009) (by John Ruggie), available at http://ap.ohchr.org/documents/sdpage_e.aspx?b=10&se=92&t=9 (last visited 3 May 2015).

[42] On a close examination, the implementation measures suggested by the GPs towards corporate fulfilment of responsibility to respect are not drastically different from the procedures set out by the Norms. For instance references to the adoption of internal rules of operation in compliance with the norms, periodical reporting on the implementation, conduct of impact assessment, and taking remedial measures such as reparation, restitution and rehabilitation find resemblance to the Norms. However, it needs to be

The PRR Framework appears to have appeased the State, corporations as well as the human rights discourse by providing what each had sought for: for business, an absolution from any formally binding legal obligation on human rights; for the State, the reiteration of their sovereignty to deal with entities within their political boundaries (irrespective of whether or not they have the capacity or willingness to regulate such entities) and for human rights discourse, the much required breakthrough from the stalemate created after the UN Norms. Consequently, the PRR Framework and the GPs had wide-ranging endorsement from diverse stakeholders, including specific businesses[43] and industries,[44] governments,[45] and nongovernmental organizations.[46] While it remains indisputable that the Framework succeeded in

---

reiterated even at the cost of repetition that whereas the UN Norms were worked in highly closed fashion and largely seen as top-down imposition; the GPs encourage companies to engage with human rights issues as a commitment that they have themselves made.

[43] See, for example, ING Congratulates UN Special Representative John Ruggie and his team on Endorsement of Guiding Principles, One Society Initiative.ORG, 24 June 2011, available at http://onesocietyinitiative. org/ing-congratulates-un-special-representative-john-ruggie-a-his-team-on-endorsement-of-guiding-principles-80 (last visited 27 August 2014).

[44] Letter of Support from the International Business Leaders Forum for the U.N. Protect, Respect and Remedy Framework, to John Ruggie, the Special Representative of the Secretary-General, (16 June 2011), available at http://www.business-humanrights.org/Links/Repository/1006814 (last visited 27 August 2014).

[45] See for example, 'Press Release, Human rights.gov, Businesses and Transactional Corporations Have a Responsibility to Respect Human Rights' (16 June 2011), available at http://www.humanrights.gov/2011/06/16/businesses-and-transnational-corporations-have-a-responsibility-to-respect-human-rights (last visited 27 August 2014).

[46] See for example, Public Statement, 'Document—United Nations: A Call for Action to Better Protect the Rights of Those Affected by Business-Related Human Rights Abuses', Amnesty International Organisation (14 June 2011), available at http://www.amnesty.org/en/library/asset/IOR40/009/2011/en/55fab4a5-fb8a-4572-93f3-67581b2dca45/ior400092011en.html (last visited 27 August 2014).

bringing back on track a discourse which was reaching a dead-end, the same has progressively been analysed more closely with respect to its contents and approach.[47]

In the context of the right to access the Internet, the normative grounding and the 'principled pragmatism' of the PRR Framework is problematic on several counts. One, the compartmentalization between the State 'duty to protect' and the corporate 'responsibility to respect' human rights existing independent of one another, does not hold good in the joint and several obligation proposed keeping in mind a decentralized Internet. A linear fashioned PRR Framework does not fit into a polycentric Internet where the State itself is a marginal player deficient of technical expertise and regulatory outreach.

Two, grounding the responsibility in 'social expectations' provides a very fragile pedestal for the realization of human rights, let alone the right to access the Internet. It tends to weaken an otherwise sound case already being made for corporate obligations in respect to the Internet. Further, it is inconsistent with the logic of human rights, which entails duties upon those who have the capacity to violate them or assist in their realization.[48]

---

[47] See Tara J. Melish and Errol Meidinger, 'Protect, Respect, Remedy and Participate: "New Governance" Lessons for the Ruggie Framework', in *The UN Guiding Principles on Business and Human Rights* (Radu Mares ed. 2012) (interrogating the theoretical underpinnings of the PRR framework and proposing addition of a fourth pillar to the framework, that of civil society participation to create a more effective framework). See generally, Surya Deva and David Bilchitz, *Human Rights Obligations of Business: Beyond the Corporate Responsibility to Respect* (2013) (The book raises critical questions surrounding the normative foundations and content of obligation with a perspective to provide more robustness to the framework). Melish, 'Putting "Human Rights" Back into the UN Guiding Principles on Business and Human Rights: Shifting Frames and Embedding Participation Rights', *SUNY Buffalo Law School, Legal Studies Research Paper Series, Paper* No. 2014–032 July 2014, available at http://ssrn.com/abstract=2475629 (exploring the possibility of a framework where empowered civil society participation could be effectively incorporated in the GPs).

[48] M. Kramer, N. Simmonds, and H. Steiner, *A Debate Over Rights: Philosophical Enquiries* (1998).

Third, if responsibility is rooted in 'social expectation', it is pertinent to first determine what is this expectation to determine the extent of responsibility. In a global world marked by competing interests and ideologies, this determination is susceptible to several contests.[49] Such relevance on social expectation as the primary mode of creating obligations is wrought with uncertainty.[50]

Lastly and importantly, if fulfilling the responsibility to respect is contingent upon bringing benefits to the company, then directors need not fulfil their responsibilities where costs outweigh benefits. Application of this approach will diminish any claims by persons with disabilities, reducing them to mere consumers. This was exactly what the enabling approach to the right to Internet implied, and was found to be problematic.

The normative assessment of the PRR Framework is inadequate to address accessibility rights concerns. Therefore, it is crucial that the approach under this study distances itself from the normative foundations of the PRR Framework. Yet, there is no harm in consulting the operative mechanisms developed by the GPs and assessing these towards the attainment of the accessibility goals. In what follows, I examine various soft-laws, mostly voluntary initiatives suggested by the GPs to nudge corporate human rights conduct under the disability lens.

Policy Commitment to Human Rights: Code of Conduct

According to the GPs, the first step for corporations in embedding respect for human rights is to express their commitments in a policy statement approved by senior level management with inputs from internal/external experts. This should be communicated

---

[49] Bilchitz, 'A Chasm between "is" and "ought"? A Critique of the Normative Foundations of the SRSG's Framework and the Guiding Principles', in *Human Rights Obligations of Business: Beyond the Corporate Responsibility to Respect* 107 (Surya Deva and Bilchitz, eds, 2013).

[50] Hart claims that such models are likely to succeed fir a 'small community closely knit by ties of kinship, common sentiment and belief and places in a stable environment'. H.L.A. Hart, *The Concept of Law* (2nd ed., 1997).

actively to the entities with which the enterprise has contractual relationships or directly linked to its operations. Thus, there needs to be coherence between a corporation's responsibility to respect human rights and the policies and procedures that govern their wider business activities and relationships.

An offshoot of policy commitment is what is known as the Code of Conduct. Whereas a policy commitment is broader in its scope, the Code of Conduct breaks down the rules in details. These are voluntary in nature and are not legally binding. The International Labour Organisation (ILO) defines a code of conduct as 'a written policy or statement of principles intended to serve as the basis for a commitment to particular enterprise conduct'.[51] The Organisation of Economic Co-operation and Development (OECD) definition is similar, referring to 'commitments voluntarily made by companies, associations or other entities, which put forth standards and principles for the conduct of business activities in the marketplace'.[52]

Although codes may take several forms, these are broadly classified into two prominent variants with further sub-classifications. The first model is one of 'public' codes established by the State through agreements under international law or through the norms for corporations.[53] Thus, such inter-governmental codes are negotiated

[51] International Labour Organisation Governing Body, Working Party on the Social Dimensions of the Liberalization of international Trade, Overview of global developments and Office activities concerning codes of conduct, social labeling and other private sector initiatives addressing labour issues, Executive Summary, GB 273/WP/SDL/1, 273rd session Geneva, November 1998.

[52] OECD Directorate for Financial, Fiscal and Enterprise Affairs, 'Codes of Corporate Conduct: Expanded Review of their Contents', Working Papers on International Investment, TD/TC/WP(99)56/FINAL, June 2000.

[53] In 1981 the World Health Organisation developed the International Code of Marketing of Breast milk substitutes. For a discussion of this, see J. Richter, *Holding Corporations Accountable: Corporate Conduct, Internatinal Codes and Citizen Action* (2001). Other codes focused on country-specific issues. The 1977 Sullivan Principles offered guidelines for companies wishing to do business in South Africa during the apartheid regime, available at www.globalsullivanprinciples.org (last visited 26 August 2014). The 1984 MacBride Principles outlined voluntary standards for businesses operating in Northern Ireland during 'the Troubles'. The MacBride Principles are designed to ensure

at international level and agreed by national governments.[54] For instance, the W3C was founded as an industry consortium in 1994.[55] It is engaged in the development of common technical web standards, referred to as the W3C Recommendation.[56] The Web Accessibility Content Guidelines developed by W3C is one of the most widely accepted international standards for accessibility.[57]

The second model is a set of 'private' codes[58] that are company specific or industry specific where corporations commit themselves, effectively in public relations terms, to standards in the above-mentioned issue areas and promise their implementation.[59] For instance, several companies (some of these being supply companies),

---

that companies are not discriminating against religious minorities in Northern Ireland and they provide an external tool for States to utilize in evaluating the actions of a particular corporation.

[54] For instance, the OECD Guidelines for Multinational Enterprises and the ILO'S Tripartite Declaration of Principles Concerning Multinational Enterprises.

[55] The origins of W3C are closely linked to Tim Berners-Lee's first attempts to connect devices in order to make knowledge more accessible. W3C is not an incorporated body having a separate legal entity. It is based on contractual relationships with its hosts and its members. Membership is open to all types of organizations whether commercial, educational, governmental entities, as well as individuals.

[56] It aims to hold the web together as a universal medium for sharing information. Its responsibilities include the documentation and consensus-building concerning web architectural principles as well as their interpretation and clarification when necessary.

[57] WACG are produced as part of the W3C Web Accessibility Initiative (WAI) see http://www.w3.org/TR/WCAG20/ (last visited 10 February 2015).

[58] Private codes are sub-classified as a) individual company codes, adopted on the firm's own initiative; b) codes issued by industry and trade associations reflecting a negotiated consensus among member firms in a particular industry; c) Multi-stakeholder codes, adopted following consultation among all those with an interest in a particular industry such as trade unions and NGOs; and d) Model codes designed to provide a benchmark of what a particular organization regards as good practice in terms of codes of conduct.

[59] The last 15 years have seen the rise of individual company codes of conduct. Levi-Strauss is usually credited as the first TNC to establish a code with comprehensive principles regarding its global sourcing and operations in

including Microsoft Corporation,[60] Hewlett-Packard,[61] Apple,[62] Facebook,[63] Google[64] have spelt their vision to create accessible products. At times, officials from these companies contribute and participate in the creation of accessibility standards at W3C.[65]

These codes have distinct advantages as a strategy for achieving the corporate observance of human rights standards (in this case accessibility concern). First, codes provide greater flexibility in norm setting and frequent updating based on experience. Evidently, corporations are closely connected to providing

---

1991. Nike followed later the same year. In May 2001 the OECD published a review of 246 codes of conduct noting that this did not cover all codes in existence.

[60] In addition to the company's vision to create accessible products and services, the company conducts and commissions research to enhance user experience. For details see http://www.microsoft.com/enable/ (last visited 10 February 2015).

[61] HP accessibility goal is to design, produce, and market products and services that can effectively be used by everyone, including people with disabilities, either on a stand-alone basis or with appropriate assistive devices. Towards these ends, HP's Accessibility Policy spells out seven key objectives—awareness raising, supporting research and development of accessible products, documenting accessibility features, involving persons with disabilities, developing guidelines, forging relationship with solution providers, supporting industry guidelines. For details see http://www8.hp.com/us/en/hp-information/accessibility-aging/policy.html (last visited 10 February 2015).

[62] For details of accessibility features of Apple products, see https://www.apple.com/accessibility/ (last visited 10 February 2015).

[63] In keeping with its mission to make the world open and connected, Facebook has released a toolkit describing accessibility efforts of Facebook including the company's efforts to monitor the feedback and sharing their work publicly. See https://code.facebook.com/accessibility (last visited 10 February 2015).

[64] Google has been creating guides and resources for developers, business to create accessible web. See https://www.google.co.in/accessibility/ (last visited 10 February 2015).

[65] For instance, staff from Google serves on the WCAG Working Group and the Web Content Accessibility Guidelines (WCAG) 2.0 and recommendatory bodies.

technical infrastructure and overall contents. In a way, they are insiders which understand 'access', both in terms of concept and practice, better than the government. It is therefore apt to have them commit to this right. Second, codes effectively create a web of transnational obligations that operate independent of the host (and the home) State consent. Also, when compared to prescriptive international instruments (which might receive limited ratification and only then with significant reservations), voluntary codes have the advantage of the potentially easier achievement.[66] For instance, when Microsoft Corporation makes a formal commitment to attain accessibility and embeds the same in its functioning, it then really does not matter whether the host country has a policy/framework to ensure accessibility or whether or not they have ratified the CRPD. The company codes prove to be an automatic route for ensuring the right to access the Internet.

Codes are also more effective in the case of corporations and products with larger public profile and greater public visibility. These are more vulnerable to adverse publicity and consumer sentiment.[67] Given the limitations of the State and patterns of globalization, a code of conduct is believed to answer the regulatory concerns for corporations.[68]

---

[66] However, empirical studies and investigations have rarely been unanimous in verifying successful application of any of these soft law measures in any particular issue.

[67] Although the content and format of these codes vary considerably, the bulk of existing codes seek to base themselves on core conventions of ILO, including prohibitions on child labour, forced labour, and discrimination in respect of employment and occupation, and protection of freedom of association and collective bargaining and other basic principles regarding the protection of health and safety, wages and hours, and treatment of women. See Xiaomin Yu, 'Impacts of Corporate Code of Conduct on Labor Standards: A Case Study of Reebok's Athletic Footwear Supplier Factory in China', 81 *Journal of Business Ethics* 513 (2008).

[68] Codes tend to address a wide range of regulatory issues. While aspects of social responsibility figure most prominently among codes, such as fair business practices, questions of internal financial control and protection of shareholder value and so on; consumer protection and avoidance of bribery and corruption, have also attained due attention. Large number of these

However, codes of conduct are often alleged to suffer from two major weaknesses—first, the characteristics inherent within the code itself and second, its practical operation. The voluntary nature of the codes often provides a weak protection when compared to the legally binding norms. Their impact depends upon private initiative and sincerity of application. Codes are influential when they enjoy wide acceptance within an industry. At times, even where industry leaders may propose and adopt a code, other firms offer a lukewarm response therefore, the codes fail to have any visible positive impact. Thus, even if the W3C set out standards of creating accessible websites, it will have little impact unless private initiative actually adopts them.

Closely tied up with the aforesaid concern is the lack of independent monitoring. While many corporations make principled commitments, it is difficult to assess their actual practice. The reluctance of many firms to include independent monitoring as an integral part of their code of conduct, raises suspicions that accessibility standards may be used as a public relations exercise. This gives an impression that Codes of Conduct is devised as a shield to avoid legal responsibility, masking traditional profit-maximizing interests through a superficial gloss of rhetoric. Under the false promises of self-regulation, public interest is deflected from stepping up hard regulatory practices that can be more effective than soft measures. Therefore, making such reputational investments will prove to be profitable only when corporations are vulnerable to a negative consumer sentiment and public markets.

Consequently, one often sees that Codes are concentrated in consumer good sectors where brand names and corporate image are very important.[69] In the context of right to access the Internet, such codes remain concentrated in corporations which are

---

invariably includes corporation response in relation to human rights, labour rights, and environmental standards.

[69] This helps explain why the large-scale retail sector, garments and footwear, toys and some food products have been the sectors where codes covering social issues have most commonly been found. They also tend to be sectors in which the cost of individual purchases is relatively low, and where production costs often make up a relatively small part of the final product price.

closely involved in providing infrastructure in terms of hardware/ software components. Evidently, such selective concentration as well as the effectiveness of the codes seriously undermines their utility as complete and adequate human rights assurance measures on accessibility.

Auditing the Corporate Position: Human Rights Due Diligence

The GPs require corporations to undertake some self-reflection[70] by undertaking human rights due diligence, a process whereby companies not only ensure compliance with national laws, but also attempt to avoid the risk of human rights violation.[71] Even as the GPs concede that this process is inductive and fact-based, it nevertheless provides broad principles. Accordingly, while undertaking a due diligence the corporation should consider four sets of factors. First, the country contexts in which their business activities take place, to highlight any specific human rights challenges they may pose.

---

[70] On-going debates fixating social responsibilities on private entities under International law culminated into appointment of Prof. John Ruggie, as United Nations Special Representative of the Secretary-General on Human Rights and Transnational Corporations and other Business Enterprises (SRSG). Ruggie's three-fold framework of a state's duty to protect human rights, a corporate responsibility to respect human rights and access to remedies was unanimously accepted by member states of the Human Rights Council in June 2008. The framework was welcomed in a joint statement by human rights NGOs as well as by the International Organisation of Employers, International Chamber of Commerce and the Business and Industry Advisory Committee to the OECD (BIAC). See the 2008 report and reactions to it at http://www.businesshumanrights. org/Documents/RuggieHRC2008 (last visited 27 February 2015).

[71] See Report of the Special Representative of the Secretary-General on the Issue of Human Rights and Transnational Corporations and other Business Enterprises, *Promotion and Protection of All Human Rights, Civil, Political, Economic, Social and Cultural Rights, Including the Right to Development: Clarifying the Concepts of 'Sphere of influence' and 'Complicity'* (by John Ruggie) A/HRC/8/16 15 May 2008.

Second, the impact their own activities may have on human within that context, in their capacity as producers, service providers, employers, and neighbours. Third, whether they might contribute to abuse through the relationships connected to their activities.[72] Fourth, the need to pay special attention to any particular human rights impact on individuals from groups or populations that may be at heightened risk of vulnerability or marginalization.

If these are translated in the context of accessibility rights to the Internet, both supply companies and consumer companies are required to undertake an access audit of their products, services, websites, and components. This kind of self-audit of the accessibility check on the technology is akin to the architectural audit of physical barriers. This allows companies to see where they stand with respect to the accessibility of their digital information. Such due diligence may further inform and guide framing the code of conduct for corporations or alternative monitoring and mitigation. Human Rights Due Diligence guides corporations in thinking critically, creatively and continually about how they are influencing human rights issues. In particular, it forces them to engage with the question whether they are a part of the problem or solution. In case of former, they seek to devise strategies for mitigation. This can then be translated into practice while putting warranties and indemnities into purchasing contracts. The collection and dissemination of positive information about accessibility will encourage others to improve and follow the best practice. Conducting due diligence enables companies to identify and prevent adverse human rights impacts. Doing so should also provide corporate boards with strong protection against mismanagement claims by shareholders.

Even where due diligence is a process well known to the companies as they routinely conduct such investigation in commercial contexts to assess, pre-empt and manage risks,[73] one needs to be cautious

---

[72] For detailed discussions, see chapter 2.

[73] See T. Lambooy, *Corporate Social Responsibility: Legal And Semi-Legal Frameworks Supporting CSR*, pp. 279–92 (2010); B. Demeyere, 'Sovereign Wealth Funds and (Un)ethical Investment', in *Human Rights, Corporate Complicity and Disinvestment* 183, pp. 211–13 (G. Nystuen, A. Follesdal, and O. Mestad, eds, 2011).

about the differences in goals and objectives when applied in a the human rights context. Due diligence investigation in commercial contexts focuses on protecting interests of the company in question. Importantly, human rights discourse is not about safeguarding the rights of companies. Rather, the focus is on protecting the rights of persons (interests of external parties). Unlike situations involving commercial matters, the targets of due diligence on human rights may not be very definite. It is, therefore, quite possible that corporations may not be too zealous while conducting such diligence.

Corporations, therefore, need a different orientation in applying due diligence tools in the context of human rights. The question is how many corporations actually undertake it? Similar to policy commitments made by supply companies, due diligence is also confined to these groups. For instance, when HP set out a seven point guideline to fulfil its commitment towards creating accessible products and services,[74] it is fairly aware about the impact its products will have on persons with disabilities.

Whereas it makes good business sense for supply companies to undertake such due diligence; end-user companies/consumer companies are less likely to engage in the same. At the most, companies may undertake generic human rights due diligence and certain human rights issue may overshadow others. Unfortunately, accessibility audit is not given due importance in a corporate set up, worse, it may be looked upon as inviting trouble. Companies must realize that acknowledging accessibility barriers will not mean causing additional burdens. Rather, it helps to create credibility of the company in the sense that the company recognizes the problem and seeks assistance to fix it.

Communicating the Progress on Human Rights Commitments: Social Reporting

Once the policy commitment has been made and due diligence undertaken, the GPs expect that corporations assess 'the social impact and ethical behaviour of an organization in relation to its aims

---

[74] For details see http://www8.hp.com/us/en/hp-information/accessibility-aging/policy.html (last visited 10 February 2015).

and those of its stakeholders. Stakeholders include all individuals and groups who are affected by, or can affect, the organization.'[75] Having made these assessments, corporations are then expected to integrate those values in their culture and management and report on performance. In short, corporations are to draw up an extensive picture of the organization's relationships with its stakeholders. This picture encompasses more than just a snapshot at a particular time—its design, development, and interpretation contribute to an on-going dialogue culture where values become vital to the organizations' self-reference.[76]

Simultaneously, corporations are required to communicate their performance to society through social reporting.[77] The rationale behind social reporting is to attain transparency in corporate behaviour and create a link between its public obligation and private choice.[78] It is largely believed to produce structural pressures to inculcate humanistic concerns into otherwise brutal global competition.[79] Such information 'can force choices (for individual action) even when the moral foundation of those choices remains

[75] Chris Nelder, 'Social Assessment', *BWZine*, The Online Better World Magazine (April/May 1996). Available at http://www.betterworld.com/BWZ/9604/cover1-1.htm (quoting Dr Simon Zadek of the New Economic Foundation, London) (last visited 27 August 2014).

[76] Bauer and Fenn categorize four approaches to social reporting. First, a report can show that the company is not doing any social harm. Second, a social report may simply show the 'subjective impressions of knowledgeable and concerned people who have collected some data and talked with many observers'. Third, the report could thoroughly review a corporation's action in specific areas of activity. Fourth, a report may attempt to 'develop sophisticated quantitative measures of social responsibility'. Raymond Bauer and Dan H. Fenn, Jr, The Corporate Social Audit, 16, p. 17 (1972).

[77] It has been argued that instead of relying upon substantive law to achieve social responsiveness by corporations, mandatory social reporting can be applied to corporate governance. D. Hess, 'Social Reporting: A Reflexive Approach to Corporate Social Responsiveness', 25 *Iowa Journal of Corporate Law* 41 (1999): 80-4.

[78] Larry Cata Backer, 'From Moral Obligation to International Law: Disclosure Systems, Markets and the Regulation of Multinational Corporations', 39 *Georgetown Journal of International Law* 591 (2008): 603-5, 625.

[79] Cynthia A. Williams, 'Corporate Social Responsibility in an Era of Economic Globalisation', 35 *U.C. Davis Law Review* 705 (2002).

contested (in the community)'.[80] Whereas social reporting may not require any changes in how directors or managers exercise their fiduciary responsibilities, it certainly creates pressure on directors about how they balance the competing demands of various constituencies. Yet, the production and dissemination of such information produces greater corporate social transparency, actuating the goal of enhanced corporate social accountability without directly undermining the traditional corporate law's goal of shareholder accountability.

Considering the subtle yet forceful pressure social reporting creates, several states have experimented with mandating social reporting. For instance, Sweden requires state-owned companies to present social reports together with other financial reports, to create an integrated basis for assessment and follow-up.[81] Following in Sweden's footsteps, the Danish government passed legislation in December 2008 requiring the country's largest 1100 companies to include information on corporate social responsibility in their annual reports.[82] Mandatory reporting would effectively give the market forces the teeth they need, since with information comes an ability to judge; judgment permits informed action; and action in the aggregate can be crucial.[83] Assessment of the authenticity of the claims in the social report by

[80] Williams, 'Corporate Social Responsibility in an Era of Economic Globalisation'.

[81] On 3 December 2007, the Swedish government became one of the first to implement a mandatory home state corporate accountability regime. It announced that, as of 1 January 2008, the state-owned companies shall present sustainability reports in accordance with the Global Reporting Initiative's (GRI) guidelines. The GRI's reporting framework contains 'general and sector-specific content that has been agreed [upon] by a wide range of stakeholders around the world to be generally applicable for reporting an organisation's sustainability performance.' Press Release, Swed. Ministry of Enter., Energy and Communications, Clearer Requirements for Information About Sustainability for State-Owned Companies.

[82] Ben Cooper, 'Danish Reporting Rules, Ethical Corp.', 26, available at http://www.ethicalcorp.com/resources/pdfs/content/20093531917_non-financial%20reporting%20feature.pdf. (last visited 2 April 2015).

[83] Backer, 'From Moral Obligation to International Law', p. 653.

an independent monitor proves to be a contentious issue. While this enhances the credibility of the report; companies do not favour such arrangements since an external monitor is often seen as interference to company's internal governance mechanisms and public infringement of market sensitive information related to the company.

Social reporting will make sense for corporations who have already made a policy commitment towards attaining accessibility. Hence, social reporting may not be useful as an independent instrumentality of corporate compliance. As experienced in the Code of Conduct, social reporting will prove to be effective where a corporation produces high end market brands more vulnerable to the scrutiny of consumers and intermediaries. However, where the structure of production is more dispersed; it is difficult to monitor and easier to manipulate the code.[84]

Thus, while the GPs propose voluntary commitment and self-regulation by corporations towards their human rights conduct, there are some limitations.

One of the major limitations of self-regulation is that these are not legally enforceable. Regardless of the legal quality as such, private norms are only applicable to those persons who have accepted the regulatory framework.[85] Often the process of rule-making is not transparent and fully democratized. Consequently, industry leaders may bear the burden of rule-making and free riders taking advantage. Such model raises many substantive questions than the one it answers. There is no clarity on how far will such self-regulation goes? This model does not offer convincing answers as to what will be its mode of enforcement or the tools of deterrence for those who violate or breach rules of the cyber community.

---

[84] Guy Mundlak and Issi Rosen-Zvi, 'Mapping the Hard Law/Soft Law Terrain: Labor Rights and Environmental Protection: Signaling Virtue? A Comparison of Corporate Codes in the Fields of Labor and Environment', 12 *Theoretical Inquiry Law* 403 (2011).

[85] See, Rolf Weber and Romana Weber, *The Internet of the Things: Legal Perspectives* (2010); Weber, *Regulatory Models For The Online World*, pp. 31, 32 (2002).

Critical Appraisal of the International Soft Law Instrumentalities

Existing international human rights law equips us with soft law instrumentalities[86] that are helpful to implement and ensure human rights conduct which operates more in terms of self-disciplining corporations rather than policing their human rights conduct. Even where normative foundations of these instrumentalities are inconsistent with the specific human rights under the present study, they are in consonance with the underlying objective of the present rights insofar as these seek a proactive engagement of corporations.

It needs to be conceded that voluntary self-regulatory mechanisms are, nonetheless, important tools which address corporate human rights violations and these softer norms and forms of regulations offer flexibility not available in the development of binding legal obligations. Human rights due diligence, thus, requires self-inspection and the Code of Conduct involves public ratification of corporate norms and commitments. This tends to place a strong relevance on self-regulation by the corporations. Some Codes of Conduct are so widely accepted that they are in essence 'binding' on corporations operating in these areas. Additionally, social reporting is seen as a platform where corporations and stakeholders can exchange notes and engage with each other positively to understand expectations and challenges involved in the process. Communication based initiatives such as social reporting, when combined with information based strategies facilitates behaviours persuasive to align norms and behaviours to human rights. These mechanisms create minimum standards of expected conduct and

---

[86] There is a wide diversity in the instruments of so called soft law. Soft law usually refers to any international instrument other than a treaty that contains principles, norms, standards or other statements of expected behaviour. D. Shelton, 'Normative Hierarchy in International Law', 100, *American Journal of International Law* 291, 319 (2006). Often it is suggested that soft law can be determined by the status of the obligation it imposes. See generally, C.M. Chinkin, 'The Challenges of Soft Law', 38, *International and Comparative Law Quarterly* 850 (1989); A.E. Boyle, 'Some Reflections on the Relationship of Treaties and Soft Law', 48 *International And Comparative Law Quarterly* 901, 902 (1999).

are bound to have a normative value that influences standards of behaviour. Even as widespread acceptance of a particular instrument may not turn soft law into legally binding principles, but it creates pressure to realign practice and operation in accordance with acceptable standards.

The effectiveness of these instrumentalities is a key concern. Does the instrument create an obligation to do or not do something? Is there apparent consent by the parties drafting or using the instrument to be 'bound' by it and if so, how might such soft law be enforced? The key criteria to consider in the effectiveness of soft law relates to whether these initiatives are 'consistent, comprehensive and implemented'.[87]

The softness of the tool does not conclusively determine their ineffectiveness in the context of the right to access the Internet. However, it is crucial to determine whether these tools will be adequate to procure corporate indulgence required under the right to access the Internet. Do they complement and/or extend existing law on the subject or is it standing in place of such law? Secondly, given the mode chosen, does it have the potential to generate compliance by corporations? An insight into the world of the Internet has demonstrated that corporations are the driving force of innovation and disbursement of technology and ideas. The accessibility goals and commitments of corporations partially tend to complement the international discourse on the evolving principles of the Internet, but it cannot be said that these tools have taken the shape of the law. Insofar as the mode of these tools is concerned, these are fraught with difficulties.

Soft law instrumentalities are found wanting on three counts: one, the limited extent of their application to supply companies; two, voluntariness and excessive relevance in business case; three, over-relevance on dialogic co-operation. This tends to give an extremely problematic message that insofar as corporations are concerned human rights are negotiable.

The self-disciplining system imbibed in these instrumentalities presupposes that corporations not only comprehend their obligation

---

[87] Bilchitz and Deva, 'Business and Human Rights: A Critical Framework', in *Human Rights Obligations of Business* (Deva and Bilchitz, eds, 2013).

to ensure access, but are also willing to proactively undertake self-introspection and commit, standardize, and internalize the same. Just like the co-operative approach, it proceeds on the basis that most corporations are 'good apples' who would come forward to address systemic discrimination and do not suffer from attitudinal barriers in the creation of an accessible virtual world order. While this may be true for supply companies, it is difficult to see how consumer companies will respond to the same. These instrumentalities are therefore limited in their scope and application to supply companies and restricted to those corporations who are directly/proximately connected to the supply of infrastructure, in whatever form. Other category of consumer companies may not take this seriously, and possibly carry on business as usual.

More disturbing is the slated 'business case' as an underlying driving force of such compliance by corporations.[88] It is suggested that it ultimately lies in the self-interest of corporations to respect human rights, which grants them 'social license to operate'.[89] In the absence of such social license they would not be able to conduct their businesses effectively. Rather, it should have been the other way round. Compliance with human rights norms should be a non-negotiable precondition for doing business, instead of becoming a matter of expediency, only being relevant when it might impact the bottom line of companies. Unless the 'trials' of the corporations in the 'courts of public opinion' culminate into economic bite in terms of heavy loss of revenues, mere 'deprivation' of 'social license to operate' may not ensure the desired behaviour. Moreover, such propositions assume that consumers value human rights and have adequate information about the human rights performance of the companies in order to reward or punish the companies. Such assumptions need not necessarily guarantee results.[90]

---

[88] It is often argued that hinging human rights compliance on corporations on the basis of economic returns is a dangerous proposition since it gives an impression that if compliance is not profitable, human rights goals need not be followed.

[89] Human Rights Council, 'Protect, Respect and Remedy', para 54.

[90] See Deva, *Regulating Corporate Human Rights Violation: Humanizing Business*, pp. 139–45 (2012).

In the process of resorting to principled pragmatism, the PRR Framework and the GPs ended up compromising the urgency of the human rights itself by setting a very low threshold. Surya Deva rightly observes that the 'dialogue-co-operation strategy' adopted by the GPs commits a fatal mistake by surrendering human rights to the power of global business and implicitly signalling that human rights are still the subject matter of negotiation and bargaining when it comes to their compliance to corporations.[91] The disability jurisprudence has struggled its way to the rights based approach and cannot afford to lose out on such surrender.

***

The examination of the human rights law framework has revealed how voluntary versus mandatory debate has resulted in a Goldilocks dilemma. Learning from the past experience suggests that over-reliance on co-operation may not lead us too far; outright imposition of obligations will also be of no avail in the absence of visible deterrence. Experience from the UN Global Compact's purely co-operative approach informs that without the complement of international legal obligations, this privatized voluntary process will prove to be mild in regulating and will enforce compliance of corporations with human rights norms. The instrumentalities under the GPs talk too softly without any visible stick. It has been already cautioned that the GPs are not intended as a tool kit, simply to be taken off the shelf and plugged in.

The Special Rapporteur to the Secretary General, Prof. Ruggie was also conscious of this limitation when he wrote, 'private governance arrangements, no matter how successful, can take us only so far. They will remain relatively small islands of progress unless their achievements are rooted in, and generalized through, the sphere of public authority.'[92] A truly pragmatic

---

[91] Deva, *Regulating Corporate Human Rights Violation*, p. 116.

[92] J.G. Ruggie, *The Global Compact and the Challenges of Global Governance*, Annual Meeting, Global Compact Learning Forum, pp. 11–13 (December 2002). See also R. Mares, *The Dynamics of Corporate Social Responsibilities*, pp. 158–64 (2008).

approach, however, must look carefully at the deep structural aspects of a given problem by establishing a common global platform for action, in which cumulative progress can be built, step-by-step, without foreclosing any other promising longer-term developments.[93]

In this respect, while normative foundations of the instrumentalities are found to be problematic, the instrumentalities in themselves can be transplanted to a certain extent to the attainment of the present right to access the Internet. It can be safely concluded that human rights laws and its instrumentalities may prove to be helpful in guiding and obtaining compliance from only a certain segment of corporations involved in the overall Internet. It is quite evident that supply companies closely associated with the provisioning of infrastructure to the Internet are quite conscious of the impacts of their products for persons with disabilities and have set out mechanisms at their own end. Present community of corporations, however, comprises of a full range; from laggards who fail to meet even minimal standards, to leaders who go beyond statutory mandate, with the majority located somewhere in-between the two extremes.[94]

The problem here is that soft law instrumentalities may not be an adequate response to the goals of addressing systemic discrimination meted out to persons with disabilities. Hence, while soft law mechanisms can be appreciated for providing some leeway to corporations to operate and regulate their conduct, these alone cannot be an effective and sustainable rights ensuring mechanism. If soft law is acting as a complement to existing hard law, a combination of the two modes of law might serve to create a greater sense of authority for the soft law than if it stands alone. Thus, in order to escape the Goldilocks dilemma, it is important to place voluntary and soft forms of regulation within a comprehensive and binding legal obligation framework to be provided by the State. Pragmatism calls for 'identifying

---

[93] Human Rights Council, 'Guiding Principles on Business and Human Rights', para 13, 15.

[94] Mundlak and Rosen-Zvi, 'Mapping the Hard Law/Soft Law Terrain'.

the specific attributes of the different challenges we face, laying out the full array of tools, and then selecting the ones that provide the best mix of effectiveness and feasibility'.[95] Having assessed international human rights framework for corporate conduct; the next chapter moves to examine domestic efforts to ensure accessibility.

[95] Remarks by SRSG Ruggie Video presentation for the conference on 'Business and Fundamental Rights: The State Duty to Protect and Domestic Legal Reform', South African Institute for Advanced Constitutional, Public, Human Rights and International Law Johannesburg, 3 November 2008, available at www.reports-and-materials.org/sites/default/files/reports-and-materials/Ruggie-remarks-South-Africa-3-Nov-2008.pdf (last visited 3 May 2015).

4

Mandating the Midas Touch
Anti-discrimination Laws and Corporations

Even where it is acknowledged that corporations hold the Midas touch to the effective realization of the right to access the Internet, one must concede that international human rights law adopts a very soft tone to human rights obligation of corporations. Moreover, with international human rights law, leaving detailed strategy to be evolved by States, one must critically question how the Midas touch should be obtained. Should the State mandate corporations through anti-discrimination laws in order to command the observance of accessibility rights? Or should the State adopt a persuasive approach that incentivizes corporations to recognize accessibility rights of persons with disabilities? I undertake a survey of the variety of instrumentalities employed by States to implement the rights of persons with disabilities, in general and the right to access the Internet, in particular. This exercise will be useful to assess the sufficiency and efficiency of the domestic instrumentalities towards the attainment of the right to access the Internet. At the same time, it will also inform the present study about the crucial legal and practical difficulties that may be encountered whilst mandating accessibility to private players. Prior to such survey, it may be worthwhile to understand how different models of disability have been informing laws and policy formulation at different points of time. Hence, the chapter begins by briefly narrating how various models of disability have been influencing State responses in terms of policy and laws for disabilities. In doing so we understand the evolution of disability laws and identify different models emerging from different jurisdictions and the approaches these adopt to seek compliance.

Theoretical Discourse Shaping Legal Recourse

Early disability discrimination law and policy was largely guided by the 'medical model' which believed that persons with impairment needed to be 'fixed' to enable them to participate fully in society.[1] Such perception encouraged regulators to devote resources to preventive, curative, and rehabilitative efforts to help persons with disabilities cope with the impairment or overcome the effects of impairments. Thus, informed by the medical model governments adopted a welfarist approach, bestowing benefits or assistance as charitable responses of 'doing special things'. Disability was commonly addressed through social security and welfare legislations, health and charity programmes. Such laws compromised the autonomy and independence of persons with disabilities[2] and simultaneously segregated persons with disabilities from the mainstream society by offering 'special' schools, institutionalized care, and employment quotas, rehabilitation.

To reverse this exclusion, the 'social model' proposed to shift the focus from the lacunae of individuals to the inadequacies of society. Accordingly, it was pointed out that the dysfunctionality of persons with disabilities was not so much on account of impairment as on account of barriers created by society and thus, efforts began to open up employment, education, goods and services for persons

[1] Anita Silvers, 'Formal Justice', in *Disability, Difference, Discrimination: Perspectives on Justice in Bioethics and Public Policy* 13, p. 85 (Anita Silvers et al. eds, 1998).

[2] See Chapter 1 for elaborate discussion.

with disabilities.[3] This scholarship and political activism around the social model resulted in the minority group model. The minority right model took root in the political movement surrounding the civil rights era in the United States in the 1960s and 1970s.[4] This model strategically sought to guarantee rights, including a right to non-discrimination. It demanded inclusion in societal structures and practices as a matter of right rather than as charity.[5] Rooted in the civil rights movement, the Americans with Disabilities Act (ADA) has been described as the pioneering model for disability discrimination legislation around the globe. In particular, the 1990s was a banner decade for disability law—more than forty nations enacted disability discrimination laws during this period.[6]

[3] The social movement was strong in the United Kingdom. It has been examined that several countries approach disability discrimination through traditional social welfare laws. For instance, disability laws in India, China, Finland, Korea, and Spain are found to have more traditional provisions on the prevention of disability and rehabilitation.

[4] The United States was exceptionally early in adopting the Rehabilitation Act of 1973 as one of its first pieces of anti-discrimination legislation for disabled persons. Yet, the United States public policy towards persons with disabilities has witnessed monumental changes over all these years. The so called 'Ugly Laws' criminalized disability. For a comprehensive discussion see, Susan Schweik, The Ugly Laws: Disability in Public (2009).

[5] Consequent to the political agitation by disability groups in the United States led to the passing of Rehabilitation Act 1973 and eventually the ADA.

[6] The United States and Canada were the first countries to adopt anti-discrimination laws and other human rights legislation for person with disabilities, with more comprehensive laws in the 1990s. See, Americans with Disabilities Act of 1990; Canadian Charter of Rights and Freedoms 1982, and Human Rights Act 1985; Disability Discrimination Act 1992 (Australia); Law of the People's Republic of China on the Protection of Disabled Persons 1990; Law on Equal Opportunities for Persons with Disabilities 1996 Costa Rica; Code Penal Article 225, 416-14 (Fr.); Disability Discrimination Ordinance, Cap. 487 (1995) H.K.; Act XXVI on Provisions of the Rights of person Living with Disability and their Equality of Opportunity (1998) (Hung.); The Person with Disabilities (Equal Opportunities, Protection of Rights and Full participation) Act 1995 India; Employment Equality Act of 1998, Equal Status Bill of 1999 Ir.; Equal Rights for People with Disabilities Law 1998 Isr.;

The paradigm shift from the medical to the social model of disability at domestic levels has now been re-classified as a human rights issue under international law. Going further than the social model, the CRPD promotes a new human rights paradigm for disability, thereby advocating a more holistic public policy agenda.[7] The human rights paradigm for disability provides that states are required to remove environmental barriers, as well as proactively enable persons with disabilities to exercise their rights.[8] The extent to which the CRPD mandate can be realized will largely depend on the translation of these rights and mandates into domestic laws and policies. While most of the states have already put in place disability inclusive interventions, the framework, scope, and application of these existing interventions differs from country to country. These interventions range from legislations to policies, directives, ordinances, guidelines and Codes.

The extent to which domestic frameworks and instrumentalities will be effective in ensuring the right to access the Internet for persons with disabilities will depend upon the current language of the legislations. It is, therefore, pertinent to make an inquiry into the existing frameworks and approaches deployed to address disability discrimination in general and the right to access the Internet in particular.

Act Related to Employment Promotion of the Handicapped 1990 S. Korea; Human Rights Act of 1993 N.Z.; Magna Carta for Disabled Persons 1991 Phil.; disability Discrimination Act 1995 (Now replaced with the Equality Act 2010); S.AFR. CONST. s. 9 1996; Protection of the Rights of Persons with Disabilities Act 1996 Sri Lanka; Law on the Prohibition of Discrimination Against Person with Disabilities in Employment 1999 Swed.; Disabled Persons Act of 1992 (Zimb.).

[7] See Paul Harpur, 'Ensuring Equality in Education: How Australian Laws are Leaving Students with Print Disabilities Behind', 15 *Media and Arts Law Review* 1, 70 (2010) (analyzing substantial problems with the operation of indirect discrimination provisions in ensuring students with print disabilities obtain their textbooks in a timely manner).

[8] Michael Ashley Stein and Penelope J.S. Stein, *Beyond Disability Civil Rights*, 58 Hastings L.J. 1203 (2007) (arguing that to be effective, both domestic and international disability rights must adopt a disability human rights paradigm).

Mandating Compliance through Anti-Discrimination Legislations

States have been placing larger relevance on the command-control form of regulation to eliminate disability related discrimination in the form of anti-discrimination laws. It is therefore, crucial to assess whether the traditional anti-discrimination law posits commands that refer to the right to access the Internet and whether these have sufficient controls to ensure compliance from corporations. Paul Harpur rightly observes that under the classic command and control regulatory model, the content of the command is critical.[9] The command will alter conduct and achieve the objective of the intervention. This command can be phrased either as rules or standards, and direction must target people who can influence the desired result, require those parties to take the necessary steps to achieve the desired outcome, while avoiding unintended consequences. In this respect, it is observed that while some anti-discrimination laws for persons with disabilities are part of a law that seeks equality for multiple groups, others focus on disability exclusively.[10] Whereas some legislations have implications for private players, others exclude private entities from its application.[11]

---

[9] Harpur, 'From Universal Exclusion to Universal Equality: Regulating Ableism in a Digital Age', *Northern Kentucky Law Review* 40(3) 529 (2013).

[10] The group law approach protects other minorities or groups such as women, homosexuals, children, the elderly, linguistic, or religious minorities that historically have been the targets of discriminatory practices. For instance, the U.K.'s Equality Act 2010.

[11] Italy has principle accessibility legislation in the form of Law 4/2004, January 9th 2004—'Provisions to support the access of the disabled to information technologies' which recognizes the accessibility rights of persons with disabilities. Article 3 stipulates that the said law is applicable to the public administrators, private firms which are licensees of public service, to regional municipal companies. Law n. 4, January 9, 2004' available at pubbliAccesso.gov.it, available at http://www.pubbliaccesso.it/normative/law_20040109_n4.htm (last visited 14 February 2015). For instance, India has such jurisprudence where private corporations are held to be not covered under Disability law. In May 2010, the Supreme Court held that the PWD Act, 1995 does not apply to any private corporation and they are not

Since most anti-discrimination legislations pre-date the information age, there are no obvious provisions regarding rights to access the Internet. While some jurisdictions attempt to read the right to access the Internet within their existing anti-discrimination laws, others are enacting new laws that directly address the accessibility of information and technology and web accessibility online.[12] In keeping with the purpose and object of inquiry of the present study, I identify three different approaches adopted by jurisdictions to address disability discrimination and examine its effectiveness to ensure compliance for the right to access the Internet.

Sanctions Based Approach

Jurisdictions such as France,[13] Finland,[14] Spain,[15] and Luxembourg[16] prohibit discrimination against persons with disabilities through criminal law. Thus, the French Criminal Code by virtue of Article 225-1 to Article 225-4 prohibits distinction made between natural persons on grounds that *inter alia* include disability; where such a distinction entails inferior treatment. What treatment

---

obliged to provide the benefits under the Act. See for details Dalco Engineering Private Ltd. v. Shree Satish Prabhakar Padhye, AIR 2010 SC 1576.

[12] For instance Spain adopted the Law of Equal Opportunities, Non-Discrimination and Universal Access for Persons with Disabilities in 2003. The 2003 Act has been unified along with two other disability laws in the General Law on the Rights of Persons with Disabilities. Similarly, the Anti-Discrimination and Accessibility Act 2008 of Norway, makes explicit references to actively promoting universal design in information and technology which extends to private undertakings that offers goods or services to general public. The AAD includes a universal design obligation, which is a minimum requirement and has been introduced as a legal standard. The breach of the obligation to universal design amounts to discrimination. For details see http://zeroproject.org/policy-type/2014/ (last visited 5 March 2015).

[13] Art. 225 Penal Code, Loi 90-602 de 12 julliet 1990.

[14] Penal Code 1995, chapter 11(9) and chapter 47(3).

[15] Art. 314 Criminal Code (Organic Law 10/1995, 23 November).

[16] Ss 454-457 Criminal Code as modified in 1997.

constitutes inferior treatment is defined by Article 225-2 which includes refusing to supply an object or a service.[17] Similarly, by virtue of Chapter 11, section 11 of the Finland's Criminal Code,[18] it is a punishable offense when a person, in the course of trade, profession, service of the general public or in an arrangement of public amusement or meeting, places someone in a clearly unequal or otherwise essentially inferior position, without good reason, owing to grounds which inter alia includes disability. In another instance, Article IX of the Austrian Einführungsgesetzzu den Verwaltungsverfahrensgesetzen (EGVG) makes it an offense to

[17] Discrimination defined by article 225-1, committed against a natural or legal person, is punished by three years' imprisonment and a fine of €45,000 where it consists: of the refusal to supply goods or services; of obstructing the normal exercise of any given economic activity; of the refusal to hire, to sanction or to dismiss a person; of subjecting the supply of goods or services to a condition based on one of the factors referred to under article 225-1; of subjecting an offer of employment, an application for a course or a training period to a condition based on one of the factors referred to under article 225-1; of refusing to accept a person onto one of the courses referred to under 2° of Article L.412-8 of the Social Security Code. Where the discriminatory refusal referred to under 1° is committed in a public place or in order to bar the access to this place, the penalties are increased to five years' imprisonment and to a fine of €75,000.

[18] Section 11–Discrimination (885/2009). A person who in his or her trade or profession, service of the general public, exercise of official authority or other public function or in the arrangement of a public amusement or meeting, without a justified reason

1. refuses someone service in accordance with the generally applicable conditions;
2. refuses someone entry to the amusement or meeting or ejects him or her; or
3. places someone in a clearly unequal or otherwise essentially inferior position

owing to his or her race, national or ethnic origin, skin colour, language, sex, age, family ties, sexual preference, inheritance, disability or state of health, or religion, political orientation, political or industrial activity or another comparable circumstance shall be sentenced, unless the act is punishable as work discrimination or extortionate work discrimination, for discrimination to a fine or to imprisonment for at most six months.

hinder a person's access to public places, buildings or services on account of disability or a comparable factor.[19]

These legislations adopt a deterrence approach to discrimination and seek to impose strict sanctions on discrimination. However, any alleged disability discrimination will constitute a criminal offense only when *mens rea is* established. The criminal law model of prohibiting discrimination is problematic as it sets higher threshold for holding the alleged discriminator accountable. Also, the negative right tone of such laws cannot be invoked to impose positive duties on relevant parties.

Reactionary Approach

The State instrumentalities, one assumes, would have the power to investigate and mandate any aspect of the life of the community where inequality and discrimination prevails or is likely to prevail. Consequently, anti-discrimination laws in general command very high confidence amongst discriminated groups to end years of discriminatory practices and derogatory treatment. Advocates of disability rights movement also have pinned hopes on the potential of anti-discrimination to alleviate discriminatory and exclusionary practices and ensure their rights and participation in society. It is, therefore, pertinent to assess the effectiveness of these anti-discriminatory laws in ensuring the right to access the Internet.

In this regard, the approach of anti-discrimination laws in the US needs to be examined in greater detail for multiple reasons. One, the ADA has the longest history and experience of disability discrimination in general and its interface with the Internet in particular. Since the US is considered to be the birth place of the Internet, it can be expected that the American legal system may have already arrived at solutions to issues related to the same. Two, the ADA is a pioneering anti-discrimination legislation which has

---

[19] Most of these attract a fine or imprisonment for specified period in case of violation.

been replicated by several other jurisdictions. Thus, not only the positive elements of the ADA but also its limitations are possibly transplanted to other jurisdictions. Three, while the US is a signatory to CRPD, other jurisdictions that have disability laws modelled upon ADA may have ratified CRPD. These jurisdictions need to be aware of the normative tension between ADA and CRPD on virtual accessibility.

It was in due acknowledgment of the fact that 'historically, society has tended to isolate and segregate'[20] Americans with disabilities and this isolation is a form of discrimination[21] with no legal recourse to redress such discrimination[,][22] that there was a felt need to enact the Americans with Disabilities Act of 1990. Recognising that Americans with disabilities continue to 'occupy an inferior status in our society, and are severely disadvantaged socially, vocationally, economically, and educationally';[23] the Americans with Disabilities Act of 1990 aimed 'to provide a clear and comprehensive national mandate for the elimination of discrimination against individuals with disabilities'.[24]

The relevant subsection of the ADA, Title III, states 'no individual shall be discriminated against on the basis of disability in the full and equal enjoyment of the services, privileges, advantages, or accommodations of any place of public accommodation.'[25] Under the existing scheme of the ADA[26] discrimination against persons with disabilities is prohibited in places of public

---

[20] 42 U.S.C. at § 12101(a)(1)-(2).

[21] 42 U.S.C. at § 12101(a)(2).

[22] 42 U.S.C. at § 12101(a)(4).

[23] 42 U.S.C. at § 12101(a)(6).

[24] 42 U.S.C. at § 12101(b)(1) (2000).

[25] 42 U.S.C. at § 12182(a) (2000).

[26] The ADA is divided into five titles. Title I prohibits discrimination in the employment context; Title II pertains to discrimination by public entities; Title III covers various types and services of private entities engaged in commerce (in 'places of public accommodation' and 'commercial facilities'); Title IV mandates the availability of telecommunications devices and relay services for persons with hearing impairments; and Title V contains miscellaneous provisions to assist in interpreting and enforcing Titles I-IV.

accommodation.[27] There exist enumerated lists of private entities which are deemed to be 'public accommodation'. This list comprises hotels, restaurants, theatres, stores, parks, museums, shelters, and gymnasiums,[28] and includes such 'other places of public gathering' and 'other places of recreation'.[29] In claim alleging discrimination

[27] 42 U.S.C. § 12182(a) (2006) 'No individual shall be discriminated against on the basis of disability in the full and equal enjoyment of the goods, services, facilities, privileges, advantages, or accommodations of any place of public accommodation by any person who owns, leases (or leases to), or operates a place of public accommodation.'

[28] The following private entities are considered public accommodations for purposes of this subchapter, if the operations of such entities affect commerce—

1. an inn, hotel, motel, or other place of lodging, except for an establishment located within a building that contains not more than five rooms for rent or hire and that is actually occupied by the proprietor of such establishment as the residence of such proprietor;
2. a restaurant, bar, or other establishment serving food or drink;
3. a motion picture house, theater, concert hall, stadium, or other place of exhibition or entertainment;
4. an auditorium, convention center, lecture hall, or other place of public gathering;
5. a bakery, grocery store, clothing store, hardware store, shopping center, or other sales or rental establishment;
6. a laundromat, dry-cleaner, bank, barber shop, beauty shop, travel service, shoe repair service, funeral parlor, gas station, office of an accountant or lawyer, pharmacy, insurance office, professional office of a health care provider, hospital, or other service establishment;
7. a terminal, depot, or other station used for specified public transportation;
8. a museum, library, gallery, or other place of public display or collection;
9. a park, zoo, amusement park, or other place of recreation;
10. a nursery, elementary, secondary, undergraduate, or postgraduate private school, or other place of education;
11. a day care center, senior citizen center, homeless shelter, food bank, adoption agency, or other social service center establishment; and
12. a gymnasium, health spa, bowling alley, golf course, or other place of exercise or recreation.

[29] 42 U.S.C, § 12181(7) (2006).

under Title III, a plaintiff must show that: (a) she is disabled within the meaning of the ADA; (b) the defendant is a private entity that owns, leases, or operates a place of public accommodation; and (c) the plaintiff was denied public accommodations by the defendant because of her disability.[30]

Since the ADA predates the Information Age, 'places of public accommodation' make no explicit reference to the Internet. With the proliferation of the Internet, there have been growing demands from persons with disabilities to extend the obligations of non-discrimination under Title III to commercial websites run by private businesses. American jurisprudence has been struggling for quite a while now with the issue on such extended application of Title III of ADA to the Internet. In order to bring business websites under the accessibility mandate under ADA, the claimant must first establish that the Internet is a place of public accommodation under Title III.[31] 'The principal point of contention is whether the term "place of public accommodation" is narrowly limited to physical places or whether it encompasses something more.'[32] This contention primarily arose in the context of disputes involving insurance policies and later on extended to websites.

In *Carparts Distribution Center v. Automotive Wholesaler's Association*,[33] the plaintiff who was the sole shareholder, president, and employee of Carparts, and was diagnosed with HIV, sued Auto Wholesaler's Association alleging that the insurance plan of the defendant that limited the benefits for AIDS-related illnesses to $25,000 which was otherwise available to the extent of $1 million for eligible plan member was discriminatory. While determining issue, whether the policy constituted discrimination by a place of

[30] *Ariz. ex rel. Goddard v. Harkins Amusement Enters.*, 603 F.3d 666, p. 670 (9th Cir. 2010)

[31] Jeffrey S. Ranen, 'Was Blind But Now I See: The Argument for ADA Applicability to the Internet', 22 B Boston College Third World (2002): 389, 390.

[32] Matthew A. Stowe, *Interpreting 'Place of Public Accommodation' Under Title III of the ADA: A Technical Determination with Potentially Broad Civil Rights Applications*, 50 DUKE L.J. 297, p. 298 (2000).

[33] 37 F.3d 12 (1st Cir. 1994).

public accommodation, the First Circuit Court examined the plain meaning of the language of the ADA and held that '[t]he plain meaning of the terms do not require "public accommodations" to have physical structures for persons to enter.'[34] Interpreting the legislative intent the Court held that by enlisting 'travel service' under 'public accommodations', the legislature contemplated the inclusion of even such service providers which did not require a person to physically enter an actual physical structure. Elaborating on this point, the Court observed that one could easily imagine the existence of other service establishments conducting business by mail and phone. It would be irrational to conclude that persons who enter an office to purchase services were protected by the ADA, but persons who purchased the same services over the telephone or by mail are not. Congress could not have intended such an absurd result.[35] Agreeing with the First Circuit's position, the Second Circuit in *Pallozzi v. Allstate Life Insurance Co.*,[36] reasoned that by guaranteeing an equal access to a public accommodation's goods and services, Congress could not have intended to limit the statute to access to physical structures.[37] The Seventh Circuit Court in *Doe v. Mutual of Omaha Insurance Company*,[38] referred to *Carparts* decision to hold that a public accommodation did not have to be a physical structure. The majority opinion held that the owner or operator of a store, website, or other facility (whether in physical space or in electronic space) that is open to the public cannot exclude disabled persons from entering the facility and, once in, from using the facility in the same way that the nondisabled do.[39]

---

[34] 37 F.3d 12 (1st Cir. 1994) at p. 19.

[35] 37 F.3d 12 (1st Cir. 1994) at p. 19.

[36] 198 F.3d 28 (2d Cir. 2000).

[37] Several cases have since adopted the First Circuit's reasoning in Carparts to hold that public accommodations need not necessarily be limited to physical structures. *Shultz v. Hemet Youth Pony League, Inc., 943 F. Supp. 1222 (C.D. Cal. 1996) Marques v. Harvard Pilgrim Healthcare of New England, Inc., 883 A.2d 742 (R.I. 2005).*

[38] 179 F.3d 557 (7th Cir. 1999).

[39] 179 F.3d 557, at p. 559. However it was held that section 302(a) of the Americans with Disabilities Act does not regulate the content of the products or services sold in places of public accommodation and does not require a

A similar conclusion was reached two years later in *Morgan v. Joint Admin. Bd., Ret. Plan of the Pillsbury Co.*,[40] in which it was held that under Title III, 'the site of the sale is irrelevant to Congress's goal of granting the disabled equal access to sellers of goods and services. What matters is that the good or service be offered to the public.'[41]

However, the Sixth Circuit Court while dealing with similar situation as *Carparts* in *Parker v. Metropolitan Life Insurance Co.*,[42] took a diametrically opposite view. Expressly rejecting the First Circuit's holding in *Carparts*, the Sixth Circuit Court went on to hold that public accommodations are limited to actual physical structures from which one can procure products or services. The plaintiff in this matter sued the employer company and its insurer company for discrimination when the insurance benefit policy provided life time coverage for physical disability but limited the same to twenty four months for those with mental disability. Rejecting the plaintiff's claim, the Court held that such a plan is 'not a good offered by a place of public accommodation.' The Court further found that public accommodation is limited to physical places, and as such 'Title III does not govern the content of a long-term disability policy offered by an employer.'[43] The dissenting judgment of Chief Judge Martin, however, cautioned that by limiting Title III to physical places 'the same technological advances that have offered disabled individuals unprecedented freedom may now operate to deprive them of rights that Title III would otherwise guarantee.'[44]

---

seller to alter his product to make it equally valuable to the disabled and to the nondisabled, even if the product is insurance. The majority found this conclusion to be consistent with *Vaughn v. Sullivan* 83 F.3d 907, pp. 912–13 (7th Cir. 1996); *Rogers v. Department of Health & Environmental Contro* 174 F.3d 431 (4th Cir. 1999); *Parker v. Metropolitan Life Ins. Co.*, 121 F.3d 1006, pp. 1010–14 (6th Cir. 1997) (en banc); *Lenox v. Healthwise of Kentucky, Ltd.*, supra; *Ford v. Schering-Plough Corp.*, 145 F.3d 601, pp. 612–14 (3d Cir. 1998) Such a stance is found to be problematic and discussed later in this chapter.

[40] 268 F.3d 456 (7th Cir.2001).
[41] 268 F.3d 456, at p. 459.
[42] 121 F.3d 1006 (6th Cir. 1997).
[43] 121 F.3d 1006, at pp. 1010, 1012.
[44] 121 F.3d 1006, at p. 1020.

The Ninth Circuit, in *Weyer v. Twentieth Century Fox Film Corp.*[45] resonated the Sixth Circuit Court's decision in *Parker*. In this case, the employee had sued its employer Twentieth Century Fox and insurance provider for violating the ADA by providing a policy that discriminated against individuals with mental disabilities over those with physical disabilities. The Court, however, held that public accommodations only applied to physical places.[46]

Thus, the American circuit courts were clearly divided in their views about the scope and extent of places of public accommodation. While the First, Second, and Seventh Circuit Courts have interpreted the term 'public accommodation' to extend beyond physical places; the Third, Sixth, and the Ninth Circuit Court opined that places of public accommodation were limited to public places and required physical structures. This circuit split had a spillover effect in the matters pertaining to websites and whether these could be included within the expression 'places of public accommodation'.

In *Access Now, Inc. v. Southwest Airlines Co.*,[47] the Eleventh Circuit Court adopted a narrow view to conclude that websites did not exist in any particular geographical location and hence, could not be 'places of public accommodation'. The plaintiffs, persons with visual impairment, contended that Southwest's inaccessible website violated the ADA since it excluded them from its digital ticket counters. Rejecting this claim, the Court held that 'the plain and unambiguous language of the statute and relevant regulations did not include websites among the [twelve specifically enumerated categories defining] "places of public accommodation"'.[48] Since websites were not expressly mentioned in the ADA or regulations, for a website to be a 'place of public accommodation', it must be connected to a 'physical, concrete structure'.[49] Accordingly, purely nonphysical establishments could not be places of public accommodation.[50]

[45] 198 F.3d 1104 (9th Cir. 2000).
[46] 198 F.3d 1104, at pp. 1114–15.
[47] 227 F. Supp. 2d 1312, p. 1317 (S.D. Fla.2002).
[48] 227 F. Supp. 2d 1312, at p. 1318.
[49] 227 F. Supp. 2d 1312, at p. 1318.
[50] 227 F. Supp. 2d 1312, at p. 1319.

Such absolute denial to read virtual places as 'place of accommodation' somewhat changed when the Northern District Court of California in *National Federation of the Blind v. Target Corp.*[51] applied nexus test to hold that the websites may be 'places of public accommodation' when there is a suitable nexus between the website and a physical store. Here, the plaintiffs brought a class action on behalf of all visually impaired Americans alleging unequal access to Target.com and that it denies the blind the full enjoyment of the goods and services offered at Target stores, which are places of public accommodation. Rejecting Target's arguments that the laws did not apply to its website because the website was not a physical place of public accommodation, the Court held in favour of the plaintiffs. The operative part of the judgment, however, in keeping with its nexus test, held that websites were *only* subject to the ADA to the extent that they offered 'goods, services, facilities, privileges, advantages, or accommodations of' a place of public accommodation, expressly finding that the websites were never, in their own right, places of 'public accommodation'. Thus, the entire website need not be completely accessible to disabled persons.[52]

[51] 452 F. Supp. 2d 946, pp. 952–3 (N.D. Cal. 2006).

[52] In *Rendon v. Valleycrest Productions, Ltd.*, 294 F.3d 1279, 1284 (11th Cir. 2002), a group of hearing and mobility impaired plaintiffs brought suit against Valleycrest Productions Limited and American Broadcasting Company (ABC). The *Rendon* plaintiffs, who were either hearing impaired or suffered from a condition that limited their finger mobility, claimed the defendants' telephone selection process for 'Who Wants to be a Millionaire' ('Millionaire') violated Title III because it tended to screen out disabled people Specifically, the selection process required potential contestants to call a toll-free telephone number and use a telephone keypad to answer a series of pre-recorded questions The court of appeals rejected the defendants' argument, 61 holding that Title III also applies to 'intangible barriers', which include discriminatory procedures that restrict a disabled person's 'ability to enjoy the defendant entity's *goods, services and privileges*'. Pointing to decisions from other circuits, the Eleventh Circuit held that the telephone selection process used by the defendants was an intangible barrier depriving the plaintiffs of the 'opportunity to compete for the privilege of being a contestant on Millionaire', which occurred at a place of public accommodation. The telephone screening process was an intangible barrier to a privilege offered by a place of public accommodation; thus, the process was subject to Title III.

The nexus test's insistence on the existence of commercial entity both in the physical and the virtual world in order to be covered within the ambit of the ADA produced somewhat anomalous results. For all practical purposes, the nexus test required corporations, say for instance, WalMart to make their websites accessible so that persons with disabilities had the freedom to purchase goods from WalMart's offline and online store. On the other hand it denied persons with disabilities opportunity to purchase products from purely web-based corporations, say, for example Amazon.com. or e-Bay.

The District court of North California has held that place of public accommodation must be a physical place. In *Cullen v. Netflix, Inc*[53] the plaintiff and other similarly situated individuals who were hearing impaired brought suit against Netflix claiming that they were unable to avail themselves of the Netflix streaming service and hence were denied equal access. Applying *Weyer*, the Court held that a place of public accommodation must be a physical place. The Court held that since Netflix was a website and not a physical entity and this website had no sufficient nexus to a physical structure, it was not a place of public accommodation. In *Young v. Facebook*[54] the District Court was approached by the plaintiff suffering from bipolar disorder alleging unlawful discrimination by Facebook. The plaintiff had opened a personal account with Facebook and subsequently created additional Facebook pages. However her account was deactivated with reasons assigned that her practices were identified as causing potential harassment to other users. It was reactivated for a temporary time with warnings issued to her. Later her account was permanently deactivated. The plaintiff sued Facebook for having unlawfully discriminated against her by terminating her account and addressing her concerns with 'automated responses' instead of a human customer service system that assists individuals with mental disabilities. Dismissing Young's complaint, the Court held that despite its frequent use of terms such as 'posts' and 'walls', Facebook operates only in cyberspace, and is thus, not a 'place of public accommodation' as construed by the

[53] 880 F. Supp. 2d 1017 (N.D. Cal. 2012).
[54] 790 F. Supp. 2d 1110 (N.D. Cal. 2011).

Ninth Circuit. While Facebook's physical headquarters obviously is a physical space, it is not a place where the online services to which Young claims she was denied access are offered to the public.

The District Court of Montana in *Ouellette v. Viacom*[55] dealt in the claims of the plaintiff who brought an action against Google, YouTube, and Myspace for having improperly identified videos uploaded by him as infringing copyright and removing his videos from the internet, thereby have violated his rights under the ADA. It was alleged that the defendants discriminated against him based on his reading disability, and deprived him of access to their internet services and their 'online theater'—a 'place of public accommodation' governed by the ADA. Rejecting this contention, the Court held that a website does not constitute a physical 'place of public accommodation' as required for a cognizable ADA claim. In the absence of a nexus between a website and a physical place of public accommodation, the relief claimed by plaintiff could not be granted.

Progressively, favourable views culminated in the Massachusetts case of *National Association of the Deaf v. Netflix, Inc.*,[56] where the Court radically held that websites were 'places of public accommodations'. In this matter, organizations representing persons with hearing impairment brought an action against Netflix, a provider of streaming videos on the Internet, for violating the ADA. It was alleged that the failure to caption Netflix's Watch Instantly service for a majority of its program titles denied plaintiffs the equal opportunity to enjoy the online service. Resorting to the nexus theory, Netflix filed a motion to dismiss, based on the claim that Netflix was not a place of public accommodation as defined by the ADA. The court rejected this argument to hold that Netflix's website was a place of public accommodation.

In a dynamic move, the Court affirmatively held that a website qualified as a place of public accommodation within the meanings of 'place of exhibition and entertainment', 'place of recreation', 'sales

[55] CV 10-133-M-DWM-JCL, 2011 WL 1882780 (D. Mont. 31 March 2011), report and recommendation adopted, No. CV 10-133-M-DWM-JCL, 2011 WL 1883190 (D. Mont. 17 May 2011).

[56] 869 F. Supp. 2d 196, p. 202 (D. Mass 2012).

or rental establishment', and 'service establishment'. Extending the concept of public accommodation, the Court held that the same need not be restricted to the actual physical structures and that the ADA can be applied to nonphysical locations.[57]

On the one hand, these contradictory court interpretations render extension of the existing provisions of the ADA to websites questionable. On the other hand, judicial decisions have doubted application of the ADA to the contents of the goods and services offered by places of public accommodation, thereby deepening the problem. It may be recollected that writing for the majority, Judge Posner in *Doe* categorically held that the ADA does not regulate the content of the products or services sold in places of public accommodation and does not require a seller to alter his product to make it equally valuable to the disabled and to the nondisabled, even if the product is insurance.[58] Similarly, the Sixth Circuit Court in *Parker* maintained that the ADA regulates only the availability of goods and services offered by a public accommodation, and not the contents of those goods and services.[59] Similarly, the respondent in *State of Arizona v. Harkins Amusement*,[60] contended that Title III did not require a commercial entity to modify the substantive content of its services and goods by providing captions and descriptive narration for hearing impaired persons.[61] The decision in *Stern v. Sony*[62] was on similar lines. The plaintiff, a person with visual impairment and

[57] A little more than one year after the Netflix litigation began, the parties settled their dispute before a ruling by the First Circuit. The terms provided for the provision of closed captions on 100 per cent of Netflix's on-demand streaming programming within two years of the agreement. *NAD v. Netflix*, Consent Decree (12 October 2012); available at: http://dredf.org/captioning/netflix-consent-decree-10-10-12.pdf (last visited 25 September 2014).

[58] *Doe*, 179 F.3d, p. 560.

[59] *Doe*, 179 F.3d, p. 1012.

[60] 603 F.3d, pp. 671–2.

[61] The Ninth Circuit Court, however, disagreed with such contention, finding that such accommodations are required under title III to prevent disability discrimination. The matter was remanded to the trial court to determine, in the light of the facts, whether the plaintiffs were entitled to closed captioning and descriptive narration subject to title III's defences.

[62] 459 Fed.Appx. 609 (9th Cir. 2011).

cognitive disability, alleged that Sony's online design of video games did not offer accommodations to users with conditions similar to his as was offered by other game manufacturers. Consequently, he was denied the full and equal enjoyment of the company's services as a user with disabilities. Deciding for Sony, the Ninth Circuit affirmed the lower court's dismissal of the application of Title III based on the finding that, as a manufacturer of gaming products, Sony was not covered by Title III.

In *Ford v. Schering-Plough Corp.*,[63] the Third Circuit followed the Sixth Circuit and held that the ADA's accessibility requirements do not extend to the products offered by companies whose physical offices are covered.[64] The Court found that the plain meaning of Title III is that 'public accommodation' is limited to places.[65] The court reasoned that this interpretation is consistent with the examples of 'public accommodations' listed in the ADA, which refer to physical places.[66] Thus, the court stated, '[t]he fact that an insurance office is a public accommodation does not mean that the insurance policies offered at that location are covered by Title III.'[67]

Such arguments and decisions seriously limit the scope and nature of accessibility envisaged. Thus, even as the ADA Title III requires access to a place of public accommodation, but it does not require that such access should be accompanied with a change in the content of goods or services provided at the place of public accommodation.[68] The purpose of the ADA's public accommodations requirements is to ensure accessibility to the goods offered by a public accommodation, not to alter the nature or mix of goods that the public accommodation has typically provided. In other words, a bookstore, for example, must make its facilities and sales operations accessible to individuals with disabilities, but is not

---

[63] 145 F.3d 601 (3d Cir. 1998).

[64] 145 F.3d 601, pp. 612–13.

[65] 145 F.3d 601, p. 612.

[66] 145 F.3d 601 and n.3 (citing 42 U.S.C. § 12181(7) (1994)).

[67] 145 F.3d 601 and n.3 (citing 42 U.S.C. § 12181(7)).

[68] See Kelly E. Konkright, 'An Analysis of the Applicability of Title III of the Americans with Disabilities Act to Private Internet Access Providers', 37 *Idaho Law Review* 713, n. 170 (2001): 736.

required to stock Brailled or large print books. Similarly, a video store must make its facilities and rental operations accessible, but is not required to stock closed-captioned video tapes.[69]

However, access to content is inherently entwined with access to websites. Without accessible content, access to the website is rendered meaningless. Judge Evans in his dissenting judgment in *Doe* astutely observed that it amounts to enterprises letting disabled customers in the door, but then refusing to sell them anything but inferior [products and services].[70] According to him the point of inquiry should not be whether Title III regulated a product's substantive design. Rather, it depends on whether an entity was discriminating against persons with disabilities in the opportunity to enjoy the substance of the goods and services. However, experience informs us that commercial entities are often unwilling to accommodate accessibility concerns on the grounds that introducing such alterations will destroy the fundamental nature of their product or service.[71] To the extent Title III requires

[69] Ford v. Schering-Plough Corp. 145 F.3d, p. 613(3d Cir. 1998) (quoting 28 C.F.R. pt. 36, app. B, p. 640 (1997)).

[70] *Doe*, 179 F.3D, p. 564.

[71] See for instance, *Colorado Cross-Disability Coalition v. Abercrombie & Fitch Co, and J.M. Hollister* 765 F.3d 1205 (10th Cir. Court 2014). The plaintiff in this matter, Colorado Cross-Disability Coalition, a disability advocacy organization in Colorado and four of its members filed complaint against J.M. Hollister LLC, operating Hollister clothing stores throughout the US. Hollister is a wholly owned subsidiary of Abercrombie and Fitch Co. The complaint alleged that many Hollister Stores included the stepped 'porch-like structure' that served as the stores' center entrance created barriers for persons with disabilities. It was therefore alleged that such physical design of Hollister's store entrances was unnecessarily relegating wheelchair users to separate and objectively different entrances than those available for other people and violated Title III of the ADA. Ruling in favor of the plaintiffs, the District Court of Colorado held that Hollister unnecessarily created a design for their brand that exclude[d] people [with disabilities] from full enjoyment of the *aesthetic* for that brand. According to the District Court by excluding customers who use wheelchairs from the porch and requiring them to use the abandoned, inferior side entrances, Abercrombie effectively relegates persons with disabilities to the status of second-class citizens. However, the decision of

that 'websites must simplify their textual design, use less complex fonts[,] and reduce unnecessary verbiage, the same would not modify the fundamental purpose of the web page.'[72] However, if Title III required business websites to change the images on their sites, it might undermine the essential purposes of the websites.[73]

This is typically an issue with several ecommerce websites. It is argued that the skill of providing clear and accurate descriptions of art work is different from the skill of simplifying provocative text. By requiring websites to provide descriptions of art work, Title III arguably converts an art website into an art commentary website.[74] While disability advocates have maintained that the ADA should apply to e-Commerce, often private enterprises are adversial to such demands.[75] Therefore, the ADA requires maintaining delicate

---

the District Court was reversed by the Tenth Circuit Court by 2:1 majority. The majority ruled that it was erroneous to impose liability on the design of Hollister Stores based on 'overarching aims' of the ADA. The majority concluded that the porches were properly evaluated under applicable design standards regulations. Abercrombie does not 'use' the porch at all and under the existing regulations, the porch was not a space that had to be accessible, and the porch did not have to be accessible as an entrance used by a majority of people.

Delivering the dissent judgment, Judge McHugh took a broad view of the mandate of the ADA. Judge McHugh held that the porch is a space that is required to be accessible and Abercrombie's use of the porch violates the ADA by denying customers who use wheelchairs the opportunity to participate and instead providing them a separate, unequal, non-integrated benefit. Unlike the majority judgment, the dissenting judgment read the Accessibility Design Standards and guidelines as requiring accessibility to all spaces in a newly constructed facility unless specifically exempted.

[72] See Colorado Cross-Disability Coalition v. Abercrombie & Fitch Co, and J.M. Hollister 765 F.3d 1205 (10th Cir. Court 2014).

[73] Adam M. Schloss, 'Web-Sight for Visually-Disabled People: Does Title III of the Americans With Disabilities Act Apply to Internet Websites?', 35 COLUM. J.L. & SOC. PROBS. 35, 51 (2001).

[74] Adam M. Schloss, 'Web-Sight for Visually-Disabled People'.

[75] The U.S. Chamber of Commerce opposes the disability advocacy position for broadening ADA Title III to include eCommerce as a place of 'Public Accommodation'. U.S. Chamber of Commerce, Brief of the Equal Employment Advisory Council, and The Chamber of Commerce of the

balance between requiring accommodation of disabilities and protecting the essence of a company's goods and services.[76]

The issue involves a conflict of the commercial interests of private players and rights and interests of persons with disabilities. This requires considering what modifications to web content are reasonable so as not to alter the fundamental nature of the product or service? What implications does it have on free speech and intellectual property rights of content owners or providers?

Such an opportunity afforded itself in *Greater Los Angeles Agency on Deafness v. Time Warner (CNN).*[77] In December 2010, the Greater Los Angeles Agency on Deafness, Inc. (GLAD) requested that Time Warner Inc., owner and operator of television service including CNN, to caption all of the videos on CNN news websites so that hearing-impaired visitors could have full access to the online videos. While such news programs were captioned at the time of broadcast; the CNN chose not to caption online video clips. GLAD contended that the service as delivered denied its members the full and equal enjoyment of CNN.com, as was provided to other users without hearing impairments.

In February 2011, CNN responded that it offered a number of text-based services and explained that CNN would be 'ready to provide whatever web access is ultimately required' by then-pending federal rule-making action regarding the captioning of online videos. Since no agreement could be reached over captioning, in June 2011 GLAD filed suit in California state court alleging violations of the California Unruh Civil Rights Act and the California Disabled Persons Act.[78] The plaintiffs sought damages, declaratory relief,

---

United States as Amici Curiae Supporting Defendant-Appellee and in Support of Affirmance (April 2003), available at http://www.eeac.org/briefs/accessnowvsouthwestairlines.pdf (last visited 26 May 2016).

[76] See Doe, 179 F.3d at p. 560 (The common sense of the statute is that the content of the goods or services offered by a place of public accommodation is not regulated.).

[77] 742 F.3d 414 (9th Cir. 2014).

[78] The Unruh Act provides that '[a]ll persons within the jurisdiction of [California] are free and equal, and no matter what their . . . disability [or] medical condition . . . are entitled to the full and equal accommodations,

and a preliminary and permanent injunction requiring CNN to take steps necessary to ensure that the benefits and advantages offered by CNN.com are fully and equally enjoyable to persons who are deaf or have hearing loss in California.

CNN raised complex issues in its defence extending to constitutional, federal, and state laws. CNN contended that mandating such captioning of excerpts compelled the company 'to speak in ways that it otherwise would not . . . altering the content and timing of CNN's video news reporting, at a substantial financial cost to CNN exclusively'. According to CNN, this was in breach of the company's constitutional right to speech, as broadly conceived by California's anti-SLAPP law.[79] Determination of anti-SLAPP motion involved two step inquiry-one, that the challenged action prevented CNN's from its valid exercise of free speech and two, that there was probability of GLAD's claim prevailing under Unruh Act and Disabled Person's Act (DPA). While deciding the matter, the Court acknowledged CNN's constitutionally protected right to publish online news videos, however CNN's anti-SLAPP motion was denied on the ground that the issue of CNN's speech merely

---

advantages, facilities, privileges, or services in all business establishments of every kind whatsoever.' Cal. Civ. Code § 51(b). The California Disabled Persons Act, Cal. Civ. Code §§ 54 et seq. provides that '[i]individuals with disabilities shall be entitled to full and equal access, as other members of the general public, to accommodations, advantages, facilities . . . and privileges of . . . places of public accommodation . . . and other places to which the general public is invited.'

[79] California's anti-SLAPP statute, enacted in 1992, Cal. Civ. Proc. Code § 425.16, provides for the 'early dismissal of unmeritorious claims filed to interfere with the valid exercise of the constitutional rights of freedom of speech and petition. Accordingly, CNN filed a motion to strike GLAD's complaint. The statute establishes a two-step analysis for determining whether a cause of action must be stricken under Section 425.16. Under the first step, the defendant is required to make 'a threshold showing that the challenged cause of action' arises from acts 'taken in furtherance of the [defendant]'s right of petition or free speech . . . in connection with a public issue'. At the second step, the burden shifts to the plaintiff to establish, with competent evidence, 'a probability that [he] will prevail on the claim[s]'.

'lurked in the background' of GLAD's action.[80] The Court was in agreement with GLAD that its action against CNN demanded nothing more than the neutral application of California's anti-discrimination laws to 'CNN's mechanical delivery process for its online news videos' without regard to the substantive content of those videos.

This decision was reversed by the Ninth Circuit Court on CNN's appeal. The Court held that even if GLAD does not request any changes to the substantive content of CNN's online news videos, GLAD, seeks to change the way CNN has chosen to report and deliver that news content by imposing a site-wide captioning requirement on CNN.com.[81] Having thus determined step one of anti-SLAPP motion in favor of CNN, the Court analysed step two. GLAD had argued that CNN's neutral policy regarding closed captioning was a 'deliberate indifference' adversely affecting persons with hearing impairment which amounted to intentional discrimination under the Unruh Act.[82] However, the Court held that such failure did not amount to intentional discrimination under the Unruh Act.[83]

---

[80] The Federal Communications Commission had also concluded that the law's captioning requirements did not significantly implicate the First Amendment based on a finding that captioning was a verbatim translation of online information that did not involve the furtherance of speech.

[81] According to the Court, GLAD's claims demanding close captioning by the CNN targets the way a content provider chooses to deliver, present, or publish news content on matters of public interest. This action is based on conduct in furtherance of free speech rights and must withstand scrutiny under California's anti-SLAPP statute.

[82] GLAD had claimed that CNN's failure to act upon knowledge that the protected rights of the deaf and hard of hearing would be violated in the absence of closed captioning of CNN.com videos amounts to deliberate indifference which in turn leads to discrimination.

[83] In addition to Anti-SLAPP motion, CNN had contended that a closed captioning requirement under the DPA imposed an unconstitutional prior restraint or an impermissible burden on its speech rights that amounts to an infringement its First Amendment Rights under U.S. Constitution. The Ninth Circuit Court held that the DPA captioning requirements would simply require CNN to express the same speech it already expresses to hearing visitors

Insofar as GLAD's claim under California's DPA was concerned, CNN contended that Californian Courts have applied the DPA only where there was a denial of physical access. GLAD contended that the question whether DPA applies to non-physical places remains an unresolved issue. In the absence of a precedent, the Ninth Circuit Court certified the matter to California's Supreme Court to determine whether the DPA's reference to 'places of public accommodation' include websites, which are non-physical places. Thus, the Ninth Circuit Court deferred the anti-SLAPP claims and application of the DPA pending California's Supreme Court Decision.

With progressive demands for closed captioning of videos on online-streaming, a complex issue pertaining to copyright laws have slowly emerged. For instance, in Norway, a university student was found liable of violating copyright law when he created and distributed for free crowd sourced subtitles in Norwegian for thousands of movie and television shows on his website. The website recorded more than one million downloads. The court found that the content of the movies and television series were copyrighted, and that the distribution of the subtitles without the consent of the owner or licensee was an illegal infringement. The student's website was subsequently closed.[84] It may be recollected that when *Netflix* was decided the company had argued about lack of control over the captioning of streaming video content belonging to third party. Netflix argued that mandating captioning would in effect amount to the creation of unauthorized derivative works by Netflix, and therefore, it amounts to an infringement of copyrights of the owners of such videos. Unfortunately, the court did not decide whether captioning was intellectual property tied to copyrighted works, owned by the creator of the programming.

---

of CNN.com and thereby rejected its defense under First Amendment. To this extent, the Court held that GLAD's claims under the DPA could withstand constitutional challenge.

[84] Available at https://www.techdirt.com/articles/20120611/121040192 77/student-fined-providing-free-film-tv-subtitles-yet-another-business-opportunity-thrown-away-copyright-industries.shtml (last visited 22 April 2015).

Thus, even where closed captioning or accessibility is mandated, compliance with such regulations may require prior permission from copyright owners.

The probable conflict between intellectual property laws and accessible formats was once again considered in *Authors Guild v. HathiTrust.*[85] The plaintiffs (individuals and organizations representing authors) claimed copyright infringement of their ownership rights on account of digital reproduction and distribution of their books owned by US universities. The HathiTrust, a service of a consortium of universities[86] in the US, had entered into a partnership with Google to create digital copies of selected library works and provide them to Universities as a part of a Mass Digitization Project. Accordingly, Google made the digital books available online through Google Books, and users were able to search the web content and view extracts or snippets of the materials. University researchers used the digital copies for data analytics and content searches within the works and to preserve the materials. The full web content was made available to persons with visual and print-related disabilities. Such digitization was challenged by the Authors Guild as violating their rights under the US Copyright Act. The Universities, however, sought defence under fair use doctrine of copyright. Recognizing that such digitization has revolutionized academic participation of the visually impaired students, the Federal District Court held that creating a full-text searchable database of copyrighted works and providing the same in accessible formats to persons with disabilities would be protected by the 'fair use' doctrine.

The rights of persons with disabilities to accessible Internet have proved to be quite complicated affair. Even where the ADA remains ambitious in its goals and the Department of Justice has taken a position that Title III applies to the Internet and covers online services so to ensure full and equal access to persons with disabilities. It is set to promulgate Title III regulations for non-discrimination

---

[85] 902 F supp2d 445.U.S.D.C. S.D.N.Y., 2012.

[86] The following universities formed the consortium: The University of Michigan, University of California, University of Wisconsin, Indiana University, and Cornell University.

in the offering of online services. In 2010, the Department published an Advanced Notice of Proposed Rulemaking (ANPR) to revise the regulations implementing Title III 'in order to establish requirements for making the goods, services, facilities, privileges, accommodations, or advantages offered by public accommodations via the Internet, specifically at sites on the World Wide Web, accessible to individuals with disabilities'.[87] However, the same are not yet effective.

In the meantime, claims under the ADA have been met with stiff resistance from commercial entities. Somewhere in February 2000, the United States Congress held hearings on the topic of how costly it would be for business websites to comply with the ADA.[88] 'Critics testified that millions of [web] pages will have to be taken down and many will be forced to stay down, due to the cost of modifications.'[89] Evidently, private entities have been taking their defences on grounds of infringement to the right to speech under the First Amendment of US Constitution or intellectual property or copyrights or citing financial implications of the accessibility mandate.

As the growing circuit split indicates, the question of whether Title III of the ADA covers non-physical places, such as websites, remains an open one. The judiciary remains divided on the interpretation of Title III of the ADA to the websites. Whereas initial attempts to apply the ADA provisions to the websites under the public accommodation rubric was shot down by the Courts,

---

[87] U.S. DOJ, 28 CFR Parts 35 and 36 [CRT Docket No. 110] RIN 1190–AA61: Nondiscrimination on the Basis of Disability; Accessibility of Web Information and Services of State and Local Government Entities and Public Accommodations,Advance Notice of Proposed Rulemaking, Federal Register, 75, No. 142, 43460, at 43462 (26 July 2010) [hereinafter DOJ Website ANPRM], available at: http://www.regulations.gov/#!documentDetail;D=DOJ-CRT-2010-0005-0001;oldLink=false (last visited 22 April 2015).

[88] Anita Ramasastry, Should Web-Only Businesses be Required to be Disabled-Accessible?, at http://www.cnn.conm2002/LAW/11/07/findlaw.analysis.ramasastry.disabled/index.htmi (last visited 17 May 2016).

[89] Charles D. Mockbee IV, 'Caught in the Web of the Internet: The Application of the Americans with Disabilities to Online Businesses', 28 S. III. U. L.J. 553 2003–2004.

over the period of time the term 'public places of accommodation' have been extended to include the virtual places of public accommodation applying the 'nexus' test.[90] However, such nexus test goes against the policy rationale behind the ADA and leaves major gaps in protection for individuals with disabilities.[91] U.S. anti-discrimination laws hold potentials to protecting the rights of, and ensuring equal opportunities for, individuals with disabilities, Government, educational, and commercial websites pose substantial accessibility challenges.[92] However, the inclusive interpretation of the ADA Title III and the expression places of public accommodation requires reach a settled position so that those seeking to establish their rights of access to private commercial websites in a surefooted manner.[93]

The American anti-discrimination law was explicitly drawn from the minority discrimination model. It needs to be appreciated for forthrightly admitting that individuals with disabilities are a

[90] The issue of web accessibility for the first time attained national attention in 1999, when the National Federation of the Blind filed a class action lawsuit against America Online (AOL). NFB alleged that AOL's services were not usable by persons with visual impairments and did not comply with the ADA title III because AOL's online sign-up form, welcome screens, and chat rooms were not usable with screen readers, which could not read text hidden within graphic displays. The law suit resulted into a settlement agreement whereby the AOL agreed to make its browser compatible with screen reader and committed to make its existing and future website accessible.

[91] Carly Schiff, 'Cracking the Code: Implementing Internet Accessibility through the Americans with Disabilities Act', 37 *Cardozo Law Reveiw* 2315 (2016): 2356.

[92] William N. Myhill, 'Law and Policy Challenges for Achieving an accessible e-society: Lessons from the United States', in *European Yearbook of Disability Law* 103 (Lisa Waddington and Gerard Quinn, eds 2010), Konkright, 'An Analysis of the Applicability of Title III of the Americans with Disabilities Act to Private Internet Access Providers', pp. 743-6; Patrick Maroney, 'The Wrong Tool for the Right Job', 2 *Vanderbilt Journal of Entertainment Law & Practice* 191 (2000): 191-2.

[93] Laura Wolk, 'Equal Access in Cyberspace: On Bridging the Digital Divide in Public Accommodations Coverage through Amendment to the Americans with Disabilities Act', 91 *Notre Dame Law Review* 447 (2015): 478.

discrete and insular minority who have been facing restrictions and limitations and been relegated to a position of political powerlessness in society.[94] Besides, the progressive approach of the US judiciary extending the ADA to ensure accessibility of the websites provides the much required breakthrough in our conception of public places. However, one needs to worry about the implicit paradoxes. The minority group model of disability has been problematic for its emphasis on the 'distinctness' of the group on account of impairments. This tends to indirectly reinforce the medical model and in carving out themselves as a 'group' the model fails to mainstream itself. Further, the minority model leads to questions over the distribution of resources. As Zola puts it, 'seeing people with disability as "different" with "special" needs, wants and rights in this currently perceived world of finite resources, they are pitted against the needs, wants and rights of the rest of the population'.[95] The US model of disability civil rights has proved to be complex and controversial. If the ADA is the template that other jurisdictions have been following, it is high time these jurisdictions brace themselves against similar challenges likely to arise in their jurisdiction. These include the challenges of mandating content accessibility on private entities, reconciling the accessibility mandate with intellectual property laws and vested commercial interests.

Anticipatory Approach

Unlike the reactionary approach of the ADA, discrimination legislations in the UK and Australia offer a guided compliance approach to reach the goals of the non-discrimination. The Equality Act, 2010 (EQA) in the United Kingdom is a generic anti-discrimination law which consolidated a number of legislative regimes and, inter alia replaced the Disability Discrimination Act,

---

[94] 104 STAT 327, 42 USC 1210.
[95] Ik Zola, 'Towards the Necessary Universalizing of a Disability Policy', 67 *The Millbank Quarter* 401 (1989).

1995 (DDA), in England, Scotland, and Wales.[96] The EQA prohibits disability discrimination in several sectors, including access to services. Whereas the EQA does not provide a comprehensive definition of what constitutes a service, section 31(2) clarifies that 'reference to the provision of a service includes a reference to the provision of goods or facilities'.[97]

Accordingly, section 29 of the EQA prohibits discrimination by the providers of services, goods, and facilities[98] whether provided

---

[96] The EQA covers discrimination on account of age, disability, gender reassignment, marriage and civil partnership, pregnancy and maternity, race, religion or belief, sex and sexual orientation. The Acts that have been replaced by the Equality Act 2010 includes the: the Equal Pay Act, 1970, Sex discrimination Act, 1975; Race Relations Act, 1976, and the Disability Discrimination Act, 1995.

[97] Section 31(2).

[98] Section 29 Provision of services, and so on.

1. A person (a 'service-provider') concerned with the provision of a service to the public or a section of the public (for payment or not) must not discriminate against a person requiring the service by not providing the person with the service.

2. A service-provider (A) must not, in providing the service, discriminate against a person (B)—
   a. as to the terms on which A provides the service to B;
   b. by terminating the provision of the service to B;
   c. by subjecting B to any other detriment.

3. A service-provider must not, in relation to the provision of the service, harass—
   a. a person requiring the service, or
   b. a person to whom the service-provider provides the service.

4. A service-provider must not victimize a person requiring the service by not providing the person with the service.

5. A service-provider (A) must not, in providing the service, victimize a person (B)—
   a. as to the terms on which A provides the service to B;
   b. by terminating the provision of the service to B;
   c. by subjecting B to any other detriment.

6. A person must not, in the exercise of a public function that is not the provision of a service to the public or a section of the public, do anything that constitutes discrimination, harassment or victimization.

publicly or privately, for payment or not. It may be noted that while section 29 prohibits service providers from harassing or victimizing persons with disabilities who seek access to or use their services, it is not very clear from the language of section 29 whether it refers to websites. However, Schedule 25 to the EQA extends the definition of Information Society Service Provider to include any commercial website or internet based provider based in Europe that has commercial relationships touching the United Kingdom.[99]

In addition to prohibiting discrimination, the EQA imposes a duty on service providers to make 'reasonable adjustments' so as to enable persons with disabilities to access their services.[100] Failure to provide such 'reasonable adjustments' can amount to discrimination.[101] While 'reasonable adjustment' is not something unique to the EQA being found in most anti-discrimination; the disability laws in the UK has always construed an anticipatory reasonable adjustment duty. This obliges duty-bearers to take steps to

---

7. A duty to make reasonable adjustments applies to—
   a. a service-provider (and see also section 55(7));
   b. a person who exercises a public function that is not the provision of a service to the public or a section of the public.
8. In the application of section 26 for the purposes of subsection (3), and subsection (6) as it relates to harassment, neither of the following is a relevant protected characteristic—
   a. religion or belief;
   b. sexual orientation.
9. In the application of this section, so far as relating to race or religion or belief, to the granting of entry clearance (within the meaning of the Immigration Act1971), it does not matter whether an act is done within or outside the United Kingdom.
10. Subsection (9) does not affect the application of any other provision of this Act to conduct outside England and Wales or Scotland.

[99] The Equality Act 2010, c.15, sch. 25 (UK).

[100] For instance, with regards to services relating to the provision of information, section 20(6) of the EQA stipulates 'the steps which it is reasonable for [an information service provider] to have to take include steps for ensuring that in the circumstances concerned the information is provided in an accessible format'.

[101] Section 21(2).

identify and remove potentially disabling aspects of their operations in advance of the actual appearance of a particular disabled person.[102] Such anticipatory conception of reasonable adjustment 'acknowledges diversity and requires those caught by its terms to recognize difference and take positive steps to accommodate it' and helps to attain 'substantive and proactive concept of equality'.[103] Lawson also notes that this anticipatory duty has 'great potential to drive systemic change'.[104] It may be examined that anticipatory duty has been recognized even under the Disability Discrimination Act 1995 of the UK (which is now repealed and replaced with the EQA). The Court of Appeal in *Roads v. Central Trains Ltd.* CA[105] confirmed that reasonable adjustment duty is anticipatory. The claimant in this matter was a wheelchair user who could not get from one platform of a Thetford station to another. While he could not use the footbridge, and a half mile road route was too difficult for him to reach the other platform. He claimed that it would be a reasonable adjustment for the railway company to provide a taxi with facilities to take an electric wheelchair, to take him between the platforms. The railway company on the other hand had offered to provide a reasonable alternative method of accessing the service, in that the claimant could go on west to Ely station and cross the tracks there. However, this suggested alternative would have added about an hour to the claimant's journey time. Rejecting this alternative of the Railway company, the Court of Appeal held that 'the policy of the DDA is not a minimalist policy of simply ensuring that some access is available to the disabled: it is, so far as reasonably practicable, to approximate the access enjoyed by disabled persons to that enjoyed by the rest of the public'.[106]

---

[102] Anna Lawson, 'Challenging Disabling Barriers to Information and Communication Technology in the Information Society: A United Kingdom Perspective', in *European Yearbook of Disability Law* 2 131 (Lisa Waddington and Gerard Quinn eds.) 2010, p. 138.

[103] Karon Monaghan, *Monaghan on Equality Law*, 6.220, 1.21 (2007).

[104] Lawson, 'Disability and Employment in the Equality Act 2010: Opportunities Seized, Lost and Generated', *Industrial Law Journal* 40(4) 359 (2011): 369, 381.

[105] (2004) EWCA Civ 1541.

[106] (2004) EWCA Civ 1541, at para 30.

However, it is pertinent to note that under the DDA, in order to invoke duty to reasonable adjustment in the context of access to services, persons with disabilities were required to demonstrate that it was 'impossible or unreasonably difficult' to use a particular service.[107] Lawson notes that the threshold so set was 'unacceptably high'.[108] Under section 20 of the EQA, however, reasonable adjustment will be invoked if persons with disabilities are placed at a 'substantial disadvantage' when accessing or using a service.[109]

[107] Section 21(1) DDA.

[108] Lawson, *Disability and Equality Law in Britain.*

[109] Section 20 Duty to make adjustments,

1. Where this Act imposes a duty to make reasonable adjustments on a person, this section, sections 21 and 22 and the applicable Schedule apply; and for those purposes, a person on whom the duty is imposed is referred to as A.

2. The duty comprises the following three requirements.

3. The first requirement is a requirement, where a provision, criterion or practice of A's puts a disabled person at a substantial disadvantage in relation to a relevant matter in comparison with persons who are not disabled, to take such steps as it is reasonable to have to take to avoid the disadvantage.

4. The second requirement is a requirement, where a physical feature puts a disabled person at a substantial disadvantage in relation to a relevant matter in comparison with persons who are not disabled, to take such steps as it is reasonable to have to take to avoid the disadvantage.

5. The third requirement is a requirement, where a disabled person would, but for the provision of an auxiliary aid, be put at a substantial disadvantage in relation to a relevant matter in comparison with persons who are not disabled, to take such steps as it is reasonable to have to take to provide the auxiliary aid.

6. Where the first or third requirement relates to the provision of information, the steps which it is reasonable for A to have to take include steps for ensuring that in the circumstances concerned the information is provided in an accessible format.

7. A person (A) who is subject to a duty to make reasonable adjustments is not (subject to express provision to the contrary) entitled to require a disabled person, in relation to whom A is required to comply with the duty, to pay to any extent A's costs of complying with the duty.

Section 212 of the EQA further clarifies that such disadvantage must be 'more than minor or trivial'.[110] Whereas the EQA has lowered the threshold from that set by the DDA, the problem is that 'substantial disadvantage' leaves a subjective criteria as to when the duty emerges.

The ambiguity in the threshold criteria of reasonable adjustment somewhere offset with the Explanatory notes contained in Schedule 2 of the EQA which elaborates that the reasonable adjustment duty, as applied to service providers, is that it is 'owed to disabled persons

---

8. A reference in section 21 or 22 or an applicable Schedule to the first, second or third requirement is to be construed in accordance with this section.

9. In relation to the second requirement, a reference in this section or an applicable Schedule to avoiding a substantial disadvantage includes a reference to—(a) removing the physical feature in question, (b) altering it, or (c) providing a reasonable means of avoiding it.

10. A reference in this section, section 21 or 22 or an applicable Schedule (apart from paragraphs 2 to 4 of Schedule 4) to a physical feature is a reference to—(a) a feature arising from the design or construction of a building, (b) a feature of an approach to, exit from or access to a building, (c) a fixture or fitting, or furniture, furnishings, materials, equipment or other chattels, in or on premises, or (d) any other physical element or quality.

11. A reference in this section, section 21 or 22 or an applicable Schedule to an auxiliary aid includes a reference to an auxiliary service.

12. A reference in this section or an applicable Schedule to chattels is to be read, in relation to Scotland, as a reference to moveable property.

13. The applicable Schedule is, in relation to the Part of this Act specified in the first column of the Table, the Schedule specified in the second column.

Part of this Act	Applicable Schedule
Part 3 (services and public functions)	Schedule 2
Part 4 (premises)	Schedule 4
Part 5 (work)	Schedule 8
Part 6 (education)	Schedule 13
Part 7 (associations)	Schedule 15
Each of the Parts mentioned above	Schedule 21

[110] Section 212(1).

generally' and, therefore, requires service providers to 'anticipate the needs' of persons with disabilities and 'make appropriate reasonable adjustments'.[111] Additionally the Statutory Code of Practice released by the Equality and Human Rights Commission to explain the EQA[112] provides that 'the duty to make reasonable adjustments requires service providers to take positive steps to ensure that disabled people can access services.' This goes beyond simply avoiding discrimination. It requires service providers to anticipate the needs of potential customers with disabilities for reasonable adjustments.[113]

However, the duty to make reasonable adjustments does not apply if it would require that service providers 'fundamentally alter' the nature of their trade, profession, or service.[114] Furthermore, the Code allows that a reasonable adjustment may factor in the service provider's financial and other resources, the amount of resources already spent on making adjustments and the extent of any disruption which taking the steps would cause the service provider. Thus, where a large company may struggle

---

[111] Explanatory Notes to schedule 2 EQA, paragraph 676.

[112] The Statutory Code of Practice for Services, Public Functions and Associations which came into force in April 2011 has been approved by the Secretary of State and laid before Parliament. The Code explicitly states that websites are included under the ambit of the EQA for the provision of services: 'Websites provide access to services and goods, and may in themselves constitute a service, for example, where they are delivering information or entertainment to the public.'

[113] To exemplify this, the Code cites a practical example of the implications of failing to make reasonable adjustments: 'A provider of legal services establishes a website to enable the public to access its services more easily. However, the website has all of its text embedded within graphics. Although it did not intend to discriminate indirectly against those with a visual impairment, this practice by the provider places those with a visual impairment at a particular disadvantage because they cannot change the font size or apply text-to-speech recognition software. They therefore cannot access the website. As well as giving rise to an obligation to make a reasonable adjustment to their website, their practice will be indirect disability discrimination unless they can justify it.'

[114] Section 2(7), schedule 2, EQA.

to justify any failure making its website accessible, a small business or a charity may have a better defence if it can show that it cannot afford or does not have the resources necessary for the development work.

Easton notes that the absence of an explicit reference to websites under section 20 of the EQA constitutes a missed opportunity to clarify the scope of the duty to make reasonable adjustments.[115] Easton calls for 'an accepted set of standards relating to the virtual environment to be validated and formalized', in order to give 'much needed clarity to the nature of accessible website design'.[116] Despite such limitations, the reasonable adjustment duty in this jurisdiction has been praised for being 'one of the strongest and most successful' in the world.[117]

Guided Compliance Approach

Australia's legislative and judicial experience with the accessibility related litigation affords useful lessons for developing Advisory notes that provide guidance for compliance in addition to the Disability Discrimination Act, 1992.[118] The landmark ruling of the Human Rights and Equal Opportunities Commission (HREOC) in *Bruce Lindsay Maguire v. Sydney Organizing Committee for the Olympic Games*[119] held that creating an inaccessible website intended for use

---

[115] C. Easton, 'Revisiting the Law on Website Accessibility in the Light of the Equality Act 2010 and the UNCRPD', *International Journal of Law and Information Technology* 20(1) (2012): 19, 25.

[116] Easton, 'Revisiting the Law on Website Accessibility in the Light of the Equality Act 2010 and the UNCRPD,' pp. 26-7.

[117] Lawson, 'Disability and Equality in Britain', p. 12.

[118] 'Disability Discrimination Act', available at Australasian Legal Information Institute http://www.austlii.edu.au/au/legis/cth/consol_act/dda1992264/ (last visited 11 June 2014).

[119] For details visit Australian Human Rights and Equal Opportunity Commission, No. H 99/115, William Carter QC, Sydney, 8, 24 August 2000, available at http://www.hreoc.gov.au/disabilityrights/decisions/comdec/2000/DD000120.htm (last visited 11 June 2014).

by general public would amount to discrimination on grounds of disability in breach of DDA.[120]

The complainant, a person with visual impairment, intended to apply for tickets for himself and his two children so as to attend the Sydney Olympic Games 2000. The event was organized by the Sydney Organizing Committee for the Olympic Games (SOCOG).[121] The complainant contended that the failure to provide braille copies of the souvenir programme and the requisite information to order tickets and an inaccessible website created by the SOCOG amounted to unlawful discrimination prohibited under the DDA.

HREOC read the provision of 'goods or services' in a broad and extensive manner. It held that the definition of 'services' under section 4, included not only the provision of 'entertainment' as a service but also services 'relating to' entertainment.[122] Since the SOCOG was providing information through its web site, it came within the ambit of section 24 of the DDA.[123] Even where HREOC conceded that SOCOG's website was being continuously developed to make it accessible; what was offered to the complainant

[120] DDA aims to eliminate discrimination against persons with disabilities as far as possible in the areas including access to premises, provisioning of goods, facilities and services and so on. By the virtue of Section 23, the DDA makes it unlawful discrimination to refuse to allow access to, or the use of, any public premises to a person on the grounds of disability. Further, Section 24 makes it unlawful for a provider of goods, facilities or services to discriminate on the grounds of disability either by refusing to provide goods, services or facilities or in the terms and conditions or manner in which these are provided.

[121] SOCOG is a statutory corporation established under legislation of the New South Wales parliament to stage the Games of the 27th Olympiad in the year 2000.

[122] Section 4 Premises includes:
  a. a structure, building, aircraft, vehicle, or vessel; and
  b. a place (whether enclosed or built on or not); and
  c. a part of premises (including premises of a kind referred to in paragraph (a) or (b)).

[123] 24 Goods, services and facilities It is unlawful for a person who, whether for payment or not, provides goods or services, or makes facilities available, to discriminate against another person on the ground of the other person's disability:

was an imperfect or limited access website. This amounted to the complainant receiving less favourable treatment, indirect discrimination under section 6 of the DDA. Further, the SOCOG could not avoid liability for its breach of section 24 of the DDA by claiming unjustifiable hardship. The SOCOG was directed to pay damages worth $20,000 AUD to the complainant in addition to other reliefs granted.

Subsequently, the Australian Human Rights Commission released a set of Advisory Notes providing detailed information about accessibility and related legal issues and advice to the web designers and website owners.[124] Although these Advisory Notes are not legally enforceable, the anti-discrimination agencies may consider them in dealing with complaints under DDA. The Advisory Note very clearly mentions that the provision of information and online services through the web is a service covered by the DDA. This requirement applies to any individual or organization developing a website or other web resource in Australia or placing or maintaining a web resource on an Australian server. It also addresses document authors and content managers in order to ensure that not only the website, but the contents on the same are also accessible.

Under the guided compliance approach, as developed by the UK and the Australian disability laws, the State seeks to engage in some form of dialogue with the duty bearers. Such a process tends to first create an understanding among the duty bearers by sensitizing them and encouraging them to anticipate the impact of their actions. It helps to avert causing damage in the first place

a. by refusing to provide the other person with those goods or services or to make those facilities available to the other person; or

b. in the terms or conditions on which the first-mentioned person provides the other person with those goods or services or makes those facilities available to the other person; or

c. in the manner in which the first-mentioned person provides the other person with those goods or services or makes those facilities available to the other person.

[124] 'World Wide Web Access: Disability Discrimination Act Advisory Notes', available at Australian Human Rights Commission, https://www.humanrights.gov.au/our-work/disability-rights/standards/world-wide-web-access-disability-discrimination-act-advisory (last visited 3 April 2015).

which then may require subsequent prolonged litigation. Whereas this approach and its effectiveness require to be tested, it is relatively a new approach which tends to advance the goals of substantive equality envisaged by the CRPD.

Critical Appraisal of Command-Control Anti-Discrimination Laws

An examination of various available models of anti-discrimination laws, brings to the fore certain inbuilt limitations of these laws regardless of the approach taken for implementation.

Scope of Application

The scope and application of the existing anti-discrimination laws in mandating accessible Internet requires more imagination. Whereas the right to access the Internet requires a broad perception of the Internet as creation of a virtual community, the extant set of discrimination laws adopts a myopic view. Most anti-discrimination laws perceive access to the Internet as equivalent to access to products and services, thereby diminishing persons with disabilities to consumers instead of citizens of the virtual world. These laws are not aimed at addressing systemic forms of discrimination. There is nothing in these laws that oblige duty bearer to change structures to accommodate diversity. Rather, they merely tend to assert negative rights without adequately spelling positive rights and consequently leave the agenda of substantive equality unfinished. The sanction in the form of litigation, fines, and penalties by the adjudicatory bodies hardly prove to be deterrence. The legislative efforts are a highly dispersed and fragmented force which does not create requisite deterrence, let alone encourage proactive engagement.[125]

---

[125] The Anti-Discrimination and Accessibility Act 2008 (AAD) of Norway stipulates a positive duty of public and private entities offering goods and services to the general public to promote universal design. However, it still

Even as the recently updated UK EQA makes explicit references to websites and experiments with a different approach to seek compliance, in the main, the effort continues to extend the existing framework to accommodate access to the Internet. Such expansive readings have often been embroiled in controversies. It is disturbing to find that even jurisdictions with relatively long experiences of and history with anti-discrimination laws, such as the ADA have given mixed signals as far as web accessibility is concerned. Under the American jurisdiction, the nexus test requires a complainant to either establish that the website was a place of public accommodation, or that there is a sufficient nexus between the service provided by such a place of public accommodation and the website. Rather than promoting substantial equality, so as to introduce systemic changes in the virtual world, such provisions have put commercial entities at loggerheads with the disability constituency.

The UK and Australian Disability Discrimination Laws make an appreciable move towards introducing a model of positive duties, instead of merely prohibiting discrimination. The effectiveness of this approach needs to be tested out in full. These legislations also continue to suffer from the problem encountered in traditional anti-discrimination laws in that they fail to focus upon all parties that can influence inclusion. For instance, creators of virtual world architecture, that is, web designers are not bearers of anti-discrimination duties. Again the anti-discrimination regimes in the UK, US, and Australia prohibit discrimination in the defined relationship which implies that those outside these definitions can lawfully engage in discrimination. While Italy expressly mandates private entities to ensure accessibility, Canada mandates only government websites.

Costs of Equality

Anti-discrimination legislation across jurisdictions is largely guided by ideals of equality and fairness. Even so, these legislations and

---

continues with the reaction based and complaint driven redressal mechanism. For details see http://zeroproject.org/policy/norway/ (last visited 5 March 2015).

the equality and non-discrimination goals are laced with costs. Consequently, policy-makers ensure that goals of equality should not impose burden on business. Therefore, anti-discrimination legislations invariably insulate duty bearers against costs with certain inbuilt defences. Thus, duty bearers should not be expected to bear 'unreasonable' expenses or to suffer 'undue hardship' as a result of having to provide equality rights. The factors that determine whether an adjustment or accommodation is unreasonable include the cost of such adjustment.[126] The most common measure is the assessment of the cost of the duty holder, rather than the positive externalities. Consequently, the discrimination may be excused if the duty holder can show 'unjustified hardship' or 'undue hardship'.

Redressal Mechanism

Typically, anti-discrimination laws excessively rely on individual litigation as a means of enforcing their precepts and in this sense places considerable burdens on individuals. It concentrates on individual retrospective fault-finding and assumes that willingness to obey the law and avoid sanctions in the form of compensation awards are sufficient means of achieving discrimination laws' ambitiously stated objectives. Thus, even where an action is brought, the focus is on remedying individual acts of discrimination after the event, not on the elimination of structures and patterns of behaviour that perpetuate discriminatory practices.

---

[126] The Canadian Supreme Court delivered a welcome judgment in this regards in *Eldrigde v. British Columbia* (1997) 3 SCR 624. The matter concerned a claim that failure to provide sign-language interpreters in hospital infringed the rights of hearing impaired. The respondents in Eldridge argued that recognition of the appellant's claim would: have a ripple effect throughout the health care field. The Court rejected this argument that to deny the appellants claim on such conjectural grounds....would denude s 15(1) of its egalitarian promise and render the disabled goal of barrier-free society distressingly remote.

In this regards, the Australian DDA adopts a fresh approach. It includes a range of measures beyond individual complaints mechanism where the state and its instrumentalities have the opportunity to work in a proactive manner. This mechanism functions at two levels. At an informal level, the mechanism provides guidance for voluntary organizational responses to rectify the social imbalance and at the formal level, they mandate legal requirements to redesign specific aspects of social life in order to bring about social justice for persons with disabilities.[127]

Deficiency in Addressing Systemic Discrimination

Much of the prejudicial treatment faced by the disadvantaged groups arises out of patterns of institutional discrimination, involving the neglect or a lack of understanding of their specific needs. Persons with disabilities have been particularly affected by exclusion from decision-making processes and subjected to paternalistic 'assistance' by decision makers. Most of the existing anti-discrimination law adopts a formal individualist approach which requires that individuals be treated alike. This emphasis on what 'equality as sameness' ignores the fact that achieving substantive equality may actually require that specific characteristics of groups be taken into account and positive steps taken to ensure their inclusion as equal participants in society.[128] The anti-discrimination model imposes no requirement to consult with disadvantaged groups in

[127] DDA is administered by HREOC and together with the Attorney General, HREOC plays a continuing role over and beyond the normal administration of an anti-discrimination law. The DDA envisaged that other than fulfilling its role as conciliator, HEROC would take the lead in developing standards designed to redress systemic discrimination and would issue guidelines to clarify the terms of the DDA such that the complaints process could be avoided.

[128] See Maria Ventegodt Liisberg, *Disability and Employment: A Contemporary Disability Rights Approach Applied to Danish, Swedish and EU Law and Policy* (Cambridge: Intersentia, 2011), pp. 23-4.

developing strategies to eliminate discrimination or in improving performance.

This makes existing anti-discrimination law of limited use in combating institutional discrimination in public authorities and private organizations. Consequently, organizations tend to take defensive steps to meet their legislative obligations, creating a culture of negative compliance. There is also the additional consequence that practices amounting to institutional discrimination may appear acceptable as they are outside the legally established definition of discrimination.

Besides the inherent peculiarities of anti-discrimination laws, entities embroiled in most litigation pertaining to disability discrimination have been consumer companies. Unlike international human rights law, which was applicable to supply companies, anti-discrimination laws are found to be used against consumer companies; both providing less than satisfactory outcome. The legislation is considered to be amongst the most effective tools to ensure compliance from corporations. The difficulty is that anti-discrimination laws tend to alienate corporations from active involvement and often blinds them towards ensuing benefits of accessibility in the form of an expanded consumer base. Tactically, therefore, it would be essential to make them a part of the overall standard setting process. Since supply companies are the ones closely associated with providing virtual infrastructure, they may be drivers of change in constructing an accessible virtual world. These may be subject to direct regulations and may also self-regulate. On the other hand, consumer companies do not lie in close proximity of disability constituency and therefore may be relatively less receptive to their concerns as is witnessed through litigations.

Thus, mandating the Midas by way of anti-discrimination law is only helpful to a certain limited extent. Anti-discrimination law is one step on the road towards the creation of an inclusive and accessible virtual world for persons with disabilities. Deconstructing the hierarchy of difference requires a systemic response and expanding participation requires more initiatives beyond the remit of discrimination law. Despite some gestures of substantive equality the narrow concerns of formal equality engage anti-discrimination legislations.[129] These legislations, therefore, provide an acknowledgment to insufficient platform for attaining wholesome accessibility. In conclusion, there is a need for other alternatives which could go towards addressing disability-based exclusion. The following portion will explore various instrumentalities that are adopting persuasive approach. In what follows is a quick survey of instrumentalities other than anti-discrimination laws often deployed by the state to ensure compliance.

Persuasive Compliance Mechanisms

Complementary Legislations to Anti-discrimination Laws

Despite the complexities and challenges encountered in the ADA with regard to the accessibility of the websites and web content, the US jurisdiction offers another non-discrimination legislation worth exploring. Recognizing the fact that persons with disabilities were not fully benefitting from technological advancement, the twenty first Century Communications and Video Accessibility Act (CVAA) was enacted. The duties in the CVAA are contained in two broad titles. Title I enshrines universal design with respect to communication devices for persons with disabilities.[130] Title II focuses on increasing access to video programming broadcast on the Internet and television for persons with disabilities.

This law targets two set of parties—one, those who produce internet-based equipment and two, those who produce material to be broadcast on the Internet or television. The CVAA thus recognizes that many barriers in society can be best removed by people who create them at the design stage and adopt a universal

---

[129] As Fredman points out, disability discrimination 'gestures' towards substantive equality, but these gestures remain imperfect. S. Fredman, 'Disability Equality: A Challenge to the Existing Anti-Discrimination Paradigm', in *Disability Rights in Europe: From Theory to Practice* 199, p. 213 (A. Lawson and C. Gooding eds, 2005).

[130] 21st Century CVAA, 47 U.S.C. §617 (Supp. V 2011).

design model to remove inequalities in the society. Section 104 is a crucial provision which creates a right to access to internet-based equipment and services. Section 716 of the CVAA requires access to Internet based communication services and equipment[131] and section 718 requires mobile phone browsers to be accessible to visually impaired persons.[132]

Section 104 has also introduced a complaints mechanism to the Federal Communications Commission (FCC).[133] Under this

---

[131] 47 U.S.C. 617 SEC. 716. Access to Advanced Communications Services and Equipment (a) Manufacturing–(1) In General–With respect to equipment manufactured after the effective date of the regulations established pursuant to subsection (e), and subject to those regulations, a manufacturer of equipment used for advanced communications services, including end user equipment, network equipment, and software, shall ensure that the equipment and software that such manufacturer offers for sale or otherwise distributes in interstate commerce shall be accessible to and usable by individuals

[132] 47 USC 619 SEC. 718. Internet Browsers Built Into Telephones Used With Public Mobile Services. (a) Accessibility–If a manufacturer of a telephone used with public mobile services (as such term is defined in section 710(b)(4)(B)) includes an Internet browser in such telephone, or if a provider of mobile service arranges for the inclusion of a browser in telephones to sell to customers, the manufacturer or provider shall ensure that the functions of the included browser (including the ability to launch the browser) are accessible to and usable by individuals who are blind or have a visual impairment, unless doing so is not achievable, except that this subsection shall not impose any requirement on such manufacturer or provider-

 1. to make accessible or usable any Internet browser other than a browser that such manufacturer or provider includes or arranges to include in the telephone; or (2) to make Internet content, applications, or services accessible or usable (other than enabling individuals with disabilities to use an included browser to access such content, applications, or services).

[133] 47 U.S.C. § 618(a) SEC. 717. Enforcement and Recordkeeping Obligations. Deadline. (a) Complaint and Enforcement Procedures– Within regulations year after the date of enactment of the Twenty-First Century Communications and Video Accessibility Act of 2010, the Commission shall establish regulations that facilitate the filing of

regime, any person can make formal and informal complaints to the FCC about any breach. While the FCC is required to resolve the complaint within a prescribed time period and can require a designer or manufacturer to remedy the breach, the FCC cannot impose any legal sanctions against such designer nor can a complainant seek damages. It is apprehended that such loose enforcement mechanism may reduce its effectiveness. However, the CVAA puts in place a different monitoring mechanism on

---

formal and informal complaints that allege a violation of section 255, 716, or 718, establish procedures for enforcement actions by the Commission with respect to such violations, and implement the recordkeeping obligations of paragraph (5) for manufacturers and providers subject to such sections. Such regulations shall include the following provisions:

1. No Fee—The Commission shall not charge any fee to an individual who files a complaint alleging a violation of section 255, 716, or 718.
2. Receipt of Complaints—The Commission shall establish separate and identifiable electronic, telephonic, and physical receptacles for the receipt of complaints filed under section 255, 716, or 718.
3. Complaints to the Commission.
   A. In General—Any person alleging a violation of section 255, 716, or 718 by a manufacturer of equipment or provider of service subject to such sections may file a formal or informal complaint with the Commission.
   B. Investigation of Informal Complaint—The Orders. Commission shall investigate the allegations in an informal complaint and, within 180 days after the date on which such complaint was filed with the Commission, issue an order concluding the investigation, unless such complaint is resolved before such time. The order shall include a determination whether any violation occurred.
   (i) If the Commission determines that a violation has occurred, the Commission may, in the order issued under this subparagraph or in a subsequent order, direct the manufacturer or service provider to bring the service, or in the case of a manufacturer, the next generation of the equipment or device, into compliance with requirements of those sections within a reasonable time established by the Commission in its order.
   (ii) No Violation—If a determination is made that a violation has not occurred, the Commission shall provide the basis for such determination.

duty holders in the form of record keeping. Section 718 imposes obligations on duty holders whereby they are required to maintain information about their efforts of implementation, descriptions about accessibility features of the product or service, consultations with individuals with disabilities.[134]

The CVAA sets performance standards to attain a desired outcome and allow duty holders to identify strategies to achieve the prescribed performance. While the performance targets set in the CVAA may not be perfect, the enactment of such targets represents a positive step by the legislature to obtain equality of outcome. This effort can thus, be categorized as an attempt to overcome the limitation of the traditional anti-discrimination laws which had been applied only to those parties who shared direct relationship with persons with disabilities. The CVAA tends to address this gap by embracing the notion that in certain situations, even without direct contact with a person with disability people have obligations to ensure the equality.

At the time of the CNN dispute, discussed above, the FCC had issued regulations under the CVAA which covered captioning of full-length programmes on television and video programmes that appeared online thereafter. It, however, did not cover excerpts of such programmes online. The state laws could therefore supplement the federal regulatory scheme for online Internet closed captioning. However, it was argued by CNN that application of California state disability law was pre-empted or precluded by the CVAA, because that federal law was the proper vehicle to address online captioning.

C. Consolidation of Complaints—The Commission may consolidate for investigation and resolution complaints alleging substantially the same violation.

4. Opportunity to Respond—Before the Commission makes a determination pursuant to paragraph (3), the party that is the subject of the complaint shall have a reasonable opportunity to respond to such complaint, and may include in such response any factors that are relevant to such determination. Before issuing a final order under paragraph (3)(B)(i), the Commission shall provide such party a reasonable opportunity to comment on any proposed remedial action.

[134] 47 USC 618(a)(5).

It contended that the federal captioning scheme for online videos was indicative of Congress's intent to preclude broader regulation of online closed captioning under state law. Consequently, the company was suggestive that the federal captioning scheme and the DPA may comprise of different requirements or deadlines for captioning which may result in creating positive repugnancy between the two laws. The Ninth Circuit Court declined to accept this argument of CNN. It was held that there was no demonstration of an irreconcilable conflict between federal law and the DPA and CNN could comply with both.

Even where the Court has cleared the air about any conflict between the CVAA and state regulation, there still remains a limitation in the CVAA. It does not presently cover online content generated by third-party advertisers and user-generated content offered on blogs or social networking website, say for instance, Facebook, YouTube, Instagram is not necessarily covered by the CVAA. This leaves out an important range of consumer companies out of accessibility net.[135]

Public Procurement

The American experience, mandating accessibility informs us that commercial entities may not be readily willing to offer accessible contents and/or components. Any compulsion through anti-discrimination legislation tends to run counter to the market sentiment and can antagonize commercial entities rather than obtaining their proactive engagement. This reluctance could be traced to deeper stereotypes and attitudinal bias prevalent in the society and the markets. The job of influencing business is made even more difficult by the many myths and perceptions heavily entrenched in the private sector around designing for accessibility. 'Accessibility' for the private sector typically conjures

---

[135] However, the CVAA remains in an evolutionary stage and necessarily offers novel features to create accessibility obligations on content providers/ service providers on the Internet.

the image of small markets, special design requirements, low-tech uncool products that are perceived to require the sacrifice of aesthetics and function to meet the needs of a few. Even more damaging for the business are the perceptions that 'designing for accessibility' will increase the cost and complexity of the product and lengthen the time for development. Corporations may be willing to undertake investments only where the potential gains tend to outweigh the risks of such investments. It need be recollected that in GLAD v. Time Warners, even where it was understood that introducing captioning would benefit the company and its customers without disabilities, the same was fervently opposed.[136] Therefore, it is crucial to recognize the fragile relationship between market responses and the accessibility needs of persons with disabilities. The truth of the matter is that market processes of negotiations, deal-making, leverage, and influence leave persons with disabilities with very little bargaining power.

I had initiated this study with a discussion as to how persons with disabilities were not considered in initial societal bargaining whilst setting up the physical world. One witness similar imbalance in the bargaining power in their commercial and market operations of creating the virtual world. Since persons with disabilities form a relatively small portion of the overall consumer pie, they are relegated to a take-it or leave-it position.

In order to address these concerns it is often considered judicious to make a business case for accessibility and stimulate the market conditions that lead to the seamless creation of accessible components and contents.[137] It is, therefore, crucial that the State throws its weight behind accessibility needs to stimulate favourable market conditions for accessibility. Insofar as the markets of information and communication technology are concerned,

---

[136] GLAD, 742 F.3d 414 (9th Cir. 2014). Text files had been shown to enhance search engine optimization (SEO), which improves online services by providing easier, effective and cost-beneficial ways to locate information, thereby enhancing the customer experience.

[137] The business case is the assessment of whether or not the gains to be made from an investment of time and money in the development of a product or service are worth the anticipated risks.

the State is seen as a major purchaser and as an outsourcer of its functionalities to the private entities. This power of the purse can be tapped to regulate and channelize the market behaviour of the private undertakings. Clearly, the State today is one of the largest buyers of products and services in the market and in that capacity has leverage over the market. The State can thus, incentivize demand of critical mass of accessible components and contents by competent producers through public procurement contracts.

Public procurement is a key contractual means through which States, as an economic actor, can influence the corporate behaviour.[138] Perceived in ordinary terms as a form of organizing business relations in a consumer market, contract laws consist of combinations of rules aimed to serve legitimate, consent-based private arrangements.[139] However, in a broader sense, contracts also have an important societal role to supply frameworks for co-operative activity. In this sense, the law of contract is a way of enforcing some kind of distributive justice within the legal system.[140] The State can therefore, bank upon this latter role of public procurement contracts to obtain desirable outcomes and make market interventions.

In the past, states have used public procurement policies to achieve certain socio-economic goals by stimulating national economic activity, improving competition in certain economic sectors and driving innovation in a particular area of technology.[141]

---

[138] Public procurement generally concerns the purchase of goods and services from the private sector contractors and vendors in a transparent and competitive bidding process.

[139] This represents 'old' model of contract based on objective manifestations of mutual assent as represented in the parties' words or conduct in a formalized dance of offer, acceptance and consideration.

[140] Morris R. Cohen, *The Basis of Contract*, 46 *Harvard Law Review* 553 (1933): 553–4.

[141] 'Socially responsible public procurement' has trailed developments in responsible supply chain management with which large private companies have experimented since the mid-1990s. See C. McCrudden, 'Corporate Social Responsibility and Public Procurement', in *The New Corporate Accountability: Corporate Social Responsibility and the Law* (D. McBarnet, A. Voiculescu, and T. Campbell eds, 2007).

Such selective public procurement uses non-economic human rights standards to evaluate the awarding of public contracts for goods or services by governments. Thus, it requires companies that wish to bid on public contracts, to make a specific level of commitment to protecting human rights. Selective public procurement may be domestically oriented[142] or even operate outside the contracting boundaries of a state.[143] While such procurement requirements act as catalyst to private players to respond to accessibility demands, the State can also integrate sanctions within procurement contracts itself by disqualifying bidders not having such expertise. Such business relationships will create effective sanctions so that businesses which depart from the accepted norms of behaviour in their peer group risk losing business opportunities or status in their community. Several jurisdictions have already put in place public procurement laws and policies that address this issue.

[142] In the United States, all contractors doing significant business with the Federal Government must certify that they have compliance programmes rooted in ethical and legally compliant cultures, based on those required in the Sentencing Guidelines. United States Federal Register, Vol. 73, No. 219, 12 November 2008.

[143] These policies either target businesses interacting with a specific country or target a specific manufacturing product or process such as child labour or a use of a particular chemical pollutant. For instance, in the US, an Executive Order from 1999 targets goods produced by forced child labour. Accordingly, public federal procurement shall include special provisions in contracts to the effect that the contractor has to certify that a good faith effort was made to determine whether forced or indentured child labour was used, and to cooperate in providing access to the contractor's records, documents, persons or premises. The sanctions on contractors are termination of contract, debarring from eligibility for future contracts and inclusion on a List of Parties Excluded from Federal Procurement. See, Executive Order 13126 Prohibition of Acquisition of Products Produced by Forced or Indentured Child Labor (12 June 1999). For the effects of this regulation, see, R. Woodard, *Sourcing: US labour 'blacklisting' a wake-up call to India?*, 20 July 2010, www.just-style.com/analysis/us-labour-blacklisting-a-wake-up-call-to-india_id108351.aspx (last visited 31 March 2015); 'US Sees Big Drop in Child Labour Use by Indian Carpet-Makers', *Sify News*, 20 July 2010, www.sify.com/news/us-sees-big-drop-in-child-labour-use-by-indian-carpet-makers-news-international-khunacfgihg.html (last visited 31 March 2015).

For instance, in a move to eliminate the barriers, the US Congress passed an amendment in the Rehabilitation Act of 1973 that requires the Federal agencies to make their electronic and information technology (EIT) accessible to persons with disabilities. Thus, by the virtue of section 508 (29 U.S.C. 794 d) it is mandated that all Federal agencies when developing, procuring, maintaining, or using electronic and information technology shall ensure that federal employees and members of the public with disabilities have access to information that is comparable to that available to persons without disabilities.[144]

Thus, section 508 creates specific binding processes to incorporate standards in federal procurement. It has also put in place compliance and enforcement mechanism in the form of reporting requirements, administrative complaint procedures and a private right of action against federal departments and agencies that do

---

[144] SEC. 508. Electronic and Information Technology (a) Requirements for Federal Departments and Agencies—(1) Accessibility—(A) Development, Procurement, Maintenance, or use of Electronic and Information Technology—When developing, procuring, maintaining, or using electronic and information technology, each Federal department or agency, including the United States Postal Service, shall ensure, unless an undue burden would be imposed on the department or agency, that the electronic and information technology allows, regardless of the type of medium of the technology—(i) individuals with disabilities who are Federal employees to have access to and use of information and data that is comparable to the access to and use of the information and data by Federal employees who are not individuals with disabilities; and (ii) individuals with disabilities who are members of the public seeking information or services from a Federal department or agency to have access to and use of information and data that is comparable to the access to and use of the information and data by such members of the public who are not individuals with disabilities. (B) Alternative Means Efforts—When development, procurement, maintenance, or use of electronic and information technology that meets the standards published by the Access Board under paragraph (2) would impose an undue burden, the Federal department or agency shall provide individuals with disabilities covered by paragraph (1) with the information and data involved by an alternative means of access that allows the individual to use the information and data.

not implement section 508. It makes a smart move towards creating market place incentives for businesses to invest in the development of accessible ICT. Whilst section 508 does not mandate business to develop accessible ICT, all such businesses who wish to sell to the US government must address accessibility in their product design. Thus, even where the law does not directly apply to private entities, it creates an indirect pressure on them to include accessible products to advance their own business.[145]

Yukins explains '[m]ore companies worry about accessibility than ever before because they covet the Federal Government's procurement dollars. The resulting advances in accessibility, in turn, have spilled over into the commercial marketplace'.[146] That is, section 508 has begun to shape industry standards among manufacturers and web developers.[147] However, the reach of section 508 remains shallow. The federal government and its subcontractors are obligated by section 508 to purchase, use, and provide accessible software, hardware, web-based information, operating systems, video and multimedia[148]—though state and local government, business and commerce, and non-profits organizations are not.

In recognition of the technological advances and convergence of technology offered by devices, the Architectural and Transportation

---

[145] Under section 508, the Architectural and Transportation Barriers Compliance Board (also known as the 'Access Board') is a standard setting body which is entrusted with task of establishing accessibility standards. Such rule making process includes consultation with specified government departments, electronic and information technology industry, and appropriate public or non-profit agencies or organizations, including organizations representing individuals with disabilities.

[146] C. Yukins, 'Making Federal Information Technology Accessible: A Case Study in Social Policy and Procurement', *Public Contract Law Journal* 33 (2004): 667, 669.

[147] Yukins, 'Making Federal Information Technology Accessible'. Cf H.M. Berven and P. Blanck, 'Assistive Technology Patenting Trends and the Americans with Disabilities Act', 17 Behavioral Sciences and the Law 47 (1999): 49 (discussing accessibility innovations by inventors and producers of assistive technologies as a rationale response to the ADA in competing for profits).

[148] Yukin, 'Making Federal Information Technology Accessible'.

Barriers Compliance Board (Access Board)[149] has proposed to update and further clarify their existing Electronic and Information Technology Standards covered by section 508 of the Rehabilitation Act of 1973, and its guidelines for telecommunications equipment and customer premises equipment covered by section 255 of the Communications Act of 1934. The existing requirement does not adequately address what is meant by comparable access to information and data. Consequently, there has been confusion over whether and how such electronic content must be made accessible. As a result, document accessibility has been inconsistent across federal agencies.

The proposed rule would incorporate, by reference, the Web Content Accessibility Guidelines (WCAG) 2.0, a voluntary consensus standard developed by ICT industry representatives and other experts. It would also require WCAG 2.0 Success Criteria to be applied not only to Web content but also to non-Web documents and software. The proposed standards replace the current product-based approach with a functionality-based approach of various products such as smart phones.[150] A functional-based approach helps to determine whether the alternative design or technology provides individuals with disabilities with substantially equivalent or greater accessibility and usability.

The web accessibility law in Italy includes provisions of prioritizing accessibility criteria in Article 4. This provision categorically accords preference to the bidder who offers best

---

[149] In accordance with section 508(a)(2)(A), the Architectural and Transportation Barriers Compliance Board (Access Board) have been entrusted with the task to publish standards that define electronic and information technology along with the technical and functional performance criteria for accessibility, and its periodic review.

[150] The functional performance criteria are outcome-based provisions that address barriers to using ICT by individuals with certain disabilities, such as those related to vision, hearing, color blindness, speech, and manual dexterity. While the existing 508 Standards provide functional performance criteria, they do not expressly define the relationship between its functional performance criteria and technical requirements. To address this gap, the Access Board proposes to clarify when application of the functional performance criteria in the 508 Standards is required.

compliance with accessibility when carrying goods and deliver services. It also mandates adequate justification for not taking into consideration accessibility requirements or the purchase of goods and supplied services. Further, Article 4 entails that entities cannot draw up contracts for the implementation and modification of the Internet websites if they fail to respect accessibility requirements and any such stipulated contract shall be null and void.

The European Union's Mandate 376 mirrors the US section 508 requirements,[151] clearly establishing directives which Member States need to follow whilst issuing public procurements. In most of the EU Member States, government contracts are an important vehicle for the promotion of environmental and corporate social responsibility, as public procurements making up 15–20 per cent of the Gross Domestic Product (GDP).[152] Therefore, ICT products and services procured within Europe are mandated to be accessible and usable by people with disabilities. Besides, the Mandate 376 seeks to harmonize web standards, functional criteria, and interoperability with assistive technologies.[153]

If closely observed public procurement can push conformity of supply companies; however, those corporations that have no close association with the government in terms of their operation will still remain untouched.

Taxation

In the past, direct and indirect taxation regimes have offered a range of incentives both for persons with disabilities and private

---

[151] See European Accessibility Requirements for Public Procurement of Products and Services in the ICT Domain (European Commission Standardization Mandate M 376, Phase 2) (12 August 2012); available at: http://www.mandate376.eu/ (last visited 27 November 2014).

[152] McCrudden, Buying Equality Draft Chapter (2009), available at: http://www.michiganlawreview.org/articles/mccrudden-buying-social-justice-equality-government-rocurement-and-legalchange (last visited 27 November 2014).

[153] Available at: http://www.mandate376.eu/doc/CEN_CLC_Report_Conformity_assessment_acc_req.pdf (last visited 27 November 2014).

entities; however, experience informs us that these have limited concentration in terms of assistive devices and employment. Thus, private entities are provided with some rebates, tax concession so as to incentivize them to employ persons with disabilities. For instance, in India a 'Scheme of Incentives to Employers in the Private Sector for providing Employment to Persons with Disabilities' was devised to encourage the private sectors to employ persons with disabilities. As per the scheme, the government would reimburse the employers' contribution to the provident fund for disabled employees earning up to Rs 25,000 for the first three years.[154] Similarly, the USA provides a tax credit to employers for amounts of premiums for disability insurance paid by the employer for its employees. However, the success or failure of such schemes needs to be empirically confirmed.

Another form of tax incentive takes shape in the form of providing relief in the excise duty/import duty where entities engaged in the production, manufacture or procurement of assistive devices for persons with disabilities. The US offers two sets of tax incentives to enable business to cover the cost of improvements in accessibility. One is a tax credit that can be used for architectural adaptations, equipment acquisitions, and services such as sign language interpreters. Popularly, it is known as Disability Access Credit, which section 44 of the Internal Revenue Code offers taxpayer who is a small business[155] when such taxpayer incurs expenditures such as readers for the customers or employees with visual disabilities, sign language interpreters, and removal of architectural barriers in facilities or vehicles and so on. The credit is equal to 50 per cent of the eligible expenses between $250 and $10,250, for a total possible credit of $5,000 each year.

---

[154] Available at http://esic.nic.in/CIRCULARS/englishbft.pdf (last visited 3 March 2015).

[155] Small business is a business that for the previous tax year had either revenues of $1,000,000 or less or 30 or fewer full-time workers may take advantage of this credit.

The second is a tax deduction that can be used for architectural or transportation adaptations.[156] Under section 190 of the Internal Revenue Code, a maximum deduction of $15,000 per year can be availed by a business (including active ownership of an apartment building) of any size, for the removal of architectural or transportation barriers, provided such renovations comply with applicable accessibility standards.[157] It needs to be carefully considered that in order to qualify, such expenditure must *inter alia* 'remove a barrier' which prevented a business from being accessible to, or usable by, individuals with disabilities, or acquire or modify equipment for use by individuals with disabilities. Thus, while renovations to the existing structures could qualify for the tax credit, the cost of constructing a new accessible building will not be eligible for any credit or deduction.

This underlying system of tax incentives can be further tweaked and transplanted to persuade creation of accessible websites and web contents. While newly designed websites or equipment could be subjected to regulations and anti-discrimination laws; tax incentives could be offered to cover the cost of refurbishing existing websites accessible.

Certification Mechanism

A certification mechanism comprises of an independent certification authority that evaluates a corporation on pre-determined parameters and where the corporation meets the prescribed standard, a requisite certificate is issued. Often these take the form of product labelling where corporations voluntarily or under some regulation are required to affix a label to a product certifying that it is made under acceptable conditions consistent

---

[156] For the sake of clarity it should be understood that a tax credit is the amount that is subtracted from total tax liability of a taxpayer whereas tax deduction is subtracted from total income of taxpayer before taxes.

[157] These incentives are in combination if the expenditures incurred qualify under both Section 44 and Section 190.

with a code of conduct. For instance, the Belgian Social Label law offers corporations the possibility to acquire a label for products if corporation production chain respects the eight fundamental ILO labour conventions. The scheme combines voluntary initiatives with legal constraints since non-complying corporations using the label are liable to criminal fines.

Such certification mechanisms have been quite popular to raise awareness and sensitize the public towards a particular targeted issue. For instance, Energy Star is an international standard for energy efficient consumer products originated in the United States. It was created in 1992 by the Environmental Protection Agency and the Department of Energy and later adapted in other countries. The energy efficiency logo is quite popular in influencing purchase preferences of electronic appliances consumers. Similarly, other range of certification mechanism exists for various industries and purpose. For instance, environmental management systems (ISO 14001), forestry conservation (FSC), recycling of electronic equipment (e-Stewards), and labour practices (AIP/FLA and SA8000). While all certification programmes involve setting of norms and monitoring by external agents, some programmes are very limited in the scope and deal with one specific issue (e-Stewards and FSC), while others are more comprehensive (ISO 14001 and FLA). Some are very demanding and make substantive requirements (FLA and SA8000), while others are more procedural and require very little in terms of substantive norms (ISO 14001).

Insofar as the virtual accessibility is concerned, the ITU, World Summit on Information Society (WSIS), Internet Governance Forum (IGF), and W3C set standards for website accessibility. Websites conforming to the W3C Guidelines are rated in accordance with their accessible features. While the accessibility rating is gaining momentum with enhanced public awareness, there is hardly any rating/certification to indicate accessibility features of products and services. As noted earlier, most supply companies closely associated with the development of hardware components of the Internet have begun to create inbuilt accessibility features. It is suggested that these features should be made visible to the consumers through product specification standards so that the consumer begin to look for them.

Corporate Social Responsibility

Whereas it is quite fashionable to seek corporate responsibility through the much celebrated principle of CSR, the concept as such has been plagued with controversy throughout its history.[158] Legal, political, social, and economic commentators have debated corporate social responsibility ad nauseam.[159] Consequently, CSR means something to all, but not always the same thing to everybody. This study does not make any attempt to get into the larger controversy surrounding theoretical and ideological basis of CSR. Rather, it proceeds on an assumption that CSR has become a modern day reality and whether willingly or unwillingly corporations have been roped in. Therefore, this discussion directly seeks to identify entry points, if any; available to accessibility concerns in a space already occupied with issues such as environment protection, gender equality, labour, and indigenous rights.

Interestingly, there are certain instances where company law creates space for directors to consider responsibility of the company towards other stakeholders (something which proponents of CSR have been demanding), without making any radical changes or compromising on the basic framework of the corporate law. For instance, section 172 of the United Kingdom's Companies Act of 2006[160] whilst entailing duty upon directors to *promote the success of*

---

[158] Some of the different theories of CSR are classified as: 1) Instrumental theories advancing economic objectives through social activities; 2) Political theories advocating corporate power and its responsible use; 3) Integrative theories expressing the necessity for corporations to integrate social demands; and 4) Ethical theories examining the morality and rightness of corporate social action.

[159] Henry N. Butler and Fred S. McChesney, 'Why They Give at the Office: Shareholder Welfare and Corporate Philanthropy in the Contractual Theory of the Corporation', 84 *Cornell Law Review* (1999): 1195.

[160] Section 172 Duty to promote the success of the company:

1. A director of a company must act in the way he considers, in good faith, would be most likely to promote the success of the company for the benefit of its members as a whole, and in doing so have regard (amongst other matters) to—

the company, requires directors to act in such a way that is most likely to inure to the benefit of its members *as a whole*, which includes, inter alia having regards for 'the likely consequences of any decision in the long term ... the impact of the company's operations on the community and the environment ... [and] the desirability of the company maintaining a reputation for high standards of business conduct.' [emphasis added]. It is pertinent to note that the phraseology 'success of the company for the benefit of its members as a whole' is susceptible to a broader interpretation than merely economic benefit. Interestingly sub-section (2) addresses situations where the purposes of a corporation include purposes 'other than the benefit of its members'. It categorically states that in such scenario 'benefit of its members' will be deemed to consist in the attainment of such purposes. In other words, benefits of members may be dissolved into other such purposes.

While this provision may not be categorized as a CSR in its pure form, it can be intelligently invoked to accommodate the concerns of stakeholders other than shareholders. It also bypasses the normative, economic, and legal constraints that are frequently placed on directors to act strictly for wealth maximization of shareholders. Thus, a company's management board may be at liberty to make certain strategic decisions pertaining to imbibing accessibility within its products or services, which may prove to be beneficial to its members as a whole ever where it may not be too

---

    a. the likely consequences of any decision in the long term,
    b. the interests of the company's employees,
    c. the need to foster the company's business relationships with suppliers, customers, and others,
    d. the impact of the company's operations on the community and the environment,
    e. the desirability of the company maintaining a reputation for high standards of business conduct, and
    f. the need to act fairly as between members of the company.
  2. Where or to the extent that the purposes of the company consist of or include purposes other than the benefit of its members, subsection (1) has effect as if the reference to promoting the success of the company for the benefit of its members were to achieving those purposes.

rewarding to the company in the short term. CSR can be subtly employed to address accessibility rights.

It appears that given the shift in disability jurisprudence from welfare to rights, exploring possibilities of enforcing virtual accessibility under the CSR rubric is self-contradictory. Does ensuring virtual accessibility imply a mere 'social' responsibility of a corporation? Does it not militate against the very ideology of the rights model which required the mandating accessibility? Even so, it needs to be conceded that CSR has a role in jurisdictions where private players have been kept out of accessibility mandate which may be influenced to realize accessibility goals through the CSR route.

***

This chapter has examined and assessed various instrumentalities available at the domestic level to implement the right to access the Internet. The examination leaves us with twin strategies—compulsion and persuasion. While anti-discrimination laws with a compulsive force may be favoured as the most effective instrumentality, ground realities of the situation, as well as the very nature of the present right demonstrate limitations of this approach.

Most anti-discrimination legislations are primarily reactive. Consequently, anti-discrimination laws stress on duties of restraint based on the assumption that agents are only responsible for inequalities which they have deliberately caused through their own prejudiced behaviour. This means that existing laws on the right to equality restraints prejudiced action, rather than ensuring positive steps to prevent inequalities from arising or to address inequalities not due to perpetrator's own actions. This hardly advances overall goals of attaining substantive equality through a rights based regime.

More recent anti-discrimination models, such as the UK, Australia, Norway, Spain have begun to realize this limitation and placed obligations on duty bearers to proactively address various forms of discrimination. Alternatively, one also comes across models where anti-discrimination laws are supported by other enactments to ensure accessibility. For instance, the Accessibility for Ontarians with Disabilities Act (AODA)[161] complements the Ontarians with Disabilities Act (ODA) to proactively eliminate barriers for persons with disabilities in all sectors of society, by placing responsibility on everyone. Even so, much of the prejudicial treatment on account of systemic discrimination remains untouched by existing legislations. Further, compliance mechanism in most jurisdictions is primarily complaint driven.

While discrimination law discourse in the context of disability is struggling to move away from influences of social welfare constructs of disability, it is problematic to pin the solution of disability inequality entirely on the anti-discrimination model. It needs to be realized that disability discrimination legislation can achieve only so much in breaking down deep-rooted structural obstacles to equality. States have sporadically employed persuasive techniques. However, given the disjunctive application of compulsive and persuasive techniques, the requisite force could not be created to make any visible dent in existing attitudes and practices towards persons with disabilities.

Both, international human rights frameworks as well as domestic anti-discrimination laws have their peculiar strengths and weaknesses to obtain compliance from corporations. While proposed international instruments are too soft in their tone, domestic anti-discrimination laws fail to address systemic discrimination deeply rooted in attitudinal stereotypes and market bias. These anti-discrimination laws are limited in the kind of corporate duty holders they target. While international human rights instrumentalities are more applicable to supply companies, domestic anti-discrimination laws tend to target consumer companies; and at times do not seek to include private companies. The former is primarily a self-propelling exercise and do not guarantee any alternative if supply companies do not engage with accessibility concerns. The latter is reactionary in nature, depending largely upon individuals with disabilities to come forward and seek a redressal, without promising any systemic change. Both options have a myopic vision.

---

[161] Accessibility for Ontarians with Disabilities Act, S.O. 2005 c. 11 [AODA].

If the corporate Midas touch is to be obtained to ensure the rights of access to the Internet for persons with disabilities, one will have to adopt a strategic mix of approaches and instrumentalities. Having fully equipped with all possible tools and with sufficient information about the strengths of each, we now go on to the drawing board to craft a strategic compliance from corporations in keeping the right to access the Internet.

5

The Interconnected Pentagon Model

From Commitment to Compliance

The discussion so far demonstrates that while goals of substantive equality envisaged under CRPD requires a structural approach to combat the prevalent structural discrimination of persons with disabilities, the regulatory challenge comprise in converting this commitment to compliance. The earlier chapters have explored international human rights laws as well as domestic laws and examined several instrumentalities and approaches deployed at both the levels to seek compliance from corporations with respect to human rights in general and disability rights in particular. However, it is found that the existing international framework, operating on the lowest common denominator of human rights standards of corporate conduct and excessively reliant upon dialogic-co-operation, cannot be transplanted to human rights and technology discourse, especially in terms of CRPD mandate. At the same time, domestic anti-discrimination laws that mostly rely on the reactive approach based on individual litigation does not adequately address systemic discrimination meted out to persons with disabilities in various aspects of physical and virtual society. Thus, international and domestic frameworks and their persuasive and punitive approaches to regulation as well as soft law and hard law regulatory instrumentalities have proved to be inadequate when applied in a disjunctive fashion. It is therefore, critical to re-conceive regulatory and design a strategy of persuasions and punishment to seek necessary compliance from corporations.

Several innovative regulatory models have been developed in the past few years. Prominent amongst these are responsive regulation, smart regulation, problem centred regulation, really responsive regulation.[1] I undertake a critical evaluation of these regulatory models through the lens of disability rights jurisprudence. Are any of these existing regulatory models helpful in attaining the goals of substantive equality and addressing systemic discrimination against persons with disabilities?

Towards this end, I examine the progressive enforcement pyramid developed by Ayres and Braithwaite that synergizes persuasion and punishment and assesses its application to ensure the right to access the Internet. The enforcement pyramid was improved upon by Gunningham in their 'smart regulation' in the form of a three dimensional pyramid. I contend that whilst responsive regulation offers a combination of enforcement options before the regulators, these pyramidal models operate in a linear fashion which is not useful to address the complexity of the polycentric virtual world with multi regulates in an emerging multi-stakeholder virtual world order.

It needs to be acknowledged that the post-modern society has become complex and fragmented systems comprising several self-referentially closed subsystems that are no longer directly accessible to one another. This complexity poses regulatory challenges before law. In order to accommodate this complexity, I explored reflexive law theory propounded by Gunther Teubner who offered appropriate structural solution to the limitations of the State and the law in a pluralistic architecture by facilitating communication with other subjects and allowing them to write rules and behaviour

---

[1] I. Ayres and J. Braithwaite, *Responsive Regulation: Transcending the Deregulation Debate* (1992); N. Gunningham, P. Grobosky, and D. Sinclair, *Smart Regulation: Designing Environment Policy* (1998); M. Sparrow, *The Regulatory Craft* (2003); Surya Deva, *Regulating Corporate Human Rights Violation: Humanizing Business* (2012).

to address their own situation which is subsequently internalized by the legal system. However, Teubner himself concedes that there exists an inherent risk of excessiveness whenever well-structured and significantly funded private bodies enter the field.[2]

This chapter offers an alternative regulatory design based on responsiveness and reflexivity in the form of an IPM. Drawing connects between the instrumentalities and joining the dots backwards, one reaches the institutions behind these to evolve an interconnected pentagon model. While conceding that each institution and instrumentality possess the capacity to influence change in varying degrees; their dynamic interaction in various combinations will prove to be more powerful. The interconnected pentagon aims to provide a regulatory mix to attain desirable outcomes by creating webs of influences. The chapter outlines that interconnected model could be deployed at various levels to attain corporate compliance in ensuring the right to access the Internet for persons with disabilities.

Regulatory Goals and Options Availed

Regulating the corporate conduct vis-a-vis human rights has always remained a challenging task. Moreover, exercising such regulation in the virtual world where corporate participants remain quite decentralized in their operation and presence,[3] adds another layer to the existing regulatory dilemmas. At the same time, it is essential to be mindful that the underlying goal of a regulatory strategy for the present problem is to seek a proactive compliance from corporations rather than preventing them from violating the right to access the Internet.

The discussion so far has demonstrated that international human rights law has been suggestive of a self-regulating enforcement strategy of human rights conduct of corporations. It is often claimed

---

[2] G. Teubner, *Constitutional Fragments: Societal Constitutionalism and Globalisation*, 56 (2012).

[3] One needs to bear in mind categorical divide between companies as supply companies and demand companies.

that self-regulation coupled with soft law instrumentalities ensures higher level of regulatory compliance and at the same time is cost-effective as it relinquishes some of the costs associated with the regulatory 'cat-and-mouse' game.[4] Such strategy is premised on the belief that the 'social license' to operate is sufficient incentive to keep corporations compliant with human rights.[5] Thus, international human rights laws do not provide any explicit incentives to obtain compliance; the question of sanctions does not even arise.

However, it has already been pointed out that internal motivation alone cannot be trusted to provide adequate persuasion. The threat of formal enforcement, even if lurking in the background plays a subtle but important role in securing compliance. What needs to be appreciated is that even in a bottom-up approach, the private sector prefers to base their rules and regulations within the framework provided by the State. The definition of rights adopted by the State provides a frame of reference to the private sector. Importantly, the State is the point at which all social demands for regulation converge, where social consensus arises. Given this characteristic, many groups not represented on the Internet, but nevertheless affected by it, can influence the government by communicating their preferences. If the Internet is completely self-regulated by the private firms that also operate on it, the system will lack inputs from other social groups. When government is included in designing a regulatory framework, consumer participation increases, which contributes to the legitimacy of the system. Therefore, when persuasion and negotiation fail, coercive measures can still be used to ensure compliance.

---

[4] Sharon Oded, *Corporate Compliance: New Approaches to Regulatory Enforcement* (2013), p. 36.

[5] Statement by Prof. John Ruggie, Special Representative of the Secretary-General on Human Rights and Transnational Corporations and Other Business Enterprises, 63rd session of the General Assembly Third Committee Agenda Item 64 (b): *'Promotion and protection of human rights: Human rights questions, including alternative approaches for improving the effective enjoyment of human rights and fundamental freedoms'*, 27th October 2008 New York, available at https://www.hks.harvard.edu/news-events/news/testimonies/john-ruggie-testimony-oct (last visited 14 May 2016).

The domestic frameworks, most often resorts to anti-discrimination laws that take a reactive route. Whereas the enforcement power of the State has been acknowledged and considered significant to obligate the corporations to conform to the rules, unlike private self-regulatory initiatives; the vital question here is whether these laws have been effective in enforcing the desirable change in corporate conduct?

The anti-discrimination laws have been applied to prohibit discrimination rather than promoting conduct that addresses the root causes of discrimination. Consequently, anti-discrimination measures alleviate the symptoms but not the ailment. The deterrence effect of such laws is limited to the cases which reach the courts. These enforcement initiatives mostly operate in a top-down manner. An over reliance on coercive techniques invariably leads to friction between the duty holders and the right holders and makes them antagonists rather than allies. The lawmakers cannot remain ignorant about the potential externalities of such regulation. If excessively enforced, the regulatees may either avoid socially desirable activities or employ excessive, costly precautions to the detriment of social welfare. This is exactly where the US anti-discrimination legislation, the ADA has been struggling. On the one hand, the extension of Title III of ADA to private websites is still not settled and on the other hand, commercial entities are often not proactive in ensuring accessibility. The accessibility mandate stands seriously challenged in the context of private websites especially media rich websites and e-commerce websites since the mandate is feared to have adverse implications on the very fundamental characteristic of such initiatives.

Whereas the anti-discrimination laws and sanctions thereunder may be classified as punishments, States also offer certain incentives in the form of public procurement priorities to accessible products and services, tax rebates, and so on; the incentives and sanctions are quite dispersed in the overall framework. Consequently, they do not have the requisite impact on compliance. Therefore, rather than applying aggressive, uncompromising enforcement measures or discrete incentives, regulators need to find a creative way to induce compliance without generating excessive social costs.

A possible solution could be suggested to obtain a mix of incentives and sanctions in order to ensure compliance.

Exploring Responsive Regulation

Over the years, several scholars have propounded innovative regulatory theories, designed strategies and models to regulate the behaviour of targeted subjects and optimize the outcome and attain desirable behaviour.[6] The theory of responsive regulation put forth by Ian Ayres and John Braithwaite[7] has proved to be highly influential in the context of corporate regulation. Ayres and Braithwaite recognized the need to 'the need to transcend the intellectual stalemate between those who favour strong state regulation of business and those who advocate deregulation'.[8] Thus, moving the debate away from 'deterrence' v. 'co-operation', Ian Ayres and John Braithwaite introduced the model of 'responsive regulation'.

According to this theory, regulators should be responsive to the effectiveness with which citizens or corporations are regulating themselves before deciding whether to escalate intervention. Thus, the trick of successful regulation is to establish a synergy between punishment and persuasion.[9] The model expounds that compliance is more likely when a regulatory agency operates in a tit-for-tat manner, aligning regulatory sanctions and strategies to the mixed motives or objectives of corporate actors in order to ensure an effective and efficient regulatory framework.

The central aspect of responsive regulation is the enforcement pyramid which envisages: a) gradual escalation up the face of the pyramid; and b) the existence of a credible peak or tip which if activated will be sufficiently powerful to deter even the most

[6] C. McCrudden, 'Corporate Social Responsibility and Public Procurement', in *The New Corporate Accountability: Corporate Social Responsibility and the Law* (D. McBarnet, A. Voiculescu, and T. Campbell eds, 2007).

[7] Ayres and Braithwaite, *Responsive Regulation*.

[8] Ayres and Braithwaite, *Responsive Regulation*, p. 3.

[9] Ayres and Braithwaite, *Responsive Regulation*.

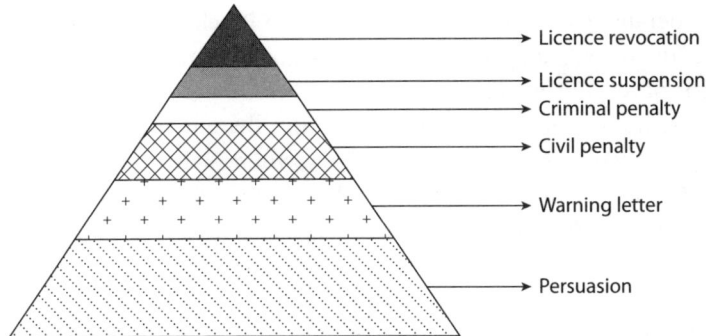

Figure 5.1 Enforcement Pyramid[10]
Source: 'Responsive Regulation: Transcending the Deregulation Debate', Oxford Socio-Legal Studies by Ayres and Brathwaite (1992), Figure 2.1, 'Example of an enforcement pyramid' (page 35).

egregious offender.[11] A pyramid of enforcement, thus, envisions persuasion and co-operation as a starting point of enforcement action. As one ascends the pyramid, variety of other regulatory responses are available so as to respond to the firm's reaction. Under this strategy, the regulatory agency approaches each firm in a co-operative, flexible manner, but turns to punishment if and when the firm clearly defects from co-operation. Once the firm begins to

[10] The proportion of space at each layer represents the proportion of enforcement activity at that level. Most regulatory action occurs at the base of the pyramid where attempts are initially made to coax compliance by persuasion. The next phase of enforcement escalation is a warning letter; if this fails to secure compliance, imposition of civil monetary penalties; if this fails, criminal prosecution; if this fails, plant shut down or temporary suspension of a license to operate; if this fails, permanent revocation of license. This particular enforcement pyramid might be applicable to occupational health and safety, environment or nursing home regulation. It is not the content of the enforcement pyramid on which Ayres and Braithwaite wish to focus rather on its form.

[11] This tip is slated as the benign big gun. Ayres and Braithwaite argue that the regulators will be able to talk softly when they carry big sticks in the form of sanctions. See Ayres and Braithwaite, *Responsive Regulation*, p. 19.

co-operate again, the agency does so too. Such strategy facilitates the 'tit for tat' response on the part of regulators which forms the basis of responsive regulation.[12]

At the top of the pyramid exists the 'Benign Big Gun', which is rarely used nevertheless it is always there.[13] In fact, Ayres and Braithwaite emphasize that regulatory agencies are often best able to obtain compliance when they are benign big guns. Thus, transcending the dichotomy between whether to punish or persuade, the enforcement pyramid suggests that regulation ought to be flexible and responsive to the objectives, goals, and history of regulatory targets. It is presumed that 'the achievement of regulatory objectives is more likely when agencies display both a hierarchy of sanctions and a hierarchy of regulatory strategies of varying degrees of interventionism.'[14] It is further presumed that strategy of persuasion will be exploited when actors are motivated by economic rationality.

However, even as Ayres and Braithwaite explore the possible advantages of co-operation between regulators and firms, they also foresee possibility of capture and corruption of regulators. In order to address such problem they suggest introducing tripartism. In simple terms, tripartism involves participation of a third player—a Public Interest Group (PIG)—into the game along with the regulatory agency and the firm. The involvement of PIGs in regulatory process is encouraged in three ways: granting the PIG 'access to all the information that is available to the regulator';[15] giving the PIG

---

[12] It should be noted that the enforcement pyramid is based on a repeat player prisoner's dilemma, under which the regulator's response (up or down the pyramid) depends upon the previous response of the regulate.

[13] According to Ayres and Braithwaite, the benign big guns are agencies that spoke softly while carrying very big guns. These agencies in the benign big gun clusters are distinguished as those having enormous power, such as the power of the Reserve Bank to seize gold, the power of Life Insurance Commissioner to shut down the business completely by revoking licenses, the power of oil and gas regulators to stop production at rigs at extraordinary costs. Ayres and Braithwaite, *Responsive Regulation*, p. 40.

[14] Ayres and Braithwaite, *Responsive Regulation*, pp. 2, 59.

[15] Ayres and Braithwaite, *Responsive Regulation*, p. 57.

'a seat at the negotiating table with the firm and agency when deals are done'[16] and granting the PIG 'the same standing to use or prosecute under the regulatory statute as the regulator'.[17]

While the pyramid of enforcement combines tools of compliance aimed at a single regulated firm, Ayres and Braithwaite concedes that there is a need to aggregate firms into industry and disaggregate firms into corporate subunits, subunits into corporate actors and individual actors into multi-selves.[18] Therefore, they also outline a pyramid of regulatory strategies that could be 'pitched at the entire industry'.[19] See Figure 5.2 below.

To begin with, the state prefers self-regulatory solutions to the industry-specific problem, however, the option is always available to escalate strategic regulatory intervention if desirable outcomes are not achieved. Therefore, there arises a need to innovate at the intermediate levels of the pyramid between self-regulation and command-control government regulation. Enforced self-regulation is suggested as striking this middle ground. It is basically understood

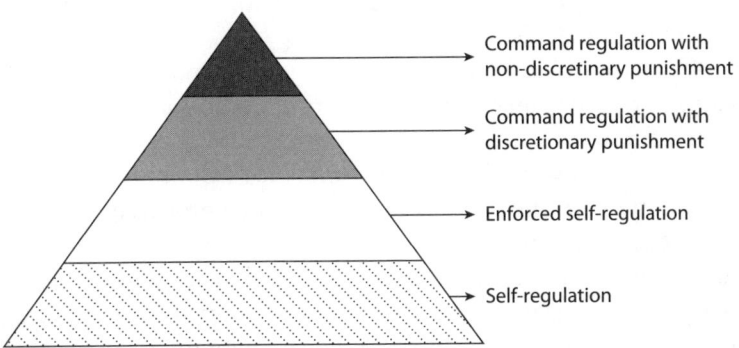

Figure 5.2 Enforcement strategy pyramid
Source: 'Responsive Regulation: Transcending the Deregulation Debate', Oxford Socio-Legal Studies by Ayres and Brathwaite (1992). Figure 2.3, 'Example of pyramid of strategies' (page 39).

16 Ayres and Braithwaite, *Responsive Regulation*, p. 57.
17 Ayres and Braithwaite, *Responsive Regulation*, p. 57.
18 Ayres and Braithwaite, *Responsive Regulation*, p. 19.
19 Ayres and Braithwaite, *Responsive Regulation*, p. 38.

as negotiation between the government and individual firms to establish regulations that are particularized to each firm. Under enforced self-regulation, the government would compel each company to write a set of corporate rules to avoid harsher (and less tailored) standards imposed by the state.[20] The regulatory agency would either approve these rules or send them back for revision if they were insufficiently stringent. At this stage in the process, PIGs would be encouraged to comment on the proposed rule. Rather than having governmental inspectors enforce the rules, most enforcement duties and costs would be internalized by the company which would be required to establish its own independent inspectorial group. Where feasible, PIGs would be represented on this inspection group. The primary function of governmental inspectors would be to ensure the independence of this internal compliance group and to audit its efficiency and toughness. The state involvement would not stop at monitoring. Violation of the privately written and publically ratified rules would be punishable by law. Regulatory agencies would not ratify rules unless the regulations were consonant with legislatively enacted minimum standards.[21]

When translated to the right to access and corporate compliance study, the enforcement pyramid will take the shape as depicted in Figure 5.3.

Thus, this pyramid will also commence from persuading the corporations in the form of taxation, public procurements, and another set of soft measures. If pure persuasions fail, the State may intervene by activating subtle forces of society in the form of mandating social reporting, developing certification mechanisms, naming and shaming techniques. Even where these fall short in creating compliant behaviour, anti-discrimination laws and laws such as CVAA can be put in place to mandate accessibility. These may have certain strong sanctions built-in that may be invoked on non-compliance of the mandate or as seen there are countries which prohibit discrimination through criminal laws. Lastly, as a severe punishment, the State may have to resort to blocking

---

[20] Ayres and Braithwaite, *Responsive Regulation*, p. 101.
[21] Ayres and Braithwaite, *Responsive Regulation*, pp. 106–7.

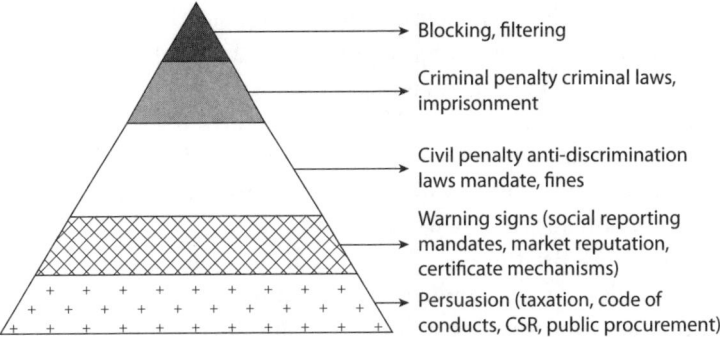

Figure 5.3   Enforcement pyramid for the right to access
Source: Author, on the basis of Figure 5.2 (immediately above) by Ayres and
Braithwaite.

or filtering online operations of such corporations unless they
are accessible.

While it is possible to create pyramids with the objective of
obtaining corporate regulation in terms of the right to access the
Internet for persons with disabilities, it is found to be problematic
once put into practice. In the context of the present issue, the
enforcement pyramid is found wanting on several counts.

One, the pyramid of strategies presupposes the uniformity
of the corporations conduct at all the times and in all contexts
operating in any particular industry and that it is possible to
generalize about the compliance trend in an industry. Thus,
it is presumed that firms or their units either co-operate or
defect. Based on the 'tit-for-tat' policy their conduct should be
met with a range of persuasive and coercive strategies arranged
in a pyramidal order. Based on this firm or industry response
as a whole, the regulator is expected to gradually scale up its
intervention. The operation of such a strategy involves the
creation of 'enforcement communities' in which the regulator
and the regulatee understand the strategy that each is adopting
and can predict each other's responses.[22]

[22] C. Parker, 'Compliance Professionalism and Regulatory Community:
The Australian Trade Practices Regime', 26 *Journal of Law and Society* 215
(1992).

Unfortunately, such predictability and generalizing trend does not appear to work in a highly decentralized virtual world and the corporations operating therein. A clear evidence of this can be obtained in *GLAD v. Time Warner*,[23] where CNN was compliant with the CVAA regulations in that it was broadcasting captioned news. It was, however unwilling to caption excerpts or clips of such previously broadcasted news on its website.

Ayres and Braithwaite also concede that all corporate actors are bundles of contradictory commitments to values about economic rationality, law abidingness, and business responsibility. Corporations have profit-motive selves and law abiding selves at different moments, in different contexts, the different selves may prevail.[24] For instance, it has been seen how the supply companies have been well aware of their accessibility impacts and have taken steps of compliance, the consumer companies have been more reluctant in imbibing accessibility goals in their products and services. Insofar as the Internet is concerned, it may not be possible to generalize about the corporations and their responses to scale up. Thus, it may require invoking different approaches to different groups within the industry. For instance, supply companies may be left with monitored self-regulation while consumer companies may require a command-control regulation with punishments. This inserts complexity, uncertainty, and unpredictability in regulatory responses.

Two, Ayres and Braithwaite acknowledge that the tit-for-tat strategy may not be effective if the target is 'pathologically irrational organisation' and a 'determinedly profit-maximizing actor'.[25] In such situations, persuasion techniques of regulators will have no impact. Rather it will lead to waste of regulatory resources and loss of time.

Three, the enforcement pyramid presupposes the existence of both persuasions as well as punitive measures at the disposal of the regulator, so as to enforce 'tit-for-tat' strategy. A foundational question therefore arises, that is, does the State have such persuasive

---

[23] 742 F.3d 414 (9th Cir. 2014).

[24] Ayres and Braithwaite, *Responsive Regulation*, p. 19.

[25] Ayres and Braithwaite, *Responsive Regulation*, pp. 29–30.

and punitive measures to ensure accessibility compliant behaviour from the corporations? Does anti-discrimination law across jurisdictions allow such multiple options or have any such inbuilt techniques? Is there any other sanction or threat available under the domestic framework apart from litigation, which may act as a sanction in terms of enforcement pyramid? It is, therefore, crucial to assess whether the State have any such big sticks apart from anti-discrimination laws when it comes to disabilities.

Four, the model presupposes that regulatees do respond to the pressures imposed by the regulators through the sanctioning. Although there is power to prosecute and to impose fines by the Courts, these are generally too low to provide deterrence. Also, one needs to concede that corporate behaviour is often driven not only by regulatory pressure, but also market forces, consumer preferences, and the sector dynamics. Often these have subtle yet effective pressure on corporations to fall in line. However, the pyramid does not refer to these parallel pressures on corporations. Blocking the online presence of the corporation amounts to an extreme step, which may not find favour either with states, markets, or community.

Further, while responsive regulation claims flexibility in regulation as its central tenet, the hierarchy of sanctions tends to jeopardize this very flexibility. Since the underlying strategy is to progressively scale up sanctions, the regulators are expected to follow certain sequence of the pyramid, thus allowing only one particular regulatory option at a time. Again, the ranking of strategies/sanctions offers little guidance to regulators in market settings as to when and where to enter the enforcement pyramid. Even if they enter the pyramid at the right time and level, the responsive regulation model does not tell regulators how long they should try one regulatory technique before moving up or down to the next level.[26] Unless persuasive techniques are fully exhausted, the regulator cannot move up the pyramid. Thus, the pyramid form of sanctions gives an impression to the regulators that they

[26] Surya Deva, *Regulating Corporate Human Rights Violation: Humanizing Business* (2012).

must always begin with persuasion keeping punishments in the background.

Such waiting time may prove to be detrimental in the present matter where the virtual world architecture is quickly taking shape. Once, the design is settled, corporations have an option to invoke 'undue hardship' as a defence since in most cases retrofitting techniques proves to be a costly affair. In other words, when the State is convinced about the irrational or irresponsive behaviour of regulatees, 'tit-for-tat' approach will tend to prove wasteful.

An important peculiarity, or rather limitation of the enforcement pyramid of Ayres and Braithwaite as highlighted by Gunningham, Grobosky, and Sinclair is that the pyramid is concerned with interaction between only two parties: State and business. Gunningham, Grobosky, and Sinclair, however, demonstrate that regulation can be carried out by quasi-regulators such as public interest groups, professional bodies, industry associations. As already discussed, one of the primary limitations of the State based regulator in a virtual world is the lack of technological knowledge and consequent modules of control. It has also been examined that whereas corporations as private entities have a dominant control of over design and architecture of the Internet, they are not the only players. One-dimensional enforcement pyramid, therefore, is not suitable in a multi-regulatee and multi-regulator industry.

In what is termed as 'smart regulation', Gunningham, Grabosky, and Sinclair propose to involve mixtures of institutions and instruments to obtain the best regulatory outcomes.[27] The pyramid of smart regulation is, accordingly, three sided and considers the possibility of regulation using a number of different instruments implemented by a number of parties. It conceives of escalation to higher levels of coerciveness not only within a single instrument but also across several instruments.[28] The three sided pyramid envisage a co-ordinated approach to regulation in which it is possible to escalate responses to non-compliance by not only moving up a single face of the pyramid but also from one face of the pyramid to

---

[27] N. Gunningham, P. Grobosky, and D. Sinclair, *Smart Regulation: Designing Environment Policy*, pp. 422–53 (1998).

[28] Gunningham, Grobosky, and Sinclair, *Smart Regulation*, pp. 300–400.

another. For instance, from a State control to a corporate control or industry association instrument. This allows creative mixes or networks of regulatory instruments and of influencing actors or institutions.

Whilst this allows flexibility of response and sanctions, it still remains a pyramid. Thus, even where smart regulation is more broad based than responsive regulation in its classical form; it nevertheless involves an escalation process. Consequently, smart regulation runs against many of the general difficulties that responsive regulation encounters. Again the co-ordination between the three dimensional pyramid is not always easy and gives rise to special difficulties of information management, clarity of messaging to regulatees, resource and time constraint, and political differences between different institutional actors. Concerns about consistency, fairness, and accountability may be even more acute than was the case with responsive regulation.[29]

Ayres and Braithwaite concede that responsive regulation is not a clearly defined programme or a set of prescriptions concerning the best way to regulate. On the contrary, the best strategy depends on the context, regulatory culture and history. Therefore, the model suggested by Ayres and Braithwaite is a new variety of regulatory options; yet the best possible solution still needs to be worked out in the context of the regulatory culture of the Internet and the goals of the disability rights jurisprudence.

Reflexive Approach to the Right to Access

The responsive regulation freed up the regulators from the dichotomous choice between co-operative self-regulation and deterrence based command-control laws. Yet it ended up stacking the available options in a hierarchical order applicable in a vertically stratified society where the values cherished by one become the command of the other. It, however, failed to acknowledge that the post-modern society has become complex and it no longer consists

---

[29] See Braithwaite, *Restorative Justice and Responsive Regulation* (2002).

of a single system. Thus, the regulatory theories somewhere overly simplify an otherwise complex regulatory field as a matter between the government as the regulator and corporation as the regulatee.

However, traditional stratification of the rulers (the State) and the ruled (the corporations) have been replaced with a multi layered and interdependent cobweb of social organizations. It needs to be recognized that the growing regulatory challenges to modern law owes itself to the deeply complex and fragmented society. In order to appreciate this complexity and non-hierarchical organization of post-modern society, I discuss German sociologist and systems theorist Gunther Teubner and his reflexive law. The systems theory develops an understanding of society as a social system made up of sub-systems of particularly structured modes of communications. Accordingly, present social order, separated into distinct subsystems based on functions such as science, religion, family life, education, politics, law, and so on. Each of these systems are further divided into sub-system having has their own world view and discourse and would form the environment for another system, leading to a diversified communication of societal (system) rationalities.[30]

Consequently, there prevails 'value pluralism' in each sub-system which appears to pull in its own direction. In other words, when certain sectors of society such as economy, politics, law, culture, and science become so autonomous that they not only program themselves, but exclusively react to themselves, they are no longer directly accessible to one another.[31] Such self-referentially closed systems only interact internally with their own elements. This makes it difficult for one system to influence the other in the way that the system intends.

This results in what Teubner dubs as 'Crisis of Interventionist State'.[32] According to Teubner, such crisis results from a substantive

[30] Gunther Teubner, *Law as an Autopoietic System*, pp. 64–5 (1993).

[31] Teubner, 'Juridification: Concepts, Aspects, Limits, Solutions', in *A Reader on Regulation* 407 (Robert Baldwin, Colin Scott, and Christopher Hood, eds 1998).

[32] See Teubner, 'Autopoiesis in Law and Society: A Rejoinder to Blankenburg', 18 L. & SOC'Y REV. 291 (1984) and Teubner, 'Substantive and Reflexive Elements in Modern Law', 17 L. & SOC'Y REV. 239 (1983).

law's inability to meet the demands placed on it by an increasing 'differentiated' society. In such autopoietic systems where systems are self-producing, self-organizing; normatively closed and cognitively open,[33] no system can act directly upon another. Subsystems interpret the commands of the legal system according to their own logic, and their responses to these directives can be decidedly non-linear. Interpreting the directive through the lens of their own discourse, subsystems often distort the message, or even undermine it altogether. Any attempt of a particular system to direct another will result in Teubner's well known regulatory trilemma: the indifference of the target system to the intervening system, or the destruction of the target system or the destruction of the intervening system itself.[34] This can lead centralized directives to misfire.[35]

This has already been experienced in terms of disability discrimination laws. The use of substantive law is likely in most circumstances to be under-inclusive and ineffective in producing meaningful changes in behaviour without risking the destruction of other subsystems (under effectiveness).[36] This tussle has been witnessed in the mandating of accessibility from supply companies and demand companies. It needs to be recounted that in GLAD v. Time Warner as well as Sony such mandating was opposed on the grounds that it tends to destroy the very design of the product/ service. Similar arguments have been forwarded in case of media rich websites or e-commerce where such mandating is seen as altering the very foundations of that sub-system. Second, substantive law may indeed turn out to be too effective and consequently destroy

---

[33] Teubner, Law as an Autopoietic System, pp. 32–43.

[34] Teubner, 'Juridification'.

[35] Jean L. Cohen, Regulating Intimacy: A New Legal Paradigm 155 (2002) ('[R]egulatory failure can be attributed to the lack of respect for the autonomy and internal logics of the regulated subsystem.'); at p. 1265 ('[S]ubstantive reform strategies often miss their mark by misunderstanding the ability of other social systems to respond.').

[36] Teubner, 'After Legal Instrumentalism? Strategic Models of Post-Regulatory Law', in Dilemmas of Law in the Welfare State 299, p. 310 (Teubner, ed., 1988).

the internal fabric of subsystems (over-legalization or juridification of society by law).[37]

However, the law was placed at a unique place from which it would constantly receive manifold communications, influences, and pressures from different parts of society, its evolution de pended on its ability to maintain this intricate relationship to its environment. Its self-reproduction depended on its constant expo sure to the forces of society, while reconstructing these signals in its own language or code.[38] Drawing on Niklas Luhmann's systems theory, Teubner argues that the complexity of modern life and society requires a new approach to regulation, that by reflexive law, in which law facilitates the internal discourse and coordination of other systems. Reflexive law reforms social practices by influencing the self-referential capacities of other social institutions.[39]

When we transplant this observation in the present study, one can identify clusters of systems—the disability constituency, the Internet, corporations, the international human rights regime, each with its own set of norms and values. If we apply the 'crisis of the state', when anti-discrimination laws are expected to ensure compliance from corporations in positive terms, it fails to influence the self-referentially closed corporations. This approach recognizes the limited ability of the law in a complex society to direct social change in an effective manner.[40] Instead of trying to suppress the complexity and diversity in society through extensive regulation,

---

[37] Teubner, 'Juridification: Concepts, Aspects, Limits, Solutions', in *Juridification of Social Spheres: A Comparative Analysis in the Areas of Labor, Corporate, Antitrust and Social Welfare Law* 3, 9 (Teubner, ed., 1987).

[38] Teubner and Helmut Willke, 'Kontext und Autonomie: Gesellschaftliche Selbstst in Law after the Welfare State: Formalism, Functionalism', cited in Peer Zumbansen, 'The Ironic Turn of Reflexive Law', 56(3) *The American Journal of Comparative Law*, Special Symposium Issue: 'Beyond the State: Rethinking Private Law', 769 (2008).

[39] Teubner, 'Introduction to Autopoietic Law', in *Autopoietic: A New Approach to Law and Society* 2 (Teubner, ed., 1988).

[40] Eric W. Orts, 'A Reflexive Model of Environmental Regulation', 5 *Business Ethics Quarterly* 779 (1995): 780 (discusses the idea to foster conditions where businesses voluntarily adopt procedures to encourage environmentally sound decision making and to monitor environmental progress).

the reflexive approach aims to guide the behaviour and promote self-regulation. Thus, the purpose of this approach is 'to foster internal reflection to force the organization to internalize outside conflicts in its own decision structure, to become socially sensitive to the externalities caused by its own behaviours and so 'to develop effective internal control structures'.[41] Reflexive approach, thereby attempts to construct internal models of the outside world with which subsystems are able to interact internally.

This approach predicts that part of the problem is lack of communication between the systems. Therefore, part of the solution involves opening up discourse, norms, values, and language with other systems so that it can be heard and incorporated. Viewed under the reflexive law lens, the UN GPs actually ended up attempting to open up several closed systems to one another; engage them with constructive mediated dialogue and in the process created an enriching text duly informed of aspirations and limitations of the involved systems which ultimately secured wide support from multi-stakeholders.[42]

While reflexive law concedes that the State and its agents remain the primary norm-generators, it considers that they are not the exclusive ones. Corporations are also major contributors to the content and shape of regulation.[43] Thus, a 'reflexive' approach gets

---

[41] References can be made to be suggested interconnected pentagon of internet governance. Reading the same under reflexive law rubric, it can be analysed as comprising of differentiated systems getting sensitive to externalities and opening up to other systems, thereby engaging in creative discourses and taking such norms which can then be internalized as its own.

[42] *Recommendations on Follow-Up to the Mandate*, Mandate of the Special Representative of the Secretary-General (SRSG) on the Issue of Human Rights and Transnational Corporations and other Business Enterprises, 2011, available at www.business-humanrights.org/media/documents/ruggie/ruggie-special-mandate-follow-up-11-feb-2011.pdf (last visited 30 August 2014).

[43] Guy Mundlak and Issi Rosen-Zvi, 'Mapping the Hard Law/Soft Law Terrain: Labor Rights and Environmental Protection: Signaling Virtue? A Comparison of Corporate Codes in the Fields of Labor and Environment', 12 *Theoretical Inquiry Law* 403 (2011) (analyses the purpose and significance of the codes of conduct and annual CSR report for improving the functioning

a corporation to reflect on how its behaviour impacts the wider society. Reflexive laws do not mandate specific technologies like traditional regulation. Nor do they require particular results like outcome-based rules. Instead, they use tools such as information disclosure, stakeholder involvement, and planning requirements to motivate companies to undertake their own, self-directed improvement efforts, while leaving it up to the corporations to determine procedures through which ultimate outcomes shall be attained. For instance, the UN GPs had suggested such reflexive human rights framework to ensure corporate responsibility to respect human rights. Such an approach concentrated on process rather than the outcome. It thus, encouraged the companies to reflect upon their human rights impact and address the same; although without creating a legal obligation.

There has been a growing emphasis on reflexive law and adoption of soft laws to this end. It is believed that such an approach introduces regulations of corporations 'that otherwise would be impossible to regulate'.[44] However, there is need to probe deeper into the validity of such claims. Certain questions naturally arise. Are these initiatives no more than a public relations exercise on the part of corporations keen to deflect criticism of their activities? Do they reflect a new form of stakeholder control over a business that is more appropriate in a globalized economy? Whether reflection alone or coupled with soft law initiatives, ensure corporate responsiveness in general? Can such soft nudging ensure the accessibility rights of persons with disabilities? It is crucial to weigh its strengths and weaknesses in the context of disability rights.

Reflexive approach undoubtedly appears useful in getting corporations to reflect on the right to access the Internet. Its application would amount to opening up the sub-system

---

of market of virtue); David Vogel, 'Private Global Business Regulation', 11 ANN. REV. POL. SCI. 261 (2008): 262 (explores the interactions between public and private regulators in the case of corporate non-financial reporting to create a series of affiliation networks. The paper assesses how the development of private regulatory networks impacts the likelihood of new public policy).

[44] A. Febbrajo, 'The Autopoietic Approach and its Form', in *State, Law and Economy as Autopoietic Systems* 30 (Teubner and Febbrajo, eds, 1992).

(corporations) to the values of another sub-system (disabilities) which will serve as a 'normative point of reference'[45] to be taken into account in the process of generating, recognizing, and connecting operations as decisions to prior decisions.[46] There is a need to be cautious in according prominence to deliberative democratic processes in total disregard of the outcome, particularly in the context of disability rights. Abandoning instrumental regulations in favour of procedural regulation without requiring particular outcomes appears to be a dangerous proposition for the heavily marginalized constituency of persons with disabilities. Therefore, an emphasis on reflexive approach should not be understood as compromising the necessity of policy-based goals and objectives of anti-discrimination laws. Moreover, the processes it relies upon, such as the Codes of Conduct, CSR are highly self-selective mechanisms that adopt certain norms and neglect others. In order to galvanize corporate responsiveness, an over-dependence upon the reflexive law approach is problematic. If corporations are expected to recognize and accommodate this diversity, the reflexive law approach as a stand-alone may not hold much promise.

Interconnected Pentagon Model (IPM): Combining Reflexivity and Responsiveness

Thus, if we step back and take a view of the discussion so far, what we have on hand are a range of soft law-hard law, persuasive-coercive instrumentalities, and voluntary mandatory, top-down-bottoms-up, deterrence-co-operative, disjunctive-stacked approaches and strategies operating nationally and internationally to seek compliance from corporations. Whereas each of these approaches, strategies, and instrumentalities have their own virtues and

---

[45] Andrew Johnston, 'Governing Externalities: The Potential of Reflexive Corporate Social Responsibility', Working Paper No. 436, Centre for Business Research, University of Cambridge (September 2012) available at http://ssrn.com/abstract=2165616.

[46] J. Achterbergh and D. Vriens, *Organisations: Social Systems Conducting Experiment* 157 (2010).

limitations, I see in all of them vital building blocks of a new strategy to ensure the right to access the Internet.

The strategy I propose is a mix of reflexion and responsiveness. Reflection will enable specialized sub-systems of society to mediate and integrate their functional role in the larger society as a whole and sensitizes them towards the values of the others.[47] Reflexive regulation prescribes inclusive procedures for parties to recognize existing and future problems and to develop their own solutions.[48] 'Responsive' regulation on the other hand, refers to a collaborative process between a regulator and the regulated interest where the co-operation of the regulated interest offers a better chance of finding a solution.[49] Explaining the interdependence of reflexivity and responsiveness, Christine Parker asserts:

> If law is to be pluralized, it must be both reflexive and responsive—it must be aimed at catalyzing processes of social coordination for people to agree on values—but it must also take up these values and apply them to the processes in order to make participation in these processes of deliberation possible in the first place and to critique their outcomes and not just the processes themselves.[50]

I am therefore, inclined to combine the core principles of responsive regulation and reflexive approach and introduce the IPM to ensure the right to access the Internet. The idea is to underscore that it is the interplay between the private regulation and state intervention which will ensure the right to access the Internet for persons with disabilities. The IPM builds upon the available regulatory models and approaches by imbibing the strengths of each of these models. It accepts the initial premise of responsive regulation that regulation should be responsive to the conduct of regulatees and that a synergy

---

[47] For more on autopoietic theory, see H. Rottleuthner, 'The Limits of Law: The Myth of a Regulatory Crisis', 17 *International Journal of Society of Law* 273 (1989); Rottleuthner, 'Biological Metaphors in Legal Thought', in *Autopoeitic Law: A New Approach to Law and Society* (Teubner, ed., 1998).

[48] David Hess, 'Social Reporting: A Reflexive Law Approach to Corporate Social Responsiveness', 25 *Iowa Journal of Corporate Law* 41 (1999): 136–40.

[49] Hugh Collins, *Regulating Contracts* 65 (1999).

[50] Parker, 'The Pluralization of Regulation', 9 *Theoretical Inquiries in Law* 369 (2008).

between persuasion and punishment is desirable for successful regulation. It also appreciates the Smart Regulation's emphasis on the mixture of institutions and instrumentalities so as to arrive at an optimal mix.

However, the IPM departs from a linear, hierarchical 'pyramid' to an interconnected 'pentagon'. This model calls for pooling in various instrumentalities and institutions available at several levels to obtain proactive corporate involvement. Such an approach calls for an integrated theory which finds references in the work of Surya Deva, who also relies on Gunninghum, Grabosky, and Sinclair, develop an optimal mix of regulatory instruments. In their book Smart Regulation, the authors sum up without using the term 'integrated', what an integrated theory of regulation aspires to achieve—

> We will argue that such single instrument or single strategy approaches are misguided, because all instruments have strengths and weaknesses and because none are sufficiently flexible and resilient to be able to successfully address all environmental problems in all contexts. Accordingly, we maintain that a better strategy will seek to harness the strengths of individual mechanisms while compensating for their weakness by the use of additional and complementary instruments.[51]

Before I elaborate on the interconnected pentagon and how it operates; let me set out the basic principles that guides the model. Since the model develops an optimal policy mix to seek corporate compliance to ensure the right to access the Internet, the same have been derived by marrying principles that guide the emerging governance models of the Internet and the ones that essentially informs the emerging disability rights jurisprudence.

Principle of Partnership and Participation

Informed by substantive equality and social model of disability coupled with the polycentric nature of the Internet, the interconnected pentagon model is based on the principles of

---

[51] Gunningham, Grobosky, and Sinclair, Smart Regulation (1998), at pp. 14–15.

partnership and participation. It thereby aims to broaden the decision-making field by involving the actors in various stages of the compliance strategy. This will help to diversify the types of expertize and experience that these new actors bring to the table. Such a regime based on engaging multiple actors and shifting citizens from passive to active roles, thereby enhancing participation, and inclusiveness and shared understanding.

At the same time, the partnership element provides a framework that enables us to view the different actors—the state, corporation, international organization, market, and civil society—as part of one comprehensive, interlocking regulatory system. A combination of participation and partnership of actors implies a shift away from the singular focus on the formal legal instruments (such as anti-discrimination legislations) and formal officials (disabilities commissions) to non-legal instrumentalities such as codes of conduct, CSR policies, tax incentives, public procurements. Such partnership and co-ordination is already somewhat visible on the international level with multi-party discourses around the Internet policy making. Of particular importance is the role of private ordering and self-regulation, particularly new instances of private standard setting, accreditation, and certification plans by independent activists, as well as monitoring by both non-profits and for-profit consulting firms.[52]

Principle of Active Citizenship

The discourse on the virtual world governance has always emphasized on creating an open and inclusive Internet. This norm of the Internet when converged with the participatory rights of

---

[52] See, for example, Lester M. Salamon et al., *Global Civil Society: Dimensions of the Nonprofit Sector*, 14 (1999); Jim Rossi, *Bargaining in the Shadow of Administrative Procedure: The Public Interest in Rulemaking Settlement*, 51 Duke L.J. 1015, pp. 1015–16 (2001) (discusses private ordering in the context of settlement of law suits); Anne-Marie Slaughter, 'The Accountability of Government Networks', 8 *Industrial Journal of Global Legal Studies* 347(2001): 352–5 (discussing the rise of trans governmental regulatory network).

persons with disabilities entails creating foundations of accessibility on the principle of active citizenship. This principle hinges upon promoting a life in the virtual community and challenges virtually constructed barriers, behaviours, and attitudes. Accordingly, the interconnected pentagon operates in keeping with this principle which perceives persons with disabilities as citizens rather than as mere consumers. Such approach ensures that persons with disabilities enjoy access to the Internet on an equal basis with others.

Principle of Shared Co-ordination

Whereas the UN PRR Framework and the UN GPs have set out a common ground for corporate conduct on human rights; it overtly relies on corporate voluntary initiatives and largely leaves States to fend for themselves to come up with requisite domestic framework. The experience of the existing domestic anti-discrimination laws, even amongst the most developed countries, has demonstrated how mandating accessibility to supply companies and consumer companies are treated as objects of regulation. They either choose to comply or conflict. This is indicative of the adversarial relations, mutual distrust and friction.

The interconnected pentagon model is based on the principle of shared co-ordination between international, national, market, community, and corporate level. This has two merits. One, it gels with the multi-stakeholderism, a norm widely accepted in the Internet governance. Two, it involves actors and stakeholders in the process of developing the norms of behaviour that will eventually change their attitude and approach towards accessibility and disability. The interconnected pentagon model thus, views traditional hierarchical top-down regulatory control as obsolete and instead establishes a co-ordinated and collaborative framework where the actors are in continuous interaction with one another. Such horizontal relationships, establish two-way communications. This ties up with systems theory which suggested opening up communication between systems and helps in creating a framework imagined, managed, and maintained by the stakeholders.

Such a collaborative process advances goals for introducing systemic changes by substantially evolving the capacities and identities of the participants over time. At the same time it ensures mutual accountability among autonomous actors committed to shared values and visions and to relationships of mutual trust and influence that enable renegotiating expectations and capacities to respond to uncertainty and change. This principle entails identifying interdependencies among actors and thereby collates shared goals. Reaching such common ground necessitates actors to perceive other actors as partners in solution by abandoning entrenched positions that construct other actors as the problem.[53]

Principle of Flexibility

It has been conceded throughout this study that disability rights jurisprudence is yet in a nascent stage as is Internet governance. There exists a yawning gap between CRPD mandate and domestic disability laws; the right to access the Internet for persons with disabilities, and its implementation. Whilst goals are clear, means to attain these goals are still taking shape. Deconstructing the hierarchy of difference requires a systemic response and expanding participation. This calls for reconfiguring existing laws, policies, and conceptions. Equality and inclusion in the Internet can only be attained with co-ordinated efforts. This in turn requires regulatory humility and flexibility in the operation of the instrumentalities. One dimension of the flexibility principle is to be understood in terms of attaining flexible combination of instrumentalities and institutions. The other dimension of flexibility principle takes the form of creating such fluid policy environment that fosters the

[53] Orly Lobel, 'The Renew Deal: The Fall of Regulation and the Rise of Governance in Contemporary Legal Thought', Research Paper No. 07-27, Legal Studies Research Paper Series, University of San Diego (2005) available at http://ssrn.com/abstract=723761 (discusses the new governance model that dislocates traditional state-regulation with more participatory, collaborative model in which government, industry, society share responsibility for achieving policy goals).

integration of corporations and stakeholders in decision-making processes along with complementing mandating laws.

Principle of Diversity and Decentralization

In keeping with the key elements of disabilities jurisprudence and the Internet, this principle calls to the model to identify the actors who effectively contribute to policy making, including disability constituency. It thus perceives disability as a facet of diversity which needs to be included rather than diminished into a minority group. It has been demonstrated how laws based on the minority model of disability have been reinforcing segregation of persons with disabilities instead of ensuring mainstreaming. The IPM emphasizes on seamless inclusion of persons with disabilities as a human diversity. At the same time decentralization which is amongst the most significant characteristic of the Internet world also needs to be reflected in the model. Consequently, the IPM imbibes a decentralized regulation which ensures horizontality of regulatory endeavours.

Envisioning the IPM

Situated in the systems theory and addressing the concerns of the crisis of the State; the IPM is so framed as to cope with an increasingly complex and volatile world.[54] Accordingly, it seeks to replace the hierarchy, control, and a culture of regulatory monologue with a more participatory and collaborative model of regulation and compliance.[55] This is peculiarly responsive to the

---

[54] See, for example, David M. Trubek and Louise G. Trubek, 'Hard and Soft Law in the Construction of Social Europe: The Role of the Open Method of Coordination', 11 *European Law Journal* 343 (2005) (outlines the debate over the relative value of hard and soft law in EU social policy and explores possibility of combination of hard and soft measures).

[55] I purport to use the term regulatory monologue to signify the unidimensional command-control form of regulation where the regulator tells the regulatee what to do and the regulatee does.

wide gaps existing between expectation and the ground reality. It is conceded that the desired outcome may not be achieved only by law. Consequently, the model weaves a co-ordinated web of instrumentalities and institutions and aims to shift from a top-down, command-and-control framework to a reflexive approach, which is process oriented and tailored to meet the horizontally networked Internet.

The model has reference to a 'regulatory space' in which many parties perform the regulatory role. It is not useful to focus purely on the state exercising its authority to regulate behaviour through law and administrative oversight. The regulatory space metaphor points out 'that resources relevant to wield regulatory power and exercise capacities are dispersed or fragmented. These resources are not restricted to formal, state authority derived from legislation or contracts, but also informative, wealth, and organizational capacities. The possession of these resources is fragmented between state and non-state bodies.'[56] Accordingly, in order to ensure the attainment of the right to access the Internet, the regulatory space is occupied by five institutions and their instrumentalities to form an interconnected pentagon which looks as follows:

Figure 5.4   Interconnected Pentagon Model
Source: Author.

[56] C. Scott, 'Analyzing Regulatory Space: Fragmented Resources and Institutional Design', *Public Law* 329 (2001): 330.

The five points of the pentagon represent five pressure points—the State, corporation, community, markets, and international organizations. Each commands leverage over certain instrumentalities. Instead of looking for the few who are formally recognized as powerful, the interconnected pentagon looks at the many whose webs of influence provoke and guide the effective implementation of the right to access the Internet.[57]

The model depicted here is an optimum combination where all possible instrumentalities are invoked in a co-ordinated manner. It is a situation where all institutions are in constant active conversation with each other so as to exchange information and communicate progress or a problem which in turn signals them which instrumentality should be now evoked. However, such an ideal situation will be attained only over a period. Nevertheless, the IPM allows each institution to serve as a point of convergence for addressing a particular purpose while simultaneously also collaborates and co-ordinates with other actors in various combinations. The strategy proposed here offers a new approach of identifying optimal combinations of instrumentalities and co-ordination of institutions. It thereby enables policy makers to avoid the excesses and inefficiencies of standalone command and control regulation on the one hand and the pitfalls of deregulation on the other.

Unlike the pyramid model of regulation where persuasions/punishment function in a linear fashion; the interconnected

---

[57] Hugh Hecklo (1978) uses the concept of 'issue network' and highlights their powerful role: 'In looking for the few who are powerful, we tend to overlook the many whose webs of influence provoke and guide the exercise of power. These webs or what we will call "issue networks" are particularly relevant to the highly intricate and confusing welfare policies that have been undertaken in recent years.... Issue networks ... comprise a large number of participants with quite variable degrees of mutual commitment or of dependence on others in their environment; in fact it is almost impossible to say where a network leaves off and its environment begins...Participants move in and out of the networks constantly.' See Hecklo, 'Issue Networks and the Executive Establishment', in *The New American Political System* 446, p. 448 (Anthony King, ed., 1978).

pentagon model allows horizontal application of the relevant measures. The model is flexible, diverse, and decentralized in that it allows application of a particular regulatory tool in isolation and at the same time can be combined with one or two other tools or all of them together. It is interesting to note that whereas this framework aims to seek corporate compliance, it does not alienate corporation. Rather, corporations are both subjects and objects of regulation. Considering the Internet as a complex social system; the entrepreneurs, consumers, policy-makers are not only participants or controllers but also adaptive agents in an integrated socio-techno economic system.[58] Even otherwise the model is in sync with the reflexive law approach in that it creates a continuous exchange of information, discourse, and creates a dialogic web between functionally differentiated systems.

Having laid out theoretical and normative foundations of the interconnected pentagon model, I next outline the operative part. The model operates at three different levels—international, national, and institutional—in combining various institutions and instrumentalities in order to ensure the rights of persons with disabilities to an accessible Internet. For this purpose, reliance is also placed on informal, non-legal tools and non-state institutions. The idea is that 'regulation' should not be seen and linked exclusively to formal law, state, and legal institutions.[59] Instead, as suggested by Ayres and Braithwaite, a sound analysis would require understanding interdependence between the state regulation and private regulation. It has already been examined how law suffers from inherent limitations in regulating corporations vis-a-vis right to access the Internet. Such limitations are natural consequences of the power dynamics, structure, and modus operandi of the corporations on the Internet where the code is law. Therefore, the IPM employs a range of informal tools and non-state actors alongside a formal set up.

---

[58] Pierre De Vries, 'The Resilience Principles: A Framework for New ICT Governance', 9 *Journal on Telecommunication and High Technology Law* 137 (2011).

[59] Gunningham, Grobosky, and Sinclair, *Smart Regulation*, pp. 229–33.

At International Level

The discussion in the earlier chapters provided information on the creation of the Internet through governmental efforts, primarily by the US Department of Defence. Yet, as it proliferated, the Internet was commercialized in the mid-1990s and governments transferred much of the standard-setting responsibilities to agencies within the cyber system. This is the period when it was claimed that the code is law. Policy making and code making were put in the hands of foras other than the State.

It has been already narrated that policy decisions and norm setting is largely deliberated in international organizations. For instance, accessibility has been discussed as policy issues in WSIS and IGF. These are international gatherings of the Information Society, where the State, corporations, civil society groups, experts, and individuals participate. Accessibility standards and tool kits have been developed by the ITU, United Nations Educational, Scientific and Cultural Organisation (UNESCO) in keeping with the CRPD.

Similarly, most Internet standards setting processes take place in non-governmental transnational settings, with membership shared between corporations, civil society, and experts.[60] For instance, the Internet Engineering Task Force (IETF) that sets the basic technical standards that define Internet functions has been identified in legal scholarship as an example of a deliberative and a co-operative rule-making environment.[61] IETF, an unincorporated association with constantly changing members, operates to set standards through negotiations open to all.[62] Michael Froomkin describes the IETF

---

[60] A. Michael Froomkin, 'HABERMAS@DISCOURSE.NET: Toward a Critical Theory of Cyberspace', 116 Harvard Law Review 749, p. 752 (2003).

[61] Froomkin, 'HABERMAS@DISCOURSE.NET'.

[62] IETF is an independent, unincorporated, international standards body. It comprise of international community of network designers, operators, vendors and researchers concerned with the evolution of the Internet architecture and its smooth operation. IETF aims to achieve technical excellence, implementation and testing, clear and concise Internet Standards Process. It has functions similar to ITU in standard-setting but exclusively related to the Internet.

model as a realization of the Habermasian vision of 'a reenergized, activist, engaged citizenry working together to create new small-scale communicative associative institutions that over time either merge into larger ones or at least join forces.'[63] W3C is another forum where experts from industry and civil society groups and individuals develop web accessibility standards.[64] Standard setting processes are thus decentered from the formal state situated elsewhere. Since such policy making and standard setting occur in the presence of and with joint participation of the State, corporation, community, and international organizations; it brings together people and institutions with diverse viewpoints.

Thus, a considerable extent of interconnection has been already at play at least at the international level. For instance, the Internet Governance Forum brings together stakeholder groups in discussions relating to policy issues related to the Internet.[65] While the IGF does not claim any negotiated outcome, it nonetheless facilitates erosion of boundaries between both policy domains and stakeholders and helps create a common understanding about the opportunities and challenges of the Internet. The IGF has floated Dynamic Coalitions including the one on Accessibility and Disability. These coalitions are informal, issue-specific groups comprising of members of stakeholder groups. Most of these activities occur in settings that focus on sustained deliberation that produce information on innovation; require sharing of good practice and experimental results; encourage actors to compare

[63] Froomkin, 'HABERMAS@DISCOURSE.NET', p. 753.

[64] W3C was founded as an industry consortium in 1994 after the invention of world wide web. W3C is engaged in the development of common technical web standards.

[65] The Tunis Agenda of WSIS prepared the way for an open and inclusive process by new forum for multi-stakeholder policy dialogue—called the *Internet Governance Forum* (IGF). See ITU, World Summit on the Information Society, 'Tunis Agenda for the Information Society', 42, WSIS-05/TUNIS/DOC/6 (Rev. 1)-E (28 November 2005), available at http://www.itu.int/wsis/docs2/tunis/off/6rev1.html (last visited 6 September 2014). The first Internet Governance Forum meeting in Athens was convened where all stakeholders and relevant parties, including governments, the private sector, civil society, and the academic and technical communities participated.

results with those of the best performers in any area; and oblige actors collectively to redefine objectives and policies.[66]

Even prior to the adoption of CRPD in December 2006, the United Nations General Assembly, the United Nations Global Alliance for ICT and Development provided the institutional framework in the form of G3ict—the 'Global Initiative for Inclusive ICTs'.[67] G3ict is a multi-stakeholder initiative that operates with a mission to facilitate the implementation of the digital accessibility agenda defined by CRPD. It includes policy makers and public sector institutions, organizations of persons with disabilities, ICT industries, the private sector, international standards development organizations, and academia. Besides, range of international institutions participate in G3ict programs including the ITU, the United Nations Department for Economic and Social Affairs (UN DESA), UNESCO, the United Nations Institute for Training and Research (UNITAR), ILO, the World Intellectual Property Organisation (WIPO), and the World Bank. G3ict is basically involved in activities of awareness raising on effective public policies, private sector initiatives; promoting regulatory, programmatic, and legislative good practices; fostering harmonization and standardization and supporting policy makers with capacity building programs and benchmarking.[68]

The proposed interconnected pentagon envisages such deliberative congregations of stakeholders, similar to G3ict and IGF. These could be informal settings as IGF or could be given a formal recognition so as to inform and inspire policy-makers in both the public and private sector to reconfigure existing policies or craft new policies and practices that create a universally acceptable accessibility policy and standard. Specifying the scope and content of private duties to ensuring right to access the Internet through an international mechanism may be more uniform and

---

[66] David M. Trubek and James S. Mosher, 'New Governance, Employment Policy, and the European Social Model', in *Governing Work and Welfare in a New Economy: European and American Experiments* 33, pp. 38–41, 46–7 (Jonathan Zeitlin and David M. Trubek, eds, 2003).

[67] See http://g3ict.com/about (last visited 17 May 2016).

[68] See http://g3ict.com/about.

more predictable than simply expecting corporations to apply a due diligence standard of accessibility.[69] But before a duty may be specified, it is necessary to have a relatively clear and uniform understanding of what the duty should be.

The proposed IPM suggests the participation of corporations to the discussion board. Since corporations could be directly engaged in the policymaking and standard setting process, they could straight away adopt universally endorsed accessibility norms, even where domestic standards are weak due to conflict, corruption, or weak governance structures. Such automatic route of accessibility helps to resolve the difficulties that States encounter on account of her 'unwillingness' or 'incapability' that resulted in governance gaps. However, this strategy presupposes that corporations are good apples who are not only willing to participate in issues concerning accessibility but also sincere in enforcing accessibility. Further, constant participation and dialogue automatically leads to sensitization and capacity building of the institutions.

At the same time, such deliberative congregations also signal to the markets about possible demands that may arise and thereby prepare them to brace up for the upcoming accessibility agenda. The markets in the virtual world are driven by standards, and in order to garner favourable mass production, economies of scale, and competition for accessible goods and services, which ultimately result in lower prices and efficient operability. Unless global markets dynamics are leveraged through uniformity and harmonization of accessibility standards, there is a greater risk of a high level of market fragmentation caused by the adoption of heterogeneous standards at country level, and disregarding international standards.[70] Policy

---

[69] See International Council on Human Rights Policy (ICHRP), 'Beyond Voluntarism: Human Rights and the Developing International Legal Obligations of Companies', 1 (2002) (International standards 'can help to harmonize rules at a time of weak national regulation. They can act as a common reference point for national law, setting benchmarks, drawing attention to core minimum requirements and establishing clearly what is not permissible.')

[70] Axel Leblois', 'Implementing the Digital Accessibility Agenda of the UN Convention on the Rights of Persons with Disabilities: Challenges and

makers and scholars have suggested that having greater uniformity of regulations addressing ICTs is likely to increase their accessibility and affordability.[71] It is also expected that more uniformity can provide greater predictability and equal rules for competition in the market.[72]

Several jurisdictions have adopted voluntary standards developed by standard organizations in their domestic laws by way of 'direct reference'. For instance, Standards developed in Australia, New Zealand, and Canada already directly have references to WCAG 2.0. On similar lines, the Access Board in the US proposes to apply WCAG 2.0 standards by way of 'reference' in its own laws. Moreover, WCAG 2.0 has progressively served as the basis for Web accessibility standards in several jurisdictions.[73] It may be recollected that the WCAG 2.0, is a voluntary body of ICT industry representatives and other experts that set standards. Since these international standards are developed after consensus building by stakeholders including industry it is believed that their incorporation in domestic laws

---

Opportunities', in *European Yearbook of Disability Law* 139, 142 (Gerard Quinn and Lisa Waddington, 2009).

[71] J. Brewer, 'The World Wide Web Consortium Accessibility Initiative', in G3ICT, *The Accessibility Imperative: Implications of the Convention of the Rights of Persons with Disabilities for Information and Communication Technologies* 161, p. 165 (G3ict, ed., 2007).

[72] K. Salaets, 'The Importance of Harmonization: Perspectives from the Information Technology Industry Council', in G3ICT, *The Accessibility Imperative*, p. 150.

[73] For instance, Germany's Federal Disabled Equalization Law requires its BITV 2.0 accessibility standards for government websites modelled on the WACG 2.0. German Federal Ministry of Labour and Social Affairs, Accessible Information Technology, available at http://www.bmas.de/DE?Startseite?stArticlehtml (last visited 22 April 2015); Advisory Notes adopted by the Australian Human Rights Commission endorses the WACG 2.0. See Australian Human Rights Commission, World Wide Web Access: disability Discrimination Act Advisory Notes, Version 4.0 at 1 (October 2010) available at http://www.hreoc.gov.au/disability_rights/standards/www_3/www_3html (last visited 22 April 2015). Similarly India and Japan Guidelines for Indian Government Websites, National Informatics Centre, available at http://web.guidelines.gov.in/tools.php (last visited 22 April 2015).

would improve clarity. Further, regulated entities are familiar with these standards which ensure easy implementation.[74] Such harmonization of domestic standards with international ones is primarily envisages creation of a larger marketplace for accessibility solutions. Such harmonization allows industry and companies to create products instead of worrying about different conflicting standards required by different countries. This attracts more offerings and increases the likelihood of commercial availability of accessible information and communication technology options.[75]

Whereas harmonization of accessibility standards in accordance with voluntary consensus building appears to ensure a consistent, predictable, simple, and globally acceptable standards of accessibility; certain technical and practical difficult questions remains unanswered. For instance, it needs to be asked if WACG standards will be applicable to user-generated content extending to those that are purely or non-profit in nature. It has already been pointed earlier that statutes such as the CVAA does not necessarily cover user-generated websites such as YouTube. The US Department of Justice propose that online service providers will not be responsible under Title III for inaccessible web content placed on their websites by individuals or third-parties that are not under their control, but they must provide their users the capability to post accessible web content.[76]

Another pressing concern in the creation of accessible content online is the likely conflict with intellectual property. The recently concluded Marrakesh Treaty has served as a good example of how the right to access published works for persons with disabilities could be ensured by forming strategic alliance between individuals,

---

[74] Refreshed Accessibility Standards and Guidelines in Telecommunications and Electronic and Information Technology TEITAC Report, April 2008, Access Board, available at http://www.access-board.gov/guidelines-and-standards/communications-and-it/about-the-ict-refresh/background/teitac-report (last visited 22 April 2015).

[75] Available at http://www.access-board.gov/guidelines-and-standards/communications-and-it/about-the-ict-refresh/proposed-rule/ii-executive-summary (last visited 22 April 2015).

[76] DOJ ANRPM at 43461.

civil society, experts, states, and international organizations. It was realized that on account of restrictive licensing under copyright laws very few electronic copies of books and texts were accessible to the print disabled. This contributed significantly to what is popularly called the 'book famine', where only an infinitesimal percentage of all published works are available in accessible formats.[77] In order to address this issue, individuals, civil society, other organizations formed a strategic alliance and collaborated in a movement to make exceptions for disability in copyright laws and voiced the issue at the World Intellectual Property Organisation.[78] In July 2008, the World Blind Union (WBU) brought together copyright experts to prepare a possible draft text of a Treaty and to address the issues faced by persons with disabilities.[79] The draft treaty proposed by WBU was endorsed by several member countries at the WIPO Standing Committee on Copyrights and Related Rights.[80] In furtherance of the WIPO General Assembly decision in December 2012, a diplomatic conference was convened which successfully resulted in the Marrakesh Treaty. The preamble of the Treaty imbibes principles

[77] Erika Lambert, 'Bread for the Blind: Ending the International Book Famine through Negotiation of an International Instrument on Access to Copyright Works for Persons with Blindness or Visual Impairment', 2, available at http://www.djls.org/20/Lambert.pdf (last visited 27 November 2014).

[78] The discussions on the need for an international treaty on copyright exceptions for persons with disabilities began in the early 1981 when WIPO and UNESCO agreed to create a Working Group on Access by the visually and Auditory Handicapped to Material Reproducing Works Produced by Copyright. In May 2002, the World Blind Union intervened at the WIPO Standing Committee on Copyright and Related Rights (SCCR) and highlighted the problems faced by persons with visual impairment in accessing books, thereby requesting WIPO to study this issue in detail.

[79] See Knowledge Ecology International, 'Background and Update on Negotiations for a WIPO Copyright Treaty for Persons Who Are Blind or Have Other Disabilities', 7 April 2011, available at http://keionline.org/node/1089 (last visited 25 November 2014).

[80] Knowledge Ecology International, 'Background and Update on Negotiations for a WIPO Copyright Treaty for Persons Who are Blind or Have Other Disabilities'.

of the CRPD in terms of equal opportunity, non-discrimination, full and effective participation inclusion, accessibility. The Treaty facilitates access to published works for persons with visual impairments[81] and requires state parties to make exceptions in copyright laws that facilitate availability of works in accessible formats. This enables State Parties to implement and realize Article 30 of CRPD that calls for equal participation including that to the digital information so that persons with disabilities could actively and freely exercise their liberty and human rights. The treaty tends to strike a balance between rights of persons with disabilities to published material and the interests of copyright owners.

If the aforesaid international scenario on accessibility is envisaged in terms of the IPM, the following picture surfaces—

It may be noted that while one finds participation from multi-stakeholders, international organizations such as IGF provides a platform where stakeholders congregate periodically to discuss normative and technical issues. However, these are all focused

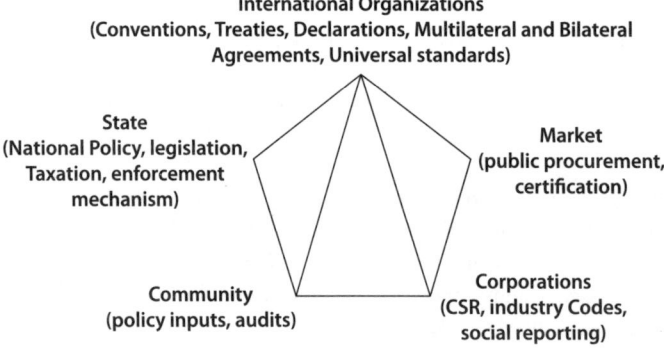

Figure 5.5   Depiction of existing international scenario in terms of the IPM
Source: Author.

---

[81] For detailed understanding on the Treaty and advocacy on the same see, Rahul Cherian Jacob, Sam Taraporevala, and Shamnad Basheer, 'The Disability Exception and the Triumph of New Rights Advocacy', 5 *National University of Juridical Science Law Review* 603 (2012).

at the tipping point—the international organization where each actor brings in their view points and concerns on the board to communicate to others. While international organizations facilitates dialogues between the members, it is desirable that these remain interconnected with one another—the state and corporations, corporations and community, and community and state so as that each actor contributes in strengthening norm setting, policy making, and standard setting that lends authority and legitimacy to the regulatory process. In the context of disability rights, it is witnessed that not only stakeholders but interconnectedness and cross-referencing between different treaty bodies are also crucial to realize the rights of persons with disabilities. Having sketched the model at international level, I next move on to the operation of the model at national level.

At National Level

External Push of the State

Despite the limited technological and regulatory outreach of States vis-a-vis the Internet, the State has made efforts to dismantle barriers through constitutional and legislative measures. Whilst domestic anti-discrimination laws remain the backbone of ensuring compliance, it is crucial to ask to whether the State can dictate corporations to design goods and services in a specific manner. Can disability discrimination laws regulate corporations to the extent of interfering with their creative autonomy?

Insofar as supply companies are concerned, state legislations can facilitate self-regulation or enforced regulation. Since supply companies are in general found to be more responsive to the questions of accessibility and often voluntarily undertake research and development of accessible line of products; the law may rely on relatively softer instrumentalities such as industry code of conduct, assessment, social reporting, and so on. Besides, the State may offer incentives such as certain tax benefits in excise, export of accessible products guided by universal designs to create accessible products and applications.

However, persuasive techniques are often found not to be working for the consumer companies. Ensuring accessibility for consumer companies remains comparatively challenging. While obligating websites run by government companies or websites of such private entities which are engaged in rendition of public service or supplying public products can be relatively easy, the real challenge lies in extending the accessibility obligation to purely private websites. Even within this latter category, those websites that are not media-rich could ensure maximum accessibility at little or no additional cost by following a set of design principles. However, it may be difficult to oblige media rich private websites or e-commerce websites where hundreds of pages and images are uploaded every minute. For instance, YouTube is largely based on user-generated content uploads and videos, most of these videos are categorized as amateur user-generated videos who lack the technical proficiency to ensure accessibility features. Similarly, e-commerce based websites upload millions of products every minute. Any regulation that requires private websites to be accessible will be accompanied by costs. Whereas the quantum of these costs may vary, it is undoubtedly severe for multi-media rich websites such as those cited here that are continuously updated. Extending accessibility obligation to private websites in ignorance of the costs or technical capacity of user would either throttle e-commerce or result into contentious litigations as experienced in the United States. Neither is desirable to advance the goals of substantive equality. Hence, one needs to attain a balanced approach.

Abrar and Dingle[82] suggest that obligations must be laid down in a more nuanced manner by drawing distinctions between (a) multimedia versus static websites, and (b) for-profit enterprises versus non-profits and individuals.[83] Since for-profit commercial websites are capable of spreading costs amongst their customers, it is viable to mandate these websites. However, imposing such

[82] Ali Abrar and Kerry J. Dingle, 'From Madness to Method: The Americans with Disabilities Act Meets the Internet', 44 *Harvard Civil Rights–Civil Liberties Law Review* 133 (2009).

[83] A for-profit enterprise, for the purposes of this proposal, is one that directly profits from the good or service sold over the Internet.

obligations on non-commercial, non-profit websites could raise risk of destroying them, and therefore such websites should be persuaded to comply voluntarily. The law needs to be responsive to the regulatee and to that end develop different degrees of regulation instead of placing a blanket obligation on all.[84] For example, services that are seen as essential should be subjected to a stronger degree of regulation and should, therefore, protect more effectively the citizenship concerns associated with the virtual world.

In this capacity, the interconnected pentagon creates a middle ground—a space of regulated autonomy—between substantive regulation and non-regulation.[85] The IPM allows adopting a command-control regulation of callous or unwilling demand corporations by imposing legally enforceable accessibility obligations through anti-discrimination laws. At the same time the interconnected pentagon model also leaves the space for laws to discern the relative capacities of different institutions by identifying other regulatees who could be delegated regulatory tasks to ensure the right to access the Internet. The model thus equips the state to invoke aid from other institutions and their instrumentalities so as to compel compliance from the laggard companies. This may take two different forms: one, encouraging private media rich websites to tie up with civil society groups or voluntary initiatives to create accessible contents; two, in situation of rampant non-compliance, to identify intermediaries and supply companies so as to make detractors fall in line.

Media rich websites could tie up with civil society and non-profit organization in order to identify and find solutions to accessibility

---

[84] According to Mortensen, a preferable approach would be to rely on 'object-specific, multi-layered regulation' that would not only respond to the regulatory challenges posed by technological convergence but also seek to safeguard the 'public interest and socio-political concerns'. Therefore, different degrees of regulatory responses should concentrate on 'infrastructures', 'network interfaces', 'carriers', 'user interfaces' and 'applications', as appropriate. See M. Mortensen, 'Beyond Convergence and the New Media Decision: Regulatory Models in Communications Law', 2 Canadian Journal of Law and Tech. 99, 101 (2003).

[85] Teubner, 'Substantive and Reflexive Elements in Modern Law', 17 *Law and Soceity Review* 239 (1983): 254, 267.

barriers. This will ensure that accessible content are created and available. There exists an alternative offered by volunteer-based site that uses a selective approach for transcription of popular videos of media rich websites such as YouTube. Through techniques that enable automatic online translation, one set of subtitles is easily and cheaply derived. These subtitles can be translated into other languages and made available to broad audiences, including the hearing impaired and non-English speakers. By expanding the user base, costs will be recouped or profits reaped and at the same time provide the best chance for accessibility of online media. Many such volunteer-based sites have emerged in the recent past to cater to transcription of popular videos.[86] Such transcriptions help to sidestep the problem YouTube faces with accessibility by prioritizing the transcription of videos that have already proven themselves popular on other websites. On similar lines, the popular social networking website Facebook in collaboration with the American Foundation for the Blind have undertaken initiatives to provide users with visual impairment more enjoyable experience of Facebook.[87] Such initiatives can either be directly supported,

---

[86] For instance, YouTube is one of the partners of Dotsub which is a volunteer-based site which aims to eliminate the language barrier in online video. For greater details see, 'About Dotsub', available at http://dotsub.com/about.jsp (last visited 24 September 2014). In another such instance, Overstream.net that relies on its volunteer user community to post transcripts of videos. The videos are found on other video-sharing websites, and the users decide which ones are worthy of transcription. Overstream avoids video-hosting and manpower costs by relying entirely on volunteers and using videos hosted on other websites. For details see, 'Overstream, What is Overstream?' available at http://www.overstream.net/whatisoverstream.php (last visited 24 September 2014). Similarly Project ReadOn allows users to post subtitled videos and maintains permanent staff that transcribes popular videos found on YouTube and other parts of the Internet. The site is funded by advertisements and sponsors. See 'Project ReadOn, About PRO', available at http://www.projectreadon.com/index.php?pg=about (last visited 24 September 2014). See P. Blanck, *Equality: The Struggle for Web Accessibility by Persons with Cognitive Disabilities* (2014).

[87] In July of 2011, the company formed the Facebook Accessibility Team to improve its support of accessibility across products. Available at http://www.afb.org/afbpress/pub.asp?DocID=aw160402 (last visited 24 September 2014).

recognized or funded by the state and corporations thought their CSR initiatives.

Alternatively, the State may impose obligations on the intermediaries and supply companies that will indirectly compel compliance from consumer companies. Given the control that some of these intermediaries have and their subtle role in creating the rule-sets, there may be a tendency to look to these intermediaries to accept responsibilities for the activities carried out on their network and to expect them to intercede in resolving disputes.

There are two prototypes of such third-party enforcers-chaperones and bouncers. Chaperones have the power to control the incentives of would-be wrongdoers, and therefore, voluntarily monitor, detect, and disrupt misconduct.[88] Chaperones are normally *repeat players* that serve many clients by acting as 'reputational intermediaries' in providing certification or verification services.[89] By verifying, ranking, or certifying monitored market players, the chaperone enforcers signal other stakeholders, such as investors and trading partners, of the trustworthiness of the monitored entity. An example could be standardization organizations that certify goods, services, or processes as meeting predetermined standards. Insofar as the accessibility of the website is concerned W3C possess a good potential to serve as chaperone enforcer. Currently, W3C issue guidelines and provide such certifications on accessibility of web content. This could be further institutionalized and granted explicit recognition with other participants such as civil society, industry associations, supply companies, and state agencies joining in. Chaperons will be of particular significance for consumer companies and accessibility compliance expected of them.

Another set of intermediaries or third parties enforcers are positioned as *bouncers* that can help to disrupt misconduct by

---

[88] See Reinier Kraakman, 'Gatekeepers: The Anatomy of a Third-Party Enforcement Strategy', 2 *Journal of Law, Economics & Organisation* 53 (1986): 61–2.

[89] See Nolan Clark, *Gatekeepers: The Professions and Corporate Governance* 2 (2006); John Coffee, 'The Attorney as Gatekeeper: An Agenda for the SEC', 103 *Columbia Law Review* 1296 (2003).

withholding necessary cooperation or consent.[90] A typical bouncer might include pharmacists who are required to refuse to deliver a controlled drug except when given a valid prescription, as well as restaurants, bars, and various shopkeepers which are required to refuse to sell alcohol and cigarettes to underage customers. Thus, bouncers are often perceived as *gatekeepers* who prevent misconduct by refusing to support it.[91]

A well-functioning bouncer-type enforcement system presupposes three basic conditions: First, there must be a 'gate' and a 'gatekeeper'; that is, there must be a service that is unavoidable for the would-be wrongdoer to perform the wrong, and a third party who is in the position to refuse to provide such a service. Second, third parties acting as gatekeepers must have the capacity to detect the potential misuse of their services by a would-be wrongdoer. And third, these third parties must be adequately incentivized to undertake their duties. As for the last requirement, bouncer-type third-party enforcers commonly receive no direct compensation for undertaking their gatekeeping duties. They are compelled to undertake an enforcement role by law and incur a duty-based liability where if they fail to fulfil their duty then sanctions will be imposed.

Such bouncers are already in use for banishing a user, removing controversial material or blocking the dissemination of a file. An example is the Australian proposal to regulate the carriage of highly offensive or illegal content over the Internet, to be administered by the Australian Broadcasting Authority.[92] Under this proposal, an online service provider could be required to remove material which does not meet the Australian classification standards. If the network functions as a gatekeeper for users in cyberspace, it is to be expected that the government may attempt 'to impose coercive sanctions on network administrators and thereby on the network rules in order

[90] This type of third-party enforcer was originally defined and analysed in-depth in Kraakman, 'Gatekeepers', pp. 53–104.

[91] See Kraakman, 'Gatekeepers', p. 63; Coffee, 'The Attorney as Gatekeeper', p. 2.

[92] Senator Richard Alston, Minister of Communications, Information Technology and the Arts, Australia, Media Release, 19 March 1999.

to implement their own government's particular preferred set of rules on behaviour in this environment'.[93]

For the purpose of compelling creation of accessible contents and websites, one may think of innovative bouncing techniques. Take for instance, Google's PageRank system. Since the very essence of the web is the linking of individual 'pages' on websites, every link represents a recommendation. The search engine, Google's PageRank system, uses an algorithm that assigns every page a rank, depending on how many other pages link to it. Furthermore, all links are not valued equally. A recommendation is worth more when it comes from a page that has a high rank itself. One of the techniques could be to insert accessibility of the website or the page to its overall valuation and ranking.

It can be seen that in addition to the classical anti-discrimination laws that creates recognition of the right to access the Internet; bringing in corporations and community based voluntary initiatives can be deployed to advance accessibility. While sanctions and judicial threats, imposition of fines may still be had to be in place; the ground situation will be positively impacted with the involvement of other players as well.

Thus, under the interconnected pentagon model, law co-exists with various subsystems, ever gauging the sustainability of the different organizations. The model serves to integrate isolated efforts at the subsystem level, co-coordinating different scales of action. The anti-discrimination laws are complemented with other private and non-law instrumentalities that facilitate information pooling, learning-by-monitoring, reliable feedback, knowledge networks, and benchmarks and indicators for best practices.

Deploying Market Forces

It has been experienced that those who continually participate in the market intercourse with their own economic interests have a

[93] David G. Post, 'Anarchy, State and the Internet: An Essay on Law-Making in Cyberspace', J. Online L. art. 3 (1995).

far greater rational knowledge of the market and interest [in the] situation than legislators and enforcement officers with regulatory concerns. In order to garner corporate compliance towards a particular human rights issue, it has often been argued that making a business case for the same, may induce requisite behaviour. However, such an approach based almost entirely on an economic perspective leaves the wider social implications associated with the right to access the Internet unresolved.[94] Placing reliance on market forces as the vehicle for the regulation of the supply of goods and services tends to alter our conception of the individual in society, demoting him from 'citizen' to 'consumer'.[95] Consequently, markets may fail to protect people from social exclusion.[96] Moreover, since interactions between individuals and service providers in the market, vary in accordance with the financial means of the public and no weight is given to substantive concerns of equality. Therefore, the market constitutes a 'seriously inadequate means of protecting citizenship rights.'[97]

Although some market players have shown leadership by developing accessible products or services, there is usually no guarantee that the Internet based manufacturers and service providers would take into account accessibility.[98] It has been a lived experience that issues such as the accessibility and development of products and services based on universal design principles 'are not on the agendas of service providers'.[99] Despite legislative mandates

[94] R. Collins, 'Realising Social Goals in Connectivity and Content', in *Regulating the Information Society* 108 (C.T. Marsden, ed., 2000).

[95] L. Whitehouse, 'The Home-owner: Citizen or Consumer?' in *Land Law: Themes and Perspectives* 186 (S. Bright and J. Dewar, eds., 1998).

[96] Whitehouse, 'The Home-owner'.

[97] T. Prosser, *The Limits of Competition Law-Markets and Public Services* 29 (2005).

[98] Prosser, *The Limits of Competition Law-Markets and Public Services*.

[99] See generally, Gerard Goggin and Christopher Newell, 'The Business of Digital Disability', *The Information Society: An International Journal* 23(3) (2007): 159. DOI: 10.1080/01972240701323572; H. Maskery, 'Crossing the Digital Divide-Possibilities for Influencing the Private-Sector Business Case', *The Information Society: An International Journal* 23 (2007).

on access, there are interested private parties who are in a position to distort the intended meaning of a legal norm to the point of turning it into its very opposite.[100]

It may be recollected that in *Stern v. Sony*,[101] the plaintiff alleged that he was denied the opportunity for equivalent enjoyment of Sony's online video games on account of his disability. Arguably, the situation may have been rectified by adding reasonable controls to adjust certain visual and auditory cues in the games. But Sony declined to consider such modifications. It may be recollected that the plaintiff Stern had alleged he cannot play Sony's video game software products as well as other gamers can. Refusing to change its products to make them easier for plaintiff's use, Sony contested the application of Title III of the ADA since the plaintiff's claim was not about inaccessibility of the product, events, but about not being enjoyable on an equal basis with other gamers. The company maintained that the law cannot mandate commercial entities to customize their products for every consumer.

The aforesaid case illustrates how law as a state instrumentality mandating accessibility on private entities may be often seen as an unnecessary interference with private autonomy and therefore, it often do not receive desirable responses from corporations. Even so, one may conveniently draw an inference that corporations respond to the markets all the time. Therefore, the interconnected pentagon seeks to harness this close relationship between the markets and corporations to accommodate accessibility rights. When viewed in isolation, markets appear to be detrimental to accessibility concerns, when collaborated with other actors it could prove to be an effective strategy to encourage companies. To this end, the model suggests other participants to offsetting the limitations created by the market. Whereas the State has always stepped in to rectify such market failures through regulatory interventions, the current model creates space for the international organization, civil society, and corporations to pitch in. Such discursive techniques of

---

[100] Max Weber, *On Law in Economy and Society* 38 (Max Rheinsteinened and Edward Shils, trans., 1954), quoted in *Sally Falk Moore, Law as Process*, pp. 56–7 (1978).

[101] Stern, 459 Fed.Appx.609 (9th Cir. 2011).

policy making and standard setting at the international level with a corporate presence in the room automatically lead to informing the markets about upcoming trends and innovative expectations. The State through its public procurement measures can provide an initial push. With the supply companies offloading accessible products and services in the market; consumer companies will also eventually end up purchasing accessible products and services. In fact, it leads to a situation where the supply companies may create accessible products and services if required by consumer companies to do so and the consumer companies may end up providing accessible products or services if the very components-contents they end up purchasing are accessible.

There may be instances, when instead of softer measures such as public procurement, demand for creation of accessible products and services can be created in the markets through community and legislative combination. For instance, the National Federation of the Blind and the American Council of the Blind (ACB), along with the US Department of Justice as an intervening party, brought a lawsuit against Arizona State University (ASU) over the University's plan to deploy electronic textbook via the Kindle DX, Amazon's reader among students.[102] The plaintiffs alleged that since the Kindle was not accessible to students with print disabilities, deployment of such reading devices amounts inequality and discrimination in education of visually impaired students.[103] ASU being a public university receiving federal funds, was obligated under the Rehabilitation Act of 1973 and ADA Title II.[104] The lawsuit was settled when ASU agreed to use more accessible devices if it chooses

---

[102] See, 'National Federation of the Blind Urges Swift Action on Recommendations for Accessible Higher Education Materials' (13 December 2011); available at http://www.nfb.org/node/948 (last visited 22 March 2014).

[103] The problem was the Kindle had limited text-to-speech capabilities. With no audio options, print disabled and visually impaired students were not able to configure the settings, select books, and use the menus because they lacked the text to speech option.

[104] See 504 of the Rehabilitation Act of 1973, 29 U.S.C. § 794, et seq. (the Rehabilitation Act) and title II of the Americans with Disabilities Act, 42 U.S.C. § 12131, et seq. (ADA).

to deploy e-book readers in future. Similarly, the Department of Justice seeking an investigation of the Baltimore City Public Schools' proposed acquisition of the Nook e-book reader.[105] As in the ASU case, the Baltimore Schools proposed to acquire Nook devices from Barnes and Noble that were not equally usable by students with print disabilities.[106] The Nook's touch screen menus and controls violated the principles of the ADA because students with print disabilities would have had to use separate devices for reading. In settling this dispute, the school district agreed to provide devices to students that would deliver equivalent information as provided by the Nook.[107]

The market sentiment has more often been lukewarm towards accessibility as a concept. As already pointed, there are deep rooted myths which need to be busted. Even where it is generally accepted that there are substantial business benefits accruing from the application of accessible design principles to all products and services irrespective of target market and user groups; as soon as the word 'accessibility' is mentioned, the doors close.[108] It may be possible to take a leaf from the environmentally friendly products and energy saving products and create an accessibility friendly product label. Just as eco-friendly products carry certain logos or energy saving appliance are evaluated based on the mark of five stars; something similar could be popularized for accessible products and services in the market. The idea is to float an alternative definition of accessible design—the Anytime, Anywhere, Anyone (AAA) Design.[109]

---

[105] See NFB release available at: 'National Federation of the Blind Files Complaint against Baltimore City Public Schools', NFB.org., (4 January 2012), available at https://nfb.org/node/944 (last visited 22 March 2014) complaint filed with U.S. DOJ, 4 January 2012.

[106] Complaint stating: 'Blind students are qualified individuals with disabilities within the meaning of the ADA. 28 C.F.R. § 35.104. Therefore, Baltimore City Public Schools may not provide them unequal or separate access to the benefits of its programs, services and activities. 28 C.F.R. § 35.101.'

[107] D. Klein, et al., 'Electronic doors to education: study of high school website accessibility in Iowa', 21 *Behaviour Science & Law* 27 (2003).

[108] Maskery, 'Crossing the Digital Divide'.

[109] Maskery, 'Crossing the Digital Divide', p. 189.

Thus, instead of pushing accessibility to the private sector, such rebranding neutralizes the stereotypical perception towards accessible products and services and at the same time create accessibility consciousness amongst consumers in general.

The AAA branding ties up with the Universalist model of disability[110] and further development of products and services that accommodates disability as diversity. The Universalist model recognizes that across the life span (and environmental conditions) everyone experiences limitations and impairments—those who do not currently have disabilities may be referred to as 'temporarily able-bodied'. This model perceives disability as a universal experience of humanity rather as a minority issue. Rather than seeing people with disabilities as a separate group in need of special protections, the Universalist model emphasizes, for instance, the benefits of accommodations, universal design, and antidiscrimination laws for everyone.

Internal Pulls

Re-conceptualizing Corporate Law

Corporations represent private law creatures, in which the public has an interest arising from functional considerations. But these political, functional considerations have a politically neutral cast, such as protecting reasonable expectations and maximizing efficiency.[111] The present corporate law is a model based on private

---

[110] An alternative model has been developed that, in contrast to the social model, views impairments as existing on a continuum and does not separate the population into people with and without disabilities. One of the originators was Zola (1989), who observed that disability is not 'fixed and dichotomous' but 'fluid and continuous'. See, I.K. Zola, 'Toward the necessary universalizing of a disability policy', 67 Milbank Quarterly 401 (1989).

[111] William W. Bratton, Jr., 'The "Nexus of Contracts" Corporation: A Critical Appraisal', 74 Cornell Law Review 407 (1989): 438 (explaining overvaluation of contractual theory of corporation, identifies its shortcomings and pursue contractual theory of firm which offers greater normatively responsiveness).

law in general and property law and contract law in particular. It remains inwards looking governing relationship between the management and shareholders and between the minority shareholder and majority shareholder. Scholarship has developed that argues that the law should free corporate managers from the shackles of profit maximization in total disregard for the interests of stakeholders other than shareholders.[112] Thus, it is suggested to make corporations responsive to the public without disturbing existing model of corporate law. This requires identification of points of intervention in corporate law where space can be created for public policy discourse and locate Achilles heels where regulatory mechanisms will be most effective.

The perception of a corporation as property of shareholders, managed by others necessitated corporate law to employ its language from agency and trust law. Hence, corporate law talks to managers in terms of agency law and trust law. Such reading of corporate law does not allow managers either to spend corporate money for purposes other than those of maximizing shareholder wealth or even to take on board any other perspective whilst arriving at decisions. However, in the present time, shareholders are not exclusive contributors of capital. With advent of tiered ownership through nominees and multi-layered mutual funds, finance portfolio of corporation has diversified. Modern day shareholders view corporations as a profitable investment option rather than an ownership unit.

The adoption of the business judgment rule, which lies at the foundation of the modern corporate law and directors' duties, marked a judicial rejection of the agency theory of corporate directors.[113] Thus, even where corporate law and its language may continue to remain the same, its foundations can be read to have inclusive meaning of ownership. Alteration in perception of corporate law can confer broader scope of management to take

---

[112] W. Werner, 'Corporation Law in Search of its Future', 81 *Columbia Law Review* 1611 (1981): 1645.

[113] Brian M. McCall, 'The Corporation as Imperfect Society', 36 *Delaware Journal of Corporate Law* 509 (2011): 516 (arguing that corporations ought to be understood in the framework of political philosophy rather than private law).

on board concerns and interests of constituencies other than shareholders. This can be a good point of intervention to engage and influence management while they still remain within their functional framework. A befitting instance, may be located in the United Kingdom which has embraced the duty approach to impose a duty on directors to take into account the interests of non-shareholders.[114]

Translating the external push and internal pulls, the following combination emerges in terms of the IPM.

It may be noted that whereas the state and markets are providing the required incentives to corporations, the state and markets are in communication with the community and obtaining the necessary inputs from the community—the state in terms of policy inputs invoked through litigation and markets in terms of demand for accessible products and services. The community can play a reactionary role here by compelling accessibility through enforcement mechanisms provided by the state such as class action or seeking judicial intervention. These are, however, external pressures that may be created in addition to the state and market forces. Similarly, international organizations and obligations and

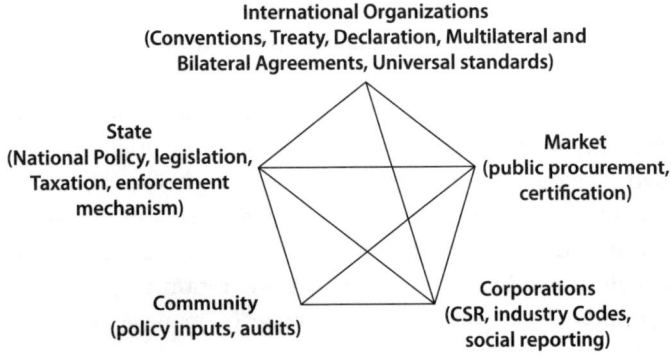

Figure 5.6   Envisioning a combination in the IPM at domestic level
Source: Author.

---

[114] South Africa Companies Act 2008, s 7(d).

norms agreed at international level feeds into the state policy and legislative and programmatic interventions.

At Institutional Level

A significant level of compliance is expected to occur from the initiatives put in place by companies themselves. This refers to consumer companies and supply companies. It is anticipated that companies will design, accessibility code of conduct for themselves. However, they would be guided by the content of regulatory initiatives at the national and international levels as well as by input from civil society. A pre-formulation consultation with the civil society is crucial, an aspect missing from the UN GPs. This marks goal setting and the same should be communicated actively to entities with which the enterprise has contractual relationships; others directly linked to its operations. Second, the companies undertake accessibility audit and maintain a record of the same. The CVAA comprise a good example of record keeping and detailing required, which can be later shared with the government or stakeholders. Third, an internal enforcement and compliance mechanism set up by the company to ensure its procurement department purchases in accordance with accessibility goals. The companies may consider creating a dedicated unit/department that looks into accessibility. For instance, Margaret Jungk proposes the establishment of a 'human rights policy unit' in corporations so that 'the humanitarian considerations are interjected into the decision making process' with consistency.[115] On similar lines, Microsoft Corporation appoints Chief Accessibility Officer who is responsible for the company's accessibility strategy and consults engineers, governments, advocacy groups, and business leaders on accessibility.

Voluntary self-regulation by the companies on an institutional level has several inherent weaknesses and some have been discussed

---

[115] M. Jungk, 'A Practical Guide to Addressing Human Rights Concerns for Companies Operating Abroad', in *Human Rights Standards and the Responsibility of Transnational Corporations* (Michael K. Addo, ed., 1999).

in greater details in the earlier chapter. Although it may not be possible to overcome all the limitations, two remedial responses are offered. First, external regulatory measures at the national and international level should ameliorate a few shortcomings of corporate self-regulation. This is the very essence of the theory of integrated regulation: complementing the weaknesses of one regime with the strengths of the other. Second, it is hoped that the involvement of stakeholders in the formulation and implementation of corporate human rights will counter some of the weaknesses.

Regulation at the institutional level is premised on the belief that the regulators have to bestow a degree of trust on corporations, which are not only rational minded but are also moral agents who bear the responsibility of their conduct.

An intriguing instance of interconnected operation can be cited in terms of Monster.com that operates a global online marketplace for job seekers and provides employer management and recruitment services.[116] Monster.com's core service allows individuals to search and apply for employment and for employers to advertise their job openings. National Federation of the Blind's concern about the accessibility of Monster.com for persons with visual impairments led to an investigation by the office of the Massachusetts Attorney General. Instead of going the litigation route, an agreement was entered into with Monster.com whereby Monster.com recognized the significance of web equality in digital content and ease of interaction. It thereby, committed to change its corporate structure and values in support of accessibility for job seekers who were persons with visual impairments.[117] In a move towards professional awareness and sensitization Monster committed to train its web technology professionals in the development of accessible and usable web content and design and also developed

[116] See Monster Worldwide, 'Who We Are', available at: http://www.about-monster.com/content/who-we-are (last visited 27 November 2014). Also see Blanck, *Equality*.

[117] See Massachusetts Attorney General, 'Monster.com First in Industry to Make WebsiteAccessible for Blind Users' (30 January 2013); available at: http://www.mass.gov/ago/news-and-updates/press-releases/2013/2013-01-30-monster-agreement.html (last visited 27 November 2014).

the 'Accessibility Guideline Manual' for all its employees involved in web programming, coding, and content development.

This agreement could be closely examined to observe how corporations could evolve several innovative initiatives leading to positive change instead embroiling in litigation. An Accessibility Committee was constituted within Monster Worldwide as an internal mechanism for accountability to ensure accessibility of the company's desktop and mobile platforms. This Committee consisted of its employees with relevant expertise who would be accountable for implementing the agreement and developing an Accessibility Guidelines Manual. The company further designated an Accessibility Coordinator to manage and review Monster's accessibility programs, the Accessibility Committee and the Accessibility Guidelines Manual, and to ensure that all new employees receive accessibility training. Monster also directly engaged its customers with disabilities to conduct annual accessibility and usability testing with human and automated testing. The Monster agreement illustrates an effort to make meaningful changes in the job hiring process—in an online service providers' attitudes and values, training, monitoring, and accountability—to ensure web equality for its employees and customers.

The kind of arrangement entered into by Monster.com could also be facilitated under the anti-discrimination law. An example of this can be found in Germany's LEDP which allows civil society representing persons with disabilities to broker agreements ('Zielvereinbarungen') with public or private enterprises. These agreements contain detailed plans and timetables for achieving barrier-free access for persons with disabilities. However, there appears to be no sanction or positive incentive to encourage organizations to conclude such agreement.

Monster.com's instance could be seen as interconnected pentagon model in operation. It exemplifies a corporation proactively engaged in ensuring substantive equality for persons with disabilities in collaboration with other actors. Thus, within the framework agreement chalked by the state, civil society, and endorsed by the company; innovative endeavours are undertaken which not only ensures effective realization of rights of persons with disabilities in the job market but also sensitized and raised awareness amongst the employees of the company. This instance, may also be analysed as responsiveness and reflexivity at play whereby company as a system engages in constructive dialogues with the state, civil society, and internalize the values of other systems within its own structure. Whereas the international organization and markets are absent in this instance, it is not far to imagine their active involvement or passive pressure in other similar models.

Thus, in terms of the IPM, at institutional level the following combination can be worked out.

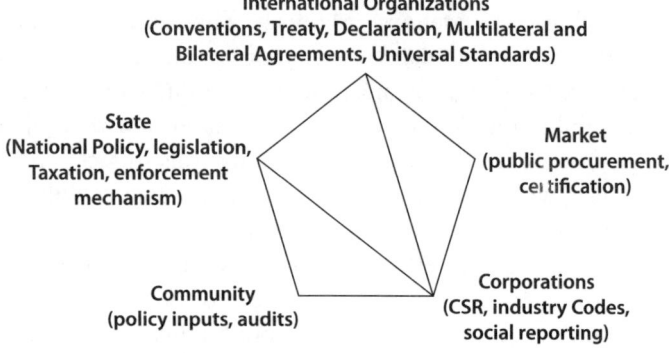

Figure 5.7 The IPM combination at institutional level
Source: Author.

This combination is suggestive of the situation where corporations having participated in standard setting internationally, draws from those principles and voluntarily chalks accessibility standards even where the state may not have notified any. Corporations may consider involving civil society consultation while finalizing its accessibility goals. Such formulations can either be mandated by the state or facilitated by the state. Having shaped the commitments, corporations are required to share information about its performance and progress as well as pending tasks with the government, markets, and community. There is also possibility of agreements entered into between corporation and civil society pertaining to accessibility standards (as was witnessed in Monster. com) which is facilitated by the state. The dissemination of company's accessibility commitment and performance will ensure to the requisite external gaze of the markets.

A Fair Assessment of the IPM

A governance and regulatory mix as envisaged through the interconnected pentagon may be subject to several criticisms. One, it may be considered to be an overly ambitious or complicated model. Two, disability rights advocates may argue that nothing short of legislative mandating compels corporations to deliver and the States may also prefer to resolve accessibility through anti-discrimination laws rather than sharing regulatory space with corporations. Three, such complex mix of instrumentalities and regulatory measures is unprecedented. Fourth, will this model guarantee complete accessibility? Let me respond to each of the objections.

It may be true to an extent that such a combination may be a time-consuming process of consensus building, bringing on board different players. There also lies the danger of a clash between fast-paced corporate culture on the one hand and the deliberative international and national bodies on the other hand; not to forget the very diverse disability constituency. When all these forces are brought to the discussion table what may emerge is a complex mix of regulation with a very limited experience of its actual operation and this in itself may be met with resistance at the stage of application.

However, it needs to be appreciated that creation of consensus presupposes differences, what is crucial is the process adopted to reconcile those differences. This reconciliatory process affords all relevant stakeholders a fair opportunity to articulate their positions and exchange views with others. Such consensus building process involves sincere attempts to understand divergent views and provide a rational before rejecting or accepting a particular view. What will eventually emerge is an unprecedented regulatory and strategic mechanism which is informed by the lived experiences of participants. Further each participant on the drawing board will be aware of the limitations, problems, difficulties and aspirations of the other. Consequently, when the model progresses from the stage of designing to the stage of implementation, each participant will have a fair amount of understanding of what to expect. In a way such an exchange will appraise the regulators and policy makers as to what is that may yield results and what other coercions may backfire. The greatest merit of such a mix comprises in identifying various pressure points and applying the right combination. It helps to develop forms of regulation in such areas that are primarily considered to be inaccessible to regulation.

Detractors of this model may question the non-hierarchical arrangement of instrumentalities as diminishing the significance of law in favour of other non-law instrumentalities. Perhaps the strongest objections may come from disability rights advocates and civil society who have been firm supporters of anti-discrimination laws as the one coercive force that compels accommodation for persons with disabilities. States may also perceive such arrangement as diminishing their sovereignty and power. Whereas I am not in any disagreement with the disability rights viewpoint over the effectiveness of a legislative mandate on accessibility; I differ with their view that it is the *only* effective instrumentality to obtain compliance. This holds true especially if corporations are required to proactively engage to create an accessible virtual world. The present model aims to address systemic discrimination towards persons with disabilities which necessitates adopting a reflexive approach. Towards this end one needs to encourage continued dialogue and deliberations between the community, corporations, state and markets. Anti-discrimination laws are mostly monologues and may not offer better opportunities of dialogues. It needs to be pointed out that even in the IPM, anti-discrimination laws occupy a significant position, though not a central position. In the model I propose, anti-discrimination laws coexist with other enforcement options in an open structured manner. Such a combine expands the regulatory imagination. The model attains legal orchestration by drawing links between institutional, national, and international levels with multiple actors through a web of strategies.

States on the other hand need to understand that even where they ambitiously mandate accessibility on all private entities, they lack practical experience required to implement the obligation. Viewed from a practical angle, it needs to be conceded that by the time international deliberations and national legislative bodies investigate, debate, vote and implement regulatory rules for accessibility issue, the technology may have been rendered obsolete. A mighty regulatory regime may force corporations to take refuge in less regulated jurisdictions. Consequently, either regulations will be redundant or be received with indifference. Any regulatory measure that is exclusively attached to the State is bound to deliver dissatisfying result. Hence it is extremely crucial that corporations, markets are made a part of the regulatory effort.

Other thorny questions arise on how to assess the effectiveness and efficiency of the IPM. This is a problem that is easier acknowledged than overcome. In many circumstances, particularly when a policy is comparatively new or untried, no objective measures of success or failure may be available.[118]

The adequacy of existing strategic initiatives for creating an accessible virtual world by corporations would be judged with reference to its efficacy. The efficacy of a norm can be tested by inquiring about the extent to which it has achieved its objectives, that is by comparing the 'actual' effect of a given norm with its 'intended' effect.[119] Thus, a strategy will be effective, if it is able to encourage, persuade, or convince not all but a sizable number of companies to take on board accessibility concerns of persons with disabilities and proactively engage to realize it.

It is likely that some companies will not be persuaded or may defy the assumption of being rational economic actors. In such situations, the IPM does not in any way prevent the State or civil society to seek compliance through anti-discrimination laws or invoke judicial remedy or impose fines or penalties. Rather, a reasonable certainty about an adverse penalty is a sine qua non for efficacy, because too much uncertainty or unpredictability might induce potential violators to take chances with regulation. In a departure from the enforcement pyramid of Ayres and Braithwaite, the interconnected pentagon allows the state and civil society to proceed against such laggards without awaiting failure of other instrumentalities. Sanctions or adverse consequences need not always come from formal judicial institutions, but may also flow from the market forces and stakeholders.

---

[118] J. Mendeloff, 'Overcoming Barriers to Better Regulation', 18 *Law & Society Inquiry* 711 (1993): 722–5.

[119] F. Tulkens, 'Human Rights, Rhetoric or Reality?', 9 European Review 125 (2001): 129.

This model facilitates gradual adoption of accessibility norms through internalization and compliance between business partners. Internalization focuses on developing a corporate culture of respect for the rights of persons with disabilities, including training individuals within the corporation and increasing internal protective measures. At the same time, interactions between corporations and subcontractors, suppliers, and other businesses could require a greater mutual respect for human rights.[120]

Evidently, there is a range of relevant motives which in combination to each other provide impetus to the corporations to comply. Primary amongst these are the economic motives, the social motives, and the normative motives. The IPM hinges on these motives and invokes them simultaneously or in various combinations in order to seek corporate compliance. Thus, the economic motives emerge from positive business strategies and avoiding negative consequences. While the former takes shape in terms of optimizing utilization of resources, business expansion, capture of greater market shares; the latter involves avoiding fines, penalties, imprisonment of individuals for non-compliance. In popular terms these are rational choices made by the corporation. Besides economic motives, corporations are often guided by social motives. The commitment to earn the respect of significant business partners, customers, employees, local communities, wider public also motivates corporations to remain compliant with law and rightful conduct. Often corporations are committed to obeying the regulations and laws for its own sake, guided by a sense of moral agreement. This is categorized as normative motive.

The interconnected pentagon seeks to invoke all these motives, in various combinations in order to obtain compliance from corporations. Thus, the code of conduct serves as a normative motive while social reporting, community audit, participation

---

[120] Deva, 'UN's Human Rights Norms for Transnational Corporations and Other Business Enterprises: An Imperfect Step in the Right Direction?', 10 ILSA Journal of International and Comparative Law 493 (2004) (arguing that whereas the UN Norms significantly improves the international response to corporate irresponsibility, the Norms also require to establish a strong enforcement mechanism and invoke multiple sanctions).

in international organizations provides the much required social motives. The markets and the anti-discrimination laws and other sanctions will generate economic motive. Since, different companies respond to different motives, the interconnected pentagon allows flexibility in application of motives either in isolation or in combination with one another.

I am inclined to accept the premise of responsive regulation in that for a responsive regulator there are no optimal or best regulatory solutions, just solutions that respond better than others to the plural configurations of support and opposition that exist at a particular moment in history. The interconnected pentagon model suggested here, does not consider state as centripetal force of accessibility rather it focuses on a multiplicity of actors involved in accessibility issue. Having assessed that traditional source of authority and hierarchical control has continuously been ineffective; it becomes imperative to look beyond the State. Co-ordination and involvement of corporation at every stage right from international standard setting, policy making and legislative subject is essential to overcome barriers created. Even at the cost of repetition, it needs to be reiterated that the IPM does not in manner whatsoever, suggest replacement of anti-discrimination laws or the command-control regulation that may be introduced by it. Rather, it co-exists with other instrumentalities and applied with full force in varying combinations. It has been rightly observed that in the absence of command-and-control regulation, regulated entities would lack any economic incentives to negotiate alternative regulatory arrangements. These must exist in the background as plausible threat. While contractarian regulation is a reform alternative to command-and-control regulation, it is also true that command-and-control regulation is a precondition for contractarian regulation.[121]

---

[121] David A. Dana, 'The New "Contractarian" Paradigm in Environmental Regulation', *University of Illinois Law Review* 35 (2000): 47 (arguing that contractarian approach to environmental regulation also comes with potential compared in terms of decreased participation from advocacy groups and stasis in regulation. The legislation should therefore, balance out these costs of contractarian approach).

A central strength of the IPM is that it appeals to both: the proactive rights-based, substantive equality agendas that support the bottom-up democratic empowerment of persons with disabilities; as well as the complex polycentric virtual world. It is of particular significance in a situation where the gap between the aspired norm and the existing reality is so large that hard regulatory provisions are meaningless. The model should thus, be understood as an attempt to envision a third way between state-based, top-down regulation and a single minded reliance on market-based norms; between centralized command-control regulation and individual free contract.

One may discover some sort of interconnectedness emerging in the existing domestic frameworks. For instance, the Australian DDA takes a comprehensive approach on disability discrimination and assigns responsibilities across society. The DDA adopted what is referred to as a 'three-dimensional approach' to ensure the rights of persons with disabilities. The first involves complaints, brought individually or collectively before the HREOC. Conciliation is the primary tool used by the HREOC. The second dimension involves the HREOC acting proactively to respond to systemic discrimination that cannot be adequately addressed through individual complaints. The HREOC is empowered to undertake public inquiries into problem areas of discrimination and to create Disability Standards. The intention was that Disability Standards would be mechanisms to educate and guide the public's attitude towards people with disabilities and rid society of the stigma and lack of understanding often faced by this group.[122]

The third dimension involves fostering a partnership between persons with disabilities and the larger community. It requires that the community takes responsibility for the integration

---

[122] Some critics find that '[i]nstead of specifying and simplifying non-discriminatory conduct ... Disability Standards have been hijacked by non-disabled stakeholders and directed towards justifying discriminatory conduct'. See Basser, L.A. and Jones, M. 'The Disability Discrimination Act 1992 (CTH): A Three-dimensional Approach to Operationalizing Human Rights.' In Disability Essays, by Peter Blanck ed. 203-33. Burlington, VT: Ashgate, 2005.

process through Action Plans. Service providers are encouraged to voluntarily develop an Action Plan, laying out the process by which the organization proposes to eliminate discriminatory practices. Rather than combating disability based discrimination through compliant driven reactive mode, this process allows service-providers to create an understanding of the impact of discriminatory practices and take steps to address inequality. The third dimension also involves Voluntary Industry Codes of Conduct. These Codes, though not specifically included in the *DDA*, have developed in response to it. Industry Codes are plans of action to eliminate discriminatory practices at an industry level. They allow the community to recognize the problems of inclusion, and allow ordinary citizens to work creatively to prevent exclusion.

The three-dimensional approach needs to be appreciated for a novel attempt to address discrimination in a proactive manner. Even so the absence of visible sanctions, the approach may fail to deliver. Unless the approach is backed by some form of legal or market based sanction, it may very little impact on the overall situation.

In another instance of the emerging interconnectedness, Spain boasts of having created the biggest public-private partnership concerning 'design for all' in the world. The Spanish government entered into a Framework Agreement with civil society groups in the country to garner co-operation and social inclusion of persons with disabilities. The purpose of the Framework is to develop a programme of universal accessibility. Towards this end, financial and technical support is created through a multi-stakeholders network. It is interesting to note that the civil society, group keeps a close watch over the development of each project and issues a quality evaluation report which is necessary to receive funding.[123] Linking availability of funds for the project subject to quality evaluation report serves as a smart strategy to ensure compliance. While the Framework can be largely seen to operate in physical spaces, similar ones can be formulated for the accessibility of the Internet as well.

---

[123] Available at http://zeroproject.org/policy/spain/ (last visited 6 March 2015).

While the aforementioned instances may not directly relate to the right under the present study, these are indicative that interconnectedness approach has already arrived on the horizon. It needs to be further engaged into and develop in a full-fledged fashion.

***

Given the past experience with corporations and disjunctive approaches, the interconnected pentagon offers a somewhat non-conventional strategy. It aims to favourably respond to compliers by leaving much space for self-regulation and innovative proactiveness to ensure accessibility. At the same time, the non-compliers are not sparred from sanction. The IPM draws from the most powerful actors to advance compliance and the cause of the disability rights. It suggests initiatives take place at the institutional, national, and international levels. This should not be perceived as undermining the State sovereignty in whichever way. Rather, the idea is to build upon the strengths of existing players and instruments to address the legal and normative lacunas. Thus, the IPM operates in a non-hierarchical, decentralization manner and addresses the existing legal lacuna in the form of aspirations and the ground situation by efficiently, leaving the shared responsibility in the hands of those closest to the problems.

Conclusion

This chapter provides a vantage point to view and understand the complexity of the present world order and future responses it calls for. It has been examined that last decade of the twentieth century witnessed three progressive trajectories in international framework— one, an acknowledgement that we are all living in a society which is constantly shaped by the evolving technologies; two, a growing acceptance towards corporations as private authority wielding public power and sharing governance space; three, the interaction of positive human rights jurisprudence with altered socio-economic and political power dynamics, continually questioning conventional perceptions of the State as the sole violator or promoter of human rights. When read in conjunction to one another, these trajectories hint towards a shift in human rights goalpost as well as goalkeepers. Thus, a compelling case is made for re-conceptualizing and reshaping the nature of the duty, re-identifying duty bearers and reconfiguring enforcement mechanisms in a society that is advancing towards digitization. I had therefore, argued that if human rights rhetoric has to ever be concretized as a reality in a technologically advanced society, it cannot disregard the non-state actors, especially corporations from its ambit.

The aforesaid argument was contextualized in terms of human rights of the most disadvantaged-persons with disabilities and obligations of the most resourceful-corporation. Juxtaposing positive human rights of the most disadvantaged to the virtual fiefdoms of the corporation provided an ideal illustration to question and examine consequences and fallacy of rejecting obligations of non-state actors in a society that is progressively advancing towards digitization.

While questions about human rights obligations of corporations and the existing international human rights framework has been often called into question, this book has sought to investigate the role of corporations in a technology driven society. The exponential growth and advancement of the Internet in the last forty years has enhanced the level of complexity and interdependencies within the society and diminished hierarchies of power. With the transformation in distribution of power in a networked society information and access to the Internet are progressively seen as indicators of measuring power. To have access to power is thus, to have access to the de facto political authorities in any given context. In addition to established political structures, the changed power dynamics progressively gives rise to new 'constituencies' of political power. These new constituencies may be a private entity, or they may be civil society.

While the trans-border nature of the global network escapes the physical boundaries of a sovereign nation-state, it is critical to ask whether the state obligations to respect, protect, and fulfil can be extended to practices in the Information Age. My interests therefore, comprised in probing whether the normative and theoretical foundations of existing human rights framework can be successfully and adequately transplanted to the human rights and technology discourse. I argued that effective realization of human rights cannot be guaranteed unless corporations' are also taken on board.

However, in order to fully appreciate the role and significance of the corporations in progressive digitized society, it is important to analyse the impact of the Internet from cultural, social and human rights dimension. Only such multifocal lens will lend the required urgency to the Internet and rights of those jeopardized on account of the Internet, particularly persons with disabilities. Disability is an inevitable condition of human life and living. The articulation of human rights of persons with disabilities in the form of CRPD is the newest in the realm of human rights and amongst the most marginalized. Hence, it is challenging to battle against the prevalent stereotypes of international human rights approaches and narrowly scoped corporate obligation and exciting to create a path breaking strategy of corporate obligation.

In this book, I have primarily focused on positive obligations of the corporation and explored the normative and regulatory options in engaging corporations in a positive fashion to the creation of an accessible virtual world for persons with disabilities. The complexity of the current world order, fragmentation of the exercise of power and control, autonomy, interactions and interdependencies, as well as the collapse of the public/private distinction, calls for innovative regulatory approach.[1] The legal and regulatory approaches require moving beyond dichotomous choice between persuasion/ punishment, top-down/bottom-up style. This book has provided strategies to reconcile seemingly conflicting rights of a marginalized group and private interests in a reflexive fashion. The specific issues that were probed, however, are merely thumbnail sketches of some more significant aspects and future agenda relating to the inclusiveness of the disadvantaged individuals, corporations, states, international human rights, and regulatory regimes.

Creation of an Inclusive World

That human rights discourse is rooted in human dignity, an absolute inner worth through which one exacts respect for oneself and for others, has been elaborated in the early discussion of this book.[2] Examination of real world situation, however, demonstrated that the effective realization of these rights often stood compromised in case of vulnerable groups. Whilst the value of human dignity is understood in terms of empowerment, autonomy, self-fulfilment, and self-realization,[3] the deprivation continues to be widespread and the distribution of resources remains unequal. Essentially a large section of human community who are marginalized and

---

[1] Julia Black, 'Decentering Regulation: Understanding the Role of Regulation and Self-regulation in a "Post-Regulatory" World', 54 Current Leg. Problems 103 (2001).

[2] I. Kant, *The Metaphysics of Morals* 186 (1996).

[3] Roger Brownsword, 'Freedom of Contract, Human Rights and Human Dignity', in *Human Rights in Private Law* 191 (D. Friedmann and D. Barak-Erez, eds, 2001).

vulnerable on account of their race, gender, age, and disability remain on the outermost periphery of life and living. Living a dignified and autonomous human life is not the entitlement of a privileged few but an inherent right available to everyone in human family irrespective of the age, gender, disability, race, class, or education. Ensuring an autonomous, self-fulfilling life for all members of human community essentially entail creating inclusiveness in every aspect of arrangements, whether physical, social, technological, political, or economic, in the designing and development stage itself. The promises of subsequent inclusion have not materialized and resulted in marginalized and excluded living devoid of participatory justices.

While certain exclusions may be more obvious, others take shape in subtle fashion. Susan Wendell raises a pertinent question on nonchalant attitudes, insubstantial on the face of it yet certainly exclusionary in its outcome by quoting an example of a typical supermarket. She astutely observes how simple lack of place to sit and rest for a few minutes in a supermarket reflects an assumption that all shoppers are strong and healthy or never likely to need to rest while shopping. Such an approach automatically excludes those who do not fit the predetermined construct.[4] And yet something intangible as the pace of life can be exclusionary for those who cannot keep up with this pace.[5]

Since exclusions are not only limited to the specific human diversity examined here, but are experienced in any age, settings, or groups; it must be addressed as a universal issue.[6] The urgency of attaining inclusiveness is not confined only in the context of disability. Rather, it is necessary to engage with the consequences of inequalities in access, social participation, and opportunities in the context of all such disadvantaged groups that are ghettoized instead of being seen as a part of human diversity. This requires

[4] See Susan Wendell, *The Rejected Body: Feminist Philosophical Reflections on Disability* 13 (1996).

[5] Wendell, *The Rejected Body*.

[6] However, it needs to be conceded that compared to other disadvantaged groups, persons with disabilities exclusions are more widespread and experienced instantaneously at very early outset in life.

appreciating a larger agenda to create an inclusive world where opportunities and participation is ensured to the disadvantaged groups. By broadening the base of beneficiaries of inclusiveness, there is an added advantage of lending greater visibility to the issue and enhance collaboration amongst the disadvantaged groups to step up the urgency of inclusion.

The effective recognition of inclusion and human dignity therefore, must accord both, protection of the right to make choices about all aspects of life, and protection from attacks on dignity in both public and private spheres of life. In order to create an inclusive world one needs to approach the architects, designers, organizers of societal structures and arrangements. Whereas the State was erstwhile discharging these functions, progressively the State has delegated public spaces and public functions to be created and operated by private actors. Thus, whether it is provisioning of health care, education, communication, security, or creating physical and virtual infrastructure, the State has either collaborated with corporations as partners or outsourced the task on agency basis. It is, therefore, vital that demands of inclusiveness and autonomy are put at the right door step.

Corporations as New Addressee of Human Rights Obligations

The globalization and onslaught of technology have lent fresh perspectives to the classic understanding of human rights. The structuring of human rights legal regime was largely dominated by a world vision preoccupied with the World Wars experiences and the sovereign power's abuse of its own citizens. Thus, existing human rights regime is primarily a response to the human suffering at the State hands. The traditional concern of international human rights was the relationship between the state and individual and according protection to the individual against the arbitrary power by the state. This relationship between the state and individual implied state obligations to protect a private party against another private party by legislation or preventive measures.

However, it has been examined that there exists a fundamental tension in the present times, created by structures of normative and regulatory state-centric conceptions steeped in post-war ideology and the practical effects of globalization which have largely diminished state authority to a large extent. Whereas globalization is premised upon flexibility, poly-centrality, adaptability, and experimental towards rapidly changing circumstances; the human rights regime is cautious, rigid, and resistant to innovation.[7]

Criticisms questioning the validity and effectiveness of a state-centric system in an increasingly diverse global order have surfaced.[8] While the corporates' human rights obligations have attained attention of international human rights law, responses are inadequate. The state and human rights regime continue to reject any formal human rights obligations on corporation at international level and instead propose to regulate corporations at domestic level. However, states are often ill-equipped or unwilling to strengthen internal laws towards this end. Consequently, human rights stand heavily compromised on account of rigidity and resistance to shift the focus even when the state is a marginalized player.

International human rights law discourse is trapped between competing claims of imposing obligations on the corporations and those rejecting it. It is submitted that such dichotomy of discourse misleads by projecting the state and corporation as contesters rather than collaborators of human rights obligation. Perhaps the vastness, diversity, and complexity of human rights issues and corporations are too overwhelming to be dealt with in their entirety. It can be suggested to adopt an incremental approach of assigning human rights obligations on corporation, beginning with those areas where corporations have an evident dominant position vis-a-vis the state. Instead of rushing towards solutions that answer in 'yes' or 'no' about corporate human rights obligations, one may promulgate a staggered inquiry into the whole question, where corporations

---

[7] P. Alston, 'Downsizing the State in Human Rights Discourse', in *Democracy and the Rule of Law*, pp. 357–68 (N. Dorden and P. Gifford, eds, 2001).

[8] Iris Halpern, 'Tracing the Contours of Transnational Corporations' Human Rights Obligations in the Twenty-First Century', 14 *Buffalo Human Rights Law Review* 129 (2008).

are obvious private authority, either natural or delegated, and progressively expand the scope of its application.

It has been demonstrated, in the context of human rights and technology, that the bilateral relationship between the state and individual has given way to a tripartite relationship between the state, corporation and individuals. Corporations as a private authority in a technologically advanced society are the most crucial guarantors of human rights. Non recognition of their positive human rights obligations has serious ramifications in terms of digital disempowerment of various segments of population. The dynamics of this relationship in the backdrop of constantly evolving themes of positive human rights compels bringing horizontal application of human rights to the forefront. Whilst this book made a case for shared human right obligations between the state and corporate in the context of the Internet; it is trite to think about this collaborative application beyond the Internet. The critical task is to identify and examine those areas where corporation hold obvious dominant position or a state-like authority.

Decentralized Regulation

As corporations continue to offer complex regulatory problems, it has been progressively realized that these problems result from several interacting factors, and policy-makers and legislators may not know as much about an industry as industry does about itself. It is fallacious to assume that any particular actor perfectly understands the regulatory requirement or has fully effective instrumentalities at its disposal. The failure to appreciate a change in understanding of the 'regulation' leads to unachieved regulatory targets.

An orthodox understanding of 'regulation' in terms of control over private activities exercised by public authorities[9] has to be

---

[9] R. Baldwin, M. Cave, and M. Lodge, *Understanding Regulation: Theory, Strategy and Practice* 3 (2nd ed., 1999). 'At its simplest, regulation refers to the promulgation of an authoritative set of rules, accompanied by some mechanism, typically a public agency, for monitoring and promoting compliance with those rules.'

suitably tweaked to provide adequate responses to the current times. Today, corporations are regulated by hugely diverse group of actors who may include shareholders, public authorities, inter-governmental bodies, trade unions, NGOs, consumer groups. The key to successful regulation is a proper understanding of influences and pressures guiding corporate behaviour and how they might be manipulated to achieve a particular aim. Corporations deal with pressures emanating not only from legal sanctions but also economic motivations that require them to meet financial expectations of investors, creditors, and chief executives, and also serves as an indicator of worth and value in capitalist society. Their social motives relates to the pressure they feel from local neighbourhoods, employees (especially from certain professions), media, and advocacy groups to engage in responsible conduct. It is often a right combination of social pressure groups and economic interest groups that provide desirable impetus for the regulatory compliance.

Given this backdrop, it is suggested to apply a broad meaning of regulation which encompasses 'any form of social control or influence, regardless of its source.'[10] Regulation need not be binding and enforceable to be effective. In the present context a broad conception of regulation is applied by widening the scope of regulation, functional at every 'layer' of interaction and at the same time acknowledging the importance of the deliberative process. More diverse actors are included in the regulatory process, as well as a strategies and mechanisms as part of the regulatory mix. It may involve direct intervention or co-regulation. The challenge is, through designing and refining a matrix of regulatory tools, to identify the most efficient and effective mix of tools to accommodate the dynamic requirements of any given context, whether that context is environmental regulation, financial services, or the franchising sector.[11]

The regulatory style therefore, may take form of a uni-dimensional pyramid, three dimensional pyramid or an

---

[10] J.A. Zerk, *Multinationals and Corporate Social Responsibility: Limitations and Opportunities in International Law* 42 (2006).

[11] Elizabeth Crawford Spencer, *The Regulation of Franchising in the New Global Economy*, 42 (2010).

interconnected pentagon as developed in this book. Whereas the first two remain centralized, the third operates in a decentralized mode. The pyramid style of compliance-oriented enforcement strategies may succeed where regulatees are equipped to understand or effectively respond to the regulator's messages of encouragement.[12] The decentralized style of regulation is effective in polycentric regulatory regimes, including those where the role of policymaking, information gathering, and enforcement is distributed between a number of organizations, particularly where they cross different jurisdictional boundaries.[13] The decentralized perspective is stimulating in that it opens up the cognitive frame of what 'regulation' is and prompt policy thinkers to consider a wide range of different configurations of state, market, community, associations, networks to deliver public policy goals.[14] This approach necessarily envisions regulation as a collaborative enterprise between multiple regulators.

The systems theory is critical in designing and accommodating the growing complexity of society and responses in the form of decentralized regulation. Baldwin and Julia rightly suggest that a decentralized approach of regulation is most often invoked in the face of five crucial regulatory peculiarities. One, complexity, where interaction between various actors in society pose unique complications of regulation; two, fragmentation, where the knowledge, power, and control of a regulatory subject are fragmented that is, no single actor has all the knowledge required to solve complex, diverse and dynamic problems; three, the autonomy and ungovernability of actors. Autonomy is not used in the sense of freedom from interference by government, rather it is the idea that actors will continue to develop or act in their own way in the absence of intervention. Four, the interaction and interdependencies between institutions and instrumentalities, where each is seen as possessing its own set of problems (needs) and

---

[12] Parker, 'Compliance Professionalism and Regulatory Community: The Australian Trade Practices Regime', 26 Journal of Law and Society 215 (1999): 223.

[13] Baldwin and Black, 'Really Responsive Regulation', 71 Modern L. Review 59 (2008): 93.

[14] Black, 'Critical Reflections on Regulation', 27 Australian Journal of Legal Philosophy 1 (2002).

solutions (capacities); and lastly, where the regulatory area/sector has witnessed a collapse of the public-private distinction in socio-political terms.[15]

Prospective Agendas

The present study has particularly brought together various lines of inquiries surrounding disadvantaged groups, their human rights in technologically advanced society and reflected upon its implications on the nature and scope of obligations and their effective realization. It is however, critical to take a look forward and flag key agendas that lies ahead.

Formulating Enforcement Paradigm for Corporate Obligation

International human rights law has been oscillating between the need to respond to emerging socio-economic realities and more specifically the heightened visibility of the corporate power in the national and international arena. It is emphasized that there is an urgent need to free international human rights law from the strangleholds of the classical Westphalian philosophies. The state cannot be allowed to privatize their way out of international legal obligations to protect and promote human rights. Similarly, corporations cannot be permitted to keep lurching in shadows and the spotlight has to be focused on corporations when they occupy state-like, dominant position. This book has identified the Internet as an illustrative area of corporate dominance. It may be possible to undertake a similar search in other spaces and sectors of obvious corporate authority.

In a fresh attempt to hold corporations accountable for human rights violations, on 26 June 2014 the Human Rights Council (HRC) adopted a resolution calling for the establishment of an open-ended intergovernmental working group (IGWG) 'to elaborate an international legally-binding instrument to regulate,

[15] Robert Baldwin and Julia Black, *Really Responsive Regulation*, 71 MODERN L. REV. 59 (2008).

in international human rights law, the activities of transnational corporations and other business enterprises'.[16] While the treaty is in early stages scholarly work have already began to surface exploring the possible form and content of a legally binding international instrument in the area of business and human rights.[17]

Even as this resolution can be seen as a renewed opportunity to bridge the normative and legal gap in corporate human rights obligations, the challenge lies in averting polarization of the issue. This study has informed how an outright rejection as well as blanket application of human rights obligations on corporations can be balanced out with staggering the imposition of obligation. It will be, therefore, critical to identify and set parameters that trigger corporate obligation, both to abstain from abuse and promote human rights. Another critical task will be the need to develop instrumentalities. Whether these ought to be generalized or sector-specific? What should be the content of these instrumentalities? Besides, one will have to worry about creating hierarchies within corporations operating in a particular industry/sector. Not all corporations are similarly placed in their financial resources, political reach, market presence, and the consequent impact on a human right under question. The human rights regime will have to be responsive to industry leaders, the recalcitrant and the laggards.

---

[16] Human Rights Council, Resolution 26/9, 'Elaboration of an Internationally Legally Binding Instrument on Transnational Corporations and Other Business Enterprises with Respect to Human Rights,' 26th Sess., 10–27 June 2014, A/HRC/26/L.22/Rev.1 para 1 (26 June 2014).

[17] Olivier De Schutter, 'Towards a New Treaty on Business and Human Rights', 1 *Business and Human Rights Journal* 41(2015) (Examining the legal and political feasibility of plausible options for a legally binding international instrument in the area of business and human rights, Schutter suggests *inter alia* imposing direct human rights obligations on corporations and establishing a new mechanism to monitor compliance with such obligations); Douglass Cassell and Anita Ramasastry, 'White Paper: Options for a Treaty on Business and Human Rights', 6 *Notre Dame Journal of International and Comparative Law* 1 (2016); Larry Cata Backer, 'Shaping a Global Law for Business Enterprises: Framing Principles and the Promise of a Comprehensive Treaty on Business and Human Rights', 42 *North Carolina Journal of International Law* 417 (2017) (suggest the range of plausible ideological choices that may serve as a starting

At the same time, future agenda essentially entails improving access to judicial and non-judicial remedies for corporate non-compliance. As of now, there exists no sanction or mechanism at international level for corporate misconduct or neglect of human rights. Developing an effective model of corporate compliance will be a significant agenda for the future.

Re-conceptualizing Corporate Law

The shift in international human rights approach to corporate obligations also necessarily leaves a domestic agenda for corporate laws. Whilst corporations remain on the private side of the line, they represent private law creatures in which the public has an interest arising from functional considerations. But these political functional considerations have a politically neutral cast, and the present corporate law model is based on private law in general and property law and contract law in particular. Given the persistent claims on corporations to perform their social and human rights obligations, the prospective challenge lies in creating a space for these goals in the current situation. How can a theoretical, legal, and normative framework be designed so that corporations could be made responsive to public policy goals without disturbing existing model of corporate law? Such an approach requires drawing up an agenda to identify points of intervention in corporate law, creating pockets for public policy discourse and locating the Achilles heels where regulatory mechanisms will be most effective. This holds

---

point for treaty drafting that is principled, classes of technical provisions and processes that the business and human rights treaty may consider); Markiewicz Graham, 'The Logical Next Step: Motivations on the Formation of a Business and Human Rights Treaty', 26 *Minnesota Journal of International Law* 63 (2017); Sara Blackwell and Nicole Vander Meulen, 'Two Roads Converged: The Mutual Complementarity of a Binding Business and Human Rights Treaty and National Action Plans on Business and Human Rights', 6 *Notre Dame Journal of International and Comparative Law* 51(2016) (suggesting that the binding business and human rights treaty and the National Action Plan under the Guiding Principles are complementary and competitive).

possibility of paying attention to the application of political and constitutional theories to corporate law with an underlying objective to provide a normative framework within which one can improve the quality of corporate decision making.[18] Such a re-conceptualization of corporate law in political theory and corporation as a political requires rigorous and systematic presentation and vision.

Humanizing the Internet Discourse

The Internet is a unique global resource and one of the largest co-operative efforts ever undertaken by humankind. The initial cooperation however, has given way to conflicting claims and interests. The situation is very chaotic. Whoever shouts loudest gets noticed first. The issues involved are too wide and too big. Negotiations have gone through a few important stages, but are still very far from completion or even from a universal agreement on what the virtual world governance should look like. We are still in the early stages of establishing principles, governance, and regulation of the Internet. How should virtual community be organized? Which social and economic values are justified in order to ensure egalitarianism in the virtual world? What norms are absolutely non-negotiable when drafting the Internet policy and governance system? To what extend should human rights perspectives inform pragmatic choices to the Internet?

Since the Internet is currently devoid of any international treaty or centralized body governing the same, it is important to think through the social, cultural and particularly human rights aspects of the Internet. The meanings and norms we attach to the Internet will be really important. In the wake of increasing internationalization and commercialization of the Internet, future research agendas must be set to attain a breakthrough in attaining and prioritizing certain non-negotiables to universal rights and governance to the Internet. Largely issues related to access to the Internet have been cornered by the issue freedom of speech and expression and market

[18] Stephen Bottomley, *The Constitutional Corporation: Rethinking Corporate Governance* (2007).

interests. However, it is suggested that discourse related to the Internet requires deeper examination through the illustration of digital divide by digging beneath the surface of access to broadband connectivity or access to low cost technology. Thus, due credence must be lent to the complexity of the digital divide from a human rights perspective and the implications of this divide. It is argued that when digital divide and issues of accessibility are construed as not only the freedom of expression and the right to privacy, but also social, economic, and cultural rights including the right to development; it lends the digital divide immediate priority and comprehensive response.

The horizons of these issues should be expanded to emphasize participation, empowerment and non-discrimination converging with human rights norms of human dignity and autonomy. The concerns about realizing human dignity in a networked society necessarily imply being alert to new forms of inequalities and injustices manifested in digital divides. It would be too simplistic to define the gap as the information haves and have nots. It is not only a gap between awareness, access, affordability, availability, and adaptability. Clearly, the digital divide is much more complex than mere lack of computers or broadband. If digital divide is continued to be seen in technology blinkers, it masks the larger human rights dimension. The diffusion of the Internet and its actual access is selective, both socially and functionally.

The policy responses and programmatic intervention will largely depend upon how the problem of the digital divide is scoped. The human rights perspectives to the Internet as explored in this book holds value for the upcoming debates regarding the Internet say for instance net neutrality. The whole discourse supporting free and open Internet and restricting creation of enclosures by an advantaged few private interests can be accorded deeper and nuanced understanding when analysed from human rights dimension. The Internet when viewed as a global commons, the disparity in diffusion is seen to affect the vital developmental goals of individuals in terms of education, employment, health, poverty alleviation. Such a broad understanding enables policy-makers and stakeholders to come up devise a finer and nuanced response to empower disadvantaged groups to effectively exercise their citizenship in a digital setting and participate in the development.[19]

Innovative Regulation

The growing complexity and interdependence between different actors, systems, and operations have challenged the conventional dilemma between centralized regulation and options of deregulation. There is a paradigm shift from regulatory to a governance mode. The regulatory system continues to be developed for different purposes and motivations. For instance, regulation for economic efficiency and consumer choice; regulation to protect rights; regulation for social solidarity, to avoid the fragmenting effects of markets and to promote universal access to public services of consistent quality and regulation as deliberation, with the major role of the regulatory institution being to provide procedural means for resolving problems, either through a forum for compromise of different views or a source of learning to seek a consensus. While these regulatory goals may not be mutually exclusive, future challenges for a regulator will lie in being informed of these motivations while designing, assessing regulatory approach, and at the same time being more experimental and flexible in finding what regulatory system works best to achieve the desired outcome. The regulatory design will require a careful consideration of the behaviour, attitudes and cultures of regulatee; the institutional settings of the different regulators; the different logics of regulatory tools and strategies and their interaction with one another.

The regulatory style therefore will have to be tailored to suit a particular situation and no one size fits all. The use of multiple rather than single policy instruments, and a broader range of regulatory actors, will produce better regulation and will further allow implementation of complementary combinations of instruments and participants. Besides the novel regulatory arenas, existing regulatory mechanisms will also have to be revisited and renewed

---

[19] Lisa Servon, *Bridging the Digital Divide: Technology, Community and Public Policy* 6 (2002).

to address contingencies, internal tensions, and dispersed power. This again is an unchartered terrain where regulators will have to be mindful of the shifting regulatory and policy issues and diagnose the mismatch between the complexity of the current situation and the state's regulatory capacities. While the present study has undertaken this inquiry pertaining to the right to access the Internet, these may be extended to employment and environmental protection laws, welfare, family, health, and education laws; policing and dispute resolution, criminal justice administration, consumer protection, transportation, information technology, corporate laws.

Thus, good regulation necessarily involves invoking different responsive enforcement strategies depending upon whether one is dealing with leaders, reluctant compliers, recalcitrant, or the incompetent. The challenge is to develop enforcement strategies that punish the worst offenders while at the same time encouraging and helping regulatees to comply voluntarily. This essentially calls for looking beyond dichotomous choice between punishment and persuasion in exclusion to each other. In a complex and rapidly evolving world order, the challenge lies in re-writing rules and regulations to obtain the desired societal outcome.

Bibliography

Books

Achterbergh, J. and D. Vriens. *Organisations: Social Systems Conducting Experiments*. 2nd ed. Heidelberg: Springer, 2010.

Allingham, M. *Rational Choice*. New York: St. Martin's Press Inc., 1999.

Archer, M.S. and J.Q. Tritter. *Rational Choice Theory: Resisting Colonization.* 1st ed. New York: Routledge, 2001.

Arend, A.C. *Legal Rules and International Society.* Oxford: Oxford University Press, 1999.

Arthurs, H.W. *Without the Law: Adminstrative Justice and Legal Pluralism in Nineteenth Century England.* Toronto: University Toronto Press, 1985.

Ayres, I. and J. Braithwaite. *Responsive Regulation: Transcending the Deregulaiton Debate.* Oxford: Oxford University Press, 1992.

Baldwin, R. and M. Cave. *Understanding Regulation: Theory, Study, and Practice.* New York: Oxford University Press, 1999.

Bardach, E. and R.A. Kagan. *Going by the Book: The Problem of Regulatory Unreasonableness.* Philadelphia PA: Temple University Press, 1982.

Barne, C. and G. Mercer. *Exploring Disability: A Sociological Introduction.* 2nd ed. Cambridge: Polity Press, 2010.

Bauer, R. and D.H. Fenn, Jr. *The Corporate Social Audit.* New York: Russell Sage Foundation, 1972.

Baxi, U. *The Future of Human Rights.* New York: Oxford University Press, 2002.

Becker, G.S. *Crime and Punishment: An Economic Approach to Human Behaviour.* Chicago, IL: Chicago University Press, 1990.

Beitz, C. *The Idea of Human Rights.* New York: Oxford University Press, 2009.

Bentham, J., ed. *An Introduction to the Principles of Morals and Legislation.* Garden City, NY: Anchor Books, 1973.

Black, J. *Rules and Regulators.* Oxford, UK: Oxford University Press, 1997.

Blanck, P. *eQuality: The Struggle for Web Accessibility by Persons with Cognitive Disabilities.* Cambridge: Cambridge University Press, 2014.

Bottomley, S. *The Constitutional Corporation: Rethinking Corporate Governance.* Aldershot UK: Ashgate, 2007.

Braithwaite, J. *Regulatory Capitalism: How It Works, Ideas for Making It Work Better.* Cheltenham, UK: Edward Elgar, 2008.

————. *Restorative Justice and Responsive Regulation.* New York: Oxford University Press, 2002.

————. *To Punish or Persuade: Enforcement of Coal Mine Safety.* Albany, NY: State Universityof New York Press, 1985.

Braithwaite, J. and Drahos, P. *Global Business Regulation.* Cambridge: Cambridge University Press, 2000.

Castells, M. *The Rise of Network Society: The Information Age: Economy, Society and Culture.* Oxford: Wiley and Blackwell, 2010.

Chalmers, D., G. Davies, and G. Monti. *European Union Law: Cases and Materials,* 2nd ed. Cambridge, University Archives: Cambridge University Press, 2011.

Clapham, A. *Human Rights in the Private Sphere.* Oxford: Oxford University Press, 1993.

————. *Human Rights Obligations of Non-state Actors.* Oxford: Oxford University Press, 2006.

Clark, N. *Gatekeepers: The Professions and Coporate Governance.* New York: Oxford University Press, 2006.

Coase, R.H. *The Firm, The Market and the Law.* Chicago, IL: The Chicago University Press,1988.

Cohen, J.L. *Regulating Intimacy: A New Legal Paradigm.* Princeton: Princeton University Press, 2002.

Collins, H. *Regulating Contracts.* Oxford: Oxford University Press, 1999.

Cotter, M. *This Ability: An International Legal Perspective of Disability Discrimination.* Hampshire, UK: Ashgate Publishing Ltd., 2007.

Deibert, R., J. Palfry. *Access Denied: The Practice and Policy of Global Internet Filtering.* Cambridge: Cambridge MIT Press, 2008.

Deva, S. *Regulating Corporate Human Rights Violations: Humanizing Business.* New York: Routledge, 2012.

Dilling, O., M. Martin Herberg, and G. Winter. *Responsible Business: Self-Governance and Law in Transnational Economic Transactions.* Oxford: Hart Publishing, 2008.

Donnelly, J. *Universal Human Rights in Theory and Practice.* Ithaca: Cornell University Press, 2003.

Feintuc, M. and M. Varney. *Media Regulation, Public Interest and the Law.* Edinburgh: Edinburgh University Press, 2006.

Finkelstein, V. *Attitudes and Disabled People: Issues for Discussion.* New York: International Exchange of Information in Rehabilitation, 1980.

Flaherty, D. *Privacy in Surveillance Societies:The Federal Republic of Germany, Sweden, France, Canada and United States.* Chapel Hill, NC: University of North Carolina Press, 1989.

Fredman, S. *Human Rights Transformed: Positive Rights and Positive Duties.* Oxford: Oxford University Press, 2008.

Freedman, M. *Capitalism and Freedom.* Chicago: The University of Chicago Press, 1962.

Freeman, S. *Reason and Agreements in Social Contract Views, in Justice and the Social Contract: Essays on Rawlsian Political Philosophy.* Oxford: Oxford University Press, 2006.

Friedman, M. *Essays in Positive Economics.* Chicago, IL: The University of Chicago Press, 1953.

Fuentes-Camacho, T. *The International Dimensions of Cyberspace Law.* Burlington, Vt: Ashgate, 2000.

Gewirth, A. *Human Rights: Essays on Justification and Applications.* Chicago: University of Chicago Press, 1982.

Griffin, J. *On Human Rights.* Oxford: Oxford University Press, 2008.

Gunningham, N., P. Grabosky, and D. Sinclair. *Smart Regulation: Designing Environmental Policy.* Oxford: Oxford Claredon Press, 1998.

———. *The Structual Transformation of the Public Sphere: An Inquiry into a Category of Bourgeois Society.* Cambridge, Mass.: MIT Press, 1992.

Habermas, J. *Between Facts and Norms: Contributions to a Discourse Theory Law and Democracy.* Cambridge, Mass.: MIT Press, 1996.

Harkaway, N. *The Blind Giant: Being Human in a Digital World.* London: John Murray Publishers, 2012

Hart, H.LA. *The Concept of Law.* Oxford: Claderon Press, 1961.

Hick, S., E. Halpin, and E. Hoskins. *Human Rights and the Internet.* Basingstoke: Macmillan, 2000.

Higgins, R. *Problems and Process: International Law and How We Use It.* Oxford: Clarendon Press, 1994.

Jacint, J. and D. Levi-Faur. *The Politics of Regulation: Institutions and Regulatory Reforms for the Age of Governance,* Cheltenham, UK: Edward Elgar, 2004.

Jaeger, P. *Disability and the Internet: Confronting a Digital Divide.* Boulder, Colo: Lynne Rienner Publishers Inc., 2012.

Jaeger, P., and C. Bowman. *Understanding Disability: Inclusion, Access, Diversity and Civil Rights.* Westport, Conn: Praeger, 2005.

Jorgensen, R.F. *Framing the Net: The Internet and Human Rgihts.* Massachusettes: Edward Elgar Publications Ltd., 2013.

Karavias, M. *Corporate Obligations Under International Law.* Oxford: Oxford University Press, 2013.

Keohane, R.O. *After Hegemony: Co-operation and Discord in the World Political Economy.* Princeton, NJ: Princeton University Press, 1984.

Krammer, M., N.E. Simmonds, and H. Steiner. *A Debate over Rights: Philosophical Enquiries.* Oxford: Claderaon Press, 1998.

Lawson, A. *Disability and Equality Law in Britain: The Role of Reasonable Adjustment.* Oxford: Hart (2008)

Lambooy, T. *Corporate Social Responsibility: Legal and Semi-Legal Frameworks Supporting CSR.* Deventer: Kluwer, 2010.

Lessig, Lawrence. *Code and Other Laws of Cyberspace.* New York: Basic Books, 1999.

Liachowitz, C.H. *Disability as a Social Construct: Legislative Roots.* Philadelphia: University of Pennsylvania Press, 1988.

Liisberg, M.V. *Disability and Employment: A Contemporary Disability Rights Approach Applied to Danish, Swedish and EU Law and Policy.* Cambridge: Intersentia, 2011.

Mares, R. *The Dynamics of Corporate Social Responsibilities.* Boston: Martinus Nijhoff Publishers, 2008.

May, C. *The Information Society: A Sceptical View.* Malden, Mass.: Polity Press, 2002.

Michael, O. *Understanding Disability: From Theory to Practice.* New York: Palgrave Macmillan, 1996.

Monaghan, K. *Monaghan on Equality Law.* Oxford: Oxford University Press, 2007.

Morris, J. *Pride against Prejudice.* New York: Praeger, 1988.

Muir-Watt, F.C. and M.W. Horatia. *Making European Private Law: Governing Design.* Massachusetts: Edgar Elgar Publising Inc., 2008.

Murray, A. *The Regulation of Cyberspace: Control in the Online Envrionment.* New York: Routledge-Cavendish, 2007.

Nussabaum, M.C. *Frontiers of Justice: Disabilities, Nationality, Species Membership.* Princeton, N.J: Princeton University Press, 2006.

Oded, S. *Corporate Compliance: New Approaches to Regulatory Enforcement.* Massachusetts, USA: Edward Elgar, 2013.

Offe, C. *Contradictions of the Welfare State.* London: Hutchinson, 1984.

Oliver, M. *The Politics of Disablement.* London: Macmillan Education, 1990.

Olivia, S. *Disability Discrimination Law.* Dublin: Thomson Reuters (Round Hall Ltd.), 2010.

O'Neill, O. *Bounds of Justice.* Cambridge University Press: Cambridge, 2000.

Parker, C. *The Open Corporation: Effective Self-Regulation and Democracy,* Cambridge, UK: Cambridge University Press, 2002.

Pickering, F.L., and A. Silvers. *Americans with Disabiliities: Exploring Implications of the Law for Individuals and Institutions.* New York: Routledge, 2000.

Prosser, T. *The Limits of Competition Law: Markets and Public Services.* Oxford: Oxford University Press, 2005.

Rawls, J. *The Law of Peoples with 'The Idea of Public Reason Revisited'*. Cambridge, MA: Harvard University Press, 1999.

_____. *Theory of Justice*. Cambridge, MA: Belknap Press of Harvard University Press, 1999.

Raz, J. *The Morality of Freedom*. Oxford: Oxford University Press, 1986.

Reinicke, W. *Global Public Policy: Governing Without Government?* Washington DC: Brookings Institution Press, 1998.

Richter, J. *Holding Corproations Accountable: Corporate Conduct, International Codes and Citizen Action*. London: Zed Books, 2001.

Ronald Deibert, John Palfry et al. *Access Denied: The Practice and Policy of Global Internet Filtering*. Cambridge: MIT Press, 2008.

Salamon, L.M. et al. *Global Civil Society: Dimensions of the Non-Profit Sector*. Bloomfield, CT.: Kumarian, 1999.

Schweik, S. *The Ugly Laws: Disability in Public*. New York: New York University Press, 2009.

Sen, A. *Development as Freedom*. New York: Knopf, 1999.

Servon, L. *Bridging the Digital Divide: Technology, Community and Public Policy*. Oxford: Blackwell Publishing, 2002.

Shirky, C. *Here Comes Everybody: The Power of Organizing without Organisations*. New York: Penguin Books, 2008.

Shue, H. *Basic Rights*. Princeton, N.J.: Princeton University Press, 1996.

Simmons, J. *Justification and Legitimacy: Essay on Rights and Obligations*. Cambridge: Cambridge University Press, 2001.

Sparrow, M.K. *The Regulatory Craft: Controlling Risks, Solving Problems and Managing Compliance*. Washington, D.C.: Brookings Institution Press, 2000.

Spencer, E.C. *The Regulation of Franchising in the New Global Economy*. Massachusetts, USA: Edward Elgar Publishing, 2010.

Strange, S. *The Retreat of the State: The Diffussion of Power in the World Economy*. Cambridge: Cambridge University Press, 1996.

Sustein, C.R. *Republic.com*. Princeton, N.J.: Princeton University Press, 2001.

Teubner, G. *Autopoietic Law: A New Approach to Law and Society*. Berlin: Walter de Gruyter, 1988.

_____. *Law as an Autopoietic System*. Oxford: Blackwell Publishers, 1993.

Turkle, S. *Life on the screen: Identity in the Age of the Internet*. New York: Simon and Schuster, 1995.

Varney, E. *Disability and Information Technology: A Comparative Study in Media Regulation*. Cambridge: Cambridge University Press, 2013.

Weber, R. *Regulatory Models for the Online World*. Kluwer International Law, 2002.

Weber, R. and Valeri, M. *The Information Society and the Digital Divide, Legal Strategies to Finance Global Access*. Geneva: Schulthess, 2008.

Weber, R.H. and Weber, R. *The Internet of the things: Legal Perspectives*. Berlin: Springer, 2010.

Wendell, S. *The Rejected Body: Feminist Philosophical Reflection on Disability*. London: Routledge, 1996.

Zerk, J.A. *Multinational and Corporate Social Responsibility: Limitations and Opportunities in International Law*. Cambridge: Cambridge University Press, 2006.

Book Chapters

Alston, P. 'Downsizing the State in Human Rights Discourse', in *Democracy and the Rule of Law*, edited by N. Dorden and P. Gifford, pp. 357–68. Washington: Congressional Quarterly Press, 2001.

_____. 'The Non-a-cat Syndrome: Can the Human Rights Regime Accommodate Non-State Actors', in *Non-State Actors and Human Rights*, edited by P. Alston, pp. 3–36. Oxford: Oxford Univesity Press, 2005.

Baade, W.H. 'The Legal Effects of Codes of Conduct', in *Legal Problems of Codes of Conduct for Multinational Enterprises*, edited by N. Horn, pp. 16–27. Boston: Kluwer, 1980.

Basser, L.A. and M. Jones. 'The Disability Discrimination Act 1992 (CTH): A Three-dimensional Approach to Opertaionalizing Human Rights', in *Disability Essays*, edited by Peter Blanck, pp. 203–33. Burlington, VT: Ashgate, 2005.

Bilchitz, D. 'A Chasm between "is" and "ought"? A critique of the normative foundations of the SRSG's Framework and the Guiding Principles', in *Human Rights Obligations of Business: Beyond the Corporate Responsibility to Respect*, edited by Surya Deva and David Bilchitz, pp. 107–37. Cambridge: Cambridge University Press, 2013.

Bilchitz, D. and Deva, S. 'Business and Human Rights: A Critical Framework', in *Human Rights Obligations of Business: Beyond the Corporate Responsibility to Respect*, edited by Surya Deva and David Bilchitz, pp. 1–26. Cambridge: Cambridge University Press, 2013.

Brownsword, R. 'Freedom of Contract, Human Rights and Human Dignity', in *Human Rights in Private Law*, edited by D. Friedman and D. Barak-Erez, pp. 181–200. Oxford: Hart Publishing, 2001.

Brewer, J. 'The World Wide Web Consortium Accessibility Initiative', in *G3ict The Accessibility Imperative: Implications of the Convention of the Rights of Persons with Disabilities for Information and Communication Technologies*, edited by G3ict Global Initiative for Inclusive Information and Communication Technologies, pp. 161–5. Georgia, USA: World Times, Inc., 2007.

Bruce Hall, R. and T.J. Biersteker. 'The Emergence of Private Authority in the International System', in *The Emergence of Private Authority in Global Governance*, edited by R. Bruce Hall and T.J. Biersteker. 2002.

Collins, R. 'Realising Social Goals in Connectivity and Content', in *Regulating the Information Society*, edited by C.T. Marsden, pp. 109–16. New York: Routledge, 2000.

Demeyere, B. 'Sovereign Wealth Funds and (Un)ethical Investment', in *Human Rights, Corporate Complicity and Disinvestment*, edited by A. Follesdal, O. Mestad, and G. Nystuen, pp. 183–221.Cambridge: Cambridge University Press, 2011.

Dutton, W.H. and M. Peltu. 'The New Politics of the Internet, Multi Stakeholder policy making and the Internet Technology', in *Handbook of Internet Politics*, edited by A. Chadwick and P.N. Howard eds, pp. 384–400. New York: Routledge, 2009.

Febbrajo, A. 'The Autopoietic Approach and its Form', in *State, Law and Economy as Autopoietic Systems*, edited by G. Teubner and A. Febbrajo, pp. 19–33. Milan: Dott-a-Guiffre Editore, 1992.

Francis, L. and Silvers, A. 'Introduction-Achieving the Right to Live in the World: Americans with Disabilities and the Civil Rights Tradition', in *Americans with Disabilities: Exploring the Implications of the Law for individuals and Institutions*, edited by L. Francis and A. Silvers, pp. xiii–xxx. New York: Routledge, 2000.

Fredman, S. 'Disability Equality: A Challenge to the Existing Anti-Discrimination Paradigm', in *Disability Rights in Europe: From Theory to Practice*, edited by A. Lawson and C. Gooding, pp. 199–218. Oxford: Hart Publishing, 2005.

Hancher, L. and Moran, M. 'Organizing Regulatory Space', in *Capitalism, Culture and Economic Regulation*, edited by L. Hancher and M. Moran, pp. 271–99. Oxford: Oxford University Press, 1989.

Hecklo, H. 'Issues Networks and the Executive Establishment', in *The New American Political System*, edited by Anthony King, pp. 87–124. Washington, DC.: American Enterprise Institute for Public Policy Research, 1978.

Hofmann, J. 'Internet Governance: A Regulative Idea in Flux', in *Internet Governance: An Introduction*, edited by R.K. Bandamutha, pp. 74–108. Hyderabad: The Icfai University Press, 2007.

Jungk, M. 'A Practical Guide to Addressing Human Rights Concerns for Companies Operating Abroad', in *Human Rights Standards and the Responsibility of Transnational Corporations*, edited by Michael K. Addo, pp. 171–86. The Hague: Kluwer Law International, 1999.

Kagan, R.A. and J. Scholz. 'The "Criminology of the Corporation" and Regulatory Enforcement Strategies', in *Enforcing Regualtion*, edited by Keith Hawkins and John M. Thomas, pp. 352–77. Boston: Kluwer-Nijhoff, 1984.

Kahn, R.E. 'The Role of Governemnt in the Evolution of the Internet', in *Revulation in the U.S. Information Infrastructure*, pp. 13-24. Washington, D.C.: National Academies Press, 1995.

Kant, I. 'The Metaphysics of Morals', in *Practical Philosophy*, translated by I. Kant, Mary J. Gregory. Cambridge: Cambridge University Press, 1996.

Keohane, R.O. and J.S. Nye, Jr. 'Introduction', in *Governance in Globalizing World*, edited by J.S. Nye Jr. and J.D. Donahue, pp. 1-44. Washington, DC: The Brookings Institution Press, 2000.

Kooiman, J. 'Governance and Governability: Using Complexity, Dynamics and Diversity', in *Modern Governance: New Government Society Interactions*, edited by J. Kooiman, pp. 35-50. London: Sage, 1993.

Lawson, A. 'Challenging Disabling Barriers to Information and Communication Technology in the Information Society: A United Kingdom Perspective', in *European Yearbook of Disability Laws Volume 2*, edited by Lisa Waddingdon and Gerard Quinn, pp. 131-48. Oxford: Intersentia, 2010.

Leblois, A. 'Implementing the Digital Accessbility Agenda of the UN Convention on the Rights of Persons with Disabilities: Challenges and Opportunities', in *European Yearbook of Disability Law Volume 1*, edited by Gerard Quinn and Lisa Waddigton, pp. 139-45. Oxford: Intersentia, 2009.

Lugones, M.C. and E.V. Spelman. 'Have We Got a Theory for You! Feminist Theory, Cultural Imperialism and the Demand for "The Woman Voice"', in *Hypatia reborn: Essays in Feminist Philosophy*, edited by Azizah Hibri and Margaret Simon, pp. 18-33. Bloomington: Indiana University Press, 1990.

MacLean, D. 'Herding Schrodinger's Cats: Some Conceptual Tools for Thinking about Internet Governance', in *Internet Governance: A Grand Collaboration An Edited Collection of Papers Contributed to the United Nations ICT Task Force Global Forum on Internet Governance*, edited by D. MacLean, pp. 73-99. New York: The United Nations Information and Communications Technology Task Force, 2004.

Malanczuk, P. 'Globalisation and the Future Role of Sovereign', in *International Economic Law with a Human Face*, edited by F. Weiss et. al., pp. 45-66. The Hague: Kluwer Law International, 1998.

McCrudden, C. 'Corporate Social Responsibility and Public Procurement', in *The New Corporate Acoountability: Corporate Social Responsibility and the Law*, edited by D. McBarnet, A. Voiculescu, and T. Campbell, pp. 93-118. Cambridge: Cambridge University Press, 2007.

Melish, T.J. and E. Meidinger. 'Protect, Respect, Remedy and Participate: "New Governance" Lessons for the Ruggie Framework', in *The UN Guiding Principles on Business and Human Rights*, edited by Radu Mares. Leiden: Martinus Nijhoff, 2012.

Myhill, W.M. 'Law and Policy Challenges for Achieving an Accessible e-society: Lessons from the United States', in *European Yearbook of Disability Laws Volume 2*, edited by Lisa Waddingdon and Gerard Quinn, pp. 103-29. Oxford: Intersentia, 2010.

Ogus, A. 'Enforcing Regulation: Do We Need the Criminal Law?', in *New Perspectives on Economic Crime*, edited by H. Sjogren and G. Skogh, pp. 42-55. Cheltenham, UK: Edward Elgar Publishing Ltd., 2004.

Prosser, T. 'Regulatory Agencies, Regulatory Legitimacy and European Private Law', in *Making European Priave Law: Governance Design*, edited by F. Cafaggi and H. Muir-Watt, pp. 235-53. Cheltenham: Edward Elgar, 2008.

Pruzan, P. 'The Ethical Dimensions of Banking: Sbn Bank, Denmark', in *Building Corporate Accountability: Emerging Practice in Social and Ethical Accounting and Auditing*, by S. Zadek, P. Pruzan, and R. Evans eds. pp. 63-83. London: Eatherscan Publications Ltd., 1997.

Quinn, G. 'The Human Rights of People with Disabilities under EU Law', in *The EU and Human Rights*, edited by Philip Alston and Mara Bustelo, pp. 281-326. Oxford: Oxford University Press, 1999.

Quinn, G. and T. Degener. 'The Moral Authority for Change: Human Rights Values and the Worldwide Processes of Disability Reform', in *Human Rights and Disability: The Current Use and Furture Potential of United Nations Human Rights Instruments in the Context of Disability*, edited by T. Degener and G. Quinn. Geneva: United Nations, 2002.

Salaets, K. 'The Importance of Harmonization: Perspectives from the Information Technology Industry Council', in G3ict *The Accessibility Imperative: Implications of the Convention of the Rights of Persons with Disabilities for Information and Communication Technologies*, edited by G3ict Global Initiative for Inclusive Information and Communication Technology, pp. 149-52. World Times, Inc., 2007.

Schutter, O. de. 'Transnational Corporations as Instruments of Human Development', in *Human Rights and Development: Towards Mutual Reinforcement* , edited by P. Alston and M. Robinson, pp. 403-44. Oxford: Oxford University Press, 2005.

Silver, D. 'Looking Backwards, Looking Forward: Cyberculture Studies', in *Web Studies: Rewiring Media Studies for the Digital Age*, edited by Ross Horsley and David Gauntlett, pp. 19-30. Arnold, Edward, 2000.

Silvers, A. 'Disability Rights', in *Encyclopedia of Applied Ethics*. Ruth Chadwick. London: Academic Press of Elsevier, 1998.

_____. 'Formal Justice', in *Disability, Difference, Discrimination: Perspectives on Justice in Bioethics and Public Policy*, edited by A. Silvers et al. Maryland: Rowman and Littlefield Publications Inc., 1998.

Steinhardt, R.G. 'Corporate Responsibility and the International law of Human Rights: The New Lex Mercatoria', in *Non-State Actors and Human*

Rights, edited by P. Alston, pp. 177–226. Oxford: Oxford University Press, 2005.

Teubner, G. 'After legal instrumentalism: Strategic models of post-regulatory law', in *Dilemma of Law in Welfare State*, edited by Teubner, pp. 299–326. Berlin: Walter de Gruyter, 1988a.

———. 'Introduction to Autopoietic Law', in *Autopoietic Law: A New Approach to Law and Society*, edited by Tuebner, pp. 1–11. Berlin: Walter de Gruyter, 1988b.

———. 'Global Bukowina: Legal Pluralism in the World Society', in *Global Law Without a State*, edited by Tuebner, pp. 3–28. Berlin: Walter de Gruyter, 1997.

———. 'Juridification: Concepts, Aspects, Limits, Solutions', in *A Reader on Regulation*, edited by Robert Baldwin, Colin Scott, and Christopher Hood, pp. 389–440. Oxford: Oxford University Press, 1998.

———. 'Juridification: Concepts, Aspects, Limits, Solutions', in *Juridification of Social Spheres: A Comparative Analysis in the areas of Labor, Corporate, Antitrust and Social Welfare Law*, edited by Teubner, pp. 3–48. Berlin: Walter de Gruyter, 1987.

Thürer, D. 'The Emergence of Non-Governmental Organisations and Transnational Enterprises in International Law and the Changing Role of the State', in *Non-State Actors as New Subjects of International Law: International Law from Traditional State Order Towards the Law of the Global Community*, edited by R. Hoffmann and N. Geissler. Berlin: Duncker and Humblot, 1999.

Waddington, L. and Diller, M. 'Tensions and coherence in Disability Policy: The Uneasy Relationship Between Social Welfare and Civil Rights Models of Disability in American, European and International Employment Law', in *Disability Rights and Policy: International and National Perspectives*, edited by M.L. Breslin and S. Yee, pp. 241–80. Ardsley, NY: Transnational Publishers, 2000.

Whitehouse, L. 'The Home-owner: Citizen or Consumer', in *Land Law: Themes and Perspectives*, edited by Susan and John Dewar, p. 186. Oxford: Oxford University Press, 1988.

Journal Articles

Abbott, K.W. and D. Snidal. 'International "Standards" and International Governance'. *Journal of European Public Policy* 8 (2001): 345.

Abrar, A. and K.J. Dingle. 'From Madness to Method: The Americans with Disabilities Act Meets the Internet'. *Harvard Civil Rights–Civil Liberties Law Review* 44 (2009): 133.

Allen, W.T. 'Our Schizphrenic Conception of the Business Corporation'. *Cardozo Law Review* 14 (1992): 261.

Amerson, J.M. '"The End of the Beginning?": A Comprehensive Look at the U.N's Business and Human Rights Agenda from a Bystander Perspective'. *Fordham Journal of Corporate and Financial Law* 17 (2012): 71.

Anderson, R.J. 'Reimagining Human Rigths Law: Towards Global Regulation of Transnational Corporations'. *Denver University Law Review* 88 (2010): 183.

Ashley, Stein and J. Penelope. 'Beyond Disability Civil Rights'. *Hastings Law Journal* (2007): 1203.

Arehart, B., and M. Stein. 'Integrating the Internet'. *George Washington Law Review* 83 (2015): 449.

Backer, L.C. 'From Moral Obligation to International Law: Disclosure Systems, Markets and the Regulation of Multinational Corporations'. *Georgetown Journal of International Law* 39 (2008): 591.

———. 'Shaping a Global Law for Business Enterprises: Framing Principles and the Promise of a Comprehensive Treaty on Business and Human Rights'. *North Carolina Journal of International Law* 42 (2017): 417.

Baldwin, R., and J. Black. 'Really Responsive Regulation'. *Modern Law Review* 71 (2008): 59.

Balkin, J.M. 'Virtual Liberty: Freedom to Design and Freedom to Play in virtual Worlds'. *Virginia Law Review* 90 (2004): 2043.

Benkler, Y. 'From Consumers to Users: Shifting the Deeper Structures of Regulation Toward Sustainable Common and User Access'. *Federal Communication Law Journal* 52 (2000): 561.

Berg, T. 'www.wildwest.gov.: The Impact of the internet on State power to Enforce the Law'. *Brighum Young University Law Review* 2000 (2000): 1305.

Best, M.L. 'Can the Internet be a Human Right?'. *Human Rights and Human Welfare* 4 (2004): 23.

Berven, H.M. and P. Blanck. 'Assistive Technology Patenting Trends and the Americans with Disabilities Act'. *Behavioral Sciences and the Law* 17 (1999): 47.

Birnhack, M.D. and N. Elkin-Koren. 'The Invisiable Handshake: The Reemergence of the State in the Digital Environment'. *Virginia Journal of Law and Technology* 8 (2003): 6.

Black, J. 'Critical Reflections on Regulation'. *Australian Journal of Legal Philosophy* 27 (2002): 1.

Blackwell, S. and N.V. Meulen. 'Two Roads Converged: The Mutual Complementarity of a Binding Business and Human Rights Treaty and National Action Plans on Business and Human Rights'. *Notre Dame Journal of International and Comparative Law* 6 (2016): 51.

Blair, M.M. and L.A. Stout. 'A Team Production Theory of the Corproation'. *Virginia Law Review* 85 (1999): 247.

Boddie, N.J. II. 'A Review of Copyright and the Internet'. *Campbel Law Review* 20 (1998): 193.

Boyle, A.E. 'Some Reflections on the Relationship of Treaties and Soft Law'. *International And Comparative Law Quarterly* 48 (1999): 901.

Boyle, J. 'Foucault in Cyberspace: Surveillance, Sovereignty, and Hardwired Censors'. *University of Cincinnati Law Review* 66 (1997): 177.

Bratton, W.W. Jr. 'The "Nexus of Contracts" Corporation: A Critical Appraisal'. *Cornell Law Review* 74 (1989): 407.

Broecker, C. '"Better the Devil You Know": Home State approaches to Transnational Corporate Accountability'. *New York University Journal of International Law and Policy* 41 (2008): 159.

Butler, H., and F. McChesney. 'Why They Give at the Office: Shareholder Welfare and Corporate Philanthropy in the Contractual Theory of the Corporation'. *Cornell Law Review* 84 (1999): 1195.

Cashore, B. 'Legitimacy and the Privatisation of Environmental Governance: How Non-state Market-Driven Governance (NSMD) Systems Gain Rule-Making Authority'. *Governance-an International Journal of Policy and Adiministration* 15 (2002): 503.

Cassell, D. and A. Ramasastry. 'White Paper: Options for a Treaty on Business and Human Rights'. *Notre Dame Journal of International and Comparative Law* 6 (2016): 1

Celli, A. and K. Dreifach. 'Postcards from the Edge: Surveying the Digital Divide'. *Cardozo Arts and Entertainment Law Journal* 20 (2002): 53.

Chinkin, C.M. 'The Challenges of Soft Law'. *International and Comparative Law Quarterly* 38 (1989): 850.

Coffee, J. 'The Attorney as Gatekeeper: An Agneda for the SEC'. *Columbia Law Review* 103 (2003): 1296.

Cohen, J.E. 'Cyberspace as/and Space'. *Columbia Law Review* 107 (2007): 210.

———. 'Cyberspace: The New Economic Orthodoxy of Rights Management'. *Michigan Law Review* 97 (1998): 462.

Cohen, M.R. 'The Basis of Contract'. *Harvard Law Review* 46 (1933): 553.

Collins, H. 'Ascription of Legal Responsibility to Groups in Complex Patterns of Economic Integration'. *Modern Law Review* 53 (1990): 731.

Dana, D.A. 'The New "Contractarian" Paradigm in Environmental Regulation'. *University of Illinois Law Review* 2000 (1999): 35.

Deva, S. 'UN's Human Rgiths Norms for Transnational Corporations and Other Business Enterprises: An Imperfect Step in the Right Direction?'. *ILSA Journal of International and Comparative Law* 10 (2004): 493.

Dhanda, A. 'Legal Capacity in the Disability Rights convention: Stranglehold of the Past or Lodestar for the Future?'. *Syracuse Journal of International Law and Commerce* 34 (2007): 429.

Dobbin, F. and A. Kalev. 'Multi-disciplinary Responses to Susan Sturm's the Architecture of Inclusion: The Architecture of Inclusion: Evidence from Corporate Diversity Programs'. *Harvard Journal of Law & Gender* 30 (2007): 279.

Drimmer, J.C. 'Cripples, Overcomers, and Civil Rights: Tracing the Evolution of Federal Legislation and Social Policy for People with Disabiliites'. *UCLA Law Review* 40 (1993): 1341.

Easterbrook, F.H. 'Cyberspace and the Law of the Horse'. *Univeristy of Chicago Legal Forum* 11 (1996): 207.

Easton, C. 'Revisiting the Law on Website Accessibility in the Light of the Equality Act 2010 and the UNCRPD'. *International Journal of Law and Information Technology* 20(1) (2012): 19.

Etling, B., R. Faris, and J. Palfrey. 'Political Change in the Digital Age: The Fragility and Promise of Online Organizing'. *Sais Review* 30 (2010): 37.

Fall, M. 'Privacy Projections of Computerized Information'. *Southern California Interdisciplinary Law Journal* 2 (1993): 170.

Fiorino, D.J. 'Rethinking Environmental Regulation: Perspectives on Law and Governance'. *Harvard Environmental Law Review* 23 (1999): 441.

Fischel, D.R. 'The Corporate Governance Movement'. *Vanderbilt Law Review* 35 (1982): 1259.

Fisher, W.W. II. 'Property and Contract on the Internet'. *Chicago-Kent Law Reveiw* 73 (1998): 1203.

Fredman, S. 'Equality: A New Generation?' *Industrial Law Journal* 30 (2001): 145.

Friedman, J.L. and G.C. Norman. 'The Norman/Friedman Principle: Equal Rights to Information and Technology Access'. *Texas Journal on Civil Liberties and Civil Rights* 18 (2012): 47.

Frischmann, B. 'Privatisation and Commercialisation of the Internet Infrastructure: Rethinking Market Intervention into Government and Government Intervention into the Market'. *Columbia Science and Technology Law Review* 2 (2000-01): 1.

Froomkin, A.M. 'Habermas@Discourse.Net: Toward a Critical Theory of Cyberspace'. *Harvard Law Review* 116 (2003): 749.

Froomkin, A.M. 'The Essential Role of Trusted Thrid Parties in Electronic Commerce'. *Orland Law Review* 75 (1996): 49.

Gilboy, J. 'Compelled Third-Party Participation in the Regulatory Process: Legal Duties, Culture, and Noncompliance'. *Law and Policy* 20 (1998): 135.

Goggin, G. and C. Newell. 'The Business of Digital Disability'. *The Information Society: An International Journal* 23(3) (2007): 159.

Goldmith, J.L. 'Against Cyber Anarchy'. *University of Chicago Law Review* 65 (1998): 1199.

Goldstein, D. and Care, G. 'Disability Rights and Access to the Digital World: An Advocate's Analysis of an Emerging Field'. *Federal Lawyer* 59(10) (2012): 54.

Grabosky, P.N. 'Using Non-governmental Resources to Foster Regulatory Complaince'. *Governance* 8 (1995): 527.

Graham, M. 'The Logical Next Step: Motivations on the Formation of a Business and Human Rights Treaty'. *Minnesota Journal of International Law* 26 (2017): 63

Greg, J.L. 'Policy-Making in the Public Interest: A Contextual Analysis in the passage of Closed-captioning Policy'. *Disability and Society* 21 (2006): 537.

Hahn, H. 'Feminist Perspectives, Disability, Sexuality and Law: New Issues and Agendas'. *South California Review Law and Women's Studies* 4: 97.

Halpern, I. 'Tracing the Contours of Transnational Corporations' Human Rights Obligations in the Twenty-First Century'. *Buffalo Human Rights Law Review* 14 (2008): 129.

Halpern, M. and A.K. Mehrota. 'From International Treaties to Internet Norms: The Evolution of international Trademark Disputes in the internet Age'. *University of Pennsylvania Journal of International Economic Law* 21 (2000): 523.

Harpur, P. 'Ensuring Equality in Education: How Australian Laws are Leaving Students with Print Disabilities Behind'. *Media and Arts Law Review* 58 (2010): 1.

———. 'From Universal Exclusion to Universal Equality: Regulating Ableism in a Digital Age'. *Northern Kentucky Law Review* 40(3) (2013): 529.

Henkin, L. 'Keynote Address: The Universal Declaration at 50 and the challenge of Global Markets'. *Brook Jounal of International Law* 25 (1999): 25.

Herik, L. and N. Cernic. 'Regulating Corporations under International Law: From Human Rgiths to International Criminal Law and Back Again'. *Journal of International Criminal Justice* 8 (2010): 725.

Hess, D. 'Social Reporting: A Reflexive Approach to Corporate Social Responsiveness'. *Iowa Journal of Corporate Law* 25 (1999): 41.

Horwitz, M.J. 'Santa Clara Revisited: The Development of Corporate Theory'. *Western Virginia Law Review* 88 (1985): 173

Humphreys, S. 'Productive users, Intellectual Property and Governance: The Challenges of Computer Games'. *Media and Arts Law Review* 10 (2005): 299.

Jacob, R., S. Taraporevala, and S. Basheer. 'The Disability Exception and the Triumph of New Rights Advocacy'. *National University of Juridical Science Law Review* 5 (2012): 603.

Jaeger, P., J.C. Bertot, K.M. Thompson, S.M. Katz, and E. DeCoster. 'The Intersection of Public Policy and Public Access: Digital Divides, Digital Literacy, Digital Inclusion, and Public Libraries'. *Public Library Quarterly* 31 (2012): 1.

Johnson, D.R. and D.G. Post. 'Law and Borders—The Rise of Law in Cyberspace'. *Stanford Law Review* 48 (1995): 1367.

Kanayama, T. 'Leaving It All Up to Industry: People with Disabilities and the Telecommunications Act of 1996'. *Inforamtion Society* 19 (2003): 185.

Kanter, A. 'The Globalisation of Disability Rights Law'. *Syracuse Journal of International Law and Com* 30 (2003): 241.

Kell, G. 'The Global Compact: Origins, Operations, Progress, Challenges'. *Journal of Corporate Citizenship* 11 (2003): 35.

Kinely, D. and R. Chambers. 'The UN Human Rights Norms for Corporations: The Private Implications of Public International Law'. *Human Rights Law Review* 6 (2006): 447.

Kinely, D. and J. Tadaki. 'From Talk to Walk: The Emergence of Human Rights Responsibilities for Corporations at International Law'. *Vanderbilt Journal of International Law* 44 (2004): 931.

Klein, D, et. al. 'Electronic Doors to Education: Study of High School website accessibility in Iowa'. *Behaviour Science & Law* 21 (2003): 27.

Knox, J.H. 'Horizontal Human Rgiths Law'. *American Journal of International Laws* 102 (2007): 1.

Kohl, Uta. 'Google: The rise and rise of online intermediaries in the governance of the Internet and Beyond'. *International Journal Law Information Technology* 21 (2013): 187.

———. 'The Rise and Rise of Online Intermediaries in the Governance of the Internet and Beyond-Connectivity Intermediaries'. *International Review of Law, Computers and Technology* 26 (2012): 185.

Konkright, K.E. 'An Analysis of the Applicability of Title III of the Americans with Disabilities Act to Private Internet Access Providers'. 37 *Idaho Law Review* 37 (2001): 713.

Kraakman, R.H. 'Gatekeeprs: The Anatomy of a Third-Party Enforcement Strategy'. *Journal of Law, Economics & Organisation* 2 (1986): 53.

L. Best, Michael. 'Can the Internet be a Human Right? *Human Rights and Human Welfare*, 2004: 23.

Lastowka, F.G., and D. Hunter. 'The Laws of the Virtual World'. *California Law Review* 92 (2004): 1.

Lawson, A. 'Disability and Employment in the Equality Act 2010: Opportunities Seized, Lost and Generated'. *Industrial Law Journal* 40(4) (2011): 359.

Lemley, M.A. 'Place and Cyberspace'. *California Law Review* 91 (2003): 521.

Lessig, L. 'The Law of the Horse: What Cyberlaw Might Teach'. *Harvard Law Review* 113 (1999): 501.

Lim, Y.J. and S.E. Sexton. 'Internet as a Human Right: A Practical Legal Framework to Address the Unique Nature of the Medium and to Promote Development'. *Washington Journal of Law, Technology and Arts* 7 (2011–12): 295.

Macdonald, R.A. 'Metaphors of Multiplicity: Civil Society, Regimes and Legal Pluralism'. *Arizona Journal of International and Comparative Law* 15 (1998): 69.

Maskery, H. 'Crossing the Digital Divide-Possibilities for Influencing the Private-Sector Business Case'. *The Information Society: An International Journal* 23 (2007): 187.

Mayer-Schonberger, V. 'The Shape of Governance: Analyzing the World of Internet Governance'. *Virginia Journal of International Law* 43 (2003): 605.

McCall, B.M. 'The Corporation as Imperfect Society'. *Delaware Journal of Corporate Law* 36 (2010): 509.

Mendeloff, J. 'Overcoming Barriers to Better Regulation'. *Law & Society Inquiry* 18 (1993): 11.

Maroney, P. 'The Wrong Tool for the Right Job'. *Vanderbilt Journal of Entertainment Law & Practice* 1 (2000): 191.

Miletello, E.C. 'The Page You Are Attempting to Access Has Been Blocked in Accordance with National Laws: Applying a Corporate Responsibility Framework to Human Rights Issues Facing Internet Companies'. *Pittsburgh Journal of Technology Law and Policy* 11 (2011): 1.

Millon, D.K. 'New Directions in Corporate Law Communitarians, Contractarians, and the Crisis in Corporate Law'. *Washington and Lee Law Review* 50 (1993): 1373.

Mortensen, M. 'Beyond Convergence and the New Media Decision: Regulatory Models in Communication Law'. *Canadian Journal of Law and Technology* 2 (2003): 99.

Mueller, M., J. Mathiason, and H. Klein. 'The Internet and Global Governance: Principles and Norms for a New Regime'. *Global Governance* 13 (2007): 237.

Mundlak, G. and I. Rosen-Zvi. 'Mapping the Hard Law/Soft Law Terrain: Labour Rights and Environment Protection: Signaling Virtue? A Comparison of Corporate Codes in the Fields of Labour and Environment'. *Theoretical Inquiry Law* 12 (2011): 603.

Netanel, N.W. 'Cyberspace Self-Governance: A Skeptical View from Liberal Democratic Theory'. *California Law Review* 88 (2000): 395.

Nien-Hsieh. 'The Obligations of Transanational Corporations: Rawlsian Justice and the Duty of Assistance'. *Business Ethics Quarterly* 14 (2004): 643.

Orts, E.W. 'A Reflexive Model of Environmental Regulation'. *Business Ethics Quarterly* 5 (1995): 779.

Palazzo, G. and A.G. Scherer. 'Corporative Legitimacy as Deliberation: A Communicative Framework'. *Business Ethics Quarterly* 66 (2006): 71.

Parker, C. 'Compliance Professionalism and Regulatory Community: The Australian Trade Practices Regime'. *Journal of Law and Society* 26 (1999): 215.

———. 'Reinventing Regulation within the Corporation: Compliance-Oriented Regulatory Innovation'. *Adminstration and Society* 32 (2000): 529.

_____. 'The Pluralization of Regulation'. *Theoretical Inquiries in Law* 9 (2008): 369.

Pedersen, W.F. 'Contracting with the Regulated for Better Regulations'. *Administrative Law Review* 53 (2001): 1067.

Pedlow, R. 'How will the Changeover to Digital Broadcasting in 2009 Influence the Accessibility of TV for Americans With Disabilities?' *Disability Studies Quarterly* 28 (2008).

Penney, J.W. 'Internet Access Rights: A Brief History and Intellectual Origins'. *William Mitchell Law Review* 38 (2011–12): 11

Pooran, B.D. and C. Wilkie. 'Failing to Achieve Equality: Disability Rights in Australia, Canada and the United States'. *Journal of Law and Social Policy* 20 (2005): 1.

Post, D.G. 'Anarchy, State and the Internet: An Essay on Law-Making in Cyberspace'. *Journal Online Law* Article 3 (1995).

_____. 'The Unsettled Paradox: The Internet, the State and the Consent of the Governed'. *Industrial Journal of Global Legal Studies* 5 (1997): 521.

Price, M. 'Free Expression and Digital Dreams: The Open and Closed Terrain of Speech'. *Critical Inquiry* (1995): 64.

Ranen, J.S. 'Was Blind But Now I See: The Argument for ADA Applicability to the Internet'. *Boston College Third World* 22 (2002): 389.

Ratner, S. 'Corporations and Human Rights : A Theory of Legal Responsibility'. *Yale Law Journal* 111 (2001): 443.

Redmont, P. 'Transnational Enterprise and Human Rights: Options for Standard Setting and Compliance'. *International Law* 37 (2003): 69.

Reidenberg, J. 'Lex Informatica: The Formulation of Information Policy Rules Through Technology'. *Texas Law Review* 76 (1998): 553.

Rossi, J. 'Bargaining in the Shadow of Administrative Procedure: The Public Interest in Rulemaking Settlement'. *Duke Journal of Law* 51 (2001): 1015.

Rottleuthner, H. 'The Limits of Law: The Myth of a Regulatory Crisis'. *International Journal of Society of Law* 17 (1989): 273.

Schiff, C. 'Cracking the Code: Implementing Internet Accessibility through the Americans with Disabilities Act'. *Cardozo Law Reveiw* 37 (2016): 2315.

Schloss, Adam M. 'Web-Sight for Visually-Disabled People: Does Title III of the Americans With Disabilities Act Apply to Internet Websites?'. *Columbia Journal of Law and Social Problems* 35 (2001): 35.

Schutter, O. 'Towards a New Treaty on Business and Human Rights'. *Business and Human Rights Journal* 1 (2015): 41.

Scott, C. 'Analyzing Regulatory Space: Fragmented Resources and Institutional Design'. *Public Law* (2001): 329.

Shelton, D. 'Normative Hierarchy in International Law'. *American Journal of International Law* 100 (2006): 291.

Silva, Alberto J. Certa. 'Internet Freedom is not Enough: Towards an Internet Based on Human Rights'. *SUR-International Journal on Human Rights*, 2013: 17.

Simpson, J. 'Inclusive Information and Communication Technologies for People with Disabilities'. *Disability Studies Quaterly* 29 (2009).

Skepys, B. 'Is There a Human Right to the Internet?'. *Journal of Politics and Law* 5 (2012): 15.

Slaughter, A. 'The Accountability of Government Networks'. *Industrial Journal of Global Legal Studies* 8 (2001): 347.

Sohmen, P. 'Taming the Dragon: China's Efforts to Regulate the Internet'. *Stanford Journal of East Asian Affairs* 1 (2001): 17.

Solomon, J.M., 'Law and Governance in the 21st Century Regulatory State'. *Texas Law Review* (2008): 819.

Stein, A.M. 'Disability Human Rights'. *California Law Review* 95 (2007): 75.

Suzor, N. 'On the (Partially) Inalienable Rights of Participants in Virtual Communities'. *Media International Australian Journal* 130 (2009): 90.

Suzor, N.P. 'The Role of the Rule of Law in Virtual Communities'. *Berkeley Technology Law Journal* 25 (2010): 1818.

tenBroek, J. 'The Right to Live in the World: The Disabled in the Law of Torts'. *California Law Review* 54 (1966): 841

Teuber, G. 'Autopoiesis in Law and Society: A Rejoinder to Blankenburg'. *Law and Society Review* 18 (1984): 291.

———. 'Substantive and Reflexive Elements in Modern Law'. *Law and Soceity Review* 17 (1983): 239.

Trachtman, J. 'Cyberspace, Sovereignty, Jurisdiciton, and Modernism'. *Industrial Journal of Global Legal Study* 5 (1998): 561.

Trubek, D.M. and L.G. Trubek. 'Hard and Soft Law in the Construction of Social Europe: The Role of the Open Method of Coordination'. *European Law Journal* 11 (2005): 343.

Tulkens, F. 'Human Rights, Rhetoric or Reality?' *European Review* 9 (2001): 125.

Tusler, A. 'How to Make Technology Work: A Study of Best Practices in United States Electronic and Information Technology Companies'. *Disability Studies Quarterly* 2 (25) (2005).

Varona, A.E. 'Changing Channels and Bridging Divides: The Failure and Redemption of American Broadcast Television'. *Minnesotta Journal of Law, Science and Technology* 6 (2004): 1.

Vazquez, C.M. 'Direct vs. Indirect Obligations of Corporations Under International Law'. *Coumbia Journal of Transnational Law* 43 (2005): 927.

Vries, P.de. 'The Resilience Principles: A Framework for New ICT Governance'. *Journal on Telecommunication and High Technology Law* 9 (2011): 137.

Wang, X. 'Time to Think about Human Right to the Internet Access: A Beitz's Approach'. *Journal of Politics and Law* 6 (2013): 67.

Waz, J. and P. Weiser. 'Internet Governance: The Role of Multistakeholder Organisations'. *Journal on Telecom and High Technology Law* 10 (2003): 331.

Weingarten, F. 'Communications Technology: New Challenges to Privacy'. *John Marshall Law Review* 21 (1988): 735.

Weissbrodt, D. 'Business and Human Rights'. *University of Cincinnati Law Review* 74 (2005): 55.

Werner, W. 'Corporation Law in Search of its Future'. *Columbia Law Review* 81 (1981): 161.

Wildhaber, L. 'Some Aspects of the Transnational Corporation in International Law'. *Netherlands International Law Review* 27 (1980): 79.

Williams, C.A. 'Corporate Social Responsibility in an Era of Economic Globalisation'. *U.C. Davis Law Review* 35 (2002): 705.

Wolks, L. 'Equal Access in Cyberspace: On Bridging the Digital Divide in Public Accommodations Coverage through Amendment to the Americans with Disabilities Act'. *Notre Dame Law Review* 91 (2015): 447.

Wood, S. 'Leverage-Based Corporate Human Rights Responsibility'. *Business Ethics Quareterly* 22 (2012): 63.

Yen, A.C. 'Western Fronteir or Feudal Society?: Metaphors and Perceptions of Cyberspace'. *Berkeley Technology Law Journal* 17 (2002): 1207.

Yukins, C. 'Making Federal Information Technology Accessible: A Case Study in Social Policy and Procurement'. *Public Contract Law Journal* 33 (2004): 667.

Yu, P.K. 'Symposium Bridging the Digital Divide: Equlaity in the Information Age: Forward'. *Cardozo Arts and Entertainment Law Jouranl* 20 (2002): 1.

Yu, X. 'Impacts of Corporate Code of Conduct on Labor Standards: A Case Study of Reebok's Athletic Footwear Supplier Factory in China'. *Journal of Business Ethics* 81 (2008): 513.

Zembek, R.S. 'Jurisdiction and the Internet: Fundamental Fairness in the Networked World of Cyberspace'. *Albania Law Journal of Science and Technology* 6 (1996): 339.

Zola, I. 'Towards the Necessary Universalizing of a Disability Policy'. *The Milibank Quarter* 67 (1989): 401.

Zumbansen, P. 'The Ironic Turn of Reflexive Law'. *The American Journal of Comparative Law: Special Symposium Issue:* 'Beyond the State: Rethinking Private Law'. 56(3) (2008): 769.

Research Papers

Andrew Johnston. 'Governing Externalities: The Potential of Reflexive Corporate Social Responsibility'. Working Paper No. 436, Centre for

Business Research, University of Cambridge (September 2012). Available at http://ssrn.com/abstract=2165616.

Don MacLean. 'Herding Schroginger's Cats: Some Conceptual Tools for Thinking about Internet Governance'. Background Paper for the ITU Workshop on Internet Governance Geneva (26–7 February 2004). https://www.itu.int/osg/spu/forum/intgov04/contributions/itu-workshop-feb-04-internet-governance-background.pdf

John C. Coffee. 'The Attorney as Gatekeeper: An Agenda for the SEC'. Columbia Law and Economic Working Paper No. 221 (April 2003). Available at http://ssrn.com/abstract=395181.

Kenneth Paul Kinyua. 'The Accountability of Multinational Corporations for Human Rights Violations: A critical analysis of select mechanisms and their potential to protect economic, social and cultural rights in developing countries'. Working Paper Series No. K33 (September 2009). Available at http://papers.ssrn.com/sol3/papers.cfm?abstract_id=1599842.

Lawrence Solumn. 'Models of Internet Governance'. Research Paper 07-25, University of Illionois. Available at http://ssrn.com/abstract=1136825.

Lawrence B. Solum and Minn Chung. 'The Layers Principle: Internet Architecture and the Law'. University of San Diego School of Law Public Law and Legal Theory Research Paper 55 (June 2003). Available at http://ssrn.com/abstract=416263.

Michael Kende. 'The Digital Handshake: Connecting Internet Backbones'. OPP Working Paper No. 32, Federal Communications Commission (2000). Available at http://www.fcc.gov/working-papers/digital-handshake-connecting-internet-backbones.

M. Stein, A. Silvers, B.A. Areheart, and L.P. Francis. 'Accomodating Every Body'. Legal Studies Research Paper No. 218. 2014 University of Tennessee (September 2013). Available at http://ssrn.com/abstract=2315271.

OECD. 'Codes of Corporate Conduct: Expanded Review of Their Contents'. OECD Working Papers on International Investment (2001) OECD. Available at http://dx.doi.org/10.1787/206157234626.

Orly Lobel. 'The Renewal Deal: The Fall of Regulation and the Rise of Governance in Contemporary Legal Thought'. Research Paper No. 07-27, University of San Diego Legal Studies Research Paper Series (December 2005). Available at http://ssrn.com/abstract=723761.

Patrick Schmidt. 'Eyes half blind: The possibilities and limits of lawyers as third party enforcers'. Paper Prepared for the Annual Meeting of the Western Political Science Association Portland, Oregon (12 March 2004). Available at http://www.allacademic.com/meta/p88159_index.html.

Tara J. Melish. 'Putting "Human Rights" Back into the UN Guiding Principles on Business and human rights: Shifting Frames and Embedding Participation Rights'. Paper No. 32, Legal Studies Research Paper Series,

SUNY Buffalo Law School (July 2014). Available at http://ssrn.com/abstract=2475629.

William H. Dutton and Malcolm Peltu. 'The Emerging Internet Governance Mosaic: Connecting the Pieces'. Forum Discussion Paper No. 5, Oxford Internet Institute, University of Oxford (November 2005). Available at http://ssrn.com/abstract=1295330.

Reports

Ben Cooper. 'Danish Reporting Rules', Ethical Corp., p. 26, available at http://www.ethicalcorp.com/resources/pdfs/content/20093531917_non-financial%20reporting%20feature.pdf.

Commission on Human Rights, Human Rights Res., 'Human Rights and Transnational Corporations and Other Business Enterprises', 59th mtg., U.N. Doc. E/CN.4/RES/2005/69 (20 April 2005), available at www.unhcr.org/refworld/doci d/45377c80c.html (last visited 27 August 2014).

Commission on Human Rights., Sub-commission., 55th Sess., 'Norms on the Responsibilities of Transnational Corporations and other Business Enterprises with Regard to Human Rights', U.N. Doc. E/CN.4/Sub.2/2003/12/Rev.2 (13 August 2003).

Commission on Human Rights, 'Promotion and Protection of Human Rights', U.N. Doc. E/CN.4/2006/97 (22 February 2006), available at http://daccess-dds-y.un.org/doc/UNDOC/GEN/GO6/110/27/PDF/G0611027.pdf? (last visited 25 August 2014)

Commission on Human Rights., Sub-commission, 'Commentary on the Norms on the Responsibilities of Transnational Corporations and Other Business Enterprises with Regard to Human Rights', P 16(b), U.N. Doc. E/CN.4/Sub.2/2003/38/Rev.2 (26 August 2003), available at http://www.unhchr.ch/Huridocda/Huridoca.nsf/e06a5300f90fa0238025668700518ca4/293378ff2003ceb0cl256d7900310d90/ILE/G0316018.pdf (last visited 25 August 2014).

Commission on Human Rights, 'Summaries of Post-Sessional Meetings and Other Activities of the Expanded Bureau During the Period from May to September 2004, transmitted by Note of the Secretariat', p. 27, U.N. Doc. E/CN.4/IM/2004/2 (28 September 2004), available at http://www2.ohchr.org/english/bodies/chr/informal/documents.htm (last visited 27 February 2015).

Human Rights Council, 'Guiding Principles on Business and Human Rights: Implementing the United Nations "Protect, Respect and Remedy" Framework', U.N. Doc. A/HRC/17/31 (21 March 2011) (by John Ruggie), available at http://www.ohchr.org/Documents/Issues/Business/A-HRC-17-31_AEV.pdf (last visited 27 August 2014).

Human Rights Council, Special Representative of the Secretary-General on the Issue of Human Rights and Transnational Corporations and Other Business Enterprises, 'Interim Report 2007 Business and Human Rights: Mapping International Standards of Responsibility and Accountability for Corporate Acts', U.N. Doc. A/HRC/4/035 (Feb. 9, 2007) (by John Ruggie), available at http://www.business-humanrights.org/SpecialRepPortal/Home/ReportstoUNHumanRightsCouncil/2007 (last visited 25 August 2014).

Human Rights Council, Special Representative of the Secretary-General on the Issue of Human Rights and Transnational Corporations and Other Business Enterprises, 'Protect, Respect and Remedy: A Framework for Business and Human Rights', p. 1, U.N. Doc.A/HRC/8/5 (7 April 2008) (by John Ruggie), available at http://www.unglobalcompact.org/docs/issues_doc/human_rights/Human_Rights_Working_Group/29Apr08_7_Report_of_SRSG_to_HRC.pdf (last visited 27 August 2014).

International Council on Human Rights Policy (ICHRP), 'Beyond Voluntarism Human Rights and the Developing International Legal Obligations of Companies'. Versoix: ICHRP, 2002.

International Telecommunication Union, 'Measuring the Information Society Report 2016', available at http://www.itu.int/en/ITU-D/Statistics/Pages/publications/mis2016.aspx (last visited 31 Augus, 2017).

Price Waterhouse Coopers, 'The UN Global Compact: Moving to the Business Mainstream, an Interview with George Kell', Corporoate Responsibility Report, vol. 2 (Winter 2005), available at www.unglobalcompact.org/docs/new_events/9.5/pwc_int_2005.pdf (last visited 25 August 2014).

Electronic Research

Anita Ramasastry, 'Should Web-Only Businesses be Required to be Disabled-Accessible?', available at http://www.cnn.com/2002/LAW/11/07/findlaw.analysis.ramasastry.disabled/index.html (7 November 2002) (last visited at 21 May 2016).

Bilal Chinoy and Tim Salo, 'Internet Exchanges: Policy Driven Evolution', available at https://www.caida.org/publications/papers/1996/nap/nap.html (last visited 25 May 2016).

Chris Nelder, 'Social Assessment, BWZine: The Online Better World Magazin (April/May 1996), available at http://www.betterworld.com/BWZ/9604/

cover1-1.htm (quoting Dr Simon Zadek of the New Economic Foundation, London) (last visited 27 August 2014).

Colin Woodard, 'Estonia, Where Being Wired Is a Human Right' (2003) Christian Science Monitor 7, available at http://www.csmonitor.com/2003/0701/p07s01-woeu.html (last visited 31 March 2015).

Danny Goodwin, 'Yahoo Search Share Sinks, Google, Bing Rise in February 2012' (12 March 2012) Search Engine Watchlt; available at http://searchenginewatch.com/article/2158888/Yahoo-Search-Share-Sinks-Google-Bing-Rise-in-February-2012 (last visited 10 March 2015).

European Accessibility Requirements for Public Procurement of Products and Services in the ICT Domain (European Commission Standardization Mandate M 376, Phase 2) (12 August 2012); available at http://www.mandate376.eu/ (last visited 27 November 2014).

Experian Hitwise, 'Data Center—Top Sites & Engines lt', available at http://www.hitwise.com/uk/datacentre/main/dashboard-7323.html (last visited 10 March 2015).

'History of the Internet, Internet for Historians, Chapter Two: From ARPANET to World Wide Web' (2002), available at http://www.let.leidenuniv.nl/history/ivh/chap2.htm (last visited 25 May 2016).

ING Congratulates U.N. Special Representative John Ruggie and His Team on Endorsement of Guiding Principles, One Society Initiative.org (24 June 2011), available at http://onesocietyinitiative.org/ing-congratulates-un-special-representative-john-ruggie-a-his-team-on-endorsement-of-guiding-principles-80 (last visited 27 August 2014).

INT'L NETWORK ON FORECON., SOC. & CULTURAL RTS., U.N. HUMAN RIGHTS NORMS FOR BUSINESS: BRIEFING KIT 4 (January 2005), available at http://www.escr-net.org/usr_doc/Briefing_Kit.pdf (last visited 25 August 2015).

Joy Liddicoat of APC, available at http://www.apc.org/en/news/access-internet-and-human-rights-thanks-vint (last visited 17 August 2014).

Letter of Support from the Int'l Bus.Leaders Forum for the U.N. Protect, Respect and Remedy Framework, to John Ruggie, the Special Representative of the Secretary-General, (16 June 2011), available at http://www.business-humanrights.org/Links/Repository/1006814 (last visited 27 August 2014).

Lisa Waddington and Matthew Diller, 'Tensions and Coherence in Disability Policy: The Uneasy Relationship Between Social Welfare and Civil Rights Models of Disability in American, European and International Employment Law,' in Disability Rights Law and Policy: International and National Perspectives 241, p. 244 (Mary Lou Breslin and Silvia Yee eds, 2002), available at http://www.dredf.org/international/waddington.html (last visited 2 April 2015).

Massachusetts Attorney General, Monster.com First in Industry to Make Website Accessible for Blind Users (30 January 2013); available at http://www.mass.gov/ago/news-and-updates/press-releases/2013/2013-01-30-monster-agreement.html (last visited 27 November 2014).

C. McCrudden. 'Buying Equality Draft Chapter' (2009), available at http://www.michiganlawreview.org/articles/mccrudden-buying-social-justice-equality-government-rocurement-and-legalchange (last visited 27 November 2014).

Message, The Secretary-General, 'Secretary-General's Message on the Adoption of the Convention of the Rights of Persons with Disabilities, delivered by Mr. Mark Malloch Brown, Deputy Secretary General,' U.N. Doc. SG/SM!10797, HR/491 1, L/T/4400 (13 December 2006), available at http://www.un.org/News/Press/docs/2006/sgsm10797.doc.htm (last visited 2 April 2015).

Press Release, Humanrights.gov, Businesses and Transactional Corporations Have a Responsibility to Respect Human Rights (16 June 2011), available at http://www.humanrights.gov/2011/06/16/businesses-and-transnational-corporations-have-a-responsibility-to-respect-human-rights (last visited 27 August 2014).

Public Statement, 'Document-United Nations: A Call for Action to Better Protect the Rights of Those Affected by Business-Related Human Rights Abuses', AMNESTYINTERNATIONAL.ORG (14 June 2011), available at http://www.amnesty.org/en/library/asset/IOR40/009/2011/en/55fab4a5-fb8a-4572-93f3-67581b2dca45/ior400092011en.html (last visited 27 August 2014).

Simon Cottle, 'Media and the Arab Uprisings of 2011: Research Notes', 12 Journalism 647, 654 (2011), available at http://www.contexting.me/files/CottleMediaandtheArabUprising.pdf (last visited 25 May 2016).

Recommendations on Follow-Up to the Mandate, Mandate of the Special Representative of the Secretary-General (SRSG) on the Issue of Human Rights and Transnational Corporations and other Business Enterprises, 2011, available at www.business-humanrights.org/media/documents/ruggie/ruggie-special-mandate-follow-up-11-feb-2011.pdf (last visited 30 August 2014).

Richard T. Griffiths, 'History of the Internet, Internet for Historians, Chapter Two: From ARPANET to World Wide Web' (2002), available at http://www.let.leidenuniv.nl/history/ivh/chap2.htm. (last visited 10 March 2015).

Robert H'obbes' Zakon, 'Hobbes' Internet Timeline', vol. 6.1 (2003), available at http://www.zakon.org/robert/internet/timeline/ (last visited 10 March 2015).

World Summit on the Information Society, 'Plan of Action, Geneva' (12 December 2003), WSIS-03/GENEVA/DOC/5-E, available at www.itu. int/wsis/docs/geneva/official/poa.html (last visited 2 April 2015).

Knowledge Ecology International, 'Background and Update on Negotiations for a WIPO Copyright Treaty for Persons Who Are Blind or Have Other Disabilities' (7 April 2011), available at http://keionline.org/node/1089 (last visited 25 November 2014).

Websites

http://www.apc.org
https://www.apple.com/
http://www.austlii.edu.au
http://www.business-humanrights.org
http://www.csmonitor.com
http://dotsub.com
http://www.dredf.org
http://www.e-accessibilitytoolkit.org/
http://www.globalsullivanprinciples.org
http://www.g3ict.com
http://www8.hp.com
http://www.ichrp.org
http://itu.int
http://www.lumn.edu/humanrights/lnks/principles11-18-200.htm
http://www.microsoft.com
http://www.nfb.org/
http://www.nsfnet.org
http://www.oecd.org/
http://www.overstream.net/
http://www.projectreadon.com
http://www.pubbliaccesso.it
http://ssrn.com/
http://tbinternet.ohchr.org/
http://www.unglobalcompact.org/
http://www.un.org
http://www.w3.org/2001/sw/
http://zeroproject.org

Index

About the Author

Neha Pathakji is assistant professor of law at NALSAR University of Law, Hyderabad, India where she teaches courses and seminars in taxation, torts, and regulatory theories. She is closely associated with Centre for Disability Studies at NALSAR University of Law. As a member of legal consultant's team, she has participated in drafting The Rights of Persons with Disabilities Bill, 2011 for the Government of India. She has also served as a researcher for Centre for Disability Studies in writing India's First Country Report on the United Nations Convention of Rights of Persons with Disability for Ministry of Social Justice and Empowerment, Government of India. She has contributed in several publications in tax laws and disability rights including second edition of the *Halsbury's Laws of India* (Direct Tax). She was awarded the 'Van Calker' Scholarship by the Swiss Institute of Comparative Law, Lausanne, Switzerland. She holds a degree from the Maharaja Sayajirao University of Baroda (B. Com, LLM) and NALSAR University of Law (PhD).